Internal Displacement in South Asia

The Relevance of the UN's Guiding Principles

Edited by

Paula Banerjee
Sabyasachi Basu Ray Chaudhury
Samir Kumar Das

Sage Publications
New Delhi/Thousand Oaks/London

First published in 2005 by

Sage Publications India Pvt Ltd
B-42 Panchsheel Enclave
New Delhi 110 017

Sage Publications Inc
2455 Teller Road
Thousand Oaks, California 91320

Sage Publications Ltd
1 Oliver's Yard, 55 City Road
London EC1Y 1SP

Published by Tejeshwar Singh for Sage Publications India Pvt Ltd, typeset in 10/12 Goudy Old Style by Prism Graphix, New Delhi and printed at Chaman Enterprises, New Delhi.

This volume is published in collaboration with the Brookings Institution—Johns Hopkins SAIS Project on Internal Displacement. However, the views expressed in the chapters are not necessarily those of the Brookings Institution or Johns Hopkins University.

Library of Congress Cataloging-in-Publication Data

Internal displacement in South Asia: the relevance of the UN's guiding principles/ edited by Paula Banerjee. Sabyasachi Basu Ray Chaudhury, Samir Kumar Das.
    p. cm.
Includes bibliographical references and index.
    1. Refugees—South Asia. 2. Forced migration—South Asia. 3. Human rights—South Asia. 4. Office of the United Nations High Commissioner for Refugees. I. Banerjee, Paula. II. Basu Ray Chaudhury, Sabyasachi. III. Das, Samir Kumar, 1961–
HV640.I515   362.87'0954—dc22   2005   2004022483

ISBN: 0-7619-3313-1 (Hb)   81-7829-443-5 (India-Hb)
          0-7619-3329-8 (Pb)   81-7829-463-X (India-Pb)

Sage Production Team: Malathi K. Ramamoorthy, Vineeta Rai, O.P. Bhasin and Santosh Rawat

CONTENTS

FOREWORD

I n today's world, the principle of national sovereignty is still the cornerstone of international relations. While international humanitarian and human rights instruments offer legally binding bases for international protection and assistance of people at risk within national borders, for the most part such people are at the mercy of their national authorities. This is particularly the case for some 25 million persons in over 40 countries, who are uprooted and at risk within their own countries as a result of internal conflicts, communal violence, or egregious violations of human rights. Additional millions of internally displaced persons (IDPs) are forcibly displaced by natural disasters and development projects. International access to them can be tragically constrained and even blocked by states in the name of sovereignty or by the collapse of states and rampant insecurity.

In the Middle East and Asia, there are 4 to 5 million persons internally displaced by conflict, and additional numbers by disasters and development projects. Many are in destitute conditions. As United Nations Secretary-General Kofi Annan has pointed out, whether the victims are forced into camps, choose to hide away in uncharted territory, or merge into communities that are often equally ravaged, internal displacement nearly always has a devastating effect on families, culture, jobs, education and the security of a stable society. Above all, it denies innocent people access to food, shelter and medicine and exposes them to all manner of violence. If left unaddressed, it can undermine state stability and spill over borders, destabilizing regions. Indeed, internal displacement, in the words of the Secretary-General, 'has created an unprecedented challenge for the international community: to find ways to respond to what is essentially an internal crisis.'

The failure to provide for the well-being and security of displaced populations often makes international involvement essential. However, to be effective, the international response must deal with, and respect, the sovereignty of states. This can be best achieved by postulating the concept of sovereignty positively, as one of state responsibility towards the people under its jurisdiction. According to this concept of sovereignty as responsibility, which the Representative of the Secretary-General on Internally Displaced Persons has regularly advocated since his appointment, states have the primary responsibility to protect and assist their populations. But where there is inadequacy of material resources, states are expected to invite or at least allow international assistance. Should they refuse, the international community, obligated by humanitarian and human rights principles, cannot be expected to stand by passively while large numbers of people suffer extreme deprivation or death. Sovereignty must entail responsibilities to one's own population and also to the international community.

Over the past decade, an increasing number of international humanitarian, human rights and development organizations have become involved in a variety of countries, reinforcing national efforts to address internal displacement. A beacon for their work has been the newly developed international standards, the Guiding Principles on Internal Displacement, presented to the UN by the Representative of the Secretary-General in 1998. Further, in cooperation with the UN, the Norwegian Refugee Council has developed a global IDP survey, an information base on IDPs. Institutionally, a special unit on IDPs has been established within the UN Office for the Coordination of Humanitarian Affairs. It is to be noted that the Secretary-General and other senior officials now regularly raise cases of internal displacement in diplomatic dialogue and also speak out when situations are severe. That situations of internal displacement can constitute a threat to international peace and security has been recognized by the Security Council, which has specifically requested to be informed when IDPs are under threat of harassment and harm. Donor governments also have begun to target more of their resources towards addressing situations of internal displacement. And at the regional level, steps are being taken by intergovernmental organizations in Africa, Europe and the Americas to monitor IDP conditions and explore regional approaches to the problem.

Less well known and written about are the initiatives being undertaken at the national and local levels to address internal displacement. In an increasing number of countries, policies and laws are being developed on internal displacement, constituting a first step toward national responsibility. In addition, civil society groups have become active in raising public awareness to the problem. Indeed, in South Asia, especially in India, academic institutions, local non-governmental organizations and other civil society groups have shown themselves to be dynamic and vibrant in trying to address the problem. Among the most notable examples is the

Mahanirban Calcutta Research Group (CRG), composed of academics, journalists, refugee experts, gender specialists, and lawyers. CRG has played a significant role in mobilizing the awareness of the academic community, and also the public, to the problem of internal displacement in the South Asia region, thereby contributing to the overall international effort to develop a more predictable and effective system for dealing with situations of internal displacement.

The process by which the current volume, *Internal Displacement in South Asia: The Relevance of the UN's Guiding Principles*, was developed is instructive. In 2000 the CRG brought together academics and NGO representatives from the different South Asian countries to examine the Guiding Principles on Internal Displacement and collaborate in a study of internal displacement in the region from the perspective of the Principles. The idea emanated from discussions between the CRG and the Brookings Institution Project on Internal Displacement, following a regional conference on internal displacement in Asia, held in Bangkok, Thailand in 2000, which recommended that academic institutions in Asia promote greater attention to internal displacement.

The CRG conceived its study as a collective research project of refugee and migration specialists from the different South Asian countries. Its aim was to expand awareness of displacement in the South Asia region as well as of the Guiding Principles. But just as importantly, it sought to develop local capacity in the region in internal displacement. In short, it aimed to create a cadre of experts in the region with understanding of internal displacement in the different countries.

In the forefront of conceptualizing and organizing the study were Professor Ranabir Samaddar (now CRG director, then director of Peace Studies at the South Asia Forum for Human Rights), Paula Banerjee (University of Calcutta and editor of *Refugee Watch*), Sabyasachi Basu Ray Chaudhury (Rabindra Bharati University) and Samir Das (University of Calcutta). With purposefulness and enthusiasm they selected a group of specialists from the different countries who travelled to the affected areas alone or in teams and prepared draft chapters on seven countries (Afghanistan, Bangladesh, Burma, India, Nepal, Pakistan and Sri Lanka). At a workshop convened by CRG in Colombo in 2003, the authors presented their findings.

The chapters in this volume look at displacement broadly, covering conflict-induced displacement as well as displacement caused by natural disasters and development projects in each of the countries. Some chapters extend to the trafficking of displaced women and children, and a special chapter is devoted to the impact of displacement on women. In all cases, an in-depth discussion and analysis are provided of internal displacement in the countries concerned. Clearly a cadre of experts has been formed, with each of the authors going on to integrate the research material into their coursework at universities, into their writings and into guiding the work of non-governmental groups and activists with whom they are associated.

Building upon this expertise, the CRG in 2003 decided to put together a two-week 'annual winter orientation course on forced migration', which opened in Calcutta in December. Co-sponsored by UNHCR, the Government of Finland, and the Brookings Project, the course contained a segment on internal displacement and the Guiding Principles, with several of the authors of the chapters in this volume serving as faculty. CRG also began to plan workshops on the Guiding Principles in the different South Asian countries.

One cannot be but heartened by the work a small group can do to mobilize academics and civil society in South Asia to a greater understanding of displacement in the region. It is significant that this volume was prepared by scholars and activists from the region, who at their own initiative decided to expand their knowledge of displacement in order to promote better policies and programmes for vulnerable populations. The study should prove valuable to governments, non-state actors, regional bodies, international organizations, and NGOs involved in the South Asia region who want to gain a better understanding of the causes and consequences of displacement and the steps needed to address the problem.

Francis Deng
Representative
of the United Nations
Secretary-General on Internally
Displaced Persons, and
Co-Director, The Brookings
Institution—Johns Hopkins SAIS
Project on Internal Displacement

Roberta Cohen
Senior Fellow, The Brookings
Institution, and Co-Director,
the Brookings Institution—
Johns
Hopkins SAIS Project on
Internal Displacement

ACKNOWLEDGEMENTS

This volume is an outcome of a two-year-long research work on the state of internal displacement in South Asia. As a research collective that works on issues of rights and justice, in this work of studying displacement, the Calcutta Research Group (CRG) had in perspective the UN Guiding Principles on Internal Displacement that bases itself on established international human rights norms. Thus, we have explored in this volume the policies in different countries of South Asia on the internally displaced people from the angle of the Guiding Principles. Our guides in this endeavour have been Francis Deng and Roberta Cohen. They have offered us valuable insights in writing the volume. We thank Roberta Cohen in particular and the Brookings Institution SAIS Project on Internal Displacement for supporting this initiative from its inception to its implementation, including the publication of the volume.

This is a South Asian research initiative. Without the active support of our collaborators from different countries of South Asia this huge task would not have been possible. We take this opportunity to thank all those who participated in this collaborative research keeping in mind that the events this book analyses are still unfolding. We thank Jeevan Thiagaraja and Dhanya Ratnavale of the International Centre for Ethnic Studies, Colombo for aiding and facilitating our discussions in Sri Lanka where we debated on the papers extensively and collectively. The volume may not have appeared without the editorial assistance of Purna Banerjee and for that we thank her. We remain grateful to CRG staff for their silent but immense administrative and technical support. This is our occasion to say thank you to all of them. From the conception of the idea to work on IDPs in South Asia to the publication of this volume we were guided, reprimanded and supported by Ranabir Samaddar. We thank him for the belief that such a complex task was possible for us to perform. To Sage Publications, and in particular to Tejeshwar Singh and Omita Goyal, our indebtedness increases with every venture.

The volume deals with issues of displacement due to development policies and massive violence that are still going on in different parts of the region. We hope that this volume will encourage policy makers, human rights and humanitarian activists and personnel, and social scientists of greater repute than us, to focus their attention on emerging vulnerable circumstances and vulnerable groups that are often overlooked. As in all our previous works, we have tried to make gender concern a cardinal feature of our analysis. Whether we have succeeded is for the readers to tell. Of course, responsibility for all acts of omission and commission remains with us.

INTRODUCTION

Paula Banerjee, Sabyasachi Basu Ray Chaudhury and Samir Kumar Das

The last two decades have witnessed an enormous increase in the number of internally displaced people in South Asia. Their situation is particularly vulnerable because unlike the refugees they are never able to move away from the site of conflict and have to remain within a state in which they were forced to migrate in the first place. Their situation seems even more susceptible to danger when one considers that there are hardly any legal mechanisms that guide their rehabilitation and care in South Asia. Only recently do we have the UN Guiding Principles on internal displacement. Keeping that in mind it becomes imperative for scholars working on issues of forced migration in South Asia to consider whether South Asian states have taken the Guiding Principles into account while organizing programmes for rehabilitation and care of the internally displaced persons (IDPs). This book is meant to be a compendium of case studies of the situation of IDPs in South Asia in the light of the already established UN Guiding Principles. The inclusion of Myanmar, still popularly known as Burma, and Afghanistan in a compendium like this might seem inappropriate. But internal displacements inside Myanmar, or for that matter Afghanistan, have their implications for not only the frontline countries but also countries which do not have any land borders with them. Besides being 'potential refugees' who can and do very often cross international borders, most of the IDPs living in these countries share ethnic continuities with the people of the neighbouring countries. The Pashtuns of northwest Pakistan, for example, seem to harbour an active interest in the affairs of their ethnic cousins living in Afghanistan and vice versa. Similarly, much of what happens inside today's Myanmar has its implications for the minorities of north-eastern India and Bangladesh. Massive displacement and the resulting plight of the predominantly tribal populations such as the Nagas of Myanmar continue to be one of the key ongoing themes of the Naga rebel discourse across the borders and the ethnic cousins of Myanmar are described by it as, 'the Eastern Nagas'. In so far as the creation of national borders could not make many of these pre-existing ethnic spaces completely obsolescent, South Asia's living linkages with West or South East Asia can hardly be exaggerated. It was this consideration that had driven us to include studies on Burma/Myanmar and Afghanistan in a compendium on predominantly South Asian countries. The established protocol of dividing this part of the world (and many other parts as well) into such apparently clear-cut regions, as South and South East Asia, Central and West Asia remains oblivious to these continuities. We cannot lose sight of these continuities while organizing our responses towards them. Thus, as the Burma case demonstrates, while international organizations are not permitted access to the affected people, cross-border initiatives from the neighbouring countries have proven effective.

VULNERABILITY

The look of pure terror on the face of the little Korku tribal girl child said it all as the elephant razed her house in the pouring rain. Her parents pleaded with the forest officials saying that they were living and cultivating the lands there for the past three decades. However, the officials said they had no alternative, since they had been instructed to evict all encroachers as ordered by the Supreme Court.[1]

The eviction of indigenous people from their land is a recurrent theme in South Asia. Be it Ranigaon, Golai, Motakeda, Somthana, Ahmedabad, Bandarban or Trincomalee, thousands of families are being evicted from their homes either in the name of conflict or in the name of modernization. They are being forced to stay in the open, in pouring rain, with a number of them suffering from malnutrition and starvation and they are fearful for their lives at most times. These unfortunate people who have been displaced once are often displaced multiple times at the hands of the powers that be. Yet, as displaced, they do not have the capacity to cross international borders, but seek rehabilitation from the powers that are responsible for their displacement in the first place. They are probably more vulnerable and insecure than the refugees. One of the leitmotifs of this book then is that those who get displaced, either due to conflict or due to development, and remain as internally displaced persons (hereafter IDPs), belong to the more vulnerable communities in South Asia.

The picture becomes clearer when one looks into the situation of the adivasis or the indigenous people in South Asia, be they the Tamangs in Nepal, the Moolvasi people in Jharkhand or the Chakmas in the Chittagong Hill Tracts (hereafter CHT). In India alone, one study testifies that 36 lakh adivasis have been displaced and only about one-third are rehabilitated.[2] If one looks at World Bank reports after 1993 on the construction of dams one gets this picture even more clearly.[3] The Sardar Sarovar Project, often described as one of the most flawed projects, displaced largely the Tadvis, Vasavas, Bhils and the Bhilalas, but very few caste Hindus. The collection of chapters in this volume also portrays a similar picture. Several studies show that the more vulnerable communities bear the brunt of displacement in most parts of South Asia. If one looks into the case of Myanmar or Sri Lanka the brunt of displacement is borne by the ethnic minorities. The northeast of India presents a slightly different picture. Among the displaced are not the national ethnic minorities but the local minorities, showing that even in the micro level the vulnerability of the local minorities continues. The chapter on displacements in other parts of India shows a third category of vulnerability belonging to the slum dwellers in urban areas of West Bengal. This book then is a commentary on vulnerable peoples of South Asia, and tries to grapple with the question of what constitutes vulnerability in the modernist project of state formation. It also deals with hierarchies of vulnerability. For example, the chapter on northeast India portrays that vulnerability is not a static process as is the case of the Chins in Mizoram. The Chins became vulnerable only in the last one decade. Therefore, these chapters collectively portray the direct relation between the post-colonial state formation projects of South Asia with the growing vulnerabilities of certain *other* groups in the region. It shows that the kind of state formation that has occurred in South Asia is dependent on the creation of exclusive spaces. The elitist project of democracy in South Asia supports a homogenized image of citizenry thereby relegating difference to the margins. But this does not mean that this elite core of democracy remains static. It is constantly negotiating spaces with the fringes and so newer elites are able to wrest power. But what remains unchanged is that power is concentrated in the hands of an elite that defines itself in opposition to the fringes. Thus, before defining citizens, these states have tried to define the alien or the *other*.[4] Thus, the *other* has a specific role in the process of state formation and it is in that mirror that we view the citizen. Ethnic, religious and class minorities are the *other* to the citizen who constantly views his relationship with the rest as oppositional. The difference becomes crucial when the privileged define themselves as a nation, thereby claiming a geopolitical space. In such an exclusive space the *others* get marginalized and are physically displaced and relegated to the fringes. This is the story that has been recounted multiple times in this volume.

But the other or the vulnerable is not a homogenous whole. It is composed of many different groups. Yet the powers that displace them also club them into a single category. As one observer comments, 'When people are uprooted because their land is wanted for economic reasons usually associated with visions of national development, their multiple identities tend to disappear: they become engendered, uprooted,' and are dealt with as undifferentiated mass of victims.[5] The displaced then become this homogenized group of victims and by becoming victims they are denied their identity. The chapters in this collection have gone against this trend. For example, the chapter on Sri Lanka speaks of how children are affected by conflict. The author tries to explicate why children should be considered as a separate category. His answer is that they constitute more than 50 per cent of the victims of conflict in Sri Lanka. The chapter also highlights the trauma of the sick among the internally displaced. Although most of the displaced fall sick due to exhaustion, they are often denied medical attention. The state considers relief as part of the security package because the displaced are not seen as individuals but clubbed into the role of the other or the alien, with the potential of becoming the enemy alien.

In the chapter on Afghanistan the author analyses how displacement affects men and women differently. Having lost the role of being the breadwinners, men often become apathetic but women face a different problem. Living in camps means that women have to share quarters with non-relatives. This is made a pretext to seriously restrict women's mobility. They are no longer allowed to move in the camp freely. Often if they need to go out they are forced to take male relatives along. What this has meant is that women are denied the feminine networks that other groups of displaced women find extremely crucial in dealing and coping with displacement.

The chapter on women's experiences of displacement portrays how women of different groups are affected differently by displacement. It highlights the experience of Kashmiri Pundit women although they are displaced in one country. It portrays how in a single geopolitical space different groups are displaced at different historical moments and how the powers that be need to constantly exclude to legitimize the inclusions. In this process of exclusion the powers that be then club the excluded together as victims. What this inadvertently reflects is that all those who have been excluded belong to the category of the vulnerable. What remains clear is that at certain historical and political moments certain groups are marked as different and vulnerable. The powers that be then negate the difference among the vulnerable and reduce individuals to the category of victims where their identity is lost and their voices are drowned.

Protracted Displacements and Citizens

The post-colonial existence of Burma has largely been influenced by military rule and the problems of ethnic nationalities, insurgencies organized by the aggrieved minorities and tough counter-insurgency measures of the military junta. What is recounted here is a sad saga of the state marking some as citizens and relegating the rest to the position of the perennially displaced. In that sense, Burma has a past that would find very few comparable counterparts elsewhere in the world. The problem of internal displacement in Burma has been looked into against this complex backdrop of the country's socio-political situation. It was not always possible to go into the official discourse on the internally displaced people in Burma as the military junta has been continuously refusing to admit the very existence of the IDPs in that country. Therefore, the chapter on Burma has mainly concentrated on a narrative history of IDPs in the country. The author has analysed the conditions and patterns of displacement in this context. The chapter reveals that Burma, being under military rule for more than four decades, has produced a large number of displaced persons in the context of ethnic minorities, development policies of the government and the cruel and inhuman relocation policy followed by the *Tatmadaw*.

The two-decade-old worst ethnic conflict between the majority Sinhalese and minority Tamils in Sri Lanka has caused immense suffering to hundreds of thousands of its citizens. As a result, men, women and children have been uprooted, dispossessed and deprived of their means of livelihood. Loss of lives, including that of breadwinners, severe and permanent disability, destruction of personal and productive assets, loss of income, psychological trauma, accompanied by alienation and isolation along with an enduring sense of uncertainty—the scars of war, particularly in relation to IDPs—go deep to produce a sociological reality and complexity that is staggering in its social, economic and psychological dimensions. To compound the crisis, fundamental human rights, democratic freedoms, and economic and social development have been gravely compromised and insecurity has become rampant. The prolonged armed conflict between the government forces and the Tamil rebel forces has very often led to relocation of the civilian families at the expense of their livelihood. The author has gone into a comprehensive analysis of these hundreds of thousands of IDPs in Sri Lanka and has analysed how citizens have joined the ranks of the dispossessed.

In the case of Afghanistan, despite efforts on a number of fronts, political resolution of the long-drawn ethno-political conflict remains elusive. Under these circumstances the ailing Afghan economy has continued to deteriorate and foster poverty and unemployment. There have been few formal-sector employment possibilities, no major rehabilitation or development projects and no major private sector investment to support income. Transit trade with neighbouring countries remains a key sector of the 'legitimate' economy. Trade in narcotics and, presumably, arms have constituted the mainstay of the 'criminalized' economy. As a consequence, a large number of Afghan citizens are displaced within their own country. The IDPs in Afghanistan also include those people displaced due to blockades that have prohibited the free movement and flow of goods, not to speak of the people affected by continuous armed conflicts between ethnic warlords and between the forces of the Kabul administration and the rebel groups.

Bangladesh also has witnessed several kinds of internal displacement in recent years. The structural violence within the state is one of the foremost causes of internal displacement in Bangladesh, as in most other South Asian countries. The unitary nature of the country's Constitution privileges Bengali language and culture over other linguistic and cultural groups. Similarly, the declaration of Islam as a state religion marginalizes the non-Muslims from the ideological mainstream, notwithstanding the equality clause. The political movement for autonomy in the CHT and the violence against minorities in the aftermath of the election in 2001 are examples of such marginalization. These are, in fact, instances of systemic internal displacement in a majoritarian democracy. This is also a story of how certain historical events are used to relegate citizens to the position of IDPs in an effort to create a homogenous nation state. The acceptance by the state of the modernization paradigm in development, accompanied by incoming international capital, has also caused displacement in different parts of the country. How disturbing internal displacement can be in a globalizing world can be understood by looking at the issue of shrimp cultivation, which the authors have dealt with in great detail. Similarly, displacement due to forced eviction by the state has been commonplace in the urban metropolises.

In the case of Pakistan, the author has discussed the problem of internal displacement under three main sections. These are: development-induced displacement, conflict-induced displacement, and natural disaster-related displacement. This comprehensive article has touched upon the problem of the persons displaced due to the construction of the Mangla dam, among others. Apart from these development-induced displacements, the author has also examined the case of persons affected due to the Kargil conflict with India. The Line of Control with India shows how the nation is collapsed within borders and citizens get displaced to maintain the legitimacy of these borders.

The chapter on India takes stock of the nature and magnitude of internal displacement on the basis of a few typologies. The author argues that while India is yet to evolve any separate legal instrument to address the problem of internal displacement and IDPs, there are nevertheless significant provisions in the existing municipal law that are frequently invoked by the appropriate authorities to deal with the problem. The IDPs, and often the organizations acting on their behalf, seek relief, resettlement and rehabilitation provided by the Indian Constitution as well as the existing laws of the land. However, the author points out that the need for a separate legal instrument is increasingly being felt since the early 1990s, not only to compile the existing laws together within a single legal instrument but also to plug the loopholes detected in them over the years. It appears from this study that India is passing through an interesting stage of legal debate and discussion and the report is prepared with a view to contribute to them. For his analysis the author has dealt with the cases of displacement in Gujarat and Kashmir due to communal frenzy and insurgency, and counter-insurgency operations of the government forces. Similarly, the issue of river-erosion-related displacement and the eviction of street hawkers in Kolkata have been discussed in the chapter at great length.

India's northeast deserves special attention due to the location and complexity of the region. Though the hills of this region were largely protected from large-scale influx of outsiders, Assam, and later Tripura, was not. Both were subjected to continuous influx from Bangladesh (the erstwhile East Bengal). While the Bengalis have already come to constitute the majority in Tripura in the years after India became independent, the Hindus and Muslims of Bengali descent account for more than 40 per cent of the population of Assam. These demographic changes have provoked fierce ethnic conflict leading to large-scale displacement of populations. On the other hand, tribes with competing homeland demands have not only found themselves pitted in conflict against the federal government but militias claiming to represent them have also fought bloody internecine feuds among themselves. The sustained deployment of government forces, the violent activities of the separatist armies and the fighting between the militia factions, often representing different ethnicities but sometimes competing for the loyalty of the same tribe or ethnic group, have led to continuous bloodletting in the region. The large-scale violations of human rights, ethnic cleansing, extra-judicial killings and rampant use of terror have all contributed to internal displacement in India's northeast. Sometimes this displacement has been visible, but sometimes not. The author of the chapter on northeast India points out that, while the displacement of the adivasis from the Bodo-dominated areas is visible, the steady displacement of the Bengalis from all over the region is rarely visible, although tens of thousands of Bengalis from the region have silently moved away to West Bengal in the past two decades. While these conflicts have regularly led to considerable internal displacement of victim populations, many of the recent migrants belonging to the minority groups are now being perceived as infiltrators. Development projects undertaken by the central and state governments have also displaced a good number of people, mostly belonging to indigenous tribes and economically weaker sections. Development-induced displacements have often contributed to deterioration of ethnic relations and exacerbated the process of conflict. For instance, the Dumbur hydroelectric project in Tripura's south district uprooted thousands of tribal people, but it benefited both the migrant Bengali fishermen (who got fishing opportunities in the reservoir lake) and urban dwellers (who got electricity from it). Similarly, in Meghalaya, the Khasi and Jaintia people have stridently opposed uranium mining by Indian government agencies in the state's Domiosiat and Wakkhaji region. The tales from the northeast reflect how the indigenous population is often pushed to the margins of citizenry and becomes the perennially displaced.

It is now known worldwide that the overwhelming majority of the internally displaced are women and their dependent children. In the chapter on displaced women in South Asia, the author has dealt with two major categories of displacement—displacement due to conflict and displacement due to developmental projects. In this framework, the author's intention is to analyse how the South Asian states have integrated gender concerns in their programmes for displaced populations. She has also analysed whether gender-specific violence has contributed in any way towards the increasing displacement in the region. The author argues that states are often weighted against women in South Asia. So even though they become citizens, their citizenship is often marginal. In such a scenario it is not surprising that they form the majority among the perennially displaced in South Asia. But do women accept such marginalization mutely? Her answer is, no. In fact, she points out that to look at women merely as victims is to see only half of the story. Accordingly, it is essential that we recognize that women, even as victims of state-sponsored displacement, attempt to organize movements to seek justice.

All these chapters together present a comprehensive study on internal displacement in South Asia. Although there are two separate articles on India, the authors concerned have dealt with the problem of internal displacement from two distinctly different perspectives as the situation in northeast India, in many cases, differs largely from that in the rest of the country. Similarly, gendered victimization is a common phenomenon in all parts of South Asia and, therefore, all the country chapters pay some attention to the issue. The chapter on women thus supplements the discussion as an incisive analysis of the situation of women as IDPs in South Asia, in general. The leitmotif often is the dichotomy between the citizens and the displaced (who might also be citizens) in the region. As has been pointed out earlier, we feel that neither the category of citizen nor that of the displaced is fixed. At times, the citizens become the displaced, and we have sought to highlight these situations.

A major contribution of this compendium is that it shows the mixed nature of displacement. Areas of developmental displacement can also be converted into areas of conflict as the case of the Chittagong Hill Tracts clearly portrays. Some areas reflect how displacement of communities can be carried out serially. For example, in Gujarat, certain communities were displaced while constructing dams, followed by the displacement of other communities due to conflict. By displacing communities the demography of the region was altered substantially. This book highlights the role of the establishment (sometimes the state and in other times the majority communities) in different areas of South Asia.

THE ETHICS OF CARE

Although the UN Guiding Principles on Internal Displacement is not a legally binding treaty it is formed of principles that are based on established legal mechanisms for aiding the human rights of the displaced people. Many of these Principles may gradually attain the status of customary international law. But as Francis Deng reminds us, 'for the time being they serve as a morally binding statement'.[6] A statement of this nature that promises to be 'morally binding' on a wide spectrum of *primarily*, national governments and, *secondarily*, other relevant international and non-governmental agencies must cut across the well-known divisions of the prevailing ethical and moral systems and elaborate itself in a way that it does not remain captive to any particular modality of moral reasoning. Plurality of such systems and modalities is helpful in building the much-needed 'moral consensus' around these principles.[7] The importance of 'moral reasoning' in initiating *organized* responses can hardly be exaggerated. That the Principles underline the necessity of organized responses does not mean that there are no unorganized (like the reflexive and instinctual) responses at all to the problem of the IDPs. But we must keep in mind that the organized and unorganized responses take on two rather distinct moral trajectories. Most of the empirical studies on unorganized, altruistic responses in general (not necessarily towards the problem of IDPs) seem to indicate their unselfconscious character. That is to say, those who care for and protect are not at the same time bothered about the fact that they are actually involved in any 'extraordinary' act that in fact constitutes 'moral reasoning'.[8] On the other hand, responses get organized, ordered and orchestrated precisely through an act of self-consciousness. It is by way of consciously entering into some form of 'moral reasoning' with others that we evolve the principles that are 'morally binding' on us. Mere abstinence or abhorrence will not do. The studies contained here focus mainly on the organized responses or maybe a lack of them and it is in the context of the organized responses that the debates and discourses on ethical and moral issues acquire some special significance. Almost all the reports included here have been written in the spirit of self-consciously deciphering the moral basis of the UN Guiding Principles and making an audit of the respective cases in their light.

Organized responses face the perpetual challenge of excising power from the ethics of care and protection. The challenge is perpetual because we hope to meet it only unsuccessfully, notwithstanding our best endeavours. There is no denying that what we do in the name of care and protection is structured in the power relations prevailing in the society. The question of care and protection in that sense can never be disentangled from that of power.[9] Samaddar, for example, points out how our humanitarian responses geared to the objective of protecting life are scripted in, and thereby reproduce, the imperial 'power of death'.[10] But the irony is that we as ethical agents always refuse to conflate what we *do* in the name of care and protection with what we *ought* to do and seldom confer moral recognition on it. The ethics of care and protection imposes on us the painful obligation of publicly denying the existence of power while at the same time being shaped and structured by it. The erasure of power is a precondition of ethics. It is important to see how we effect the erasure through the language of 'moral reasoning' in our attempts at making the Principles 'morally binding' on us. The Guiding Principles too take particular care in ensuring that 'humanitarian assistance is carried out in accordance with the principles of humanity' and is not made subservient to any other reasons—'political and military reasons, in particular'.

The common thread that sutures the studies included here is their moral language and what emerges from the pages of this book is the wide variety of moral reasoning offered by various authors in justification of their advocacies for care and protection of the IDPs. First of all, there is the *rights-based argument*. Care and protection, according to this argument, will be construed as our 'duty' in so far as the 'well-being' of the IDPs becomes 'a sufficient reason for holding us to be under this duty'.[11] The problem recognized by almost all the exponents of this argument is that the right against displacement is not an end in itself and cannot per se be regarded as a 'sufficient reason' for holding us—the non-IDPs who are also not in any way responsible for their displacement—under this duty. Sufficiency of reason does not reflect itself in the same way as in the two advocacies for the right against displacement and, say, the right to life. If one's displacement becomes a necessary condition for another's enjoyment of the right to life—often understood as decent life—we can say that the former is derogable, while the latter is not. Thus, the right against eviction routinely carried out ín the metropolitan cities of South Asia—whether in Dhaka or in Islamabad or elsewhere—has to contend with the argument for development and decent life defined in these countries as a 'collective goal of the community as a whole'.[12] The successful assertion of the right against displacement therefore entails some form of compromise with 'the collective goal'. Many of those who were evicted from the banks of the Beliaghata circular canal of north Kolkata had been living there for more than one generation. Yet as the India study emphasizes, all of them were the illegal occupants of land. In the absence of any legal title, they are unlikely to be able to sustain their claim to land in the first place, in any court of law.[13] The UN Guiding Principles too present the right as only a limited right against *arbitrary* displacement. Thus, as the Bangladesh study points out, the ruling of the High Court on the famous Agargoan eviction case did not make eviction as part of urban planning 'illegal'; but it ordered for the provision of 'alternative accommodation'. While we cannot compromise with the 'collective goal', we can certainly reduce the sufferings of the displaced through compensation, relief and rehabilitation. Conversely and by the same logic, we should be prepared to accept that the importance of the same right will vary if it ever becomes a necessary condition for the enjoyment of one's non-derogable rights, including that to life. What if it becomes impossible to carry out displacement without simultaneously violating 'the rights to life and freedom from cruel, inhuman or degrading treatment'? What if displacement involves violation of the victims' right to life and livelihood as in the case of the pavement dwellers of Mumbai?[14] Displacement in that case is bound to be illegal for it leads to derogation of a non-derogable right enshrined in law. By basing itself on the rights-based argument, the ethics of care and protection remain dependent on the contingent nature of the relationship between the right against displacement on the one hand and any of the non-derogable rights recognized by the court of law on the other. An argument is made almost in all the chapters contained here, to locate the rights of the IDPs within 'a radical democratic perspective', redefine the lines of derogability and non-derogability and thereby extend the sphere of their rights beyond the given limits of law by constantly waging and organizing political struggles.[15] Thus, to cite an instance, the report on internally displaced women underlines the imperative necessity of women's participation in making decisions and organizing responses that affect them and their families. To our mind, this actually turns the rights-based argument on its head by basing rights on ethics and not vice versa.

This takes us to the heart of our second argument. According to it, care and protection always follow the established lines of community and kinship. Organizing responses beyond these lines proves particularly difficult especially on the margins of South Asia. Studies on northeastern India and (northwestern) Pakistan illuminate the preponderance of kinship and community lineages in defining the terms of relief and rehabilitation. When in the early 1990s thousands of Raijas, Kalpars and Ahmedans were displaced as a sequel to the continuing inter-tribal feuds in Pakistan, they fled to the nearby provinces of Punjab and Sindh. There the leaders of the Legharis and the Khosas refused to provide shelter to the displaced tribes 'as they did not want to annoy the Chief of the Bugti tribe'. The *community-based argument*, as the case studies point out, evidently has its limits: in the course of organizing the responses, it can not only reinforce the traditional lines of rivalry, but can re-enact the inequities and asymmetries otherwise internal to these bodies. The report on Afghanistan shows how aid and assistance help in reproducing and even in some cases accentuating gender asymmetries. But it also gives us examples of how informal support structures across traditional kinship and community networks develop inside the IDP camps. Reports on India and Myanmar emphasize how life in camps, allocation and utilization of aid and assistance for the IDPs reinforce and resuscitate the kinship and community lineages and become the fertile ground for future tensions and strife.

The limits of the community-based argument are sought to be overcome by what we call *the humanitarian argument*. A somewhat old-fashioned version of the argument looks upon care and protection as a form of 'moral exercise' that we require for making our individual selves 'pure and perfect'. Helping others, according to this version, is a form of self-help, of achieving one's higher moral self.[16] The objective of self-help does not however rule out the necessity of organized responses. Learning to work with others is also a means of helping oneself, and the proponents of this argument recognize the importance of institutions and organizations in accomplishing this objective.[17] Today, however, the humanitarian ethic seldom turns on one's own self. Instead it considers others as equal moral agents in the sense that they are as much entitled to 'purity and perfection' as we are. Viewed in this light, our care and protection are a tribute to their moral entitlements, of which they are otherwise deprived. The humanitarian ethic thus has two presuppositions: first, displacement in South Asia cannot be fathomed without the metaphor of home for it is not simply where we live or to which all of us are morally entitled like many other objects of our social existence, but it is the fountainhead of *all* our moral entitlements. Almost all the South Asian societies make a distinction between the home we simply live in and the *home* (e.g. *ghar* in Marathi or *aamar gharkhon* in Assamese) that helps shape what we aspire to become and therefore invests us with our moral identities.[18] Any involuntary displacement is a disjuncture between home and *home*, between what we are and what we want to become, between our senses of lack and fulfilment. Most of the studies included here amply demonstrate the inadequacy of modern legal provisions in safeguarding and protecting the right to *home* in the second sense, so much so that many actually displaced tribes have been retrospectively reclassified as nomadic and homeless groups by the state. In northeastern India, for example, many Santhals displaced as a result of the inter-tribal clashes in the proposed 'Bodoland' could not return to their homes; they have been living for generations on the land that the Supreme Court of India upheld as a 'forest reserve'. Second, should a conflict arise between our moral entitlements and their moral entitlements, humanitarian ethic settles for a minimalist course. Those of us who have taken care of the IDPs will be under a moral obligation only, if by taking care and protecting them, we 'do not sacrifice anything of comparable moral importance', that is to say, our own right to life and livelihood.[19]

As we see, the variations in the tenor and accent of our 'moral reasoning' can hardly be overlooked. But they should not be blown out of proportion. The rights-based argument may well be subsumed under the humanitarian argument or, for that matter, the community-based argument, though of course it will be difficult to accommodate the community-based and the humanitarian arguments within the same moral philosophy. In many ways, the arguments cut across each other and can hardly be considered mutually exclusive. While in our 'moral reasoning' we face the challenge of extricating ethic from power, all the studies, without any exception, point out how the practice of care and protection continues to be governed by power and security considerations. Nowhere is this more sharply evident than in those cases of displacement in which the state remains involved as one of the conflicting parties. Thus, the 'welfare centres' in Sri Lanka or the 'camps' in Nepal or Afghanistan sheltering the IDPs represent sites where war is continued 'by other means'. The budgetary allocation is paltry and irregular. The camp-dwellers are deprived of the non-derogable freedoms the Guiding Principles propose to secure. Life is poor and insecure. The report on India views camps, sheltering especially the Kashmiri Pundits and the Muslims of Gujarat, as the hothouses of communal unrest. The Afghan case is most blatant of all: it shows how, with the breakdown of law and order and the inability of the Kabul-based interim government to establish political order across the country, protectors sometimes become looters. 'Moral reasoning', on the other hand, makes it imperative on each of the authors to renegotiate the foundations of care and protection and sever their connection from power. The Sri Lankan case, for example, makes a distinction between care and durable solutions and argues that care and protection are no guarantee for a durable solution to the blood-soaked conflict that has ripped this small island nation apart. The search for any durable solution ironically makes us confront power and negotiate its terms. Our attempts at disentangling ethic from power too are a power game.

RESPONSIBILITY

If the state-centric nationalistic approach has meant the exclusion of minorities and has produced a large number of refugees in the post-colonial states in Asia and Africa, the state-centric national security perspective and development paradigm have not done any better. The people displaced against this backdrop might have got some relief if they had been able to cross international boundaries. Crossing the international boundary may entitle them to 'refugee' status, thus providing them at least a fig leaf of relief and rehabilitation in an alien land. But wretched are those who remain internally displaced. They remain at the mercy of the same state and administration whose policy might have sent them on the run. According to all estimates, the number of IDPs is rising compared to the refugees seeking shelter in another country. South Asia is no exception to this. But, so far, no systematic and comprehensive study has been carried out. Only a few brief, and sometimes sketchy, reports and articles are available on the plight of the IDPs in South Asia. This book hopefully will fill that awful and disturbing vacuum.

The authors contributing to this volume have not only gone through the nature of the extent of displacement in their respective studies, they have also provided recommendations to minimize the insecurity of the displaced. A few authors have also suggested some early warning systems as preventive measures to forestall the displacement at the very outset. Most of the essays have dealt with the issue of responsibility; not merely who or what is responsible for such massive displacements, but rather who takes responsibility for the displaced.

This volume is a collaborative endeavour. A small group of South Asian scholars, journalists, social scientists and activists got together under the aegis of the Calcutta Research Group as they felt the need to address the situation of IDPs in South Asia, particularly in the post September 11th period. This was also the time when Gujarat witnessed the killings and displacement of Muslim minorities. The situation in both Sri Lanka and Nepal was tense. There was increasing fear among women's groups in Sri Lanka that in the period of the ceasefire it would be the women who would be pushed back into the high security zones in the north and east, even though these areas are infested with landmines. Although there was a ceasefire in Nepal between the state and the Maoists it was at best tenuous. Further, the state refused to acknowledge that the number of IDPs was fast increasing. Keeping these developments in mind the group decided to investigate how far the South Asian states are sensitive to the needs of the IDPs and whether the UN Guiding Principles are being adhered to in any extent. Today a volume of this kind has become even more essential as ceasefires in two areas in South Asia have broken down. It is time for us to recognize that unless we can continue the peace process, the situation of IDPs will not be in any way improved. And unless the situation of IDPs is addressed and justice achieved, there will not be any lasting peace in South Asia.

NOTES

1. Pradip Prabhu, 'Tribals Face Genocide', *Combat Law: The Human Rights Magazine*, Vol. 1, Issue 4 (October–November 2002), 73.
2. Stan Swamy, 'New State, Dying Hopes', *Combat Law: The Human Rights Magazine*, Vol. 2, Issue 1 (April–May 2003), 83.
3. Lyla Mehta and Bina Srinivasan, 'Balancing Pains and Gains: A Perspective Paper on Gender and Large Dams,' A Working Paper of the World Commission on Dams (unpublished) prepared for *Thematic Review*, Cape Town. http://www.dams.org/, 2.
4. Paula Banerjee, 'Aliens in the Colonial World', in R. Samaddar (ed.), *Refugees and the State: Practices of Asylum and Care in India 1947–2000* (New Delhi: Sage, 2003), 69–105.
5. E. Colson, 'Engendering those Uprooted by Development', in D. Indra (ed.), *Engendering Forced Migration: Theory and Practice* (Oxford: Refugee Studies Programme, 1999), 25.
6. Francis Deng's 'Preface' to Walter Kalin, *Guiding Principles on Internal Displacement: Annotations* (Washington, DC: American Society of International Law, and the Brookings Institution, 2000), vi.
7. Peter Penz describes it as 'middle level analysis' that situates itself between boundary-conscious ethical and philosophical systems on the one hand, and simple and boundary-blind 'moral intuitions' on the other. He also calls for 'engaging different theoretical perspectives in a "dialogue" with each other'. Peter Penz, 'Development, Displacement and International Ethics' (2000, mimeo).
8. Kristen Renwick Monroe, *The Heart of Altruism: Perceptions of a Common Humanity* (Princeton: Princeton University Press, 1996), 197–215.
9. Foucault, for example, shows how the modern self 'constitutes' and 'empowers' itself and thereby becomes a 'subject' through these acts of caring and protecting others. See, Michel Foucault, *Ethics: Essential Works of Foucault 1954–1984*, Vol. 1, edited by Paul Rabinow (London: Penguin, 1994), 269–80.
10. Ranabir Samaddar, 'In life, In death: Power and Rights' (2003, mimeo). See, his 'Caring for the Refugee: Issues of Power, Fear and Ethics', in Ranabir Samaddar, 'Three Essays on Law Responsibility and Justice', SAFHR paper 12 (Kathmandu: South Asia Forum for Human Rights, 2002), 42–60. See also, *Refugees and the State: Practices of Asylum and Care in India 1947–2000* (New Delhi: Sage, 2003), Introduction, 21–68 ff. Sudipto Ghose's study on a sample of Ramakrishna Mission and Rotary International

organizations based in Calcutta points out how 'social service discourse' in India is *powered* by non-altruistic (like personal, and caste) considerations. See, Sudipto Ghose, 'Some Aspects of Social Service in Contemporary India', unpublished M.A. dissertation, University of Calcutta, Kolkata, 2002.

11. Joseph Raz is perhaps the most eloquent exponent of this argument. I have paraphrased his words to suit our specific context. See, Joseph Raz, *The Morality of Freedom* (Oxford: Clarendon, 1986), 166–68.

12. Ronald Dworkin calls these rights, 'principles' that are always pitched against 'policies' or 'collective goals'. See, Ronald Dworkin, *Taking Rights Seriously* (Cambridge, Mass.: Harvard University Press, 1977), 82–5.

13. In a similar study on the Mumbai pavement dwellers, the author points out: 'The state has never included them in any census as a matter of policy, because it views them merely as intruders into or encroachers of private/government property. ... The only way the state approached them was by dislocating them, demolishing their hutments, demonising them and by keeping them away from its network of entitlement and rights'. See, Bishnu N. Mohapatra, 'A View from the Subalterns: The Pavement Dwellers of Mumbai', in Rajesh Tandon and Ranjita Mohanty, *Does Civil Society Matter? Governance in Contemporary India* (New Delhi: Sage, 2003), 297.

14. Bishnu N. Mohapatra raises the same question. See, Bishnu N. Mohapatra, ibid.

15. Niraja Gopal Jayal, 'Displaced Persons and Discourse of Rights', *Economic and Political Weekly*, XXX (5), 31 January 1998, PE 30–PE 36.

16. For example, the 'omission of the virtues of positive social service' is central to the ethics of the Hindus. See, Susil Kumar Maitra, *The Ethics of the Hindus* (Kolkata: University of Calcutta, 1963), 9.

17. See, *The Complete Works of Swami Vivekananda*, Vol. I (Kolkata: Advaita Ashrama, 1994), 72–80.

18. Contemporary anthropological researches on home in South Asia in general and India in particular point to this disjuncture. See, Salmon Rushdie, *Imaginary Homelands: Essays and Criticism 1981-1991* (London: Granta, 1991). Also, Yasmin Saikia, 'A Name without a People: Searching to be a Tai-Ahom in Modern India,' unpublished Ph.D. dissertation, Dept. of History, University of Wisconsin, Madison, 1999, 65–66. Also, Irina Glushkova and Anne Feldhaus (eds), *House and Home in Maharashtra* (Delhi: OUP, 1998).

19. See, for example, Peter Singer, 'Famine, Affluence, and Morality', in Stephen Cahn and Peter Markie (eds), *Ethics: History, Theory and Contemporary Issues* (New York: Oxford University Press, 1998), 800.

Chapter 1

Afghanistan: The Long Way Home

Mossarat Qadeem

The eyes of the dove are lovely, my son! But the sky is made for the hawk.
So cover your dove-like eyes and grow claws.

Pushto proverb

Afghanistan, at the crossroads of Central Asia, has been subjected to a series of invasions dating back as far as the sixth century BC. The invasions continued well into the late 1970s, when the Afghans heard the roar of Soviet tanks. The agony and difficulty for the Afghans is not as yet over. Today, they are facing the worst humanitarian crisis of modern history.

Afghanistan is a land of diverse philosophies and ways of living, from the communists to religious fundamentalists. Afghanistan has remained a focal point of ideological radicalism for years, with little place for moderates. Besides, there is a diverse ethnic distribution and a tribal split in Afghanistan. There are no exact statistics available for its population and ethnic distribution. However, the current published estimates assume a total population of about 22,600,000 in 1996 (excluding refugees). The ethnic composition in 1990 was assumed to be about 40 per cent Pushtun, 25 per cent Tajik, 19 per cent Hazara and 6 per cent Uzbek—with other ethnic groups making up 12 per cent of the population.[1] Muslims comprise 99 per cent of the total population of Afghanistan, approximately 80 per cent of them belonging to the Sunni sect living mainly in the central, south and east of Afghanistan. The remaining 20 per cent are Shi'a followers, concentrated in central and western Afghanistan. With no ethnic group having an overall majority in Afghanistan, the ethnic and sometimes ideological tensions have prevailed for decades now. The civil war in Afghanistan has not only been long, it has been brutal as well, costing the lives of thousands of Afghan people. The ethnic groups, after their areas were captured and recaptured by rival factions, are now faced with complete displacement. Such incidents include massacres and mass arrests of civilians, brutal ill-treatment of detainees, disappearance of many young men and some young women.

LOOKING BACK

In 1993, Burhanuddin Rabbani was selected to lead the country in what was supposed to be a revolving presidency among the various militia commanders. The presidency, however, never revolved. Rabbani, a Tajik, ruled until the Taliban threw him out in 1996. President Rabbani's control of Afghanistan was tenuous and at times did not even include all of the capital itself, let alone the rest of the country. Outside of Kabul, militia warlords carved much of Afghanistan into private fiefdoms based largely on traditional ethnic and tribal divisions. The militias that had fought together against the Soviet army now turned on each other. Pushtun commanders threatened Kabul from the south; Hazara resistance groups held parts of Kabul itself, including the area around the university, and Kabul was bombed more than once by the Uzbek groups in the north. The country was again mired in sectarian conflict.

Refugees began returning to Afghanistan from Pakistan and Iran in 1992. Both asylum-giving countries exerted strong pressure on the refugees to return since, as far as they were concerned, the war that had created the refugees was over. In addition, a change in government in Pakistan led to increased pressure on Islamabad to end the 'refugee problem' in Pakistan. Pakistan closed camps, offered incentives to the Afghan refugees to return to Afghanistan and tried several times to close the border to Afghans seeking entry into Pakistan. But since fighting erupted again, repatriation was largely unsuccessful; many of those who tried to return were forced to leave again as the fighting intensified.

By the mid-1990s, a large internally displaced population had developed. Relief agencies opened several camps for the displaced in the Jalalabad area. Other camps were opened in the area around Mazar-i-Sharif in the north and in Herat in the west, near the Iranian border. These camps housed over 400,000 displaced persons. The rise of Taliban to the cadres of high authority in Afghanistan in 1996 was a new chapter in Afghan politics. Economic decline exacerbated the level of poverty and economic hardship throughout the country.

Table 1
Human Development Index

Life expectancy	Mortality rate for children under 5 yrs	Illiteracy rate	Percentage of undernourished	Access to improved water sources
40 years	25.7 per cent	64 per cent	70 per cent	13 per cent

Source: UNDP, 8 October 2001.

Due to a lack of available estimate of income per capita, Afghanistan has not appeared in the UNDP's Human Development Index since 1996. It then ranked as number 169 of a total of 174 countries.[2]

On top of the political unrest, the regional drought too emerged as one of the dominating factors affecting the socio-economic situation in the medium term. It came at a time when much of the population was already highly vulnerable. Some, particularly in the central highlands, had to sell their assets or go into debt to cope with reduced crop production in 1999 and 2000. Lack of assets and the high level of dependence on agriculture and livestock raising meant that many families had nothing to fall back on. The migration of people from drought areas to urban areas, particularly to Herat, resulted in fewer job opportunities.[3] Significant economic resources were diverted for the continuation of the war at the expense of civilians. Military employment offered an opportunity of economic survival to many young men and their families. At the same time, the absence of effective and legitimate institutions of governance allowed the development of large-scale criminalized economic activities, linked in particular to narcotics production and marketing. The nation's transportation and communication system, heavy and small-scale industries, education and agricultural infrastructure are the most seriously damaged sectors. This economic decline has exacerbated the level of poverty and economic hardship throughout the country. Largely dependent on subsistence agriculture, the country has witnessed diminishing income levels, declining food security and reduced access to essential services. In addition, a wide range of disparities exist between different regions and within each region.

Despite efforts on a number of fronts, political resolution of the conflict remained elusive. Under these circumstances the ailing Afghan economy continued to deteriorate. There were few formal-sector employment possibilities, no major rehabilitation or development projects and no major private sector investment to support income. Cross-border trade through Iran and Turkmenistan expanded as Afghanistan adjusted to the suspension of flights and border restrictions with Pakistan. Trade in narcotics, and presumably arms, constituted the mainstay of the 'criminalized' economy. Overall, serious human rights violations continued to occur and citizens were precluded from changing their government or choosing their leaders peacefully. Armed units, local commanders and rogue individuals were responsible for political killings, abductions, kidnappings for ransom, torture, rape, arbitrary detention and looting. Prison conditions were extremely poor both in Taliban and anti-Taliban controlled areas. Summary justice was common. Various factions infringed on citizens' privacy rights. Both Taliban and anti-Taliban forces were responsible for the indiscriminate bombardment of civilian areas. Masood's forces continued rocket attacks against Kabul. Civil war conditions and the unfettered actions of competing factions effectively limited the freedoms of speech, press, assembly, association, religion and movement.[4]

In Taliban areas, strict and oppressive order was imposed and stiff punishments for crimes prevailed. The Taliban's religious police and the Ministry for the Promotion of Virtues and Suppression of Vice (PVSV), enforced their extreme interpretation of Islamic punishments, such as public execution for adultery or murder, and amputation of one hand and one foot for theft. For other infractions, Taliban militiamen often decided right or wrong and meted out punishments such as beatings on the spot. The Taliban government imposed a strict version of sharia, Islamic law, on the country, prohibiting a wide range of public activities. Many of these prohibitions were particularly designed to restrict the freedom and rights of women. Under this interpretation of Islamic law, women were forced to comply with the discriminatory policies of the Taliban who imposed severe restrictions on their education, employment and freedom of movement. Tens of thousands of women effectively remained prisoners in their homes, with no scope to seek the removal of these restrictions. Women who violated these restrictions were punished severely and their families held responsible for their behaviour. Displaced women who had no shelter in which to maintain their privacy were doubly disadvantaged.

Even before sharia was imposed, the patriarchal society of Afghanistan required that women depended on close male relatives to survive. Women were not allowed to appear in public with men who were not close relatives. This restriction created particularly severe problems for widows who had no male family members to help or protect them. Since women are defined by their relationship to a male member of their family, displaced females who had no male relative present, either because the men stayed behind, were arrested or were killed, were particularly vulnerable. A widow's brother or close male relative of her deceased husband would often protect her by marrying her, as men are permitted four wives under Islamic law. This form of protection increased among the displaced population, though it was by no means a complete solution to women's considerable problems.

Defining Internally Displaced Persons

'In defining internally displaced persons (IDPs) in Afghanistan, a distinction is made between principal internal displacement and secondary internal displacement'.[5]

Principal internal displacement includes victims of conflict who chose to remain in Afghanistan rather than flee to neighbouring countries. It also includes people displaced due to blockades that have prohibited free movement and the flow of goods. The resulting economic insecurity has forced many of these people to leave their homes. This group faces the loss of property rights, access to land and livelihoods.

Secondary internal displacement includes other groups such as pastoral nomads, estimated in 1979 to number 800,000. Nomads normally fall outside the definition of IDPs and some nomadic groups, such as the Zala Khan Khel, opted for external exile. Others remained in Afghanistan but were prevented by landmines and other war-related factors from exploiting traditional pastures. Also included are repatriating Afghan refugees who returned from Pakistan and Iran between 1992 and 1993. They could not reach their places of origin due to the resumption of conflict between the different warring factions.

Causes and Patterns of Displacement

The causes of internal displacement in Afghanistan have been: Soviet invasion in 1979; start of civil war in 1993; drought and famine of 1996; US air strikes in 2001; anti-Pushton violence since Northern Alliance regained power in 2001.

Soviet Invasion in 1979

Traditionally Afghans are a highly mobile people. Their patterns of displacement accentuate the normal patterns of movement and as a consequence there have been continuous movements in and out of Afghanistan. Even within the context of the mobile Afghan society, the major population shifts experienced over the past 23 years represent a significant state of disruption. During the Soviet occupation the most immediate and obvious cause was the bombing of villages and the destruction of harvests, livestock and, of course, people. Although often people did not flee at first, the momentum of mass movement increased with the fear and terror that followed each event. Fear of reprisals following a resistance operation, house-to-house searches, checking operations, recruitment of young conscripts, punitive operations conducted by both sides and the abduction of young girls were some of the reasons behind these mass movements. In the most recent offensives in the Panjshir valley, a repeat of 15 years ago, village evacuation, sometimes forced, has preceded bombardment or attack. The areas most affected are strategically significant: towns, lines of communication and military strongholds where entire valleys or mountain areas are affected.

During the 1979 Soviet invasion the displacement of people was an incidental effect of hostilities and those displaced could count on the support from their government, the Mujahideen factions and fellow citizens. The spirit of solidarity vanished when the factional conflict set in; in such a situation particular groups within the population were characteristically identified with the enemy and deliberately targeted. The majority of these displaced persons were totally empty-handed, exhausted, sick or wounded, traumatized and separated from the rest of their community or family. As the duration of their displacement increased, new challenges arose regarding how to meet their different needs, be it in the form of security, education, job opportunities or political rights.

During the 25 years of displacement, four major patterns of internal movement have developed: movement towards the mountains nearest to the area abandoned; refuge in major cities such as Kabul, Jalalabad and Herat; refuge in Pakistan; and for populations in the southwest, refuge in Iran.[6]

Total Number of IDPs

Obtaining exact data has been very difficult due to the warring situation in Afghanistan. Distinguishing between drought and conflict-induced displacement has not been easy especially in regions such as Mazar-e-Sharif and Kabul where both groups of victims are mixed together. The internally displaced are integrated with host populations making identification difficult to the extent that some members of the local population have also been known to masquerade as IDPs in order to obtain assistance. The frequent movement of IDPs has also complicated estimates.[7] Finally, the ongoing displacement and limited access to needy populations in several regions of Afghanistan (e.g. Dar-e-Suf), due to bad weather or volatile security conditions, further complicate the task of getting a comprehensive picture of the situation in terms of figures. The UN estimated that the total number of people displaced at the end of the year 2000, ranged between 600,000 and 800,000 persons and included displacement caused by drought and conflict.[8] The total number of conflict-induced IDPs at the end of 2000 was estimated to range between 300,000 and 400,000.[9] Included in the conflict-induced figures are an estimated 100,000 people displaced since 1999 such as those in Kabul, the Panjshir valley and northern Hazarajat.[10] According to the OCHA, up to 1,000,000 people were displaced either by conflict or drought before the 11 September events in the USA.

It is variously estimated that around 5 million Afghans remain displaced, either internally (some 1 million) or as refugees in neighbouring countries and elsewhere (nearly 4 million). These numbers have been generated over the past two decades in three basic phases. Whereas in the 1980s, large displacements resulted from the Soviet invasion and the ensuing war, internecine conflict was the main cause during the 1990s. Over the past four years, displacement has been a consequence of the effects of a prolonged and severe drought, which was most acute in the western and northern regions, and continuing internal conflict between the Taliban and Northern Alliance forces along the northeastern frontline and in various pockets in the central and highland regions.

The threat of the US attacks started to trigger population movements away from most urban areas towards remote villages and border regions. Eastern and central regions were particularly affected. As of 19 October, 2001 the total number of IDPs (displaced by conflict and/or drought) is estimated at 1,160,000.[11] Straight addition shows that about 470,000 people have left their homes, and the majority of them are internally displaced inside Afghanistan. In addition, the totals represent only new IDPs and do not include at least 100,000 old IDPs from 1999, such as those in Kabul, Panjshir and northern Hazarajat, or the many waves of displaced people over the years, who have sought safety in the capital city, Kabul.[12] Moreover, these totals do not take into account all displacement that is likely to have occurred, such as within remote districts to other remote districts (e.g. Ghor); into urban centres but outside the camps (e.g. Herat); or into Iran. Therefore, this total number of IDPs should be assumed to be reasonably accurate for now, and if anything, on the low side. The pattern of displacement follows the pattern of fighting.

Characteristics of Displacement

The distinction between 'conflict-induced' and 'drought-induced' IDPs is an oversimplification of Afghanistan's complex internal displacement problem. Many drought-induced IDPs may not have become displaced had conflict not undermined their normal support capacities.[13] Moreover, the overall national food-security crisis has created widespread levels of acute vulnerability where the only survival strategy is to become 'local' IDPs at or near internationally assisted IDP camps. Indeed, one of the overriding concerns expressed by almost all humanitarian actors is the dilemma they face in providing even the most basic levels of assistance to IDPs, especially in light of the fact that such assistance will likely create new IDPs drawn from among the local vulnerable populations. This situation is compounded by the fact that in many areas IDPs are living with host families who are equally destitute and in need of assistance. Moreover, in many cases, IDPs living with host families are not included in registrations and, by extension, in food distribution.

Notwithstanding the above, an important distinction must be made between those able to return to areas of displacement caused by conflict (where mines are one of the primary constraints to return) and those that were displaced by drought (where the availability of agricultural inputs and the vagaries of climate are the primary constraint). Hence, in much of the south, southeast and central regions, returnees require a basic provision of shelter kits and mine action in their villages in order to re-establish themselves, while in the north and west, return is a much more uncertain and precarious challenge given the risk that ameliorated drought conditions may only be a temporary phenomenon.[14] Table 2 shows the pattern of displacement which follows the pattern of fighting.

US Strikes and Displacement

It is estimated that there were more than 1 million internally displaced and more than 4 million internally stranded people within Afghanistan before the threat of reprisals following the terrorist attacks on the USA. An estimated 400,000 people were living in these camps, in squalid conditions with little water, shelter or sanitation. In August 2001, Medicines Sans Frontiers estimated that 20–40 people were dying each day.[15] Some reports stated that people left their camps and headed for the Iranian border, in the hope of finding better provision there. Initially, the threat of a US-led military strike on Afghanistan and increased Taliban

Table 2
Overview of Main Displacements (1992–2000)

Period of displacement	Reason for displacement	Number of displaced	Displacement site	Place of origin
1992–93	Fear of reprisal from Islamic militias	400,000	Mazar-i-Sharif and Jalalabad	Kabul
1992–93	Combat	200,000	Kabul	Surrounding provinces
1995	Flight from the Taliban	180,000	Kabul and Northern Afghanistan	Southern areas
1997	Fighting in the provinces near Kabul and in the north.	600,000	Kabul and Mazar-i-Sharif	Areas near Kabul and in the northern provinces
1998	Fighting in and around Mazar-i-Sharif	50,000	Mountainous areas in the north	Uzbeks and Hazaras living in Mazar-i-Sharif
Summer 1999	Fighting north of Kabul in the Shomali plain	100,000	Panjshir valley	Tajiks from Shomali plain
Fall 1999	Fighting in the Shomali plain	12,995	Kabul, ex-Soviet embassy compound	Tajiks from Shomali plain
Fall 1999	Fighting in the Panjshir valley	100,000	Northern provinces	Tajiks from Panjshir valley
Fall 1999	Fighting around Talaqan in Takhar province (a Tajik stronghold)	16,000	Areas around Faizabad	Tajiks from the Talaqan area
Winter 2000	Fighting in the Hazarajat	60,000	Near Behsud or Pul-i-Khumri	Hazaras and Tajiks from Bamiyan area
Summer 2000	Fighting in Panjshir valley and Shomali plain	50,000	Kabul and Panjshir valley	Tajiks from the Shomali plain and the Panjshir valley
Summer 2000	Fighting around Talaqan in Takhar province	15,000	Badakhshan area	Tajiks from Talaqan area

Source: United States Committee for Refugees (USCR), June 2000; United Nations Resident Coordinator Office (UNRCO), March 2000; Bashir/Agence France Presse (AFP), 7 August 2000.

repression caused hundreds of thousands of people to flee from their homes, particularly in major cities. A quarter of the population of Kabul and half the population of the southern Afghan province of Kandahar, the headquarters of the Taliban, were said to have evacuated. While reports indicate that many of those who had left the cities returned, the huge number of Afghans who were displaced prior to the events of 11 September remain displaced and in great need of assistance. It was reported that a group of over 20,000 displaced Afghans who had been waiting at the border with Pakistan near the city of Quetta, despite reported attempts by the Taliban to stop people from leaving Afghanistan, have either found alternative routes into Pakistan or have moved and dispersed into other areas of Afghanistan. Prior to 11 September 2001, the number of IDPs was estimated by UNOCHA at some 900,000, with particularly heavy concentrations of newly displaced persons in the north and west. Their number is believed to have risen as a result of the conflict during October and November 2001, to around 1.2 million—much of the increase being experienced in the central and southeastern regions and along the Pakistan border. However, given the fluidity of the situation over the past six months, and the protracted absence of international observers, these numbers are but crude and largely unverifiable estimates.

Attempts are now under way to ascertain more reliable statistics on IDPs through registrations conducted by International Office for Migration (IOM) and United Nations High Commissioner for Refugees (UNHCR) and their partner NGOs. The present paucity of detailed/verifiable information on IDPs continues to constrain the planning and response capacity of humanitarian actors supporting return movements and/or providing assistance to the displaced. Furthermore, it hampers the capacity of agencies to provide timely and objective information to IDPs concerning conditions in areas of potential return.

Rapid assessment exercises and the production of detailed district profiles are currently ongoing in potential areas of return using standardized survey instruments. When completed, these assessments will generate much of the urgently required information at regional, provincial and district levels, including such data as: population numbers, places of origin, time/length of displacement, ethnic group, conditions of vulnerability, assistance needs in areas of displacement and prospects and expectations for return. However, the exercise appears to be carried out at varying intensities and sometimes with diverse methodologies and/or actors in each region.[16]

Table 3
Summary of IDP Data Aggregated at Province Level

Province name	No. of locations	No. of families	No. of persons
Badakhshan	1	1,600	11,200
Baghlan	4	1,026	7,200
Balkh	42	23,671	165,728
Bamiyan	2	1,700	11,900
Hilmand	29	993	6,951
Hirat	5	29,412	205,900
Kabul	2	47	333
Kandahar	86	19,435	136,110
Khost	154	2,544	17,808
Kunar	9	1,051	7,357
Kunduz	10	3,538	24,800
Laghman	191	15,251	106,826
Nangarhar	226	14,095	98,676
Nimroz	7	2,701	18,916
Nuristan	17	509	3,563
Paktya	26	633	4,431
Samangan	1	1,000	7,000
Sari Pul	1	2,028	14,200
Takhar	6	4,628	32,400
Uruzgan	60	410	3,085
Wardak	1	3,000	21,000
Zabul	81	2,276	15,932
Total	961	131,548	921,316

Source: Afghanistan Internal Migration Sources (AIMS), March 2002.

Displacement of Pashtun

In northern Afghanistan, the ethnic Pashtun minority that had been closely identified with the Pashtun-dominated Taliban has been effectively left out of the new power arrangement. Most of the Taliban leadership comprised Pashtuns from southern Afghanistan. As soon as the Taliban collapsed, Pashtun communities were quickly disarmed across northern Afghanistan, and soon faced widespread abuses at the hands of the three ethnic militias—Junbish, Wahdat and Jamiat—as well as by armed Uzbeks, Tajiks and Hazaras taking advantage of the imbalance of power created by the sudden disarming of Pashtun communities. Throughout northern Afghanistan, Pashtun communities faced widespread looting, beatings, abductions, extortion, and incidents of killing and sexual violence. In some communities, these abuses have continued for months. In addition, Pashtun communities have been stripped of their assets, impoverished and displaced by the abuses, and face a difficult future.[17] Targeted violence and looting by ethnic militia against ethnic Pashtuns has led to the internal displacement of thousands across northern Afghanistan, with most moving from rural areas towards cities and towns that have larger concentrations of Pashtuns and where they believe there is greater security.[18] Since early January 2002, the newly displaced Afghans—the majority of whom have been Pashtuns—have sought refuge in Pakistan, mostly at the Pakistani border town of Chaman. While Pakistan's borders have been officially closed since the fall of 2000, some of these displaced persons have taken up residence in private homes; others live in camps for IDPs or in abandoned villages.[19]

The human rights abuses perpetrated against Pashtuns, together with a worsening humanitarian situation in certain areas, were at the root of this recent flight of Pashtuns. Pashtuns consistently reported fleeing because of ethnic persecution. By early January, for instance, the Pashtun families were fleeing the southwestern city of Herat because of harassment, telling officials of the UNHCR that 'the soldiers were looting in the city and forcing people belonging to the Pashtun tribe to pay them money.'[20] The IDPs claimed that they were persecuted, robbed and intimidated because of being Pashtuns in ethnically-mixed villages in northern Afghanistan, often at the instigation of local commanders. Some IDPs said that they were forced off their land, their houses were looted, they were violently attacked, and some said their relatives were killed.[21] Pushtuns from the camp for internally displaced persons at Spin Boldak, south of Kandahar, said the area was 'teeming with gunmen and bandits' since the collapse of the Taliban regime.[22]

The Pashtun minority in the north had suffered throughout the Afghan conflict. Like the other Afghans they had been exposed to all sorts of hardship, destitution and deprivation. Today when the rest of the Afghans are heaving a sigh of relief and looking forward to a better future, these Pashtuns are paying for the crimes of others.[23]

General Condition of the IDPs

IDP families, whether settled in the city or camps, continue (for a variety of reasons) to feel insecure. The IDPs living in Kabul city belonging to the same village/district have, in many cases, grouped themselves in host area or with families, which has been quite significant in planning livelihood-support activities. The majority of those interviewed[24] are able to occupy rooms in relatives' homes in Kabul city without payment. The rest pay on average US $2 per room per month. Two-thirds of those interviewed in-habit living quarters that are felt to be a risk to their health (insecure structures, often with no windows or floor covering, and inadequate ven-tilation). Mattresses, pillows and household utensils are the items most commonly borrowed by IDP families from their hosts/relatives. Most of them have been relying on such loans, and also cash contributions. An absence of fuel for cooking/heating is a major problem, and many are reduced to burning rubbish, with an inevitable impact on their health. Most families have some access to an outside space or yard, but often without the possibility of cultivation.

The majority of IDP families in Kabul city, having no potential bread-winner (i.e. with female or disabled head of household), find life too hard to cope with. The widespread loss of assets and sources of livelihood (i.e. agricultural production) has required IDP families to find manual work to obtain cash. Both IDP and host families have a high proportion of chil-dren between 5 and 15 years old, some of whom are forced to work. Some of the IDPs have family members who are working outside the country but remittances from them are insignificant. So begging remains the only way through which some IDP families earn money, but it is only possible to meet a fraction of the estimated needs of a typical family in this way.

The IDPs living in camp areas belong to different villages, clans and tribes. This is not a traditional community set-up. There are group lead-ers in each camp who are a part of camp management. They work to-gether with the authority running the camp. Nearly all IDPs in a camp have a (military) guard that is responsible for the security of the camp citizens. The Ministry of Repatriation (MoR) is permanently present in the camp. People can easily report to the camp management, which in turn can report automatically to the UNHCR protection officer, and if necessary to the UN security officer through UNOCHA.[25] The manage-ment also reports any issues to the MoR and the military guards. Informa-tion about any mishap in the camps may come from the medical teams in the camps. They report through the UNHCR protection meeting. There is a permanent contact possible between these agencies and the camp management. In emergencies the management is called in.

The camps have had their difficulties when more than one military faction was present and operating in the camp. The military people are probably as poor as the IDPs. Often we got messages that 'soldiers' were involved in looting, bribing, etc.[26] There is no legal system in place in the camps; people have to seek redress from institutions in town. But most of the camps are quite far away from towns. 'Judicial recourse is possible in theory only; none of us has knowledge of cases where IDPs have taken the opportunity to put in a claim. No one will ever submit any accusation if there is a possibility to avoid it,' says an IOM official in Maslakh camp. The shortage of food is another big problem faced by the IDPs. I interviewed a group of people in the Sar-e-Pol camp in Afghanistan. The situation is drastic. There are more children in feeding centres than ever before. The numbers of severely malnourished have increased. Mortality rates have doubled and the numbers of displaced have risen. Of all the families surveyed in 2001, almost half had not received food aid. A lack of food in some camps is forcing people to return home. There are also reports of local international agency staff members telling the IDPs that they must immediately leave or risk losing assistance.[27]

The issue of food has emerged as one of the biggest problems at Maslakh camp. In April 2002 the World Food Program (WFP) began distributing bread instead of wheat. There are different explanations for this change. According to an Afghan WFP employee, 'It is time for the IDPs to return to their homes. If we give them bread each day, then there is no reason for them to stay. If we give them wheat, then they will be encouraged to stay.'[28] The WFP's official explanation for the change is to eliminate corruption in the distribution system of wheat. In many cases, block leaders were collecting the wheat and selling some of it instead of giving it to the intended beneficiaries. Since the IDPs began receiving bread instead of wheat, there have been no reports of diversions. In response to complaints by camp residents about poor quality bread, WFP has initiated quality control measures in the mills and bakeries. In addition, according to a recent UN press release, WFP is possibly faced with a massive food shortage throughout much of Afghanistan. Addressing WFP's Executive Board in Rome for the first time since his appointment, James T. Morris said the Agency's Afghan reconstruction programme has a 46 per cent budget shortfall. 'We are extremely concerned that such high priority emergencies have fallen this far short on funding,' Mr Morris said.[29] In one of the camps visited by the author, the women fetch water from a distant spring and then store it in an uncovered muddy pond. They use this water for cooking and drinking, which is not safe. Many of the IDPs said that they are unable to afford the costs of healthcare. There is a growing risk of malnutrition among young children of the more vulnerable IDP families. The UN Development Program (UNDP) is still not active in the western provinces and, according to one international official, 'UNDP is conspicuous by its absence.'

The camps near Herat shelter 80,000 IDPs. The conditions in these camps are grim. The largest camp, Maslakh, is home to 40,000 people crammed together, three families to each small tent. In winter the temperature drops to below zero Fahrenheit and there is heavy snowfall. Many of the adults and children lack warm clothing, especially adequate shoes and socks. A graveyard full of children's graves testifies to the rigours of life in the camps. Many of these deaths result from exposure to severe cold conditions. Many of the men attempt to supplement the meagre aid they receive by gathering firewood to sell or by journeying by foot or bus 10 miles into the city to seek day labour. At best, they earn a few cents a day. Although Herat remains relatively untouched by the civil war going on elsewhere in Afghanistan, economic opportunities are extremely limited.

Most of the IDPs in Herat cited the drought as the reason for their displacement.[30] Without food to last the winter in their homes, they banded together in village and family groups to travel to the IDP camps. They reported travelling on foot and in trucks for up to 12 days to reach the camps, spending all their remaining resources during the journey. In the summer of 2002, all said they would return to their homes if sufficient rain fell to make agriculture possible and if they had the means to plant a crop and to survive while they waited for a harvest. The Afghans who reached the IDP camps in the winter of 2001 could be considered the lucky ones. The condition of those who stayed back in their inaccessible villages remains unknown. WFP has a far-flung system of food distribution, but many areas of the country are inaccessible due to lack of roads or poor security. Most of the IDPs in Herat, for example, come from areas which cannot be reached by international food aid. In general, due to difficult and dangerous working conditions, there is a shortage of local and international NGOs on the ground in Afghanistan to implement relief and development programmes. This is a serious constraint as the international community attempts to address the appalling humanitarian situation in Afghanistan.

There are no schools in IDP camps but income-generated schemes have been initiated by some of the NGOs. In Mazar-e-Sharif and Herat most of the IDPs are skilled in carpet weaving so NGOs provide them with a kit for carpet weaving to start their own work and to generate some money. Similarly some IDPs from Herat are skilled in making silk stoles. The NGOs give them the silk worm seeds initially and then the IDPs make thread and later weave stoles from it.[31]

An International Relief Committee (IRC) staff member working in Maslakh camp explained that IDPs need better information about their right to stay in the camp or return to their place of origin, and about what they would find when they return.[32] In some camps the workers of international agencies are being pressurized by the IDPs as they want to go back home and do not want to be delayed. For the return of IDPs we need funding for transportation and for reintegration kits (water container, tools, seeds, two to three months' ration and some fuel), says an International Office of Migration (IOM) official.[33] IOM and the UN High Commissioner for Refugees are planning to open an information centre in the camps soon.

THE VOICE OF THE UNHEARD: AFGHAN WOMEN AND THE CHANGED SCENARIO

IDPs come from different backgrounds and experiences. The changes brought about by loss of status, death of loved ones, loss of valuable property and life's savings, in addition to being displaced, result in immense adjustment difficulties. Children and women are particularly vulnerable in such turbulent times as they are faced with multiple burdens and have a lower social status.

Afghan IDP households contain more complex mixtures of kin-related women because so many men have perished during the long conflict in Afghanistan. It is not uncommon to find compounds run by charismatic matriarchs responsible for up to 8 to 10 married and widowed daughters and daughters-in-law, with a legion of children. Other homes are sometimes under the charge of a man's second wife, who is responsible for the well-being of the first wife, bevies of middle-aged single or widowed female relatives and an assortment of all of their children. Sometimes nuclear households without full-time males in residence cluster around the homes of respected female elders. The variations are endless, but all illustrate how these women have adjusted themselves to the changed circumstances. The fortitude of these women is admirable, but with the passage of time symptoms of stress are evident. Strained, incompatible relationships within extended households are exacerbated by the unaccustomed physical closeness of living arrangements and the more than normal dependency on resources outside the family. A woman's pride and self-esteem, engendered by shared contribution to the family welfare is utterly shattered by the realization that her role is so diminished that she can no longer harvest crops or shear sheep for wool to be spun and woven. Rations are doled out to by foreigners, creating a sense of dependency that is abhorrent to both Afghan men and women. There have been great changes in the lifestyle of Afghan females. Female IDPs have experienced the imposition of strict behavioural codes. IDP camps are not kin-related, as were most villages in Afghanistan. Any movement of women out of their compounds is viewed as risky and generally allowed only with a male relative as escort. Afghan women symbolize their family's and society's honour, with Pashtun communities, in particular, placing a high value on women's chastity.[34] Control of the woman is basic to the honour of the Afghan man and an agnatic family. The honour (*namus*) of the family is embodied in the honour of its women; the maintenance of family honour requires control as well as protection of women and family, house and land. Seclusion in *purdah* (veil) is an ideal, closely connected with the concept of family honour. Veil (*burqa*) is a part of Afghan tradition and has played a positive role in the basic protection of women. None of the women find that purdah restricts their work and, contrary to what an outside observer might think, the women do not believe that purdah locks them up in their own separate universe, it merely keeps out men.[35]

In an effort to help themselves women gathered informally in groups or cooperatives. These groups were modelled on the traditional living arrangements in Afghan society, where women live much of their lives apart from men in groups related by birth or marriage. In the traditional household compounds, sisters, sisters-in-law, mothers, grandmothers, daughters, and, in some cases, multiple wives form tight bonds and develop informal networks outside the home. Displaced women in desperate situations formed similar bonds. In these groups of unrelated women, food and other resources are shared and labour is divided: some women look after children while other women search or beg for food. Since women beyond their childbearing years are somewhat freer to move around in public, they represent the group in society. Some groups number only a few women; others can include more than two dozen women, including children. These groupings, however, have become the source of new problems: traditional Afghan society views unattached women, especially those living together, as sinful. They are assumed to be prostitutes. Why else, the traditional thinking claims, would they have no men with them? While there have been reports of prostitution among displaced women, evidence suggests that it is a rare occurrence.[36]

These female IDPs continue to face serious threats to their physical safety, which denies them the opportunity to exercise their basic human rights and to participate fully in the rebuilding of their country. Many children have been separated from their families during mass population movements. Some have lost family members and the family unit has been broken up. This has left these children vulnerable and lacking protection. Some of the IDP children were recruited as soldiers. Even before the October 2001 crisis, children in Afghanistan were acutely vulnerable. Their health and nutritional status is particularly deplorable, and government's capacity to deliver basic health and education services is virtually non-existent. As children flee their homes, their access to education is further hampered.[37]

Individual Voices

Conflict has become a kind of ritual for the Afghans now. I interviewed a number of IDPs in different camps and areas. These interviews present a snapshot of life of the displaced in Afghanistan over the last 23 years.

Neelofur, age 9:

My mother says peace is very beautiful, but I have never seen it in my country. And I want it. Sometimes I think that peace is a bird that flies over every other country except Afghanistan. Peace must be angry at us. It won't come. But I will be happy if it comes. I am so tired of war. Please promise us you'll end it.

Zarlashta, 12-year-old, mother and brother killed on first night of American bombing in October 2001:

America has killed my mother. Can it give me my mother back? In war, people lose mothers. I don't want war. How can I keep my hope for the future? Come and see my life. It's terrible. I perform all those duties that my mother used to do. I cook and clean and wash and all the time the memories of my mother stay with me.

Arsala, a 12-year-old boy in a camp in Mazar-e-Sharif recited a poem written by him in his native language Dari:

Oh god, anger has engulfed the whole world,
And this destruction has prevailed upon my house.
Everything is devastated.

Baghbala has been destroyed.
Shehre-No is also destroyed.
All the countries have united and have brought miseries to us and all our people have become helpless.
Do they have the heart to feel and the eyes to see our sufferings?

An IDP from Maslakh camp in Herat, Mr Malang Jan said:

I feel let down by America. I don't know about other people. The only reason why I say this is because we the Afghans fought the American war against the Soviets & took the bullets on our bosom. Now it's the same America that bombarded us, killed us and displaced us.

Zarghona, a 39-year-old woman who had to leave her home twice (first during Soviet invasion in 1979, when she had to go to Pakistan, and subsequeatly due to American bombardment of her village) says, 'The experience of becoming displaced is awful, truly wrenching. It is impossible to convey the misery of it.'

Mohsin Saeedi, 54-year-old male, alleges that the international agencies are all one and the same: 'You eat, I eat.' According to him, the commanders and the Intergovernmental Organizations (IGO), NGO staffs have all ganged up against the mafia.

Saleh Ahmed, a landowner who lost his three sons between 1979 and 2001 says:

We have seen only destruction and human deaths in our life. We are not afraid. My first son died while fighting against the Russians in 1983. I left my home. I lost all my possessions. I went to Pakistan for six years but I don't like living in another country. Nobody has a right to make me leave my country for any reason. I lost my two sons due to American bombardment in October 2001.

Fatima, a 30-year-old woman says:

Fear of American bombardment emptied villages in batches. The hardest thing when the bombardment started was the fear and panic. We thought of escaping but there was nowhere to go as Pakistan had closed its borders. We stayed near Pak-Afghan border in cold weather where

I gave birth to a baby girl who died two days after due to cold and hunger, as I couldn't feed her.

A 35-year-old Kuchi[38] woman said:

My neighbours and I don't want to go home. We don't have land or houses. We used to be farmers and have animals. When the drought first started, we borrowed money from some rich people in our village so that we could live. They took our land when the money was not paid back. We can't return unless we have money to pay them. We hear that this camp will be closed. We will have to go to another province and look for work. If we can't find work, then we will beg. We can't go home. I came here 1 year and 7 months ago because of the drought in Badghis. After I arrived here, I became a health educator with one of the NGOs here. I am illiterate, but they trained me how to teach people here about hygiene and paid me well. Many people have left Maslakh to return home, but around 50 families have come back to Maslakh because the situation is very bad in their villages. Most of us don't have land and no one will hire us to work on his land. Before I came here, we used to have animals. This is how we survived. Now I don't have animals, but at least I have a salary. If the IOM [International Organization of Migration] tells us that we have to leave, I will go to Iran because I can't return home. People have returned to their homes by choice, but in the last few months there has been no wheat distribution so people now feel they are being forced to return to their homes. I want to tell the world that if they want us to return to our homes, they must help us to survive once we arrive and to start our lives again.

Seventy-year-old asthmatic Barawar could not get medicines for the last two and a half months but still he collects wood and sells them to make some money to buy medicine: 'I have repeatedly asked the doctor in the camp to give me medicine but I am not a young beauty to allure them.'[39]

Jameela Gul, a 40-year-old widow says:

My husband died in the camp in December 2001and left me with two young daughters aged 11 and 12. I had no money to bury him so I went to a rich man in the camp to request him to lend me some money for the burial. At that time he gave me the money without any conditions. But the very next day he came to my tent and said 'either you give me money right now or marry me'. I didn't have the money so I married him. After a month or so when I came back from fetching water he was taking his clothes [off] and both of my daughters were standing naked. I fought with him and later in the dark of the night when the whole camp was asleep I killed him and left the camp. My daughters told me that he had been sleeping with them whenever I would go out.

I would like to mention here that despite the cultural barriers to reporting sexual violence in Afghanistan, being a woman I was able to gather testimony from several rape survivors and witnesses. In one case, a Pashtun woman from Balkh city, recounted how she and her 14-year-old daughter were brutally gang-raped by Hazara soldiers.

Heaven Looks Down on Afghans: Human Rights, Guiding Principles and IDPs

Decades of war have had a devastating impact on traditional coping mechanisms and means of survival. Growing poverty and the limited availability of, and access to, basic social services mean that the vast majority of not only IDPs but also common Afghan men and women are denied their basic human rights. Indeed, it is all too apparent that the poor, the vulnerable and the marginalized, who for the most part constitute the same group, suffer a formidable human rights deficit. They are unable to enjoy such fundamental rights as the right to food, adequate shelter, health, education and a means of livelihood. In addition, they have little or no possibility of judicial recourse and are largely denied the possibility of shaping decisions that affect them. The combination of widespread poverty and protracted conflict, including the deliberate abuse of civilians and means of livelihood, continues to take an incredible toll. Deplorable socioeconomic conditions, coupled with the direct and indirect impact of the war, make Afghanistan one of the most deadly places on earth, particularly for women, children and others made vulnerable by years of unceasing conflict and growing impoverishment.

Violations or denial of rights are a root cause of displacement and related vulnerability. War-torn Afghanistan has the poorest human rights record. The IDPs have been exposed to all sorts of repression and oppression. The right to life is the most fundamental human right[40] but in case of Afghan IDPs they were deprived of life by their own security forces.[41] During the Taliban regime, males and females of the same IDP families were forcefully separated and women and girls taken away by them are still missing.[42] Serious violations of international humanitarian laws are being committed. Young persons have been arrested, detained or taken away against their will by different organized groups or the government authorities and the whereabouts of these people are still unknown.[43] Violations go largely unpunished, as there is an almost total lack of accountability on the part of the authorities. This impunity is compounded by the lack of systematic monitoring and collection of information on violations and abuses in Afghanistan. There is no uniform legal system prevailing in the country. The interim government's rule is limited to Kabul. They don't have the power and money to control other areas. Every commander has his own domain, which he rules according to his own will.[44] The provinces are run by independent governors, and most of them have their own administrative and legal set-up. In such an anarchic situation not only the IDPs but all the people of Afghanistan are denied the right to judicial recourse. There is no legal procedure to punish the criminal or help the victim. There are incidents in which members of armed groups abducted Pashtun IDPs, in Mazar-i-Sharif and on the outskirts of Baghlan city, and left them after beating them for hours. This is in total contrast to Principle 12 of the Guiding Principles.[45]

Some of the families in Mazar-i-Sharif camps sold their children to westerners for money.[46] 'They would be brought up as Christian children,' says Mr Ibrahim Saleemi, an NGO worker in Mazar-i-Sharif. Destitute parents accept money in exchange for allowing their children to go off with strangers who promise them work as domestics, camel jockeys or labourers. The parents believe they are acting in the best interest of their families.[47] In nearly every camp there are at least five hundred orphan children. In some cases, relatives or acquaintances take these children to Pakistan where they are often lured into illicit and illegal trades.[48] Child protection agencies are trying to stop this heinous business but so far they have not been successful because of the mafia-like protection provided by the camp commanders to the brokers.[49]

Afghanistan traditionally has been a diverse country; the war has rendered it even more complex. Despite Afghanistan's compulsory education law for males and females passed in 1919, illiteracy rate is very high among Afghan women particularly. The literacy rate for Afghan women is only 8 per cent.[50] The camps have no schools, as providing education is of secondary importance for the authorities as well as IDPs.[51] Their immediate concerns are food and shelter. A joint statement by Medicines Sans Frontier and Mediciness du Monde reported that the nutritional status of long-term IDPs at Maslakh camp was worse than that of the new arrivals.[52] The finding suggests that the IDPs are not receiving enough food.[53] The agencies reported widespread corruption and criminal activities in the camps especially linked with food distribution.[54] The aid community also faces difficulties in maintaining unhindered access to all IDPs in need of assistance; in a number of instances, the right of IDPs to receive assistance has been denied, in contravention of international law.[55]

Human rights issues in Afghanistan are not well understood or defined. Perceptions about human rights issues in the field may differ from those noted at the international level. Available data are inadequate; particularly, violence against women is seldom reported but that does not mean that violence against women does not occur. In Afghan culture, a woman, or a male relative, would not report an incident of gender violence.[56] An IOM official in Malakh camp states:

> It took us a while before we realized that no one deliberately would insult someone else if the latter is not caught red-handed. One should be aware that the tribe system is still in force and means a lot more than whatever we, western people, may be used to in terms of justice and jurisdiction. Here, any accusation goes farther than the person, farther than the family; it concerns the clan, the tribe. An accusation may endanger not only the accuser but also his/her relatives.[57]

For the camp management the difficulty starts when one tries to get evidence. Besides, women in the camps do not have ways to report abuses in a confidential, appropriate manner. Women have been raped in the camps in Mazar and Herat, according to relief agencies. The International Rescue Committee has documented over 60 cases of sexual violence against women in Mazar IDPs camp.[58] The IDPs' world is a hard world, food is a major issue and sexual favours, asked and/or offered may not be excluded in the struggle for life.[59] Some of these women are being frequently coerced by the commanders or group leaders into providing sexual acts in return for essential food, shelter or other form of assistance.[60] These forms of gender-specific violence breach not only many of the human rights and humanitarian laws[61] but the Guiding Principles[62] as well. In some camps prostitution serves as one of the few forms of economic support for women heads of households, as there are a lot of widows and single women in the camps.[63] An organized prostitution network operates in some camps and at the same time some women/men are working on an individual basis as well. However, prostitution by men cannot be totally excluded.[64]

The interim government has the primary duty and responsibility to establish conditions, as well as provide the means, so that internally displaced persons should return voluntarily, in safety and with dignity, to their homes or places of habitual residence.[65] But the interim government does not have the means to make the resettlement possible. Although the Guiding Principles on Internal Displacement have been translated into local languages, there was little awareness of the Principles on the ground. The law seems to cover many aspects relating to the right to life, prohibitions on torture, hostage-taking, contemporary forms of slavery, subsistence rights and many aspects of religious rights. In these areas, the hardships experienced by Afghan IDPs indicate a lack of willingness on the part of the authorities to observe and implement existing obligations rather than lack of clarity about or absence of relevant norms. In a country like Afghanistan where the authority of the interim government is limited to a particular area and the rest of the country is run by commanders and warlords, rights-based humanitarian action and protection of legal rights is still a far cry.[66] A Human Rights Adviser, whose office is under-funded and under-staffed, supports the UN Coordinator. In the framework of the UN Special Mission to Afghanistan (UNSMA), a Civil Affairs Officer is currently working in Afghanistan. There is a need for improved collaboration and information-sharing mechanisms between UNSMA and other humanitarian actors. UNHCR has also a considerable capacity with regard to protection, but so far the focus of its activities has been on returning populations.

RECOMMENDATIONS

The starting point is that internally displaced people have the same rights as any others living in the same country. In fact, their particular situation requires special measures to be taken so that they can benefit from these rights; it should be legitimate and useful to articulate the specific application of the law. As the human rights law is binding on state actors only, the IDPs in Afghanistan lack protection and are the victims of aggression because the violations most of the time had been perpetrated by non-state actors.[67] If serious human rights violations with regard to IDPs are taking place in Afghanistan the reason is not inadequate legal protection but rather the unwillingness of state and other non-state actors to observe obligations.[68] However, United Nations Coordinator Office (UNCO), possibly through the Emergency Task Force, must work to ensure the development of a comprehensive protection strategy for displaced population in Afghanistan, aimed at ensuring effective monitoring capacity on the ground.

UNCO should continue to undertake advocacy with authorities for safe and unrestricted access of humanitarian agencies to all populations in need;[69] promote and assist in the return of IDPs to their home areas as soon as possible; expand protection services and security in the camps. There should be gender-based violence-protection programme in the camps to raise awareness; and provision of income-generating and skills-building activities for women in camps and upon return to home areas.

UNHCR should strengthen its activities on the ground to monitor population movements throughout Afghanistan, including displaced persons. Other relevant agencies should continue to monitor conditions of displaced populations within the purview of their programmes.

UNCO and UNSMA should strengthen collaboration and information-sharing; survey households to determine food security and nutritional status;[70] UNCO and humanitarian agencies should strengthen the dissemination and implementation of the Guiding Principles on Internal Displacement; humanitarian agencies and NGOs should strengthen awareness of, and support for, a rights-based approach, ensuring it is translated into rights-based programming; and OHCHR should identify dedicated resources to support the work of the Human Rights Advisor.

It would be useful in each situation of Afghan IDPs to designate an institution or task force to monitor people's needs on an ongoing basis, to reveal their main problems as well as priorities and plans for the future. In this way, operational planning and preparedness may be improved. For instance, when internally displaced people decide to return from camps without waiting for the establishment of any organized programme of return, one or both parents may need to work on their houses and land before the rest of the family can follow. With advance knowledge of such decisions, the process can be facilitated and additional food provided for those who return.

The authorities must be made aware that internally displaced people, like all other citizens, have rights, the entitlement to which they have not lost by virtue of having been displaced. Knowledge and understanding of the law is a prerequisite for its proper application. Unless more determined and committed action is taken by the international community and the relevant Afghan authorities to address the underlying causes of poverty and to invest in programmes that will strengthen the coping capabilities of the poor, the human rights challenges faced by the Afghans will continue to increase.

The problems at certain camps and people's reticence to return to their places of origin point to the need for assistance agencies to augment and eventually replace emergency aid with longer-term development interventions in rural areas. International development agencies need to work with, and eventually replace, UN emergency agencies to help ensure that returnees can survive in their places of origin.

As returns of refugees and displaced persons are taking place more rapidly than anticipated, donors must respond to the urgent additional needs of UNHCR and IOM to help people go home and provide assistance to communities with high numbers of returnees.

The emergency agencies and NGOs in Herat are heavily burdened and they need inputs and support from development agencies.

Donors should recognize that WFP needs additional, large donations of food to meet the emergency needs in Afghanistan this year and plan accordingly.[71] Donors, including the World Bank and development agencies, should collaborate to expand programmes, which will enable Afghan refugees and IDPs to return to their homes as soon as possible and to resume farming. For example, the distribution of seeds to returning farmers is a necessity, but resources to provide seeds are now grossly inadequate. Donors should support the timely creation of a diverse and human rights-trained Afghan national army and exclude from it commanders and troops responsible for war crimes or serious human rights violations.[72] Humanitarian assistance must reach northern Pashtuns and other minorities displaced by ethnically targeted violence.[73] It must be made possible for IDPs to participate in elections and measures must be taken to enable them to register and vote outside their home communes. Donors should support efforts to strengthen monitoring and protection activities, including staffing of UNHCR and of the office of the Human Rights Adviser.[74] The International Security Force should be deployed all over Afghanistan and its duration should be for a longer period.[75] Agencies collecting data should distribute findings to all agencies working with IDPs.

THE PATH AHEAD

The unarmed from Badakhshan to Farah and Jawzjan to Kandahar want peace but the armed ones do not want it because they know that when peace prevails they would not be able to survive.[76] The IDPs are faced with a multitude of problems when considering the question of return, each problem being quite sufficient to prevent the return from taking place. Their fears are that an insecure environment in the home area will expose them to capture, beatings, killings, occupation of their land and houses, as well as discrimination in terms of employment.[77] (Many fighters buried their guns when the Taliban took over. As soon as the Talibans were driven out, they dug up the buried weapons and some of them began robbing and looting homes. In Kabul there were over 1,000 robberies in one month and a number of murders after the departure of the Taliban.) Whereas the existing political environment in Afghanistan, including the commitment to peace and democracy by the Interim Administration and the international community's support to this process, provides the foundations for an end to displacement and exile, some of the underlying causes of displacement have yet to vanish completely, whilst others remain latent or are even on the verge of re-emergence. Hence, there is still a need to promote among national, regional and local authorities a basic understanding of the Guiding Principles on IDPs in order to raise awareness of the special needs and human rights of IDPs.

During early 2001 there were reports of increasing insecurity in several areas which resulted in looting, diversion of assistance in camps to non-beneficiaries, rapes and other forms of serious human rights violations. In particular, ethnic Pashtun minorities in the northern and western provinces were singled out.[78] This resulted in scores of Pashtun families fleeing their villages and seeking protection in Pashtun majority areas in southern and central Afghanistan or even attempting to cross into Pakistan. There were also reports in 2002 of some Uzbeks being harassed in Pashtun areas. These incidents have produced a significant wave of fresh displacements during the tenure of the Interim Administration, and, as such, are a cause for much concern. The risk is that what some may interpret as ominous yet isolated acts of revenge for perceived past violations under the Taliban, may actually trigger an upsurge of ethnic tensions that may eventually spread to minorities throughout the country. Consequently, unless immediate and forceful preventive and remedial measures are applied, minorities may become apprehensive about returning to areas dominated by other ethnic groups.

The International Security Assistance Force (ISAF) troops should be deployed beyond Kabul, particularly to areas of ethnic tension as a deterrent measure to prevent further displacement. It is noteworthy that in most peace-building and reconstruction operations, demobilization, disarmament and reintegration (DDR) is an integral part of recovery and building trust and reconciliation within war-torn communities. It is recommended, therefore, that high priority be given to the formulation and implementation of a DDR programme as this will strengthen the will of the people to return to a secure environment. Unless confidence and security are restored, people will not return to their places of origin and the country will remain in a state of social instability and poverty. Reconciliation and confidence-building measures are therefore important elements in any attempt to achieve lasting solutions.

Furthermore, it is necessary that a capacity be created to monitor, document and map all local conflicts, tensions and human rights violations as a prerequisite for preventing displacement and ensuring rapid remedial response. It is, therefore, important that the UN Assistance Mission in Afghanistan (UNAMA), in support of the national human rights commission and in collaboration with all UN agencies with protection interests and expertise, establishes and sustains such a capacity.[79] In this regard, it is also important that IDPs be also supported in gaining a political voice in local and regional affairs and especially to ensure that they are adequately represented on the Loya Jirga. Return is also seriously constrained by the levels of destruction of homes; the widespread distribution of mines and other unexploded ordnances, as well as ongoing localized military operations. In addition, some provinces from where thousands of refugees and IDPs originate are still labelled by the UN as no-go 'red zones' for security reasons. Therefore, agencies can neither conduct needs assessments nor initiate preparations on the ground for returns. In order to facilitate the voluntary return of displaced people and refugees, it is critical that main areas of return are prioritized under the security agenda.

Despite these constraints, the international agencies should focus on the humanitarian intervention in Afghanistan and help in the return of IDPs and refugees in safety and dignity. This, however, does not pre-empt the need for ongoing continued contingency planning, as well as maintaining adequate protection to those IDPs who decide to remain in their host communities for the time being.

NOTES

1. Encyclopaedia Britannica Online, 1994-98.
2. UNDP, 8 October 2001. The HDI is an annual index produced by UNDP's Human Development Report Office, and is based on indicators for health, education and income.

3. UN Office for the Coordination of Humanitarian Affairs (UNOCHA), 17 November 2000, *UN Consolidated Inter-Agency Appeal for Afghanistan 2001*.

4. Interview with an International Committee of the Red Cross (ICRC) official in Peshawar on 8 May 2002.

5. National Resource Centre (NRC) publication 1998.

6. World Food Programme (WFP), October 1999, WFP Assistance to Internally Displaced Persons, Country Case Study on Internal Displacement, Patterns of Displacement in Afghanistan.

7. Office for the Coordination of Humanitarian Affairs, 17 October 2000.

8. Integrated Regional Information Networks (IRIN), 5 March 2001/UNOCHA, 6 April 2001.

9. UNICEF, 8 March 2001; USCR, 2 February 2001; IRIN, 8 February 2001.

10. Office of the UN Coordinator for Afghanistan, 19 January 2001.

11. DFID, 19 October 2001.

12. Data collected from a UNHCR official in Kabul in April 2002.

13. The institution of the family is very strong in Afghan culture and they normally support each other but the continuous conflict has stressed the families and the system is on the verge of decline.

14. IDP Unit-Office for the Cordination of Humanitarian Affairs, 28 March 2002, 3.

15. Report of Medicines Sans Frontiers September, 2001.

16. IDP Unit-OCHA, 28 March 2002, 2–3.

17. The author interviewed only a fraction of those victims, but their accounts are representative of the suffering of many more. Those interviews are included in the section entitled 'Individual Voices' in this book.

18. Also see *Human Rights Watch* report released in New York, 9 April 2002.

19. The government of Pakistan has allowed vulnerable refugees, identified as such by Pakistan border guards, to enter at Chaman in fixed quotas starting from November 2001. On several occasions the number of arrivals into Chaman was far larger than the daily entry quotas set by the government. Even with the difficulty in gaining entry into Pakistan, 47,000 Afghans sought refuge in Pakistan between January and 8 March 2002.

20. 'New influx of Afghan refugees arrives at Chaman Border Crossing in Pakistan', UNHCR News, 29 January 2002.

21. Louis Meixler, 'Thousands of Ethnic Pashtuns Fleeing Northern Afghanistan,' Associated Press, 21 February 2002.

22. A staff member of ICRC told the author in April 2002 in Kabul.

23. A three-person team appointed in February by Hamid Karzai, the chairman of Afghanistan's interim government, to investigate abuses against northern Pashtuns had documented cases of summary executions, beatings, sexual violence, abduction and looting that have been committed since November 2001, when non-Pashtun Northern Alliance forces regained power in the north. But Chairman Karzai's capacity to implement the team's recommendations is limited. Key power in the north remains in the hands of regional warlords and local commanders, some of whom hold high offices in the interimgovernment.

24. The author conducted a survey of the IDPs in Kabul city in April 2002.

25. In case of Herat the IOM (International Office for Migration) manages the camps. Other camps are managed by other IGOs and NGOs.

26. IOM officials in Herat in an interview with the author gave this information in May 2002.

27. Engineer Abdu-Razzaq, Administative Officer of Coordination of Afghan Relief (COAR), an Afghan NGO, told the author during an interview on 7 May 2002.
28. Report of Refugees International (RI), April 2002.
29. Report by RI advocates Larry Thompson and Michelle Brown, 'Afghanistan: IDP Returns Outpace Reintegration Assistance', May 2002.
30. Interviewed an IDP from Herat, 14 April 2002.
31. Mrs Shamim Anwari, programme officer/publication incharge, Coordination of Afghan Relief (COAR), an Afghan NGO working inside Afghanistan, told the author in May 2002.
32. Engineer Abdullah, Field Coordinator Officer, Peshawar Coordinator of IRC (PECO IRC), interviewed by the author, May 2002.
33. An IOM official in Islamabad, interviewed by the author in May 2002.
34. Hafizullah Emadi, *The Politics of Women and Development in Afghanistan* (New York: Paragon House, 1993), 22; Anna M. Pont, 'Eat What You Want, Dress the Way Your Community Wants: The Position of Afghan Women in Mercy Corps International Programme Areas,' A *Mercy Corps International Report* (May 1998), 2–4.
35. Hanne Christensen, 'The Reconstruction of Afghanistan: A Chance for Rural Women', United Nations Institute for Social Development (UNRISD) Report, Geneva, 1990).
36. However, the author was told very confidentially by some women NGO workers in camps in the north that a number of women indulged in prostitution to get some favours from the commanders of the camps.
37. Save the Children Fund (SCF), Save the Children Emergency Section, 10 October 2001.
38. Kuchis are nomadic herders, usually Pashtuns.
39. Principle 4 in Guiding Principles reads: 'Certain internally displaced persons, such as children, especially unaccompanied minors, expectant mothers, mothers with young children, female heads of household, persons with disabilities and elderly persons, shall be entitled to protection and assistance required by their condition and to treatment which takes into account their special needs'.
40. As affirmed in Article 3 of the Universal Declaration. Article 6(1) of the International Covenant on Civil and Political Rights (ICCPR) states that: 'Every human being has the inherent right to life….' Also see Common Articles 3's prohibition of 'violence to life and person' of persons 'taking no active part in active hostilities'.
41. The militia and the forces of the commanders, particularly in the north, killed many Pashtun IDPs and took away young girls from the camps.
42. A brother-in-law of one such missing girl revealed during my visit to the camp in Kabul.
43. See Declaration on the Protection of All Persons from Enforced Disappearance, adopted without a vote, 18 December 1992, General Assembly Resolution 133, Official Records of the General Assembly, Forty-Seventh Session. Supplement No 49, at 207, United Nations document A/47/49 (vol.1) (1993).
44. Ahmed Najim, an IRC field officer in Maslakh.
45. Principle 12 of the Guiding Principles: '(1) Internally displaced persons shall be protected from discriminatory arrest and detention as a result of their displacement. (2) In no case shall internally displaced persons be taken hostage'.
46. Principle 11/2 of the Guiding Principles reads: 'Internally displaced persons, whether or not their liberty has been restricted, shall be protected in particular against: Slavery or any contemporary form of slavery, such as sale into marriage, sexual exploitation, or forced labour of children'.

47. Judy A. Benjamin, 'Post Taliban: Changed Prospects for Women?', in *A Study on the Situation of Women and Girls in Afghanistan* (UN Coordinator's Office, Afghanistan, February 2002).

48. The Afghans in Pakistan engage these boys in commercial sex trade. According to the Vienna Declaration, supra note 4, Part 11, para. 48, there is a particular need to address exploitation and abuse of children in difficult circumstances.

49. Street Children: Afghan NGO, Academy Town, Peshawar.

50. Office of the AID representative for Afghanistan strategy, p. 4, March 1998.

51. Principle 23, Section I of Guiding Principles clearly states:

    1. Every human being has the right to education.
    2. To give effect to this right for internally displaced persons, the authorities concerned shall ensure that such persons, in particular displaced children, receive education which shall be free and compulsory at the primary level. Education should respect their cultural identity, language and religion.
    3. Special efforts should be made to ensure the full and equal participation of women and girls in educational programmes.
    4. Education and training facilities shall be made available to internally displaced persons, in particular adolescents and women, whether or not living in camps, as soon as conditions permit.

52. Médicins Sans Frontièrs (MSF) and Médecins du Monde (MDM) presented Mrs Ogata with their written statement about conditions in the camp during her January 2002 visit to Herat on behalf of the Japanese government.

53. Article 25 (1) of the Universal Declaration proclaims the right of everyone to a standard of living that is adequate for the health and well-being of the person and his/her family, which include *inter alia*, food, clothing and housing.

54. This is in contravention of Principle 18 of the Guiding Principles, which says that at the minimum, regardless of the circumstances, and without discrimination, competent authorities shall provide internally displaced persons with and ensure safe access to:

    1. essential food and potable water;
    2. basic shelter and housing;
    3. appropriate clothing; and
    4. essential medical services and sanitation.

55. UNSG, June 2001 (incorrect and incomplete citation).

56. Historically, some of these communities have sanctioned 'honour' killings in which a woman is killed by her own relatives for bringing 'dishonour' upon the family by conduct perceived as breaching community norms on sexual behaviour, including being a victim of sexual violence. Also see Emadi, *The Politics of Women*, pp. 16, 23; Benedicte Grima, *The Performance of Emotion Among Paxtun Women* (Karachi: Oxford University Press, 1998), pp. 150–54, 163–65.

57. The camp manager of Maslakh camp, Herat conveyed to the author in May 2002.

58. A field officer of IRC working in Afghanistan gave the statistics to the author in April 2002.

59. The IOM officials In Afghanistan told the author in May 2002.

60. Malalay, an IDP at Mazar-i-Sharif told the author in an interview in April 2002.

61. Rape, forced prostitution and other forms of gender specific assault and ill-treatment are prohibited in Article 27 of the Fourth Geneva Convention, which extends to protected persons also. See, United Nations Declaration on Violence Against Women, supra note 6, No. 19, para 7(b).

62. Principle 11, Section I of Guiding Principles reads: 'Every human being has the right to dignity and physical, mental and moral integrity. Internally displaced persons, whether or not their liberty has been restricted, shall be protected in particular against: (a) Rape, mutilation, torture, cruel, inhuman or degrading treatment or punishment, and other outrages upon personal dignity, such as acts of gender-specific violence, forced prostitution and any form of indecent assault'.

63. At the root of this phenomenon, there is often a discriminatory allocation to men of all essential food, water and non-food items.

64. IOM officials working in IDP camps in Kabul told the author in May 2002 that men are often involved in this act for two reasons: sexual pleasure or other sort of favours from persons concerned.

65. Principle 28, Section V, Guiding Principles on Internally Displaced Persons.

66. The interim government itself continues to commit human rights abuses.

67. Francis M. Deng, 'Internally Displaced Persons Compilation and Analysis of Legal Norms' (United Nations, New York, 1998), 77.

68. Present international law seems to protect sufficiently most of the specific needs of the internally displaced persons.

69. International Council of Voluntary Agencies (ICVA), October 2001, 'Responding to the Afghan Crisis: Making the Same Mistakes', *Talk Back*, Volume 3-5.

70. Post-Taliban Afghanistan, *op. cit.*, 16.

71. Refugees International, *op. cit.*, 2002

72. Senior Inter-Agency Network on Internal Displacement, 'Findings and Recommendations,' *Mission to Afghanistan* (April 2001), 18-25.

73. Human Rights Watch Press Release, 7 March 2002

74. Senior Inter-Agency Network on Internal Displacement, 3 May 2001

75. See International Crisis Group (ICG) report published March 2002. Also see ICG President Gareth Evans' statement: 'The failure of the major western powers to summon the political will to expand ISAF risks seeing Afghanistan again slide toward factional fighting.'

76. Stated by Eengineer Abdur Razzaq, Administrative Officer, COAR, Main office, Chinar Road, Peshawar. Interviewed by the author in Wardak, April 2002.

77. While interviewing an IDP at Kabul, he said that if different ethnic groups are in strong position in his area, he will be exposed to all sorts of discrimination and this fear prohibits him and his family from moving to his village.

78. The author interviewed some Pashtun families while they were fleeing from Jawzjan because the Hazara (an ethnic group in Afghanistan) asked them to hand over their girls. They left the village overnight.

79. Internal Displacement Unit, Office for the Coordination of Humanitarian Affairs, 28 March 2002, 'The IDP Situation in Afghanistan'.

CHAPTER 2

PAKISTAN: DEVELOPMENT AND DISASTER

Atta ur Rehman Sheikh

INTRODUCTION

D isplacement of communities from their ancestral lands has been integral to the developing economies of South Asia. The heavy emphasis on large-scale projects for infrastructure development of the country has led to the displacement of millions in South Asia. Added to them are large number of people who are victims of conflicts and natural disasters. According to UN refugee agency, there are an estimated 20–25 million Internally Displaced Persons (IDPs) around the world.[1] In Asia, there are about 5 million IDPs.[2] Pakistan is also host to a large number of IDPs, about whom little is known in official handbooks or the chronicles of development sector in the country. The present study is a preliminary attempt to provide an overview and analysis of the phenomena of displacement caused by development, conflict and natural disasters in Pakistan. The study has been divided into following sections namely: (a) development-induced displacement; (b) conflict-induced displacement; (c) displacement due to the natural disasters; (d) relevance of UN Guiding Principles on Internal Displacement; and (e) conclusions and recommendations. In each section an overall picture is attempted through the presentation of some representative case studies. Legal situation in terms of policies, legislation, institutional framework cum capacity, gaps as well as role of civil society and international institutions has been analysed to a significant extent. A cross-spectral analysis of gender issues has also been included in the study. In terms of methods, the study draws on secondary as well as primary sources. Case studies, interviews and field observations have been conducted, wherever possible, within the limitations of time and resources.

POLITICAL CLIMATE

On the eve of independence in 1947, Pakistan was predominantly an agrarian country with a minuscule industrial base and a tiny service sector. The newly independent state had to face numerous political and economic shocks. Integration of different ethnic groups into one nation and resettlement of 7 million refugees from India were priority issues, apart from other pressing financial problems. From the outset, the approach towards industrialization and modern technologies was assumed to be the panacea of development, as the mere dependence on agriculture produce would not make the state viable and stable. Over the last five decades, whether under civil or military rule in Pakistan, the emphasis has been placed on such development to be now included among the Newly Industrializing Countries (NICs).

The process of industrialization and modernization in Pakistan officially culminated during the era of President Ayub Khan (1958–69) known as 'Decade of Development'. According to Omar Noman (the author of *The Political Economy of Pakistan*), Pakistan was considered to be a model capitalist economy in the 1960s. Although the decade stands out for best performance in terms of economic growth, it failed to address the issue of equitable distribution of resources among all classes and mitigate the grievances of marginalized sections of population as well as participation in political processes. The independence of Bangladesh (former East Pakistan) in 1971 was the result of protracted suppression of social, political and economic rights of Bengalis. Similar policies and approaches prevailed in the succeeding decades of 1970s through to the 1990s. The issue of provincial autonomy and the due share of the federating units in national resources are still on the agenda and yet to be resolved. In the wake of the then USSR invasion of Afghanistan, the issue of provincial autonomy and democratic set-up became latent, as USA and its allies were more generous to the military regime in Pakistan, that helped them settle their score with USSR in Afghanistan. Pakistan hosted more than 3 million refugees from Afghanistan. Pakistan gained a lot in terms of financial and military aid by extending support to USA in Afghan–Soviet war.

At the same time, Pakistan had to pay a high social price by inheriting a host of problems in the form of gun-running, drug trafficking, rise of sectarianism, deterioration of law and order, etc. Pakistan has been generous enough to host more than 3 million Afghan refugees for over two decades, although the international aid ceased after 1995 on the pretext of 'donor fatigue'. Despite the fact of being generous towards Afghan refugees, Pakistan is not a signatory to the 1951 Convention Relating to the Status of Refugees. Following 11 September Pakistan stood by the Coalition against Terrorism and provided logistical support to USA for military operations in Afghanistan. A fresh wave of thousands of Afghan refugees entered Pakistani territory in the wake of American air strikes.

Despite all odds, growth rate almost remained 6 per cent per annum except in the early 1990s. However, the growth patterns remain lop-sided. The result is that agriculture contributes merely 24.4 per cent towards the GDP, while remaining contribution comes from manufacturing and service sectors as S. Akbar Zaidi has pointed out in his book *Issues of Economy in Pakistan*. In the 1990s there was sharp criticism, by the international development and monetary institutions, of the unimpressive situation with reference to social development. Particularly following the end of cold war era, the international monetary institutions have been pressing and emphasizing the need to devote more resources for social sector needs and development. More and more development programmes are being initiated to eradicate poverty, illiteracy, population explosion and narcotics in the overall context of good governance. But Pakistan is still to go a long way to achieve the goals of sustainable development and social justice.

DEVELOPMENT-INDUCED DISPLACEMENT

Large dams have been declared the bedrock of Pakistan's agricultural economy and industrial base from the early decades of its national policy and planning. Pakistan has built 81 large, medium and small dams across the country since 1947.[3] These development projects (large- or small-scale) have given rise to a huge number of displaced populations who are facing acute problems with regard to land acquisition, resettlement, rehabilitation, compensation and environmental depletion. Impoverishment risks noted in the report of World Commission on Dams are conspicuous by their presence in all dam projects. Concern for resettlement of uprooted communities has always been secondary in project plans and the experience has shown that the implementation of resettlement action plans continued to be faulty and poor.

We can argue, despite the differences in nature and scale of dams, the problems and issues faced by displaced people show similar patterns. For example, the victims of Tarbela dam are still waiting for their compensation, while at the ongoing Ghazi Barotha Hydropower Project (which has been declared as the model project) resettlement plans await implementation in an integrated manner. Several observers have noted serious inconsistencies in the award of compensations and rehabilitation measures. It is important to make the observation that owing to the pressures of donors and mandatory guidelines provided by them to deal with the resettlement issues, the resettlement action plans for all dams have incorporated general guidelines in the overall design of development projects. But specific guidelines relating to community participation, consensus building, timely compensations, integrated approach towards resettlement, among others, have largely been ignored. Without having a comprehensive plan for development of rehabilitation and resettlement, the government has launched another ambitious hydropower project named 'Vision 2025', which is likely to add to the number of displaced in the country. Various small and big dams, water reservoirs, upgrading of existing dams, among others, have been planned in the proposed 'Vision 2025' programme. Apart from dam building, numerous other developmental projects have been planned, like expressways, highways, roads, canals and water reservoirs. As a result, Pakistan's record on the scoreboard of forced eviction of the people, lack of comprehensive plans for resettlement and rehabilitation of livelihood, undervalued compensation, delayed payment, relocations and problems of integration of dislocated communities is quite dismal.

An overview and analysis of specific issues relating to the development-related displacement in the country is in order. It presents some of the major convincing case studies demonstrating the patterns and situation of internally displaced persons with reference to large dams, irrigation and highway projects.

Mangla Dam

Mangla dam was constructed in the district of Mirpur in Azad Jammu and Kashmir (Pakistani-controlled Kashmir) and commissioned in 1967. Mangla dam is the world's third largest earth-filled dam and first large dam built as a part of Indus Basin Project, following the treaty between India and Pakistan on the use of water from the Indus River and its tributaries. Official statistics quote displacement of 5,000 persons, while independent figures show displacement of around 30,000.[4] The dam was built with the financial assistance of World Bank.

There had been strong reaction by the people of Mirpur when the project was initiated, but the government promised them a good package. The then president, Ayub Khan, himself went to the site and met leaders and people of the area. Overall 81,000 people of Mirpur city and nearby villages were affected.[5] The displaced persons were resettled in Punjab and Sindh provinces. Thousands were encouraged to migrate to the UK. However, a substantial number of families settled in Punjab and Sindh have not got possession of their allotted lands so far and thus numerous cases are lying pending in the courts as their lands have been grabbed by the local influential people. Another section of affected people are those settled in the districts of Jhang and Khushab. Even after three and a half decades they are still without ownership rights and they do not have electricity or drinking water supply in their colonies.[6]

The government of Pakistan approved the controversial Mangla Dam Raising Project in 2001. The raising of the dam by 40 feet is meant to augment the efficiency of the dam. The proposed project is included in the long-term development programme 'Vision 2025' of the military government. The raising of the dam height from the present 380 feet to 420 feet would increase the storage capacity by 3.1 million acre-feet and enhance its energy output by 18 per cent. As per the estimate of the WAPDA (Water and Power Development Agency), 40,000 people of Mirpur City and suburbs would be affected by the project. The government of Azad Jammu and Kashmir had expressed serious reservations over the proposal and according to official estimates, 7,000 houses would come under water after the execution of the project. The cost of the project is Rs 53 billion, including Rs 20 billion required for resettlement of the affected people. The authorities are also considering construction of dikes and embankments to minimize the project's effects on the settlement of the people.[7]

Following the official announcement, the people of Mirpur City reacted strongly to the project and a series of protests took place. An Anti-Mangla Dam Extension Committee has been formed to stop the implementation of the project in the district. The Kashmiris settled in the UK decided to raise the issue in the UK and other European countries. They also threatened to go on hunger strike in front of the Pakistani Mission in London.[8] Despite the assurances of the authority of the comprehensive resettlement plan and efforts to minimize the effects on cultivable land, the people of Mirpur City and the government of Azad Jammu and Kashmir stuck to their reservations. In these circumstances the federal government had to defer the project. Various local NGOs and the Anti-Mangla Dam Extension Committee have taken up the cause of potentially affected people.[9]

The project remained a non-starter for quite sometime. WAPDA has not been able to muster sufficient support of the people and the government of Azad Jammu and Kashmir for the project. However, WAPDA continued its work on survey on resettlement assessment to determine the extent of the population and property to be affected as a result of the proposed project. The authorities have spent Rs 16.875 million till April 2002 for carrying out the survey.[10] On the other hand, the minister for Kashmir Affairs and Northern Areas set up two committees (in the presence of the prime minister and senior officials of Azad Jammu and Kashmir) for resolving issues related to resettlement and compensation. The minister said that the project would be launched after resolving all pending issues.[11] An unusual meeting of the steering committee attended by President General Pervez Musharraf, the minister for Kashmir Affairs, WADA high officials, President and Prime Minister of the Azad Jammu and Kashmir (AJK) was held recently. It was decided to prepare a new package of compensation for the affected, evolve consensus and address the reservations of the people of the area before work on the project began. A sub-committee has been entrusted the task of preparing a new package for the people affected in 1967 and review the issues of redress regarding their grievances. The committee will also work out comprehensive resettlement plan for the newly affected.[12] In a 2002 session of AJK Legislative Assembly, despite the strong opposition of the members of the Assembly, a seven-member committee was formed to develop a consensus on the proposed project.[13]

However, towards the end of 2002, the president of Pakistan inaugurated the project by announcing a generous package for the persons affected and royalty for government of Azad Jammu and Kashmir. The cost was estimated to be Rs 57 billion, as compared to original cost of Rs 53 billion. New estimates revealed that instead of 40,000 people, 44,000 people would need to be relocated while 8,000 houses would come under water. According to the resettlement plan the newly-affected people would be paid Rs 300,000 with a plot of five *marla* while the old affected would get Rs 200,000. The government of AJ & K would be paid Rs 700 to 800 million per year as royalty.[14]

Tarbela Dam

Tarbela dam was launched in 1967 with the financial assistance from the World Bank and this was another mega project of that decade. At the outset it was assessed that 80,000 people would have to be dislocated and 100 villages would be submerged by the water reservoir. But towards the end of the project, 96,000 people had been displaced and 120 villages came under water.[15] The construction of Tarbela dam involved acquisition of 329 sq. km of land for the reservoir structures and other facilities. Tarbela Dam Resettlement Organization (project NGO) was set up for acquisition of land, disbursement of compensation, evacuation of affected population and their resettlement. Policies on matters related to land acquisition, compensation and resettlement were laid down in a high-level meeting in 1967 chaired by the then president of Pakistan.[16] Provincial governments of Punjab and Sindh were directed to allocate 60,000 acres of land (30,000 acres each). Only Punjab could provide the land asked for in that meeting whereas the government of Sindh allocated only 10,667 acres. Out of the 667 families who were issued allotment letters in the late 1970s by the Sindh government, over 250 families have not been given possession despite the fact that most of them had already made payments. The affected people who went to Sindh province to get possession of land had to face retaliation from the local people. Similarly in Punjab a majority of those who were allotted land were either forced by the influential people of the area to vacate the land, or were compelled to dispose of their allotted land, as it was difficult to utilize or cultivate it.[17]

In 1990, the federal government conducted a study on the recommendation of World Bank on the issue of outstanding resettlement. The study came up with two major findings that were hindering the resolution of resettlement of displaced families: inadequate compensation and non-availability of housing plots. The cost of settling the two issues was estimated to be Rs 1.66 billion for compensation and Rs 3.5 billion for providing sufficient residential plots. However, the Water and Power Development Authority (WAPDA) has not been able to raise the sum of Rs 5.16 billion to settle the issue.[18]

In 1996, a team of representatives of the World Bank held meetings and gathered information regarding litigations affecting Tarbela dam. The World Bank team submitted a detailed report with recommendations. The findings of the team revealed that 3,000 cases are pending for the last 26 years. A social organization for 'Mutasirin Tarbela Dam' (organization for the affected) kept raising the issue at different levels. The properties were acquired under Land Acquisition Act, 1894. The compensation package included land for land, provision of residential plots and free transportation. Apparently the package was satisfactory and hence there was no protest against it when the project was started off. However, the promised package of economic and social rehabilitation never materialized as envisaged. A comprehensive resettlement programme was prepared but it fell into difficulties for a number of reasons such as reluctance to settle in other provinces and undervaluation of their acquired lands. About 2,100 families are still waiting to get their claims settled even after the lapse of more than 35 years.[19]

An independent study has exposed the prevailing situation with regard to resettlement as being primarily due to the inefficiency and inconsistencies of the institutions concerned. The government of Pakistan had set up a commission in July 1998 to review the entire resettlement plan in the context of history, along with current status of outstanding resettlement issues relating to Tarbela dam. The commission came up with the recommendation that a new fully fledged exercise on the resettlement of those affected, probably on the pattern of Ghazi–Barotha Hydropower Project, be undertaken (ADB's Regional Technical Assistance [RETA] Project). Given the situation, the World Bank (being one of the donors for Ghazi–Barotha Hydropower Project) has put in conditionalities for the provision of funds for the said project. In view of the pressure from the World Bank, the military government has expedited the process of settlement of the displaced families by pursuing the case more vigilantly. The governments of the NWFP, Punjab and Sindh have been directed to allot 2,607 acres, 14,200 acres and 7,100 acres, respectively, to over 1,700 dislocated families eligible for getting alternative land. But again this did not work out and all three provinces have clearly shown their inability to spare lands for the affected. Consequently as a last resort, now, the federal government is prepared to pay cash compensation to all claimants.[20]

The Report of the World Commission on Dams has taken up the case study of Tarbela dam. The report found out that of the 96,000 physically displaced people enumerated for the Tarbela dam, two-thirds qualified for replacement agricultural land in Punjab and Sindh provinces. Of these, some 2,000 families or approximately 20,000 people did not receive land when the land provided by Sindh fell short of what was promised. Similarly affected people did not receive adequate compensation to buy alternate land. Resettlement and restoration of livelihood of affected people were largely ignored.[21]

Ghazi–Barotha Dam

Ghazi–Barotha Hydropower Project is currently the most important project, where a comprehensive resettlement plan has been incorporated in the overall project. The objective of the project is to generate low-cost hydropower with minimal environmental and resettlement impacts in Pakistan. The assessment of social and environmental impact was carried out and recommendations were incorporated in the project. It is stated that potential significant social effects of the project due to displacement of families and loss of private land were largely avoided during site selection, sometimes at a considerable cost.[22] Total persons affected are 21,653. They include 1,778 persons that did not own any land (126 tenants, 26 lessees of state land, 105 fishermen, and the rest, herders, landless farm workers and others). The number of persons who would lose all of their land is 3,412. About 110 scattered dwellings will have to be resettled for the civil work, and an estimated 15–20 dwellings for right of way. The number of families to be affected is 179.[23] The project includes development of three resettlement villages in the project area. It was expected that impact of land acquisition would largely be mitigated by the provision of irrigated land on the spoil banks and by measures of fair and prompt compensation.[24] It was further envisaged that the social and economic impact would also be substantially minimized by the implementation of the Regional Development Plan which would ensure that the project-affected families would have a standard of living at least equal to that which they had before the project.[25]

Under the Loan and Technical Assistance Grant Agreement between the government of Pakistan and the Asian Development Bank, the implementation mechanism stipulates that the Ghazi–Barotha Project Organization (GBPO) will be expanded and restructured. The restructured organization will include the Environmental and Social Division. The Environmental and Social Division will be responsible for resettlement action plan.[26] The agreement also stipulates that a project non-governmental organization (PNGO) will assist in establishing contacts with the local population, particularly in regard to matters related to land acquisition and compensation, formation of tube-well users' association and allocation of developed spoil bank. The PNGO will also assist in monitoring the social aspects of the resettlement action plan during construction and operation of the project.[27] Ghazi–Barotha Taraqqiati Idara (GBTI) has been set up as the PNGO by WAPDA and consortium of funding agencies. It is registered under the Companies Act, 1894. WAPDA has provided Rs 100 million as seed money with assurance of providing an additional amount of Rs 176 million for the implementation of the integrated rural development plan. Its objectives are to promote the participatory development of the communities, villages, lands and settlements directly or indirectly affected by the Ghazi–Barotha Hydropower Project, and such other adjacent or nearby communities as may be designated from time to time by the Company's Board. It also safeguards the affected people's rights and provides them facilitation, mediation, and support in handling matters of resettlement and compensation.[28]

The Ghazi–Barotha Resettlement Plan's objectives conform to the Asian Development Bank's resettlement policy objectives. The action plan provides for upgrading of institutional capacity in the overall framework of the project to effectively deal with and facilitate the resettlement process through the project resettlement organization, appointment of Land Acquisition Collectors, formation of PNGO to be funded by WAPDA with the mandate of establishing village level grass-roots organizations; formation of Project Field Teams for facilitating the entitled persons in the materialization of their entitlement; organizing activities for women and the landless in training, credit and self-employment; administer the integrated rural development plan; assist in the formation of project contact committees in each village; appointment of monitoring consultants and external panel of experts.[29]

In general, the Ghazi–Barotha Hydropower Project was expected to be a model project for future initiatives as it was addressing issues and problems being ignored by earlier mega dam projects by ensuring community participation at all stages and in all phases. Transparency of compensation process, resettlement housing, employment, training and credit schemes, and environmental protection under the integrated rural development programme was implemented. However, in 2002 the National Accountability Bureau (NAB) and the Regional Accountability Bureau (NWFP) launched an inquiry into the irregularities and malpractices in awarding of compensations and they termed it as the biggest 'Land Acquisition Scam' in South Asia. The officials of both bureaus said that payment of compensation was made at highly inflated rates for low category of land, non-existing facilities, infrastructure and orchards. WAPDA officials and landowners are involved in it. Although Land Valuation Assessment Committees were formed to assess the value of land being acquired, their role has been termed as dubious. All this was done with the connivance of Land Valuation Assessment Committees, Land Acquisition Collectors, officials of Agriculture Department and landowners of the area. Investigation is under way and 200 affected people, including 80 women, have been accused of receiving excessive land compensation. Among them 20 are in the custody of National Accountability Bureau. The affected are being harassed and chased by the police.[30] The affected began a protest campaign against this treatment, which was covered by the press. The NAB organized a protest in front of the World Bank office in Islamabad where 300 women, some of them with their infants, presented a memorandum to the World Bank officials about the mal-treatment.[31] The affected held the World Bank responsible for their miseries as the Bank, right at the start, had promised to resolve all their issues. In response to this investigation being carried out by NAB, and as a result the protest campaign by the affected families, the World Bank has sent a letter making it clear that 'if you have any further questions or issues regarding investigations, you may contact the Secretary of Ministry of Water and Power or Chairman or NAB officials directly.'[32]

Kalabagh Dam

Kalabagh dam has been controversial for more than two decades. The political leadership in the smaller provinces and the civil society are up in arms against the project. There have been strong reservations and doubts regarding the claims and justifications of the proposed dam in terms of water availability, food security and energy production, environmental implications, community displacement and rehabilitation, technical and financial feasibility. Particularly the civil society organizations have critiqued the proposed large dam from a sustainable development perspective, as it entails adverse environmental effects and involves large-scale community displacement.[33]

The total estimated population to be affected by the dam would be 83,000 from two provinces (48,500 in Punjab and 34,500 in North West Frontier Province or NWFP). A comprehensive resettlement plan has been designed to provide alternate irrigated lands to the affected families. The affected population would be resettled in 27 extended and 20 model villages where modern facilities of water, electricity, roads, dispensaries, schools and other civic amenities would be provided. The estimated cost for resettlement is Rs 20 to 25 million. The proposal claimed that the affected would enjoy an improved environment. The owners of the land on the reservoir periphery above normal conservation level of 915 feet would also be compensated, as their lands could be flooded once in five years. Although they would remain owners of their respective lands, they would not claim damages to crops for occasional flooding. It is claimed that the resettlement package is in fact the most innovative and attractive than those previously designed for Mangla and Tarbela dams and the displaced communities would find themselves in a better socio-economic environment.

The Kalabagh dam project became an extremely political issue ever since it was launched by the then military regime in the 1980s. NWFP and Sindh provinces have serious reservations about the project. NWFP fears that the very project would aggravate the situation in Peshawar and Naushehra districts in case of recurrence of floods as in 1929. It would cause salinity and waterlogging in the nearby districts and large arable lands would be submerged, as well as cause dislocation of large number of people. The province of Sindh seems more vulnerable and thus more reactive to the proposed project. The province asserts that the project would render the province into a desert, as there would be no surplus water to fill the Kalabagh reservoir, which would consequently affect agriculture, fish production, threaten the mangrove forest, accentuate sea water encroachment and affect the environment in general in lower Sindh.[34]

Following the resolutions passed by all three provincial assemblies against the construction of the dam and concerted pressures from regional political parties as well as from civil society organizations, the succeeding governments have not dared commence the project in spite of the fact that the country needs more electricity. In the face of the pressure from political parties and other civil groups in the other three provinces, the Kalabagh dam could not be included in the 'Vision 2025' programme. But in an interview to a Sindhi newspaper, the *Daily Jang*, on 23 September 2002, President General Pervez Musharraf said that Kalabagh dam was vital for the country and would be launched at a suitable time once the government had succeeded in evolving a national consensus on the issue. In a television interview in September 2002, the chairman of WAPDA has clarified that Kalabagh dam is part of the Vision 2025 programme. [35]

Islamabad Capital Territory Case

Islamabad capital territory was created to develop a new capital for the country. The Capital Development Ordinance was promulgated in 1960. Although as per the Constitution of the country, housing and urban planning is a provincial subject, in the case of Islamabad, the federal government was directly involved. The ordinance provided specific powers to the Capital Development Authority (the authority was created through the Ordinance) for land acquisition and payment of compensation. Section 22 of the Ordinance expressly states, 'All land within the specified areas shall be liable to acquisition at any time in accordance with provisions of this chapter.'[36] Apart from cash compensation paid according to the regulations, the affected were also given additional compensation in the form of land available on concessionaire rates. Under this policy 194,000 acres have been allotted to 17,481 eligible displaced persons.[37]

However, Capital Development Authority (CDA) policies have been inconsistent and modifications in regulations and policy have continued from time to time to meet the needs of the city. But there have been irregularities and anomalies in resettlement and compensation packages and as a result more and more legal problems have emerged and affected people have gone into litigation. As a matter of fact, the discretionary power at the disposal of the chairman of CDA created a number of problems. The chairman exercising his power entered into agreement with different groups of affected people with some getting extra benefits, with the result that the non-beneficiaries have felt discriminated against and have resorted to litigation (RETA). There are a number of cases pending with the courts and complaints for meagre compensation have been many. There were also numerous cases where disputes between the CDA and the affected took place and police force was used for eviction. In July 2002, a clash took place between CDA officials, accompanied by a team of police, who came to undertake development work in D-12 area (village Sri Saral) and residents of the village. The police opened fire that killed two villagers and more than 60 were injured. The villagers claimed that they had not been paid compensation for their land on which development work had started. The village of Sri Saral has a history in terms of non-receipt of compensation. Compensation awards were announced in 1968 and then in 1969 but most people did not get compensation. Again in 1985, an award list was prepared but 272 canals of land were yet to be acquired by CDA and the officials wanted to take possession of it.[38] Later on, police registered an FIR against the 430 residents of the Sri Saral village. Till 31 July 2002, the police had arrested 70 people, including 20 women. But women were released following the instructions of the high officials.[39] The development work in Sri Saral was officially suspended and proceedings in the Judicial Commission began. The incident drew wide condemnation as political parties and civil society organizations deplored the brutal acts by the state machinery.[40] According to another newspaper report, there were over 5,000 affected people who are waiting for land compensation. The residents of villages, which include Dharak, Bheka Syedan, Moza Kalanger, Dheri Kila, Moza Barkhzad, Moza Kataria and Moza Noorpur Shahan, are still awaiting residential plots as per the policy of the CDA.[41]

National Motorway Network Project

The Motorway Project was launched in the first tenure of the Pakistan's Prime Minister Mohammad Nawaz Sharif (1991–93). The aim of the project was to connect the northern and southern areas of the country. The proposed project consisted of a total of 10 projects. The construction of Lahore–Islamabad motorway began as the first stage. It was completed in 1997. The total estimated cost of the project was US $986,900,000. But the actual cost was far higher for the 350-km-long motorway between Lahore and Islamabad. Ironically no environmental impact assessment (EIA) was undertaken at any stage of the project, which was required under Environmental Protection Ordinance, 1983. The project was implemented and co-financed by Daewoo Corporation of South Korea.[42]

The motorway project was apparently politically motivated and the situation further aggravated when a clash of interests between the military elites and the ruling party began to surface, which resulted in the ousting of Mohammad Nawaz Sharif and induction of Benazir Bhutto as prime minister. Construction work remained suspended for sometime during the tenure of the government of Pakistan Peoples Party for political reasons. During the second tenure of Mohammad Nawaz Sharif (1997–2000), the construction work was completed in abnormal haste and chaos. There were certain problems with the design of the project, particularly with regard to social side of it. Thousands of families living on the periphery of the newly-constructed section of the motorway faced extreme difficulties which included division of their lands, stoppage of water supply lines, blockage of the approach ways to their lands, blockage of approach ways to cattle grazing grounds, blockage of paths between graveyards and human settlements and, of course, displacement of people. The project was carried out with such irresponsibility, haphazard planning and utter haste that it disturbed the entire cultural habitat and livelihood patterns of the area. Those affected by the project were all farmers. The farmers were paid between Rs 107,000 to Rs 120,000 per acre on an average. The process of payment to the farmers began a year after the acquisition of land. The sad aspect of the compensation was that it was paid only to the affected whose lands were acquired for building metalled road.[43]

Greater adverse impact was faced by women who equally participated in the economic activities of the family, particularly in livestock care, harvesting of crops, seedling, fetching drinking water and providing food to male members in the field, and numerous other field tasks, apart from household chores. Now that the land had been divided on either side of the motorway and there were no direct approach ways, one had to travel long distances to reach the land for cultivation. As a result the women became marginalized and affected economically. The mobility of the women was greatly reduced. Community ties and interaction were shattered owing to the design of the project that did not address the adverse social impact on the displaced communities.[44] The official plan contained a number of passages, water drains and other facilities that do not exist on the ground. The design's requirements were bypassed, perhaps to reduce costs. In some cases families were displaced twice as the design of project was modified. The motorway project is a sorry example of projects creating displacement in recent times.[45]

Lyari Expressway Project

Lyari Expressway is yet another big infrastructure development project initiated by the military government that would dislocate a population of 203,200 and cause a loss of Rs 3.54 billion to the urban poor in Karachi (Pakistan's biggest city in terms of population and geography). Around 40 years ago migrant workers from different parts of Pakistan began to settle in Lyari, while a village called Hassan Aulia has been inhabited by the Baloch tribe for 200 years, along the river Lyari. Owing to urbanization and pressure of population, the river turned into a sewage channel for the city. Presently more than 200,000 people live along the river and on the river bed.[46] The Northern Bypass was planned in 1980 to link Karachi Port to the Karachi Super Highway, which connects the city to north of Pakistan. The purpose of the bypass was to shift the load of port traffic to Super Highway (about 20,000 heavy diesel vehicles pass through the city). But the Northern Bypass never took off. In 1989 the government came up with the proposal to construct Lyari Expressway along the Lyari river. The proposal met with strong criticism and resistance from the NGOs and other civic groups of the area. In 1995 and 1996 following a dialogue between citizens and the representatives of the government, the Lyari Expressway Project was cancelled.[47]

In June 2000, however, the military government decided to resume work on both projects: Northern Bypass and the Lyari Expressway. Mr Arif Hassan (an expert on urban development issues of Karachi) has declared the project un-valid. He has said that while government is constructing Northern Bypass, there is no justification for building the Lyari Expressway. He has further said that the Lyari Expressway is in no way a priority for the city. Rs 5 billion is being spent on the project when there are no bus terminals for the city. 'I am totally against this project because this is not required', he has emphasized.[48] In all 25,000 houses, 3,600 shops and commercial units, 50 mosques, 5 churches, 8 temples, 10 schools, 38 clinics, 1 hospital and 66 factories would be bulldozed. Appallingly, a 112-year-old mosque in the village has also been among other buildings marked for demolition. The City District government of Karachi, prior to eviction, announced that all 71,000 to 72,000 displaced families would be resettled or compensated according to the law. They would be given alternative plots (each measuring 80 square yards) in three townships.[49] But in practice the government is violating the national law on a massive scale. Resettlement plan has not been designed and all information is being kept secret. Notices of eviction were not served and demolition was started on short notice. The operation of demolition was conducted with the support of army and rangers personnel present on location, and when residents protested they were tear-gassed and beaten by them. Although there are a great number of residents who are illegal settlers, there are still thousands of residents and commercial enterprises that are legal and have valid lease agreements and ownership documents issued by the government. The displaced families who have been allotted land (on locations far away from the area) and given compensation for construction of houses are minuscule in number. Apart from distance, resettled locations lack utility services. Women, particularly widows, are facing hardships as it is difficult for women to go from one office to another to get their compensation or get their land allotted.[50]

All big and small NGOs including Orangi Pilot Project Karachi, Human Rights Commission of Pakistan, Pakistan Institute of Labour Education and Research, and Lyari Nadi Welfare Association (a coalition of 45 community-based organizations [CBOs] of the area), have been against this project and when this project was re-launched there were strong pressure group activities on the part of civil society but nevertheless the government was determined to carry out the project at all costs. Originally the city district government (or Government of Sindh) was to implement the project but ever since the military government took over, this was handed over to National Highway Authority. Despite sharp criticism by civil society organizations the Authority has not provided the design of the project so far. All details related to the project are being kept secret. The project has created a lot of confusion among displaced communities, and above all they were not taken into confidence at any stage of the project. The project is a real human disaster where citizen's rights were violated on such a scale.[51] A letter was also written by the United Nations Special Rapporteur on Adequate Housing to the president of Pakistan, pronouncing his grave concern about the resumption and further continuation of the Lyari Expressway Project, which would affect the livelihood of thousands of people. Amidst the sharp criticism from social and political circles, the Advocate General of Sindh (province) is reported to have defended the Lyari Expressway Project on the grounds that the Asian Development Bank is funding the project. On the other hand, the country director of Asian Development Bank in Pakistan has denied that ADB is funding the project.[52] According to Ms Parveen Rehman, Director, Orangi Pilot Project (an NGO with considerable experience in sanitation and low-cost housing projects), the legalities involved with the Land Acquisition Act, 1894 have been blatantly violated:

> The act allows the government to take away any leased or notified land but even for that there is a certain process to be followed, which the government conveniently pushed aside. It did not publish any gazette notification, nor held any public hearing on the issue. The affected have to be given compensation according to the market value of the acquired land. Right now everybody has been promised 80 square yards plot regardless of the size of the property they had previously.[53]

The estimates mentioned above do not include social and psychological cost of evictions. In most of the cases people have lost jobs, children have lost their schools and everything has been turned to rubble.[54]

Legal and Policy Issues in Displacement

In Pakistan, most of the development projects, including small ones, have required large areas of land, causing dislocation of human settlements and disturbing the livelihoods of the dislocated people. The rural communities have been major victims of development in a way. In addition, people from semi-rural and urban areas are also suffering the negative impacts of development. Such projects have always been related to construction of airports, seaports, military installations, campuses, industrial units, housing schemes, canals, highways, roads and, particularly, large dams. In the overall context of the development projects, problems remain the same regarding compensation, resettlement and rehabilitation and making good the loss of livelihood. The Land Acquisition Act, 1894 is the principal general statute, laying down the framework for exercise of the right to eminent domain of the state. The right of eminent domain has its constitutional foundations in article 24 of the Constitution of Islamic Republic of Pakistan. The Land Acquisition Act, 1894 has been the de facto policy regarding resettlement and compensation to the project-affected persons. It lays down procedures for acquisition of private properties for public purposes and their compensation. Resettlement needs in today's perspective are not addressed by the act or for that matter in any other law of the country.[55] The Land Acquisition Act, 1894 is 110 years old and continued to be the general land acquisition law in Pakistan since 1947. It has been amended from time to time. In the subcontinent, the first land acquisition law was promulgated in 1870 (Act X of 1870). It was amended and then replaced by the Land Acquisition Act, 1894. The 1894 Act is the basic law; however, in the absence of a national resettlement policy, it has been amended and updated differently in all four provinces. The nature of the differences is primarily procedural but the overall spirit of the act remains intact. The act does not differentiate between different projects in terms of: (a) land acquisition for developmental or non-developmental purpose; (b) whether land acquisition involved forced displacement or not; and (c) scale and nature of different projects. The act treats all types of projects alike. Given the scale and nature of different projects, the package of compensation and resettlement plans varies from project to project. Another reason for this variation is inadequate sources of funding, which include donor funding—national or private. Usually foreign donor funded projects entail a good package of compensation and resettlement plans, as World Bank-Asian Development Bank guidelines and directives have to be followed, while in nationally or privately funded projects, resettlement plans are largely ignored or inadequate and untimely compensation is extended.[56]

The following laws were adapted in the Land Acquisition Act, 1894 for specific purposes. The adaptation was meant to serve the purpose of certain sectors by tailoring the law to the requirement of each sector particularly related to urban sector development. Some of the significant laws are:

Land Acquisition (Mines) Act, 1885
Telegraph Act, 1885
Railway Act, 1890
Electricity Act, 1910
The West Punjab Thal Development Act, 1949
Punjab Soil Reclamation Act, 1952

Karachi Development Authority Order, 1957
Capital Development Authority Ordinance, 1960
Lahore Development Authority Act, 1976
Hyderabad Development Authority Act, 1979
Punjab Development of Cities Act, 1977
Baluchistan Acquisition of Land Act, 1974

Apart from the laws listed above, rules of business have been framed for procedures to acquire land. In the Punjab province, Punjab Acquisition Rules, 1983 have been enforced. These rules amply elaborate the provisions of 1894 Act in addition to ensuring that the acquisition of land is justified.[57]

The 1894 Act or any other law is not comprehensive enough and thus does not cover the entire issues related to resettlement, except the compensation part of it. Over the years, the act has undergone numerous modifications by the federal and provincial governments as well as the respective courts. All four provincial revenue departments have their own interpretations of the act. The land acquisition collectors come up with their own versions. Since the act does not address the resettlement issues, recourse has to be taken by ad hoc arrangements in unavoidable circumstances. All this causes serious socio-economic problems and psychological trauma to the affected people. Particularly, the act does not address the livelihood issues and cultural aspects of the affected people in case of vulnerable groups like landless people, especially artisans and fishermen, in addition to women and children of displaced communities.

As far as refugees are concerned, Pakistan performed the task of managing exodus of refugees fairly well in 1947, and then in 1979, in the case of Afghan refugees. In 1947, Refugee Rehabilitation Finance Corporation (RRFC), a refugee rehabilitation agency, was established for the settlement process, which really provided a useful experience for settlement and resettlement issues. The second substantial experience was following the then Soviet invasion of Afghanistan in 1979, when more than 3 million refugees crossed into Pakistan. Pakistan has been able to manage such a large number of refugees with internal and international support. The USA and Saudi Arabia provided huge financial and material support during the Soviet–Afghan war.

But, despite experiences of such magnitude in dealing with refugees and being a member of UNHCR's Executive Committee,[58] Pakistan is not a signatory to the 1951 Convention on Refugees. All kinds of refugees are regarded as illegal aliens. They are dealt with under the Foreign

Act, 1946 enacted by the British. However, in the case of 7 million migrants from India in 1947 some rules, regulations and laws were made and devised to rehabilitate them. The Displaced Persons (Compensation and Rehabilitation) Act, 1958 laid down procedures for the resettlement of refugees from India.

Following the 11 September attack on the USA, a campaign was launched against terrorism wherein Afghanistan was attacked by the USA to eliminate so-called terrorists. Pakistan took measures to put its house in order by taking stock of refugees in the country. Since 1980 the Afghan refugees were allowed to do business and move freely in the country. It created a host of political and social problems in terms of law and order in Pakistan. But their prolonged stay in Pakistan, extending over more than two decades, made it difficult to keep track of Afghan refugees, as they were mixed up with the local population, particularly in big cities like Islamabad, Peshawar, Karachi, Quetta and Lahore. Therefore, the National Alien Registration Authority under the Foreigners Amendment Ordinance 2000, was framed for the registration of refugees, asylum seekers and migrant workers so that they can be issued work permits, and stay, or be repatriated, if needed, afterwards.

In Pakistan, displacement owing to development presents a grim scenario that includes landlessness, unemployment, homelessness, marginalization, lack of food, loss of common resources and breakdown of social networks. These risks are in sheer violation of the UN Guiding Principles on Internal Displacement or, for that matter, other international human rights instruments. The situation becomes all the more critical in the absence of national policy and adequate laws on resettlement and compensation issues. The key issue in development-induced displacement is the absence of national resettlement policy and a law that can address the problems of fair and timely compensation, rehabilitation, restoration of livelihood and participation of affected communities in the decision making at all stages of the project. Apart from lack of commitment of government towards the implementation of resettlement guidelines, there are other factors that negatively impact IDPs. These include the absence of community participation and inadequate funding for compensation or purchase of land for displaced people. Furthermore, it also includes incompatibility of ethnic background, clash of interest between the host community and resettled families, and lack of support services as well as social organization processes to integrate the resettled population in the local communities. All these inadequacies exist across all projects.[59]

Under the Pakistan Environmental Protection Act, 1997, Clause 12, Initial Environmental Examination (IEE), an environmental impact assessment (EIA), is mandatory where the project is likely to cause an adverse environmental effect. This clause has been operationalized vide IEE/EIA Regulation 2000. The proponent of a project is responsible to submit the IEE/EIA to the concerned EPA. This process came into force from 1 July, 1994 and the projects planned prior to 1994 were not covered under Pakistan Environmental Protection Act, 1997. The responsible EPA has the powers to take legal action against proponents of project who do not comply with the rules and regulations set under the act. Environmental tribunals are functional and cases could be referred to these tribunals. Under the act, Pakistan Environmental Protection Agency (PEPA or Pak–EPA) has also developed a regulated procedure as far as monitoring, evaluation and environmental impact of new projects are concerned. This includes public hearing on EIA reports submitted by the proponents. The proponents are held responsible to submit EIA report whether coming up in public or private sector; this includes projects of dams also.[60] For a comprehensive resettlement policy, EPA had initiated a consultation process in 1999 with the collaboration of Asian Development Bank's Regional Technical Assistance Project.[61] The process was meant to review the current status of resettlement policies, practices, review of land acquisition laws and discussion with stakeholders, and study of relevant literature so that a framework for a resettlement policy could be formulated. A draft report on 'Resettlement Policy and Practice: Review and Recommendations' was prepared by SEBCON (Private) Limited for the Pakistan Environmental Protection Agency.[62] The ADB Regional Technical Assistance (RETA) Project on Resettlement Policy and Practice, which began in seven Asian countries (Bangladesh, Indonesia, Nepal, Pakistan, People's Republic of China, the Philippines and Vietnam), was launched in September 1998. Its primary aim is to assist these countries in making resettlement policies and legal framework that assure protection of rights of those affected by development projects. RETA–I has been completed, which has produced a review of existing resettlement policies and practices and a draft policy framework. A number of workshops were held in the past at the federal and provincial levels as part of the consultation process. Now ADB has assisted in RETA-II, which focuses on updating of draft policy, regulatory framework and guidelines for implementing of resettlement policy and amendment/new legislation. It was expected that RETA-III (2002) would be designed to build institutional capacity.[63] However, since the proposed policy and the law have not been adopted, RETA-III has not been launched.

A briefing session on the second phase of Resettlement Policy was held on 18 July 2001. The minister for Environment, Local Government and Rural Development chaired the session. The representatives of Planning and Development Division, Asian Development Bank, World Bank, and the local consultants were present. During the session, the draft Resettlement Policy/Regulatory Framework and Guidelines, along with different options to amend existing Land Acquisition Act, 1894, were discussed. The legal consultant made representation on various aspects of the draft of National Resettlement Policy vis-à-vis provisions of the Land Acquisition Act, 1894. This was done to safeguard the interests of the affected having no land. On the basis of the findings of the study, a draft National Resettlement Policy was prepared. It was circulated among all the provinces and discussed with the provincial authorities. It was also subjected to scrutiny and discussion in different workshops held at federal and provincial levels in which representatives of the governments, donor agencies, NGOs and other stakeholders participated. The Draft Policy and Enabling Law have been revised by incorporating the views of all the stakeholders, which was presented in the National Workshop organized on 12 January 2002 at Islamabad. During the workshop, all the stakeholders participated in the discussions and gave their views on issues involved in the proposed National Resettlement Policy and the Enabling Law. The recommendations made in the workshop were incorporated and it was reiterated that the federal government would seek the endorsement of the provincial governments on the proposed documents. Based on these two documents, a country report was prepared which was presented in the Regional Workshop held in Asian Development Bank head office Manila from 18 to 20 February 2002. The draft National Resettlement Policy and the Enabling Law documents have been fine-tuned to incorporate the outcome of the regional workshop. The formal endorsement/comments of provincial governments are still awaited.[64]

Response of Civil Society

In recent years some NGOs have come forward to do advocacy on behalf of those affected by development projects, particularly water-related projects. They are few in numbers but they have evolved networks and the building of their institutional capacity to address issues related to development-induced displacement. Their activities include: policy advocacy, awareness raising, research and pressure group activities.

Sungi Development Foundation (SDF) is the pioneer organization for taking up specific issues related to displacement, resettlement and compensation in Pakistan. SDF has made successful intervention in various projects which include: GBHP, families still displaced by Tarbela dam, those affected by Chotiari Reservoir, Chashma Right Bank Canal Project, etc. SDF continues its advocacy of issues relating to displacement and environment with government and other international agencies like WB and ADB. SDF has also taken the initiative to form Pakistan Network of Rivers, Dams and People and plays a critical role in strengthening the network by providing support to its member organizations. Sungi Development Foundation has given critical inputs in the Indus Basin Study conducted by the World Commission on Dams.

Pakistan Network of Rivers, Dams and People is the leading network taking up issues of displacement owing to construction of dams and it has membership in all four provinces. Its member organizations have been active in promoting the process for formulation of national resettlement policy. The network has made effective intervention in different dams' projects, regarding mitigation of environmentally adverse impact and the dislocation of people. In addition to local support, the network also elicits support from international organizations working on the involuntary resettlement and forced displacement issues.

Human Rights Commission of Pakistan (HRCP) has also played its role in raising the issues of refugees and environmental refugees in the overall context of human rights. This is done through its publications and press statements. It provides consultations at both the national and regional level. HRCP is one of the active organizations on the issue of Lyari Expressway Project.

Apart from these apex organizations working at the broader policy level, some community-level organizations are also working for the protection of the rights of those affected in various projects like Anjuman-e-Mutaasireen Tarbela Dam (for Tarbela dam) Anti-Mangla Dam Committee (for Mangla dam), DAAMAN (for Chashma Right Bank Canal Project), Anjuman-e-Tahafuz-e-Haqooq (for GBHP Right Bank), Dharti Dost Tanzeem (for Chotiari dam), Anjuman Mutasireen Islamabad (for the capital city), etc. International Union for Conservation of Nature (IUCN) has undertaken various initiatives in terms of research, consultation and training workshops on dams and displacement in the context of environmental degradation. Urban Resource Centre, Shehri and Orngi

Pilot Project are in the forefront in Karachi in taking up such issues as dislocation and making effective interventions at public and policy levels. Apart from specific research on resettlement or displacement by the consultants, the research done by civil society organizations or otherwise is conducted in the context of environment or ecology. The displacement issues are secondary. Similarly, there is a dearth of studies done with gender perspective. Gender disaggregated data are seldom available in any development project involving displacement.[65]

The social and political groups working towards provincial autonomy also raise issues of displacement and livelihood in their respective provinces. Various forums in Sindh, NWFP and Balochistan are particularly active in this regard. Implications of displacement on women and children are an underreported and underdocumented aspect. There is no specific study available to address or document specifically the gender perspective in this phenomenon. But the interviews with some social activists, working for those affected by Mangla and Tarbela dams, who shared their experiences, help to throw some light on the gender dimension. They may be summarized as follows.

The cash compensation generally disempowers women, just because women do not handle cash or for that matter have control over financial resource within the family. Therefore, the decision to spend the money lies with the men of the family. Being mostly in the informal sector and without much skill, and mainly involved in menial jobs, women do not have many choices to invest the compensation amount in some productive small business where they can earn their livelihood. The women in agriculture have to face harsh impact as, in the case of loss of land and other common resources of livelihood, they have fewer choices at their disposal for future. The only choice is to migrate to big or small cities for domestic work or other odd jobs for survival. All of this severely impacts on the health and nutrition of women, as well as on their children, who remain without education during this process of change. The disintegration of social network of the displaced community further makes them vulnerable. Landless tenants meet the same fate by migrating to cities to work as unskilled labourers and other such underpaid workers. Moreover it has always been difficult for women who were heading their families, to pursue their cases with the departments dealing with compensation or allotment of land because of problems of mobility and social constraints.[66]

CONFLICT-INDUCED DISPLACEMENT

Political conflicts are another significant factor in displacement of population. Since Independence, Pakistan has witnessed various armed political and military conflicts that have caused displacement. The conflict-induced displacement increased significantly from 1970s onwards, as the insurgency in Balochistan, uprisings in Sindh and battles between militant Mohajirs and the security forces on the streets of Karachi rocked the entire country. The secession of East Pakistan (now Bangladesh) led to extreme cases of violence and mayhem, due to which thousands of people were displaced from their homes. Apart from that, there were two wars with India in 1948 and 1965; a limited war between India and Pakistan over Kargil in 1999 also forced a large number of people out of their homes. Periodic escalation of tension between India and Pakistan has also resulted in displacement of thousands of people residing along the border areas.

Unlike India, ethnic movements or movements of provincial autonomy in Pakistan did not turn into armed conflicts except in the case of Balochistan and Sindh. All these conflicts were not of such magnitude that they resulted in displacement of population on a larger scale, although the insurgency in Balochistan in 1973, following the military operation to curb the insurgency, resulted in migration of more than 5,000 families in Barkhan area of Balochistan alone. Of them, about 2,000 families settled in Afghanistan as refugees while another 3,000 families moved to Sindh province or urban areas of Balochistan.[67] Likewise, in early 1990, ethnic conflicts displaced 1,200 families from 'no-go areas' (held by Mohajir Qaumi Movement-Haqiqi, a rival political faction of Muttahida Qaumi Movement) in Karachi (Sindh).[68] The president of Pakistan directed the government of Sindh to rehabilitate the displaced families as well as evacuation of unauthorized occupation of their properties.[69]

Significant research material is available with reference to conflicts in Pakistan but there is lack of information regarding IDPs. Similarly reports in the press are more focused on other details of conflicts and strife than aspects of displacement. In this section we will restrict ourselves to some ongoing conflicts wherein patterns and scale of displacement can be assessed with reference to conflict. The three case studies that follow will describe and analyse the IDPs in Balochistan, Azad Jammu and Kashmir, and in the southern Pakistan–Indian borders.

Bugtis Tribal Feud

The conflict escalated in 1993 and a group of Kalpar tribe was forced to leave their homes because of a running feud as frequent armed clashes began to occur between the Kalpars and the Bugtis. The prolonged feud between the Bugti and the Kalpar and Raija tribes (sub-tribes of Bugti) compelled the latter to take shelter in other provinces. The newspapers reported the displacement of 600 families. Several persons of Kalpar and Raija tribes were allegedly killed and their houses were besieged and burnt. Rival Bugits cut off electricity, water and other facilities. Being influential and virtual ruler of the Dera Bugti (a tribal district in Balochistan province), the succeeding governments could not intervene effectively and hence the uprooted tribes had to face all sorts of miseries and hardships.[70] More than 7,000 Kalpars have since been forced to take refuge in various parts of the country mainly in Larkana (Sindh) and Multan (Punjab).[71]

The feud began when the cousin of Nawab Akbar Bugti (the chief of the Bugti tribe and the chairman of the Jamhoori Watan Party, a leading regional political party of Balochistan province), Mir Ahmadan, became chairman of the Dera Bugti district in 1979. Mir Ahmadan, unlike Nawab Akbar Bugti, adopted a pro-people politics by taking numerous initiatives for public development works. He succeeded in getting sanctioned electricity supply, a road from Dera Bugti to Kashmore via Sui, and supply of gas, which, at that time, was not available to the local people although it was explored in 1952 and supplied to other parts of the country from here. All these initiatives really annoyed the tribal chief as they shrank his political space in the area. He resorted to oppressing the opponents on one pretext or another.[72]

To counter the opposition of the tribal chief, Mir Ahmadan formed an alliance comprising other local chiefs of small tribes. The alliance was not able to win any electoral seats till 1991 but the margin of victory of the chief's candidates continued to shrink. That factor was a matter of concern for him. In 1992, local government elections were held in the province and the Ahmadani alliance won two seats unopposed, out of 11 seats. A tough fight was expected on the remaining seats. The Nawab's men allegedly killed Humza Bugti (member of the alliance and a leader of the Pakistan Peoples' Party) on the polling day. The election to the local government was postponed in the district.[73] As per the tribal tradition, the father of the deceased, Hamza Qadir Bugti, took revenge by killing the most loved son of the Nawab, Salal Bugti. This resulted in the never-ending catastrophe of killing and forced migration of a section of the tribal population. Ahmadan and his fellow-tribesmen had to face hardship because they had to desert their houses, jobs and lands. Initially thousands of Kalpars fled the area to save their lives. Their houses were attacked with rocket launchers, guns and other firearms. According to newspaper reports they had to bury the dead bodies in the premises of their houses as the tense situation could not allow them to take them to burial sites. Some women of the Ahmadan and Raija tribes were allegedly abducted by the Nawab's men.[74]

In these circumstances thousands of Raijas, Kalpars and Ahmadans were compelled to move to the nearby provinces of Punjab and Sindh. The government and the state did not take any steps to ease the situation or protect the vulnerable tribes people. Only one section of Raija tribe was escorted by the Frontier Constabulary to DG Khan district of Punjab and left there, on its own. The chief of Esani branch of Khosa tribe, Sardar Asif Nadeem, provided them shelter in hilly area of Dallana village falling under his chieftainship. Among the 1,600 displaced persons, more than 600 settled in Dallana village, a number of them settled in the cities of DG Khan and Multan districts, while a substantial number moved to Sindh province. The other tribal chiefs in Punjab, namely, Sardar Farooq Kahan Leghari (the head of the Leghari tribe and ex-president of Pakistan) and Sardar Zulfiqar Khosa (the chief of Khosa tribe and the then provincial minister of the Punjab province) simply refused to provide shelter to the displaced tribes, as they did not want to annoy the chief of Bugti tribe. At one point the provincial minister and the head of the Khosa tribe asked them to leave the area as it could jeopardize the situation further owing to proximity of the Bugti tribe.[75]

In 1993, the Pakistan Peoples' Party came to power and the displaced tribes people was resettled in the district (Dera Bugti). But again in 1997 they were removed from the town of Sui (Dera Bugti) for fear of impending clashes with dominant Bugtis. The feud became increasingly violent and endangered the nearby gas fields. During this period they were provided financial help from Zakat Fund (financial support for deserving and destitute) but there were reports of embezzlement by the state functionaries and it was not ascertained that the money reached the displaced community. During the Nawaz Sharif government, in 1998, the financial assistance and rations were reportedly stopped. About 600 displaced persons were living in Dallana village (far-flung and without health facilities) in district DG Khan, while thousands other were scattered in other districts of Sindh and Punjab provinces. The people living in Dalana (DG Khan) faced many hardships. During winter there were reports of death of some children owing to the freezing cold. Particularly, displaced women went through hard times owing to the frequent forced travel and unavailability of medical facilities. Another group of the displaced tribe has been reported to be settled in Larkana and Sukkur districts of Sindh province. A significant number has been living in DG Khan, Multan and Rahim Yar Khan districts of the Punjab province.[76]

The role of the state institutions in mitigating the problems of the displaced population amounted to criminal negligence. Both the federal and the provincial governments did not take steps to resolve or rehabilitate the uprooted tribespeople, although the Jamat-e-Islami (a leading religious political party) and some other social service organizations lent a helping hand by providing much-needed blankets, food items and essential medicines. Jamat-e-Islami also made efforts towards reconciliation between the rival tribes. The national and, at some points, international media played a critical role in raising the issue in the print and electronic media. The Human Rights Commission of Pakistan also took notice of it and sent letters to the federal and provincial governments, asking them to resolve the conflict at the earliest. In mid-2002, the federal government planned to resolve the issue by settling the displaced people in Sindh province. The government of Sindh was asked to assess the feasibility for the settlement of displaced tribe. However, it was reluctant to provide land for the displaced people as it could create law and order problem in the province and therefore resorted to delaying the federal government's plan. The government was cautions because frequent clashes and long enmity between the two sides, posed a threat to the important and sensitive installations in Sui gas-fields in Dera Bugti. As per the plan, the first batch of 6,400 persons of Kalpars was to be relocated in 2002.[77] No headway has been made regarding their relocation even in 2004.

Displacement along the Border

Since 1947 Pakistan and India have fought three declared wars in 1948, 1965 and 1971 and some other low intensity wars like Kargil war in 1999. All these large- and small-scale wars played havoc in terms of human displacement on a massive scale along the border. Pakistan shares a long border with India (1,800 miles), other than the Line of Control in Azad Kashmir (Pakistani-held Kashmir).

Subsequent to the attack on Indian parliament on 13 December 2001, India began to build up troops along the border on a massive scale to respond to the alleged cross-border terrorism by Pakistani-backed terrorists in India and Indian-controlled Kashmir. In view of the Indian threat to launch war, Pakistan also planned to deploy troops at the border. As a result more than 1 million army personnel were deployed on both sides. Deployment of artillery and infantry and installation of other military outfits continued in the ensuing four months. Pakistan and India recalled their respective high commissioners. Apparently preparations for an all-out war were under way. While the tension continued to increase, the prime minister of India Atal Behari Vajpayee stated, 'The time has come for a decisive fight'. In view of the prevailing situation, the United Nations asked its officials to evacuate their dependents at the earliest. Many other governments also issued warnings to their nationals to leave the war threatened zone and advised not to travel in this region. Many embassies in Pakistan pulled out its non-essential staff. The British High Commission closed its visa sections in Lahore, Karachi and Islamabad, in addition to reducing its staff for security reasons.[78]

The border areas of Punjab and upper Sindh were badly hit by the movement and camping of the troops. The people of these areas suffered enormous physical, economic, social and mental loss. There was a heavy movements of troops reported in the newspapers, particularly in Sialkot working boundary, Lahore, Narowal, Kasur, Okara, Bahawalnagar and Cholistan sectors, in addition to LOC (Line of Control).[79] In Bahawalpur district, apart from deployment of troops, many government buildings were evacuated for defence needs. Likewise in Sindh province, troops were deployed at the borders of the Desert (Thar) Region (Rajasthan–Thar border) and anti-aircraft guns were fixed. The entire Mirpur Khas division was put on high alert.[80] This was the biggest military build-up since the war in 1971.

The large-scale mobilization of troops, including artillery and infantry, sent shudders down the spine of people living along the Pak-India border. It really created a wave of panic among the residents of rural areas along the border. Consequently thousands of people migrated to safe areas for fear of impending war. Tapan K. Bose, in a letter to the editors of all newspapers in India and Pakistan regarding the uprooted people along the border areas quoted the figure of 20,000 displaced persons on both sides. Residents themselves vacated many villages, whereas a number of villages were evacuated by the army personnel. In

Shakargarh-Zafarwal sector (district Narowal) alone all villages within the radius of 5 km were evicted. As a result, 300 villages were vacated, which displaced 350,000 people in that district.[81] A similar situation was reported from other sectors where villagers fled for safer areas. In Lahore district over 100,000 villagers had left border areas by January 2002.[82] Military personnel dug up trenches that destroyed the standing crops while landmines were laid down in the radius of 5 km. Heavy military troops stationed at the border villages used the manpower for shifting of heavy artillery and construction of bunkers, but no compensation was paid. Moreover the army used their electric tubewells and cattle without any kind of payment.[83]

Intermittent shelling and skirmishes between the two armies seriously disrupted the lives of people living in the border areas. There were reports of many deaths and injuries particularly in Sialkot and Narowal sectors. Anti-personnel and anti-vehicle landmines were laid down on a large scale that caused injury or death to many civilians and cattle. According to two separate news reports, seven persons (including two women) were killed by the shelling, while three children were seriously injured in a landmine blast.[84] There were scores of other people who got injured or died owing to shelling and landmines. The shelling also damaged the houses and buildings near the borders.[85] Most of the forward areas along the border had been used as pastures, but because of landmines thousands of herders lost their livelihood and there was a shortage of fodder for the animals. Since animals were the only source of income for them, they were really in bad shape. Many of them sold their animals at throwaway prices.[86] The Human Rights Watch's report states that both India and Pakistan have emplaced large number of anti-personnel and anti-vehicle mines along their common border in one of the largest mine laying operations anywhere in the world since 1997.

The situation was not any different for the displaced families in Sindh province. In early 2002 residents of border areas (sub-districts of Umerkot, Diplo, Chachro, Nagarparkar) began moving to safe areas following the large deployment of Indian troops in Rajasthan, an Indian state bordering Sindh. There was widespread fear that war would break out between India and Pakistan. The district officials said that villagers had not been asked to vacate. They had done it on their own.[87] Rubi Ramdas (Member District Council, Mirpur Khas, Sindh) was interviewed on 31 May 2002.

She gave the following information regarding the displaced people in her district:

People from border areas began to come in January but returned after normalcy. But again they had to come back in early May. They were able to settle in *Kachi abadies* (squatter settlements), in cities of Umar Kot, Mirpur Khas. They got rented houses or stayed with their relatives. A number of them moved to Badin, Sukkur and Thatta districts in search of livelihood. Apart from anticipated war, major reason was the security of women who are always vulnerable in the presence of stationed regiments of army. They are sometimes abused by the army people. Since the main professions of the displaced are agriculture and livestock rearing, they could only survive by selling their animals. They could not harvest their crops because of threat of war and also because their movement near the border was restricted by the army people. The agony and problems of the migrating families were underreported in the local and national press. No NGO has been able to do anything for them in mitigating their grievances. The District Administration has equally ignored them. They were provided no relief or support in kind or cash. The children had to stop going to schools and health facilities were not available.[88]

Ms Azeem Khatoon (Member District Council, Khairpur district, Sindh) too was interviewed and she said that some villages along border of district Khairpur were vacated by people themselves while some villages were evacuated by the army. People had to migrate to areas near cities with their livestock. They could not bring their stock of wheat that they stored to use throughout the year. They lived in rented houses or with relatives. Some migrants were able to build houses of their own with the assistance of the local chief of their tribe. They mainly settled in different *tehsils*, namely Nara, Mirwah and Khairpur.

The deployment of troops seriously disrupted the community life in a big way as, in most of the cases, the entire village had to move to other areas far from the border. The displaced people were accommodated by their relatives and friends and in some cases took shelter in government buildings like schools, dispensaries and hospitals, or got rented houses in the cities. Children's education was discontinued. Children and women were the worst sufferers of the conflict, as they had to face all kinds of hardships. The loss due to the deployment of troops was not only suffered by the farming communities but also a large number of skilled artisans and daily-wage labourers.

Relief, Remedies and Measures

The government of Pakistan has reportedly no policy on conflict-induced displacement and there has not been any consistent mechanism or structure to manage the affected in such cases. Neither the national nor provincial government has any mechanism to avoid or manage such displacements. In the case of displacement owing to conflict or strife ad hoc arrangements are made. The measures available are inadequate, as they do not address the problem in an integrated manner. In the case of the impending war-displaced families, no consistent policy was adopted to manage the thousands of them. Neither compensation nor a decent resettlement or camps for them could be provided. Reportedly only in Narowal district, a few relief camps were set up to accommodate the displaced people. But supplies within the camps were of poor quality and conditions deplorable.[89] President General Pervez Musharraf addressed a rally in Gujranwala in connection with his referendum campaign. Since a large number of people came from Narowal and Sialkot districts, the president announced that the government would compensate the people who suffered losses owing to mobilization of troops and installation of military outfits in Narowal and Shakargarh (18 April 2002). The governor of Punjab announced a relief package for the villagers of border areas who had not been able to cultivate their land due to movement of troops and landmines. He also announced the waiver of the water cess of the affected farmers.[90] As a result, the government of Punjab declared over 6,000 revenue estates and villages as 'calamity hit' due to drought conditions and the deployment of the army in border areas. In districts Lahore, Okara, Narowal, Bahawalnagar, Sialkot and Kasur 448 revenue estates were declared 'calamity hit' owing to deployment of army troops along the border villages.[91] Earlier in response to the president's announcement, revenue minister of Punjab, Malik M. Aslam Khan, also declared 367 villages of Punjab as calamity hit. With the declaration of calamity-affected areas, the dues of agriculture income tax, water rates (*aabiana*), development cess and local rate were remitted. The villages included: 75 of Lahore, 44 of Narowal, 49 of Okara, 104 of Bahawalnagar and 95 of Sialkot. Moreover, the agricultural loans taken by the farmers from these areas were deferred for one year and advance loans for next crop allowed.[92] The city district government of Lahore directed the executive district officer (education) that all students evacuated from the border areas should be admitted to the government schools close to the places they had resettled in.[93] The district government of Sialkot announced a Rs 15 million compensation package for the people affected on the border villages by shelling and firing during the last 25 years.[94]

As per the new local government system of 2001, the district governments are supposed to take action in times of emergency and catastrophe. The Local Government Ordinance, 2001 clearly entrusted the district governments with distribution of relief funds and goods to the calamity-affected, and formulation of recommendations, when an area was declared as calamity hit.[95] District governments in Punjab and Sindh located near the border were not able to manage the crisis appropriately. The scale of displacement was much higher, while district governments had meagre resources to deal with it. Districts governments are dependent on provincial governments in situations like these. The provincial governments too could not devise effective strategies required to mitigate the problems of the displaced population.

Initially the number of affected people in the border areas was under-reported by the national press, but as the scale of migration increased, extensive reporting of the phenomenon began. But few civil society organizations took up the issue at any level. The Human Rights Commission of Pakistan (HRCP) and AGHS Legal Aid Cell, Labour Party Pakistan, Pakistan Muslim League (Quaid-e-Azam) raised the issue only in the press or made some visits to the border areas for fact finding. Khurshid Mehmood Qasuri (vice president of the Pakistan Muslim League [Q] and now foreign minister) demanded that a commission should be set up to resolve the problems of and provide compensation to, the displaced population of the border areas.[96]

IDPs in Kashmir

Since 1947, successive waves of refugees from Jammu and Kashmir in India have migrated to Pakistan-held Kashmir and assimilated in the local population. Apart from deaths and horrific injuries, thousands of Kashmiris have left their villages across the 740-km Line of Control (LOC), which divides the mountainous region between Pakistan and India. For instance, almost 20,000 people in the Neelum valley, having to face artillery exchanges or small fire arms from across the border, remain continually on the move, shifting from settlement to settlement to avoid fighting.[97] Similarly there have been a significant number of internally displaced persons, but because they live with their relatives and friends they are not readily identifiable.[98] The terms 'refugees' and 'internally displaced persons' are used interchangeably in the press and official documents, and this further makes it more difficult to assess the numbers of displaced persons. In 1947, 1.5 million refugees crossed into Pakistan-controlled Kashmir and various districts of Pakistan itself. During the 1965 and 1971 wars, 50,000 people came into the territory controlled by Pakistan.[99]

Since the start of disturbances or conflict in Jammu and Kashmir in India from 1989, which were accompanied by massive attacks and counter-attacks between the insurgents and Indian security forces, a large number of Kashmiri families have fled their homes and sought refuge in the Pakistan-held Kashmir. The governments of Pakistan and that of Pakistan-held Kashmir have taken measures to provide them with all kinds of assistance. As such, each refugee family is provided with tent, monthly subsistence allowance and education allowance for children. Special medical centres have been established to provide them with appropriate healthcare. The majority of IDPs in Pakistan-held Kashmir live near the Line of Control and thus are vulnerable at all times. According to the Pakistan-held Kashmir's Refugees Rehabilitation Department, the number of refugees who migrated to Pakistan-held Kashmir in 1990 and afterwards is more than 12,000. Those who are registered with the department are about 12,784, while many others remain unregistered. The Pakistan-held Kashmir government and the government of Pakistan have been trying to get these refugees recognized by the United Nations so that they can get international humanitarian assistance. However, so far no progress has been made.[100] On the other hand, the refugees living in these camps are not satisfied with the facilities and arrangements. There have been frequent protest demonstrations by the refugees for proper facilities and assistance at the camps.[101] Currently there are nearly 18,000 refugees living in 15 camps in Pakistan-held Kashmir.[102] In 2002 the Ministry of Finance and Rehabilitation of the Pakistan-held Kashmir announced various facilities and privileges for the Kashmiri refugees which include monthly subsistence allowance of Rs 1,500 for each family living in the 15 camps, and establishment of a medical board for health services, special allowance for refugee students in educational institutions and provision of land to rehabilitate the homeless refugees.[103] According to the HRCP report, the nine years of militancy and military action in Indian-held Kashmir created a refugee population in Pakistan of about 400,000 people, 35,000 of whom are still unregistered.[104]

As well as refugees living in camps, the Kashmiris who entered Pakistan or Pakistan-controlled Kashmir from Jammu and Kashmir in India before 1971 were offered land, assistance, and citizenship by Pakistan.[105]

As a result, a large number of the Kashmiri refugees are living in Pakistan. The majority of them have their own houses and hundreds of them have been allocated land in different districts. A plan is under way in district Toba Tek Singh for 2,300 families, displaced during 1965 war in AJK, to be given ownership rights of houses.[106] In district Gujranwala 500 families of Kashmiri refugees were awarded landownership rights in 1996.[107] Reportedly, there are thousands of Kashmiri Muslims who have migrated abroad, mostly to Britain, as a result of the conflict in Kashmir.[108]

During the summer of 1998 Indian armed forces' constant firing across the Line of Control, rendered thousands of people living along the LOC homeless. There had been intensive shelling and firing across the LOC which continued for months. At least 300,000 people were affected, while over 100,000 people were displaced in Neelum valley, Bhimber and Nakial (Jhelum valley).[109] In one of the sub-districts (Athmuqam) of district Muzaffarabad about 80 per cent of the population fled from their homes due to the continued firing and shelling across the Line of Control in 1998.[110] The Human Rights Commission of Pakistan (fact-finding mission) reported the displacement of 1,600 families (12,000 men and women, and 900 children) around the Kharmang town on the Line of Control; the displaced group trekked all 247 km up to Sakardu (Northern Areas). The mission also reported the deplorable conditions of the camps established in Sakardu, where medical services were non-existent and supply of water and food was substandard.[111] The Pakistan-held Kashmir government was quite unprepared for the situation and thus there was chaos in dealing with such a large number of displaced families. Apart from lack of institutional capacity to deal with migration of this scale, there was dearth of resources to provide relief services to the displaced population.[112]

During the Kargil war in 1999, when Pakistan and India exchanged heavy fire near the LOC, an estimated 40,000 people in Pakistan-controlled Kashmir were displaced. In another statement, the minister for Kashmir Affairs and Northern Areas reported that there was a displacement of 4,000 families.[113] The Human Rights Commission of Pakistan's estimate of IDPs was around 104,564.[114] Displaced families of the Kargil conflict were settled in different villages and given Rs 3,000 per family per month.[115] Similarly in Baltistan (Northern Areas) 5,000 people were rendered homeless because of constant shelling.[116] Hundreds of Kashmiris have been killed, injured and maimed in the fresh hostilities. According to Agence France Press, 26,000 people fled the areas for safer places.[117] However, the Pakistan Army always encourages or compels the people of Kashmir to remain settled in the places near the LOC so that

Pakistan can maintain its claim on the territory. This is against The Hague Convention, which expressly states that, 'Population shall not be used as shield or as military objectives from attacks.'[118]

Relief and Rehabilitation of Kashmiri IDPs

The government of Pakistan-held Kashmir is primarily managing the refugees and the IDPs in terms of relief and supplies. The government of Pakistan gives financial and material assistance as and when needed. The ministry for Kashmir Affairs and Northern Areas is a full-fledged ministry that deals with issues related to Pakistan-held Kahmir. Whenever there is a severe refugee pressure, a separate relief fund is launched for public donations by the AJK and Pakistan governments. The local authorities, with the cooperation of the Pakistan Army, handle all the refugees and IDPs. The Refugee Rehabilitation Department in the Pakistan-held Kashmir is responsible for operations regarding relief and rehabilitation of displaced persons and refugees. Overall, the conditions in the camps (and elsewhere) providing relief to the IDPs have always been deplorable and unsatisfactory as reported in the press frequently.[119]

Numerous other national and international organizations also extend support to the refugees and IDPs in Pakistan-controlled Kashmir. These organizations include International Committee of Red Crescent (ICRC), Islamic Relief International, Adventure Development Relief Agency (USA), World Assembly of Muslim Youth (Saudi Arabia) and Organization of Islamic Countries (OIC). Various local and national groups, including political parties, also contribute in times of emergencies. Moreover the Kashmiri diaspora and migrant workers in other countries also send financial and material support time and again. The office of the United Nations High Commissioner for Refugees does not provide any support to Kashmiri IDPs or refugees.

DISPLACEMENT DUE TO NATURAL DISASTERS

Pakistan is one of the most disaster-prone countries in South Asia where one form or another of disaster continues to strike the less developed regions of the country. According to the World Disaster Report 2002, out of 184 countries Pakistan stands at number 56. The type of disasters includes floods, drought, cyclones, earthquakes and landslides that have the potential to disrupt social and economic life on a massive scale. The government predominantly views disaster in an isolated manner, merely as an event that requires emergency relief, once it has hit an area. The predominance of state institutions with sole mandate for managing disasters, is a clear manifestation of an approach that lacks sustainable solution towards disaster mitigation and preparedness. As a result, there are little or no institutional arrangements in the government or non-government sectors that can cope with natural disasters in an adequately planned manner. Despite the long spell of droughts, for instance, in certain regions of Pakistan, the government and the non-governmental organizations have not been able to launch a comprehensive programme to deal with it. Although millions of dollars of aid have come in for relief and rehabilitation, few programmes have been launched to anticipate and prepare for the adverse impacts of drought on a sustainable basis.

In this section, an overview of the natural disasters in Pakistan is made along with an analysis of their impact on displacement of people from the calamity-stricken areas. The role of government and non-governmental organizations in disaster preparedness and mitigation is also analysed.

Disasters and Displacement in Pakistan

Pakistan has faced acute drought conditions in Balochistan, Sindh and in certain areas of Punjab and NWFP. A four-year-long dry spell from 1998 to 2001 caused havoc in terms of loss of human lives, livelihood and habitat. The following districts suffered from the drought:

- Twenty-six districts of Balochistan
- Six districts of Sindh (particularly Thaparkar)
- Ten districts in Punjab (particularly Cholistan, an arid zone)
- Nine districts in NWFP (including the tribal areas) [120]

According to an independent assessment, around 1 million people left their homes in search of food, water and fodder in Balochistan alone (Brig. [Retd] Shafqat Mehmood, Provincial Coordinator Drought Control, Balochistan). In Sindh over a hundered thousand were homeless while thousands rendered displaced in Cholistan (Punjab). In Tharparkar (Sindh), the situation of protracted drought and scarcity of water has been a chronic problem resulting in hunger and poverty. In 2001, 70 per cent from scheduled castes and 20 per cent from other castes migrated to Barrage Belt (districts near Sukkur Barrage) along with their cattle in search of food, water and fodder. [121] There have not been any official figures available regarding the number of deaths. However, the International Red Cross (IRC) estimated that by August 2000 around 1,500, and very possibly almost double this number of people, had died. The displacements of thousands of people, a majority of them nomads, and the loss of entire herds of cattle, which wiped out the means of living for hundreds, were reported by IRC according to the HRCP Report 2000. The national economy was estimated to have suffered a loss of US $2 billion due to drought and water shortage in 2001.[122] The IFRC estimated that, at least 3.4 million people had been affected in Balochistan and Sindh. In these circumstances the federal government established an emergency assistance policy as well as special relief fund for victims of drought, and donated Rs 900 million to Balochistan and Sindh provinces in 2000.[123]

According to the HRCP Report, Balochistan emerged as the worst affected region in the country due to the drought. It was adversely affected by the drought of 2000, and scanty rains in 2001 significantly worsened the situation. The provincial government declared almost all districts as 'calamity hit', with the exception of the urban parts of some districts.[124]

According to a field report by Aurat Foundation, Pakistan, hundreds of families in different villages of district Chagai were forced to migrate to other areas, while in some cases the entire population of a village left their homes because of shortage of water and fodder for their animals.[125] Moreover, the farmers and herders were either forced to sell their animals at throwaway prices or they died from the effects of weather conditions.[126]

In Balochistan, the government and the other national and international agencies took notice of the situation but it was too late, and the initiatives taken by them were inadequate and insufficient. Two million cattle in Balochistan perished by the time aid came. Disaster control measures were haphazard. Various relief camps and relief centres were set up in the affected areas. At the relief camps arrangements were made but reports said that there was mismanagement and corruption. Therefore, by and large, in all cases there was gross violation of human rights where government could not provide for basic life sustaining items like food, water and shelter to its citizens.[127]

In other provinces, the situation was not dissimilar. In Punjab province, the worst affected area was Cholistan (desert) where 300,000 people had to migrate to other areas and 30 to 40 per cent of the livestock perished.[128] Almost the entire population of livestock had migrated during the 1999–2001 drought after suffering mortality rate of 5 to 7 per cent.[129] Other districts in Punjab province, which were partly affected by drought, included Attock, Jhang, Chakwal, DG Khan, Rajanpur, Mianwali, Rawalpindi, Gujrat, Multan, Bhakkar and Khushab. In district Rajanpur 90,000 people of Dhundi state area migrated to green belts with all their livestock.[130] Cholistan and other affected areas of different districts in Punjab were declared calamity hit by the provincial government in July 2002. The number of villages declared calamity hit was 3,437 in 2001.[131]

In Sindh, even official figures show that a total of 1.3 million people and 2,664 villages in the arid zone of Tharparkar, Umerkot and Dadu districts where affected by the drought of 2000 and 2001. In 2,664 'calamity-hit' villages, 1.3 million people and 5 million cattle were affected.[132] The UN Office for Coordination of Humanitarian Affairs (UNOCHA) in one of its reports pointed out that Sindh and Balochistan had still not recovered from drought that affected them from November 1999 to July 2000 and were thus least able to battle the existing situation.[133] The drought also forced about 600 families to migrate and settle in the Quetha's suburbs.[134] In view of the famine-like situation, the government of Sindh declared various districts as 'calamity-hit areas'. The districts of Tharparkar, Dadu, Mirpurkhas, Badin and many other sub-divisions in the province were declared calamity-hit.[135]

Some parts of NWFP districts were also affected by the dry spell. These areas were DI Khan, Karak, Chitral, Lower Dir, Shangla, Sawabi and Lakki Marwat. Various villages of these districts were declared calamity-hit by the provincial government.[136]

Apart from drought and famine there are numerous other recurrent natural calamities, and already vulnerable communities become the major sufferers. Floods have been the main feature occurring every year, but since the construction of dams and water reservoirs, the level and frequency of this form of disaster has not been on such a damaging scale. It is obvious, though, from the data of last five decades that the scale of destruction is high and capability of state institutions to deal with such calamity is inadequate. From 1950 to 1998 Pakistan suffered a loss of US $5,000 million, 60,000 villages were affected and thousands of people were dislocated due to floods. The floods in 1992 killed more than 2,000 people, while thousands became homeless. Similarly in 1995, a total of 485 people lost their lives, 60,683 houses were damaged, 26,997 cattle were killed and thousands of people were displaced. In the March 1998 floods in Balochistan more than 2,000 people died or were reported missing, 4,000 houses were damaged and 7,500 cattle perished.[137] The rains in July 2001 caused a lot of damage to the residents of the twin cities of Islamabad and Rawalpindi. According to the official figures, 71 people died in the flash flood in Nullah Leh, out of 1,936 houses affected, 841 were completely destroyed while 742 animals perished.[138] In another calamity in the NWFP, torrential rains and subsequent flash floods caused havoc in at least 11 districts of the province. More than 500 houses collapsed, hundreds of acres of crops were destroyed and hundreds of people were displaced. Reportedly 23 people died and 17 were injured.[139] The breach in Rohri Canal inundated 35 villages, rendered 50,000 persons homeless, besides destroying standing crops of cotton, sugar cane and chillies, and orchards spanning over 20,000 acres. A similar breach had occurred in June 2000 but despite complaints and reports by people, the Irrigation Department failed to strengthen the embankment of the canal.[140]

The severe tropical cyclone (02–A) caused heavy damages in southeastern Sindh in May 1999. The cyclone was heading towards Karachi when it changed course and thus coastal areas of Thatta and Badin districts were severely ravaged. Independent sources put the loss of life at over 1,000 as compared to official figures of some 200 dead and 20 missing. Over 80,000 houses simply vanished from the face of the earth. The Meteorology Department and other concerned departments failed to inform people of the impending disaster. There was then no evacuation of the people living in the coastal villages.[141] The Pakistan Army and Navy took part in the rescue operations. More than 14,000 homeless people were accommodated in 31 relief camps set up by the provincial government. The federal government allocated US $1 million for rescue operations in the affected area (JICA website). In 2001, the tropical cyclone (01–A), hit the coastal belt of districts Thatta and Badin. Several villages were inundated due to the cyclone. More than 20,000 people were evacuated from the coastal areas by the district administrations of Thatta and Badin. According to the administration, 3,210 persons in district of Thatta and 5,198 in district of Badin, including women and children, were sheltered in the relief camps. More than 7,000 persons took shelter in houses of their relatives and friends.[142]

The sea intrusion in Sindh province and land erosion along the rivers, all over the country, is also one of the causes of displacement and migration. In coastal area of Sindh, 122,360 acres of land had been submerged under the sea water in the districts of Thatta and Badin. Similarly the 1,850 sq. m of the delta region covered with mangroves was reduced to 1,000 square metres due to degeneration over a decade.[143] The communities depending on the mangroves for their livelihood have been forced to migrate to urban areas for survival. The sea intrusion too has rendered hundreds of farming and fishing communities vulnerable in terms of habitat and economic survival, coupled with increasing non-availability of sweet water downstream Kotri and Indus Delta.[144] Regarding displacement due to the land erosion, Mr Ahmed Malik (president, Indus Welfare Society, Chachran Sharif, Rahim Yar Khan district) shared the following facts:

Chachran Sharif is situated along the river Indus in district Rahim Yar Khan. It's a town with a population of 30,000. Agriculture is the main profession. Over the years about 40 villages have been affected by land erosion. The process of erosion is still going on. Every year there are floods or the river changes course and the land is eroded or submerged. Earlier the district administration established relief camps, those affected by the floods were provided with food and other essential items. But cases of erosion, when lands are being washed away and so uneven that they cannot be cultivated, are never addressed by the government. Consequently the families of the erosion-affected villages have to migrate to urban areas to earn their livelihood because they do not have resources to level their lands or in some cases reclamation. The males work as casual wage labourers and women work as domestic servants. Among those 10,000 displaced from these villages 7,000 are settled in Karachi alone, living in shanty towns. Majority of these peasants had 5–10 acres of land. On the part of government no compensation was paid or rehabilitation plan launched, so that they might continue with their century-old profession. Even the Malya (revenue) was not written off. All these 40 villages had an average of 50 families but now only five to 10 families are living in each village. Some of these villages have been so severely affected by erosion that they are completely extinct. Although the river erosion is an ongoing process, the government has not been able to come up with comprehensive plans to prevent it and programmes to rehabilitate the affected communities living on the river banks.

Earthquakes are another form of natural disaster that have caused damage on a massive scale over the years whenever they have occurred. According to the Punjab University Earthquake Centre's scientists 40 per cent of the earth's seismic activity occurs in this part of the globe, and Pakistan lies entirely in this seismic belt which has suffered big catastrophes in the past.[145] For instance, thousands of people died in the 1974 earthquake in Swat and Besham. The early 2001 earthquake in southeast Sindh (Hyderabad, Badin and Tharparkar) rendered over 1,000 families homeless. According to an estimate, about 500 villages were affected by the earthquake in Tharparkar and Badin.[146] At least 19 deaths were reported. The deputy commissioner of Thar confirmed that 109, 714 houses had been damaged and 11,000 were totally destroyed. Insufficient relief efforts meant that the tents sent in could provide shelter to only a few thousands of the victims.[147] Although the government of Sindh and various other non-governmental organizations provided relief in terms of food, shelter and medical aid, it still remained insufficient and could not reach all those who were affected.[148]

Mechanisms for Disaster Management

There are various state institutions, which are all only loosely responsible for disaster management, thus hampering proper coordination and flow of information. Moreover, these institutions lack necessary training, logistical and financial support, resulting in mostly ad hoc, incoherent and inconsistent disaster management policies.[149] All emergency operations regarding relief are carried out and compensations dealt with under the West Pakistan Natural Calamities and Relief Act, 1958. An Emergency Relief Cell was established in 1977. This cell functions under the Cabinet Division. The primary responsibility of the Cell is to collect information about disasters, monitor losses and provide relief and compensations. In each province a Relief Commissioner is appointed and a Relief Department has been established under the Board of Revenue. All these departments directly receive grants from the federal government.[150]

Federal Flood Commission is the federal body with a mandate to monitor and manage floods. However when there is a flood disaster or other calamity, all provincial departments which include irrigation, agriculture, railway, livestock, and so on work in close coordination. Particularly, Pakistan Army plays a key role in dealing with natural disasters. During floods the army's help is always sought. The Civil Defence Departments also deal with emergencies in all four provinces. It has a district level network but it is virtually ineffective in managing any kind of disasters. Inadequate resources and outdated equipment and lack of proper training restrict the department's ability to deal with fire operations. In a press briefing, the governor of Punjab admitted that the department had certain resource constraints and was thus unable to manage crises of scale.[151] Provincial Ushar and Zakat Departments also provide relief (in cash and kind) through the relief departments.[152] Pakistan Meteorology Department operates 73 meteorological observatories all over the country.

The main task is the weather forecasting to avoid natural calamities (Amjad Bhatti, Coordinator, Journalists Resource Centre). Pakistan is also a signatory to the UN Convention to Combat Desertification since 1994. A National Plan of Action was designed to combat desertification and drought as mandated by the Convention. However, nothing significant has come out of it. [153]

In the wake of emerging needs of disaster mitigation on a longer-term basis, the government has come up with various plans at the national and provincial levels. The National Programme for Disaster Management was launched in 2000. The main thrust of the programme is to build capacity of vulnerable communities to sustain disasters and thus save property and lives. [154] In 2002 the federal government allocated Rs 6 billion for the implementation of the Drought Emergency Relief Assistance (DERA) programme to mitigate the impacts of dry spell, while in 2001 the government had allocated Rs 7 billion for drought mitigation. All the provincial governments have been involved in the programmes and activities designed and executed in 85 drought-stricken districts under the DERA. Various projects and activities have been prepared under the programme, which includes farm water management, drinkable water schemes, construction of farm roads and projects that can support agriculture, and livestock sustenance. [155] The government of Pakistan, the Asian Development Bank and the World Bank jointly fund the programme.

Response of Civil Society

The federal and the provincial governments have taken various initiatives and steps with the support of international organizations to deal with the crisis related to natural disasters. But the predominant approach has always been relief and assistance rather than to address the underlying causes to minimize the vulnerabilities. Since 1999 various multilateral and bilateral donors are involved in responding to looming disasters, particularly drought. The World Bank, the Asian Development Bank, International Federation of Red Crescent, USAID, Catholic Relief Service, Church World Service, World Food Programme, Action Aid, Caritas, UNDP, UNICEF, Japan International Cooperation Agency (JICA), OXFAM, embassies and high commissions in Pakistan and numerous other international, national and local organizations are doing their bit to cope with different natural disasters. Furthermore, Bahn Beli, Thardeep, Journalists Resource Centre, Pattan Development Organization, Sustainable Development Policy Institute, Sungi Development Foundation and a number of other organizations are also working on disaster mitigation through policy advocacy, and some of them are also into service delivery support to affected communities. Various other charitable, religious and political groups also become active whenever emergencies occur. These groups mobilize funds to make food and clothing arrangements for the affected people. Special relief funds are also launched by the prime minister or the president for donations from the public for specific calamities. The Disaster Mitigation Network has also been launched by some civil society organizations to raise issues related to disaster in the context of sustainable development for disaster preparedness and prevention.

Given the patriarchal order in Pakistani society, women and children are more vulnerable and suffer more than men. The Report on the Drought Situation in Sindh (2001) prepared by Pattan Development Organization, Islamabad, explicitly analysed this dimension:

> There is no doubt that drought has affected all those living in drought affected areas; nevertheless, the impact of drought situation on women is worst due to their socio-cultural and economic positioning within the family and the community. The workload on women has increased manifold due to the scarcity of water, loss of male employment in the agricultural sector and their subsequent migration to other cities in search of work, ill health of animals and members of their families.

Dr Farzana Bari and Sarwar Bari wrote in a research article 'Impact of Drought on Women':

> The oversight of gender in dealing with the present situation of drought in the country is quite striking. There is no evidence that the government has made any effort so far to assess the impact of drought on women. The absence of female staff in relief operations and need assessments, despite availability of a large number of female teachers, health workers present in these areas who could have been involved in such exercise, indicates the gender blindness of our administrators and policy makers responsible for drought management.[156]

The report on 'Livelihood Options for Disaster Risk Reduction in Thar' prepared by Journalists Resource Centre, Islamabad, in 2002 narrates that the women who don't migrate have the responsibility to take care of family and animals. Due to insufficient food, women and children face many visible and invisible diseases.[157]

RELEVANCE OF THE UN GUIDING PRINCIPLES

The UN Guiding Principles on Internal Displacement are based on existing international humanitarian laws and human rights instruments, and are also compatible with the guidelines provided by the World Bank and Asian Development Bank. There is a dire need to take strategic action for the lives and future of those who are displaced by development, conflict and natural disasters. Similarly, the losses of economic potential incurred by affected people should be reduced and redressed. In addition, they should be assisted to develop their full economic, social and cultural potential. However, in Pakistan, it may be submitted that UN Guiding Principles exist only in sheer violation across the board. The Principles relating to protection and assistance of displaced persons before, during and after the displacement have been starkly violated in almost all events of displacements caused by disasters.

The Principles, which are of particular relevance to Pakistan, include numbers 3, 5, 6, 7, 8, 9, 18, 19 and 23, especially with reference to displacement due to the development, conflict or natural disasters. Principles 3 and 5 entrust obligations on national governments and international actors for the protection and assistance of IDPs. Principle 6 is related to the conditions that lead to displacement, but which may be prevented or avoided. In Principle 7 it is proposed that comprehensive measures need to be taken before relocation of the affected population. Principles 8 and 9 again stress on the relocation of affected people in a manner that does not violate the basic rights of affected people, particularly the indigenous people, minorities, peasants, pastoralists and other groups under particular obligation. Principles 18 and 19 address the norm of adequate standard of living and provision of commodities essential for survival, in addition to medical services for physical and mental ailments of the displaced people. Principle 23 sets forth that every human being has a right to education and thus it is critical to provide the same to all displaced children with special emphasis on the education of women and girls. The Guiding Principles put special emphasis with regard to vulnerable groups like the disabled, children, female-headed households, the landless, ethnic minorities, herders, etc. Principles 28, 29 and 30 are focused on the return and resettlement of the IDPs, laying special emphasis on recovery of the affected communities, including appropriate compensation in case of loss of property and possessions.

In the absence of comprehensive policy and legislation in Pakistan, the Guiding Principles can provide a framework for formulation of the same. Other than that, Pakistan is signatory to various other international instruments that bind it to undertake mitigating measures regarding displaced population. Currently those affected are not getting adequate assistance on a sustained basis. And the available mechanisms are sporadic, inconsistent and ad hoc. Pakistan is a signatory to various international instruments, which include Geneva Conventions, 1949 (with all its additional and optional protocols), the Convention on the Elimination of All Forms of Discrimination Against Women (CEDAW), the International Convention on the Elimination of All Forms of Racial Discrimination (ICERD), the Convention on the Rights of the Child (CRC), Discrimination (Employment and Occupation) Convention (DC), and the Convention on the Suppression of the Traffic in Persons and of the Exploitation of the Prostitution of Others (CSTPEP).[158] The Geneva Conventions directly relate to humanitarian assistance and rehabilitation measures during conflict situations and Pakistan is bound to undertake action in such occurrences.[159]

CONCLUSIONS AND RECOMMENDATIONS

It is apparent from the scenario presented regarding IDPs in Pakistan that efforts and initiatives to ensure protection and assistance of displaced communities have been totally inadequate and ad hoc. Although there are interventions by civil society organizations, these are too recent and limited to have made any substantial impact on national policy and laws. Despite the fact that the state bears the responsibility for ensuring the protection of the displaced persons, the overall strategy on the part of government has been 'case to case approach' towards development projects which involved resettlement and conflict-related migration for shelter and food. Thus, the state has to come up with up-to-date laws and inte-grated policies, incorporating sectoral and gender needs, to assist and protect the citizens from the adverse implications of displacement and violation of human rights.

Issues related to IDPs have come to surface since 1990s, but in Paki-stan minimal work has been undertaken and nothing significant has been done so far in terms of initiatives for research, advocacy and training programmes on the issues of displacement. There is general lack of aware-ness, information and data regarding IDPs. The terms refugee, IDP and all other 'immigrants' are referred interchangeably. Particularly the media persons use it in a broader sense, rather than employ different terms for different categories of displaced persons in legalistic definition. They consider refugees to be those who has been forced to leave their usual place of residence by circumstances beyond their control. More often than not, the refugees referred to are actually IDPs.[160] Following are some recommendations for ensuring protection of IDPs in Pakistan in the context of the Guiding Principles. These are by no means comprehensive recommendations since more detailed work is required to be done to formulate specific recommendations:

- Legislation, meeting current needs and comprehensive policy is required, as stated in international conventions and the Guiding Principles, so that measures can be taken and mechanisms developed to deal with displacement caused due to development projects, conflicts and natural disasters.
- More initiatives and efforts are needed to enhance capacities in documentation, database building, advocacy and lobbying in the context of the Guiding Principles in order to work out strategies to protect IDPs at all levels.
- In view of the limited awareness about the UN Guiding Principles on Internal Displacement, widespread dissemination and promotion of the Guiding Principles should be undertaken across the board. NGOs and media may be involved in this connection.
- Help should be sought from international organizations in terms of technical and financial support to deal with displacement issues. Particularly, capacity building of existing state and non-state institutions is needed to cope with the IDPs' crises.
- Local government institutions should be delegated more powers and resources to deal with natural disasters and emergencies related to conflict-induced displacement. It is critical that a long-term programme based on a sustainable approach be launched so that the underlying causes of natural disaster can be targeted and removed, rather than continued pumping of relief in time of emergencies.

NOTES

1. UNCHR, *The State of the World's Refugees: The Challenge of Protection* (New York Penguin, 1993).
2. Ibid.
3. Zafar Afghani Khan, 'Distribution of Water among the Provinces: A Crisis', *Jang* (29 Jan. 2001).

4. Tappan K. Bose, *Protection of Refugees in South Asia: Need for a Legal Framework* (Nepal: South Asia Forum for Human Rights, 2000).
5. Zafar Mughal, 'Kalabagh Dam v/s Mangla Dam', *Daily Khabrain*, 2 August 2001.
6. *The News*, 25 Jan. 2001.
7. *The Dawn*, 31 July 2001.
8. *The Business Recorder*, 23 March 2002.
9. Arif Malik, Coordinator, Citizen Action Committee, Mirpur.
10. *The Dawn*, 9 July 2002.
11. *The Dawn*, 26 July 2002.
12. *Daily News*, 3 Aug. 2002.
13. *The Dawn*, 10 Sept. 2002.
14. *The Dawn*, 4 Aug. 2002.
15. World Commission on Dams (WCD), *Dams and Development: A New Framework for Analysis* (London: Earthscan Publications, 2000).
16. 'Pakistan Resettlement Policy and Practice: Review and Recommendations', prepared for Pakistan Environmental Protection Agency in 2000 by SEBCON (Pvt) Ltd under Regional Technical Assistance No. 5781 funded by Asian Development Bank.
17. Intikhab Amir, 'Waiting in Distress', The Review, *The Dawn*, 1–7 November 2001.
18. Ibid.
19. *The Dawn*, 1–7 July 2000.
20. *The Dawn*, 30 July 2002.
21. WCD, *Dams and Development*.
22. SEBCON, 'Pakistan Resettlement'.
23. Ibid.
24. Ibid.
25. Ibid.
26. Ibid.
27. Ibid.
28. Ibid.
29. Ibid.
30. *The Dawn*, 24 Apr. 2002.
31. *The Dawn*, 1 Aug. 2002.
32. *Daily News*, 7 June 2002.
33. CEESP/SDPI Website, www. sdpi. og
34. 'To build or not to build Kalabagh Dam,' *The News* seminar on 19 July 1998.
35. Interview telecast on PTV, 23 Sept. 2002.
36. SEBCON, 2000, 'Pakistan Resettlement Policy'.
37. Ibid.
38. *The News*, 6 Aug. 2002.
39. *The Dawn*, 30 July 2002.
40. *Daily News*, 31 July 2002.
41. *The Dawn*, 14 Apr. 2002.
42. UNESCAP Website, http:// www.natural-resources.org/minerals/cd/index.htm
43. SEBCON, 2000, 'Pakistan Resettlement Policy'.
44. Mr Amajad Bhatti, Coordinator, Journalists Resource Centre, Islamabad.
45. Mujahid Hussain, 1999, *Motorway: People's Lives and the Lahore-Islamabad Section*, Lahore: Shirkatgah.

46. Rabia Asif, *The News*, 21 July 2002.
47. Newsletter, 2002, *Facts and Figures*, Vol. 10, Urban Resource Centre, Karachi.
48. Rabia Arif, 'Express woes', *The News*, 21 July 2002.
49. *The Dawn*, 19 Jan. 2002.
50. Rabia Arif, 'Express woes', *The News*, 21 July 2002.
51. *Facts and Figures*, 2002.
52. *The Dawn*, 6 Sept. 2002.
53. The Review, *Dawn*, 22–28 August 2002.
54. Aquila Ismal, *Evictions* (Karachi: City Press, 2002).
55. SEBCON, 'Pakistan Resettlement Policy'.
56. Ibid.
57. Ibid.
58. UNHCR, *The State of World's Refugees*.
59. Khalid Hussain, Coordinator, Development Vision, an organization working on water and resettlement issues, interviewed on 30 June 2001.
60. Pakistan Environment Protection Act, 1997.
61. SEBCON, 'Pakistan Resettlement Policy'.
62. Kamran Sadiq, Chief Executive, SEBCON (Pvt) Ltd. Information made available via e-mail on 15 Sept. 2002.
63. Zia ul Islam, Director (EIA/Mont), PEPA. Information made available via e-mail on 17 Sept. 2002.
64. Ibid.
65. Saba Gul Khattak, Executive Director, SDPI. Information made available via e-mail on 12 January 2002.
66. Arif Malik, Coordinator, Citizens Action Committee, Mirpur, Amir Shah of Society Mutaasireen-e-Tarbela, Haripur.
67. Sheikh Asad Rehman, Journalist/political activist.
68. *The Dawn*, 9 Nov. 2002.
69. *The Dawn*, 30 Nov. 2002.
70. *The Jang*, 19 Dec. 1997.
71. Riaz Gamb and Ghulam Mustafa, 'Lost Roots,' *The News*, 11 Jan. 1998.
72. Nadeem Saeed, 'For How Long Will They Remain Shelterless?', *The Dawn*, 23 Dec. 1997.
73. Ibid.
74. Ibid.
75. *The Jang*, 19 Dec. 1997.
76. Hassan Mansoor, 'Sindh does not Want Kalpars on Its Soil', *Weekly Friday Times*, 6 June 2002.
77. Ibid.
78. *The Dawn*, 22 May 2002.
79. Ibid.
80. *The Nation*, 21 May 2002.
81. *Daily Business Recorder*, 21 Jan. 2002; *Jang*, 2 June 2002.
82. Ahmed Waleed, 'Waiting to Return Home', *The News on Sunday*, 20 Jan. 2002.
83. *The News*, 19 Jan. 2002.
84. *Daily News*, 9 June 2002; *The Dawn*, 24 March 2002.
85. *The Dawn*, 24 May 2002.
86. *Daily Business Recorder*, 21 Jan. 2002.

87. *The Dawn*, 7 Feb. 2002.
88. Dr Rubi Ramdas, Member, District Council, Mirpur Khas (Sindh), and Ms Bachal Kubber and Ms Azeem Khatoon, Members, District Council, Khairpur district (Sindh) were interviewed on 31 May 2002.
89. *Daily Sahafat*, 2 June 2002.
90. *Daily News*, 30 May 2002.
91. *Daily Times*, 1 July 2002.
92. *The Dawn*, 16 Mar. 2002.
93. *The Dawn*, 15 Jan. 2002.
94. *The Dawn*, 1 June 2002.
95. *Local Government Ordinance 2001*, Lahore: Mansoor Law Book House.
96. *Daily Sahafat*, 10 September 2002.
97. OCHA, IRIN Report, 27 May 2002.
98. www.idpproject.org
99. *Daily News*, 20 Dec. 1999.
100. *The Dawn*, 9 Dec. 1997.
101. *The Muslim*, 27 Oct. 1997.
102. *Daily News*, 6 Jan. 2002.
103. *The Dawn*, 30 Oct. 2002.
104. State of Human Rights in 1999, HRCP.
105. www. Idproject.org
106. *The Dawn*, 27 June 1998.
107. *The Frontier Post*, 25 Jan. 1996.
108. www.idproject.org
109. *Daily News*, 24 July 1998; *The Dawn*, 9 Dec. 1998; *Daily News*, 22 June 1999.
110. *The Dawn*, 24 Apr. 2000.
111. *The Dawn*, 18 Aug. 1998; Human Rights Commission of Pakistan, *The State of Human Rights in 1998* (Lahore, 1999).
112. *Daily News*, 15 Oct. 1998.
113. *The Muslim*, 3 Dec. 1999.
114. HRCP Report, 1999.
115. Ibid.
116. *Daily News*, 31 Aug. 1999.
117. http://www.refugees.org/world/articles/wrs02_Scasia2e.cfm Pakistan (Dordrecht: Martinus Nijhoff and Geneva: Henry Dunant Institute, 1985).
118. Jean Pictet, *Development and Principles of International Humanitarian Law*
119. *Daily News*, 31 Aug. 1999; Pakistan Bar Council-Human Rights Committee's briefing to the press on 15 May 1999.
120. *Daily News*, 15 May 2001.
121. *The News*, 19 Apr. 2001.
122. *The Dawn*, 16 Apr. 2001
123. JICA website
124. *The Dawn, Economic and Business Review*, 9-15 Sept. 2002.
125. AF Field Report 2000.
126. *The News*, 25 Aug. 2001.
127. HRCP Reports, 2000 and 2001.
128. *The Nation*, 5 Feb. 2001.

129. *The Dawn*, 15 May 2002.
130. Ibid.
131. *The News*, 11 Aug. 2002.
132. Amjad Bhatti, 'A Graveyard of the Destitute', *The News*, 4 Feb. 2001.
133. HRCP Annual Report, 2001.
134. *The Nation*, 2 July 2002.
135. *The Dawn*, 21 July 2002.
136. *The Nation*, 3 May 2002.
137. Research and Reference Section, Jang Group of Publications, *Jang*, 11 Jan. 2002.
138. *The Dawn*, 23 July 2002.
139. *The Dawn*, 16 Sept. 2002.
140. *The Nation*, 5 Aug. 2002.
141. *The Dawn*, 18 May 2001.
142. *The Nation*, 30 Jan. 2001.
143. *The Business Recorder*, 5 July 2001.
144. Ibid.
145. *The Nation*, 13 Feb. 2001.
146. *The Nation*, 22 Feb. 2002.
147. HRCP Annual Report, 2001.
148. *The Dawn*, 23 Feb. 2001.
149. Amjad Bhatti and Madhavi Malagoda Ariyanbandu, *Disaster Communication* (Islamabad: Journalists Resource Centre and ITDG South Asia, 2002).
150. *Jang*, 3 July 2002.
151. *The Dawn*, 30 May 2002.
152. *The Dawn*, 14 Sept. 2002.
153. Shafqat Munir, 'New Threats to Sustainable Development', *The News on Sunday*, 23 June 2002.
154. *The News*, 23 Aug. 2002.
155. *The News*, 23 June 2002.
156. Farzana Bari/ Sarwar Bari, *The News*, 13 July 2001.
157. Amjad Bhatti, JRC documents
158. *The Tribune*, 'Newsletter No. 58', May 1999
159. http://www.icrc.org/Web/eng/siteeno.nsf/htmlall/Pakistan? Open Document
160. UNHCR, *The State of the World's Refugees.*

CHAPTER 3

INDIA: HOMELESSNESS AT HOME

Samir Kumar Das

This chapter proposes to take stock of the nature and magnitude of the internal displacement in contemporary India, in the light of the 1998 UN Guiding Principles on Internal Displacement. While India is yet to evolve any separate legal instrument to address the problem of internal displacement and internally displaced persons (IDPs), there are nevertheless significant provisions in the existing municipal laws that are frequently invoked by the appropriate authorities to deal with the problem. The IDPs, and often the organizations acting on their behalf, seek relief, resettlement and rehabilitation provided by the Indian Constitution as well as the existing laws of the land. However, from the early 1990s the need for a separate legal mechanism has increasingly been felt to not only compile the existing laws together within a single legal instrument but also to plug the loopholes detected in them over the years. The Working Group on Displacement attached to Lokayan for example prepared a Draft National Policy on Developmental Resettlement of Project-Affected People sometime in the late-1980s.[1] India, in short, is currently passing through an interesting stage of legal debate and discussion and this chapter seeks to contribute to them. This is in conformity with one of the basic ideas that led to the formulation of the UN Guiding Principles. The Principles do not constitute 'a binding instrument' although they 'reflect and are consistent with international humanitarian law and analogous refugee law'.[2] Its objective was to 'help create the moral and political climate needed for improved protection and assistance for the internally displaced'. As David A. Korn points out:

> Although the Guiding Principles reflect and are consistent with international law Deng and his colleagues deliberately chose not to seek for them the status of a binding legal document. It was felt that a

non-binding instrument would be most realistic and also quickest way to proceed. The instrument could attain authority through use and help create the moral and political climate needed for improved protection and assistance for the internally displaced while avoiding confrontation with governments opposed to binding legal instrument if such were to be considered necessary.[3]

It is in the spirit of creating and developing an appropriate 'moral and political climate' that this chapter has been written. Its purpose is to take part in the ongoing debates and discussions on one of the most sensitive problems the world is facing now, rather than to take on, confront and put the authorities to task. While the problem is universal, affecting almost every single nation-state all over the world, of course with varying degree and intensity, it is still considered so much national and domestic in its scope that the process might take some time 'to attain the status of customary international law'.[4] IDPs, unlike refugees, do not cross international borders and do not pose an international problem. Since it is still within the territorial jurisdiction of the nation-state that the displacement takes place, any hardening of posture in this regard runs the risk of prematurely closing the debates and discussions and of throttling the general climate of political and moral discourse. It is through the power of a moral and political discourse that the 'governments and the other controlling authorities' are reminded of their 'obligations' towards these people.[5] In the words of Roberta Cohen and Francis Deng: 'The definition of sovereignty should be broadened to include responsibility: a state can claim the prerogatives of sovereignty only so long as it carries out its internationally recognized protection and assistance to its citizens.'[6]

Another important objective of this chapter is to relate the Guiding Principles to the concrete cases of displacement in the country, so that the victims become aware of their 'rights' in this regard. In many cases, the authorities are reluctant to fulfil their 'obligations' precisely because the victims do not assert their rights often enshrined in and guaranteed by the existing municipal laws and seek remedies against arbitrary encroachment on them. The Guiding Principles approach the problem from the point of view of the IDPs[7] and make them (as well as 'those responding to their plight') aware of their 'rights'. This chapter is prepared with the objective of raising their level of awareness and consciousness in this regard. While the authorities are required to fulfil their obligations, an enduring and viable regime of rights is predicated on an ever-conscious and vigilant public who first of all *claim* their rights and then express grievances whenever they are encroached upon and violated. Viewed in this light, the Principles aim at helping the IDPs in articulating themselves as rights-bearing, conscious and vigilant public who are capable of exerting moral and, wherever possible, legal influence on the appropriate authorities. In keeping with the spirit of the Guiding Principles, this chapter aims principally to work for the creation and consolidation of a moral community across the world.

Before we make any headway, it is necessary to note at least two major limitations of this chapter: First, while we are required to take note of India as a whole, we will exclude the northeastern region from the scope of our inquiry in order to avoid duplication.[8] Second, for our convenience, we follow the case study method in order to highlight some of the major trends in the nature and magnitude of internal displacement in India. The cases are selectively chosen with a view to provide us with a fairly balanced representation of the phenomenon of internal displacement in a country like India. Of course, the chapter is in no way confined only to the cases mentioned here. We refer to other cases as well but our references to other cases are brief and sketchy.

DEFINITION AND TYPOLOGY

The Guiding Principles define the IDPs in the following terms:

> For the purpose of these Principles, internally displaced persons are persons or groups of persons who have been forced or obliged to flee or to leave their homes or places of habitual residence, in particular as a result of or in order to avoid the effects of armed conflict, situations of generalized violence, violations of human rights or natural or human-made disasters, and who have not crossed an internationally recognized State Border.

Several features of this definition stand out as important. First, displacement according to this definition is always measured in terms of one's movement from 'home or place of habitual residence'. The definition does not seem to take into account those cases in which self-employed persons are displaced from their habitual places of work. The workplace displacement sometimes leads to involuntary migration to areas which offer better prospects of livelihood. Second, while there is certainly an element of force or involuntariness in one's displacement from home or place of habitual residence, the sources of such displacement spelt out in the definition are by no means exhaustive: The words 'in particular' indicate that the listed examples are not exhaustive.[9] The most important thing to be noted in this connection is that displacement might take place in order 'to avoid' the situations described in the list. The IDPs are entitled to the rights and safeguards enshrined in the Guiding Principles, whether these situations actually take place or not after they are displaced from their homes or places of habitual residence. In simple terms, these situations do not have to subsequently take place in order to justify their enjoyment of these rights and safeguards. Third, IDPs, unlike refugees, have not crossed an internationally recognized border. Internal displacement is 'exodus within the borders' as much as the IDPs are the 'homeless at home'.

In this context, it may be helpful to refer to the typology of internal displacement in India and in South Asia in general, that we had developed a few years ago.[10]

1. **Development-related displacement:** This again may be divided into two subcategories—direct and indirect. By direct displacement we refer to those cases where the installation and commissioning of development projects lead to a direct displacement of people who have inhabited these sites for generations together. In India alone, between 1955 and 1990, as a result of the installation of such projects as mines, dams and industries, wildlife sanctuaries and others about 21 million people were internally displaced.[11] The Narmada River Valley project, described as 'the world's greatest planned environmental disaster', envisages the construction of 30 major dams on the Narmada and its tributaries and 135 medium-sized and 3,000 minor dams. Of the total number, two of them have already been built. The focus of the Narmada Banchao Andolan (Save Narmada movement) is mainly, though not exclusively, on the Sardar Sarovar Project (SSP), which happens to be the largest scheme of the total project. In all, 297 villages are to be submerged by the reservoir: 19, 33 and 245 villages in Gujarat, Maharashtra and Madhya Pradesh respectively. Though accurate estimates of the number of people displaced are not yet available, a minimum of 23,500 people in Gujarat, 20,000 in Maharashtra and 120,000 in Madhya Pradesh are expected to be displaced by the reservoir.[12] Indirect displacement emanates first of all from a process whereby installation and functioning of projects continuously push up the consumption of natural and environmental resources, thereby depriving the indigenous people of the surrounding regions of their

traditional means of wherewithal and sustenance. Nor can they be accommodated by these projects in gainful ways.

2. **Ethnicity-related displacement:** On the one hand, we know of cases where an ethnic community lays its exclusive claim to what it defines as its 'homeland' on the ground that it is the 'original inhabitant' of the land. By the same token, the outsiders have no right to settle there. In the 1960s, several thousand Tamil, Gujarati and Hindi-speaking factory and dock workers as well as small business persons and daily-wage earners were forced out of the city of Bombay (Mumbai) by the activists of Shiv Sena, a pro-Marathi Hindu radical group that led the sons-of-the-soil movement in Maharashtra.

3. **Border-related displacement:** (*a*) Sometimes disputes over internal and external 'borders' i.e. between two or more districts, provinces or constituent states of the Indian Union become so fierce that they often turn into major border skirmishes. As a result, the bordering villages are evacuated at the instance of the government. (*b*) Conflicts along the border between two nation-states, which have at times metamorphosed into full-scale wars (like those between India and Pakistan), have been responsible for major displacement along the Line of Control (LOC) in the west.

4. **Externally-induced displacement:** (*a*) As the migrants pour in, they put pressures on land; cause unemployment, particularly rural unemployment; create environmental problems and foment inter-ethnic tensions, thereby disturbing the demographic balance and posing a threat to the language and culture of the native people. As a consequence, they fall prey to explosive nativist outbursts and become soft and easy victims of torture, harassment, deportation and even death. (*b*) As immigrants from across the international borders pour in, and get themselves haphazardly settled in such public places as railway tracks, fragile embankments (*chars*), reserve forests and sanctuaries, the state finds it imperative—often at the insistence of the 'native' people—to evict them and clear these areas of 'illegal' settlers. External migrants are thus subjected to some successive rounds of displacement from the land that they had slowly made their own.

5. **Potentially displaced persons** (PDPs): It is necessary to make a separate category of potentially displaced persons in order to refer to those who are invalid or infirm, or people suffering from terminal ailments, orphaned children or widowed women who are basically too weak to move to a new place. A significant percentage of them are too poor to meet the minimum costs of migration. They are in a displaced-like

situation and ironically are far less fortunate than those who could migrate to safe and secure areas. The following report on the Bhagalpur (in Bihar) riots may serve as an example. It tells us why many of the PDPs are not likely to survive:

> Rajpur is a village in Sabor, 15 kilometres from Bhagalpur. Muhammad Muzibullah Quadari in his late sixties recalls the black Friday of 27 October 1989. Scores of people from the eastern and northern sides invaded the village at around 2 pm. It was a massacre. People ran helter skelter and in only one hamlet the youths resisted the attackers and chased them away. But the houses were already in flames.[13]

Case Studies

This report makes a study of three recent cases of displacement in India. The communal riots of Gujarat in February 2002, the new wave of militancy in Kashmir since the early 1990s, firing across the LoC and the military build-up in 2001–2 have led to a massive displacement of people particularly belonging to the minority communities. While in the case of Gujarat, the Muslims had to bear the brunt of internal displacement, in Kashmir, militancy is reported to have evicted the minority of Pundits. Although at one level, they narrate experiences opposite to each other pertaining to the Muslims and Hindus, respectively, they are actually two sides of the same coin for they point to the fact that the minorities more than the other sections of population are at risk. Internal displacement in short takes a toll more on the minorities. Thus to cite an example, Ajai Raina, himself a Kashmiri Pundit displaced in Kashmir in the early 1990s, presently works with the displaced persons of Gujarat and argues that being displaced himself he is better equipped to deal with a crisis like this than any of his co-workers. As he observes:

> But I find a strange similarity between an uprooted Kashmiri Pundit and the inhabitants of the lane (gully) of Kasai in Gujarat. The Pundits in the Kashmir valley [too] are a minority. In fact, somewhere or the other, all of us are minorities, isn't it?[14]

This in fact not only shows how the minorities at myriad levels of the nation's social and political life are at grave risk, it also warns against the commonly understood association of the concept of minority with the Muslims of contemporary India.[15]

While both Gujarat and Kashmir have by now become an integral part of our public agenda, the phenomenon of displacement in West Bengal, though it had assumed alarming proportions in recent years, is yet to attract any significant public attention. Compared to many other cases of similar nature, the extent of displacement here, as we will have to see later, is not all that great. But the case makes an interesting study because it tells us why displacement in spite of being a hard reality does not become part of our public agenda. In other words, there are reasons to believe that the cases become eligible for being part of our public agenda when there are factors in addition to the purely humanitarian considerations. First, while mainstream vernacular media report on displacement of persons as a result of floods, erosion of the river banks, eviction as part of urban planning, subway extension and mega-city project, their reporting suffers from some important deficiencies. Many of these reports are of one-shot nature in the sense that they are carried as and when they take place. Seldom is there any reference to the post-displacement state of the IDPs and their resettlement and rehabilitation. West Bengal, particularly Calcutta (now Kolkata), has the living tradition of little magazines run mostly by young and socially committed students and sections of intelligentsia albeit with relatively shorter shelf life. Interestingly, the phenomenon is highlighted by them rather than by the mainstream media affiliated to big business houses. They usually form small discussion groups in order to run their magazines and conduct these surveys more often than not from out of their own pockets. Unlike West Bengal, both Gujarat and Kashmir have received wide media attention from the national as well as the international press. Second, while the poor and the weaker sections of the population are required to bear the brunt of displacement whether in Kolkata or in other parts of West Bengal, displacement here is yet to acquire any overtly communal character. Displacement due to communal clashes, though not non-existent, is mostly limited to some peripheral pockets of Kolkata and is not of any significant magnitude. It is true that no reliable estimate is available on displacement along an all-West Bengal scale. However, by all accounts it represents only a small fraction of the total number of IDPs in the state. Moreover, in most cases, the displaced persons are reported to have come back to their homes or places of habitual residence as soon as the dust storm gets settled. Camp life is of extremely short duration. The Kashmiri Pundits who left Kashmir in the early 1990s are yet to return to their homes.

In simple terms, displacement in West Bengal does not seem to have fractured the nation on its seams; whereas, nowhere is communal divide so sharp and grievously pronounced as it is in Gujarat and Kashmir. The communal divisions in Gujarat do not always coincide with the stratification along class lines. For example, the Bohras of Gujarat (a sect amongst the Muslims) are reported to have been the special targets in the recent spate of riots for they are believed to constitute the economic backbone of their community. It is very difficult, if not impossible, to brand the Kashmiri Pundits uniformly as a poor and economically backward community. What is interesting to note is that public agenda continues to be dictated by the imperatives of nationhood. IDPs become a *problem* only when they pose a problem to the nation. Third, the West Bengal case also shows that, left to themselves, the IDPs are not in a position to raise their voice and assert their rights. In fact, as we will argue, displacement also results from a certain dissipation and erosion of social capital that is required for any mobilization and articulation of IDPs' demands. Obviously, civil society institutions play an important role in helping them voice their demands. The fringe groups, as we have pointed out, are very active in this regard. But there is a significant reluctance on the part of the mainstream Bengali civil society to take up their cause and focus on their demands, let alone fight for them. It is obviously beyond the scope of the present chapter to find out why the civil society in West Bengal is not as active and alert as it is in some other parts (for example the Narmada Banchao Andolan in Gujarat, Maharashtra and Madhya Pradesh) of India. Besides, international response to the problem of internal displacement 'is largely ad hoc' and dictated by various other non-humanitarian concerns. As Francis Deng points out: '... many agencies pick and choose the situations in which they wish to become involved; no organization has a global and comprehensive mandate to protect the displaced'.[16]

The Birth of a Problem

Internal displacement is neither new nor unprecedented in India. But its recognition as a problem is certainly new. In the early years of Independence (1947), there was little protest against big dams in India. The 1950s witnessed the construction of large river valley projects like the Bhakra Nangal in Punjab, the Damodar Valley project in Bihar and West Bengal, the Tungabhadra project on the Andhra Pradesh–Karnataka border and the Rihand dam in Uttar Pradesh, etc. Each of those projects ousted thousands of people, and yet there was very little opposition. According to a report, an estimated 527,000 persons have been displaced by armed conflict and inter-ethnic strife. However, the number is only a small fraction of the 21 to 33 million Indians displaced by development projects, primarily the construction of big dams.[17] Of late there have been some significant studies explaining why internal displacement was not regarded as a problem during the early years of Independence. In contrast to the Narmada case, there was no reaction to the Bhakra in Punjab. Interestingly after almost four decades, the Bhakra oustees are finally mobilizing themselves through such organizations as the All-Party Bhakra Oustees Rights Protection Committee, the Bilaspur River Development Committee and the All-Party Citizens' Action Committee. This may be attributed to a combination of at least three major factors: First of all, a strong nationalist consensus could be built around the discourse that looked upon the construction of dams as a prerequisite for development. Displacement was seen as an unavoidable corollary of development and the priority was given to easing the economic impact of displacement through compensation.[18] Since there was hardly any 'widely accepted alternative developmental paradigm', it was possible on the part of the nationalist elite to evolve such a consensus without much obstruction.[19] During the last 50 years, some 3,300 big dams have been constructed in India. Jawaharlal Nehru, India's first prime minister, for example, described the dams as 'the temples of modern India'. Second, as the cost of displacement was offset by the gains consolidated by the green revolution that enormously augmented the agricultural productivity especially during the initial years, there was hardly any protest against displacement.[20] Third, it would be wrong to say that there were no protests whatsoever against the construction of big dams. For example, in March 1946, when the foundation stone of the Hirakud dam was laid, the peasants of Sambalpur district of Orissa who were to be displaced organized anti-dam demonstrations. But the agitation fizzled out 'in part due to the co-option of its leaders by the Congress (party that led India to Independence) and the administration'.[21]

As the nationalist consensus started getting eroded over the years, the development model that was hitherto almost uncritically accepted by the political elite faced criticisms from some quarters of the Indian public. The big dams and assimilation of the diverse and heterogeneous sections of people into the so-called nationalist mainstream were the two major planks of the development model that received a severe jolt as a result of these criticisms brewing in the body politic since the late-1980s.[22] Internal displacement was no longer seen an unavoidable problem of national development; it started being seen as a problem that could surely be taken care of, if not completely avoided, had an alternative model of development been followed in India.

THE KASHMIR SCENARIO

Though the Kashmir problem started with the Partition in 1947, the attack on the temples of the valley in 1986 signalled a warning to the minorities, forcing them to seriously think about moving out from their place of birth. The desecration, defilement and burning down of over four dozen Hindu shrines in south Kashmir part of district Anantnag in 1986 forced some Pundit families to purchase land in Jammu and elsewhere and this started a process of settling down outside Kashmir valley. Mohammed Khan, the Amir of Lashkar-e-Toiba—a militant organization operating in Kashmir—reportedly declared: 'Our jihad is strictly confined to non-Muslims, particularly Hindus and Jews, the two main enemies of the Muslims'.[23] The year 1986, in short, marks the watershed in the history of internal displacement in Kashmir. It was in early 1990, during Governor Jagmohan's few months in office, that most of the Pundits fled from the valley. The government is often accused of having encouraged migration of Hindu Pundits in order to 'isolate' the Muslims so that it could 'freely deal' with them. According to Pankaj Mishra, 'many Kashmiris believe that he wanted the Hindus safely out of the way while he dealt with the Muslim guerrillas'.[24] Even as late as 1990, a team of representatives drawn from such organizations as People's Union for Civil Liberties, Citizens for Democracy, Radical Humanist Association and Manav Ekta Abhiyan visiting the Kashmir valley, noted with concern:

> It is necessary to mention that whenever local papers appear, there is always an appeal on behalf of the Mujahadeen, particularly in Urdu press, on the front page, requesting the Kashmiri Pundits to return to their valley. In this appeal the Muslims are warned against occupying, tampering with or selling of any movable or immovable property belonging to Kashmiri Pundits. So far the local Muslims have lived up to what they say in this regard, and in quite a few cases, the keys of the houses belonging to Kashmiri Pundits are also left with them.[25]

According to the US Committee for Refugees, 'as many as 350,000 people have been displaced within India as a result of the long-standing conflict in Kashmir'. While a majority of them happen to be Pundits, there are Muslims and Sikhs amongst those who have been displaced by the conflict. Most of the Pundits left their homes between January and May 1990 when a new wave of militancy engulfed the entire valley. The Committee quotes Mr B. D. Babyal, the government's deputy commissioner for relief who said that there were more than 29,000 registered displaced families (some 240,000 people) in the state mostly in the Jammu region. Of these, 25,700 families are Hindu Pundits, while 1,500 and 1,800 are Muslims and Sikhs, respectively. Of the 29,000 displaced families living in Jammu, some 14,200 families (some 595,000 people) receive government assistance as displaced persons. Another 14,800 families (almost all Hindus) are headed by former government employees to whom the government of India has continued to pay full salaries (or retirement benefits as the case may be) since 1990, even though most of them are not working in any government jobs. Mr Babyal tells the Committee that the government of India spends Rs 26 million (US $597,000) per month on financial and food aid for the displaced. Those living outside camps and receiving governmental assistance are given a cash payment of Rs 1,800 (US $41) for families of four or more, in addition to a food ration of rice, flour and sugar. The Committee also reports that most displaced Kashmiris in Jammu lived in tents even after six or seven years after their displacement. But over the years, many have obtained rented accommodation in Jammu, Delhi or even abroad. The government took the initiative of constructing some 4,600 single-room, semi-permanent houses for those who were forced to remain in camps. According to Mr Surinder Kher, vice president of the Kashmir Samiti based in Delhi, an estimated number of 21,000 displaced Pundit families (about 1,00,000 persons) are dispersed throughout the city, living mostly in private accommodations, of which some 2,000 to 3,000 continue to stay in 14 camps. Those living in camps receive Rs 1200 per head (US $46) per month plus electricity and water.[26] Mr Francis Deng, the Special Rapporteur on IDPs, in one of the sessions of the UN Human Rights Commission held on 11 April 2002, pointed out that his office had taken note of the phenomenon of internal displacement in Kashmir.

While what we have just discussed in the foregoing paragraph may be bracketed under the heading of ethnicity-related displacement, a good deal of displacement in Kashmir comes under the border-related type. The Line of Control (LOC) that separates India-administered Kashmir from its Pakistan-administered counterpart, from Dras in north Kashmir to Rajouri in the Jammu division, is not accepted by the concerned nation-states as international borders. As a result, it has remained a bone of contention posing an obstacle to the improvement of the relations between the two nations. Continuous exchanges of artillery and light-weapons fire across the LOC have resulted in the major displacement of population in both sides. Interestingly in some bigger towns, like Uri and Poonch, people have become so used to exchanges of fire that they have remained in their homes.[27] It shows that the decision to flee one's home is dictated by a situation when one is left with no other alternative. They continue to live in their homes, sometimes at grave risk, and learn to live under war-like conditions, and leave their homes only when all options are exhausted.

The five-month long stand-off between two regional nuclear powers arising from the 13 December 2001 attack on Indian parliament led to the massive build-up of nearly 1 million troops on the international borders and the LOC. According to a report, this resulted in the displacement of about 100,000 on both sides of the LOC. While most of the displaced people were staying temporarily with friends and relatives, several thousands of them had been camping in buildings such as schools, a commercial centre and a disused factory. After consultations with the civilian authorities of the Indian state of Jammu and Kashmir (J & K) and working in close cooperation with local members of the Indian Red Cross Society, the International Committee of Red Cross (ICRC) assessed the needs of some 2,600 families living in public buildings in the districts of Jammu, Rajouri and Poonch. On the basis of its findings, between 25 January and 1 February 2002, the ICRC distributed family parcels consisting of food (lentil, sugar and oil), hygiene products and blankets to these displaced families.[28] The military stand-off also led to extensive mining operations along the 1,000 km long LOC and international border with Pakistan. The army is believed to have plugged, 87 infiltration routes from across the borders and LOC by packing them with mines. According to rough estimates, 200 landmine victims were recorded between Rajouri and Poonch border areas alone, constituting a length of 300 km between 1947 and 1989. Some years back an army spokesman had confirmed that there were 51 minefields near the LOC in Kupwara district with a minimum of 100 landmines in each field. In a stretch of 12 km of land, at least 5,000 landmines have lain buried for decades. This is the reason why according to Anuradha Bhasin Jamwal 'the villages at the fringes are abandoned and empty'.[29] Over 10,000 explosions have taken place over the last 13 years and 1,151 deaths, including those of security personnel, have been registered. While the government of India has announced an ex gratia relief of Rs 500,000 and relief of Rs 75,000 for the victims who are killed and maimed respectively in militancy-related explosions, the border residents who are killed in landmine explosions are entitled to the ex gratia relief of Rs 100,000 and the permanently disabled persons to not more than Rs 10,000 only. The compensation for the killing of each cattle is Rs 400 only. About 100,000 persons, according to Jamwal, have taken shelter in various camps. Despite relief of Rs. 10,000,000 announced for the border villagers, an effective mechanism was yet to be devised for the disbursement of the said amount. With an estimated population of about 500,000 in the border villages, most of whom are feared to have been displaced in the midst of the conflict, the amount would work out to Rs 20 per head and that too for just a day. Moreover de-mining is not only going to take time but is expensive.

Internal displacement in Kashmir has, first of all, contributed to a communal polarization in the state. The government of India has raised armed Village Defence Committees (VDCs) in areas closer to the LOC to serve as the first step of resistance against the 'infiltration' of militants from across it and also for taking quick responsive action in case the villagers are attacked. In fact, the move was preceded by a series of attacks on the innocent villagers in remoter parts of the state along the LOC. But the government is often accused of being discriminatory and biased in supplying arms to the villages. It is believed to have not only widened the distance but also caused armed communal clashes between the communities of Kashmir particularly in such districts as Doda, Udhampur, Poonch and Rajouri. The same move is believed to have been initiated by the state of Pakistan. Ishaq Zaffar, a senior minister from Pakistan-administered Kashmir has actually made an appeal for the people to stay in their towns and villages and build what he called defensive positions. The use of civilians to serve as defence shield seems to represent a situation that we designate as potential displacement, in which the persons are compelled to stay at their homes and places of habitual residence when it is not safe for them to do so. On the other hand, some of the organizations claiming to represent the displaced Kashmiri Pundits have expressed their resentment against the indiscriminate attacks on their community. In a memorandum dated 11 September 2000 submitted to the UN Secretary-General, one such organization, namely the Panun Kashmir Movement (PKM) points out that the scenario in Kashmir has 'assumed a shape of cultural onslaught on the minority by the majority'. The 'onslaught' according to the memorandum amounts to 'a well planned, designed aggression on the existence, culture and distinct identity of the community'. While claiming that such 'aggression' continued unabated for the last 700 years, it raises the demand for a separate 'homeland' for them:

The establishment of a homeland for all the seven hundred thousand Kashmiri Hindus in Kashmir will be a deterrent against the creation of disorder and aggression on the aborigines and indigenous minorities living in various far-off pockets of the world. The Pundits as a distinct cultural identity can maintain their cultural ethos only when their right to live in a compact and cohesive manner within a specific territory in their homeland in Kashmir valley is accepted and the Constitution of India is made applicable fully to that territory with full political power in their hands along an economic mechanism which can retain the community in the land of their origin on lasting basis.[30]

According to Dr Ajay Chrangoo, chairman of the Political Affairs Committee of PKM, much more invisible is the 'grabbing' of land and property owned by the Pundits in a concerted attempt to displace them. As he argues: 'The less talked about and much more hidden components are engineered purchase of land and properties in targeted areas of Jammu region, fraudulent and illegal grab of Hindu properties and most significantly, the demographic invasion of Jammu city'.[31]

Besides, protracted militancy in Kashmir has not only taken a toll on human lives and property but caused various forms of psychological disorder and trauma amongst the survivors and also the displaced. Several NGOs have opened up special trauma care centres in different parts of Kashmir. What is most appalling is that the people in the camps frequently complain of being watched by all shades of people and subjected to constant surveillance. Thus the feeling that they are objects of 'political football' has gradually grown amongst them. Mishra refers to Gautam, a displaced Pundit, who angrily remarks: 'We are like a zoo, people come to watch and then go away'.[32] Displacement has in many ways made life difficult for the Pundits. The community used to sub-zero temperatures had to adapt overnight to temperatures above 44 degrees Celsius. It has disrupted the precious academic years of the children and younger ones of the families that have been displaced. It was the Shiv Sena government in Maharashtra that came to the rescue of this community and extended open support to it by introducing a special quota for its students in all professional colleges.

THE GUJARAT SCENARIO

The state of Gujarat in recent years has been a standing witness to almost all varieties of internal displacement hitherto mentioned. The floods of Morvi, the earthquake in Bhuj (January 2000), the construction of the Sardar

Sarovar Dam as part of the Narmada project, the anti-Dalit (the downtrodden) riots of the early-1980s, the successive waves of communal riots of varying degree and intensity, including the attacks on Christians in 1999 particularly, and the one during February–March 2002, have led in their combination to an incredibly massive displacement of people, particularly the minorities and the weaker sections of the population. In this chapter, however, we propose to confine ourselves to an analysis of the recent riots of Gujarat for they are in a certain sense, unprecedented in post-colonial India. First of all, as Asghar Ali Engineer has put it, 'Gujarat carnage represents the peak of communal violence in independent India.' Both in terms of its intensity and magnitude, it has been the worst of all the earlier riots of post-colonial India. While 700 persons lost their lives according to official estimates, several non-governmental organizations estimate that the actual number of the victims might be over 2,000. Never before in the history of post-colonial India has an entire community been singled out, targeted and sought to be exterminated and wiped out in such a blatant manner. Amnesty International in its report for example notes: 'Some form of organization and planning of the crimes committed is repeatedly suggested by survivors, eyewitnesses, relief workers, political commentators and members of extremist Hindu organizations themselves'.[33]

The idea was to break the economic backbone of the minority community. Some of the specimens of hate literature that came out even in the national press, for example, ask the Hindu traders to desist from dealing and transacting with the Muslims. When there is a silent and effective ban on buying and selling of goods and services from the minorities, the minorities as a community cease to remain an economic force. According to a Confederation of Indian Industries (CII) survey, the first few days of rioting cost Gujarat a loss of about Rs. 20,000,000 belonging predominantly to the minorities. As riots rolled on, the figure according to Communalism Combat rose up to Rs 35,000,000. [34] The visible symbols of the minority existence were subjected to destruction. Even the heritage sites were not spared. 240 dargahs and about 180 mosques were destroyed in course of these riots. Amnesty International also notes with concern the 'unprecedented brutality' experienced in course of these riots. In many cases, men and women were bludgeoned to death with heavy and blunt-looking stones, killed by screwdrivers, tridents, etc. or were simply burnt alive by bursting gas cylinders or dousing petrol or any other inflammable material on them. Women were the particular targets of attack. They were the victims of rape and other sex-related forms of assault. Mahasweta Devi, an eminent Bengali litterateur reporting on these riots has coined the term 'sexual terror' in order to describe how women were coerced into submission through all this.[35] Women were raped in front of their children or even other family members by assailants in most cases known to them.[36] Even children were not spared. As Salman Rushdie has put it, 'the murder of children is something of Indian speciality'.[37] The children made to experience the riots are deprived of their child-hood. Sonu, a displaced Muslim child for example, rues the fact of miss-ing some of her close friends who incidentally are Hindus.[38] According to Priyanka Kakodkar, there were about 42,000 children in relief camps in early May 2002, of which 30,000 were in the camps of Ahmedabad alone.[39] Besides National Human Rights Commission notes with concern that it was for the first time that 'rural and tribal areas' were also affected by the riots. More than 1,200 villages in the districts of Panch Mahal, Mehsana, Sabarkantha, Bharuch, Bhavnagar and Vadodra witnessed mob attacks on the minority communities leading to large-scale exodus. One must recognize that there were, of course, cases of displacement amongst the Hindus. The National Human Rights Commission for example, visited a relief camp operating from Suryadas temple where 106 Hindu families comprising 471 members have been living since 28 February 2002. The point is not that the property and the lives of the minorities were never the targets of communal frenzy before. It is rather the other way around. It did not seem to emanate so much from the urge to exterminate an entire community as much to acquire the land and property left by them. Destruction was only incidental to this vested interest. A comparison with the earlier riots may be attempted in this connection. The Bhopal riots of 1992 for example were reportedly driven by the same interest of destroying the shanties evacuated in course of riots. To quote a report:

> We have listed at least 25 places (*jhuggis* or slums) where they were completely or partially burnt. Some of them were unauthorized. Most people who were displaced in the anti-encroachment drives of recent years have once again become victims in these riots. In fact, the de-struction of *jhuggis* became the 'God-given' opportunity for those who wanted the place cleared. The victims of Acharya Narendra Deva Nagar for instance, discovered that through what were once their *jhuggis*, the BHEL (Bharat Heavy Electricals) is building a boundary wall and lay-ing sewage lines.[40]

These examples are by no means rare. The reports on the Kolkata riots of 1992 prepared by such organizations as Nagarik Mancha and Association for the Protection of Democratic Rights indicate the same. In fact, the Kolkata riots are important because there were very few casualties.

Second, according to Asghar Ali Engineer, it was 'for the first time' that the state machinery 'was directly involved in it'.[41] The National Human Rights Commission in its report accused the government of having 'failed in taking appropriate anticipatory and subsequent action to prevent the spread and continuation of violence'. Police officers who took initial steps to quell the riots were transferred. According to Harsh Mandar, himself a civil servant who tendered his resignation in protest against the government's role in Gujarat violence, Mr Rahul Sharma, a police officer, who fired upon some attackers in order to save about 400 lives of young Muslim students in a madrasa, was served with such a transfer order.[42] In the words of National Human Rights Commission: '... public servants who had sought to perform their duties diligently and deal with those responsible for the violence had been transferred at short notice to other posts without consulting the Director-General of Police, over his protests.' Sometimes the police misdirected the people fleeing from their houses during communal riots and deliberately exposed them to the attackers waiting for them. Sahmat indicts the state in these terms:

The collusion of the state was absolute. Firstly, the state administration and the police failed to protect the lives and properties of Muslim citizens, even when several people complaining about mobs attacking their homes and shops contacted them. Secondly, in many cases BJP, VHP and Bajrang Dal leaders including Ministers actually led the mobs and supervised the killings and destruction. And finally, the Administration is now busy in ensuring that the victims are denied of an iota of justice. While the role of the national print and electronic media has been applauded widely for its coverage of the violence and exposure of government's negligence, the local Gujarati media has hardly attracted adequate attention.[43]

Third, the riots also point to the shrinking space of civil society institutions in the state. It actually shows how civil society institutions built over the years with great care cannot withstand the crescendo of communal riots and pathetically crumble in the face of such onslaughts. As a result, a riot-torn society is literally left in the lurch to fend for itself. Relief, resettlement and rehabilitation as a result take on the same communal lines and in some sense they seem to be an extension of the same divide that once escalated into full-blooded communal frenzy and attacks.

As a result, social bridges are not built and the wounds done to the social body are never taken care of and healed. This is what made the participation total in these riots. Even the educated sections of the Hindu middle class consisting of the medical practitioners, teachers, advocates and engineers took an active part in these riots and indulged in unbelievable atrocities.[44] Teesta Setalvad of Communalism Combat for example asks:

> Where also amidst the savagery, injustice, and human suffering is the 'civil society', the Gandhians, the development workers, the NGOs, the fabled spontaneous Gujarati philanthropy which was so much in evidence in the earthquake in Kutch and Ahmedabad? The newspapers reported that at the peak of the pogrom, the gates of Sabarmati Ashram were closed to protect its properties, it should instead have been the city's major sanctuary. Which Gandhian leaders, or NGO managers, staked their lives to halt the death-dealing throngs? It is one more shame that we as citizens of this country must carry on our already burdened backs, that the camps for the Muslim riot victims in Ahmedabad are being run almost exclusively by Muslim organizations. It is as though the monumental pain, loss, betrayal and injustice suffered by the Muslim people is the concern only of other Muslim people, and the rest of us have no share in the responsibility to assuage, to heal and rebuild.[45]

Of course, there are exceptions to this generally noted trend in matters of relief and rehabilitation. In most cases, courageous and moving interventions by personal friends, neighbours and even strangers in defence of the helpless across the communal divide were the only silver lining in an otherwise stark and abject scenario. Professor Bandukwala, the professor of Physics at the M. S. University of Baroda, known for his secular credentials has admitted that in times of crisis, his Hindu neighbours came by his side and protected him at great personal risk. Even village ties played an important role in forestalling riots. Keshubhai Patel, the *sarpanch* (headman) of a village, for example, narrated how there were persistent phone calls asking for the feasibility of springing attacks and how he took initiatives in protecting as many as 41 Muslim families.[46] The report prepared by the Citizens' Initiative cites many such examples of cross-cutting neighbourhood ties.

While the event that triggered off the worst-ever communal orgy in post-colonial India should by no means be considered as the sole cause, it was nevertheless an event that was and continues to be projected to fire up the communal passions. It seems that the ground was already ripe for the articulation of the rivalling communal archetypes to make tempers run high and the event provided the necessary spark in order to ignite them. The first event was certainly not to be confused as the first cause as the official version would have us believe.[47] Sahmat for example points out that the theory of spontaneous Hindu upsurge against whatever had happened in Godhra hardly holds water.[48] It all started on 27 February 2002 when the train called Sabarmati Express had halted at a little-known Godhra railway station and a section of *karsevaks* riding the train[49] were reportedly involved in an altercation with some vendors at the station. While there are different versions of the story,[50] the fact is that 57 persons were burnt alive as the compartment carrying them was set on fire. This is believed to have set off the communal fuse and the violence continued unabated for nearly 40 days. That Gujarat was bracing for some kind of turmoil is evident from the preparations even before the event took place.[51] Godhra has a long history of riots. Even as early as in 1981, there was one in this otherwise sleepy place.[52]

There were about 20 relief camps run in the capital city of Ahmedabad alone. Official figures estimate that about 50,000 people were (some of them still are) living in camps spread across the city. Some NGOs concerned with relief work estimate the figure to be as high as 75,000. Large camps like Aman Chowk and Shah-e-Alam Dargah housed between 8,000 and 9,000 persons and smaller ones like those in Nagoripatel Ni Challi, Sundaramnagar, Arasapur Pathrewali Masjid sheltered up to 4,000 persons. Outside Ahmedabad, various community leaders and NGOs reported that at least 40,000 people were (some of them are) living in similar conditions in relief camps situated in cities like Baroda, Rajkot, Godhra, Khera, Mehsana, Chota Udaipur and Kalol, as well as in nearby towns and villages. On 14 March Haren Pandya, the minister of state for revenue placed the official number of the relief camps all over Gujarat at 91. Even after that, a fresh spate of riots broke out in Ahmedabad and other parts of the state. On 30 March, the number of camps in the state was estimated to be 102. In the first week of April, some 120,000 victims of both communities were still to be found taking pitiable refuge in makeshift relief camps run by the NGOs with little official assistance.[53] Existing reports on some of the camps run for the internally displaced persons tell us the following stories—each violating the relevant UN Guiding Principles:

1. **Direct attacks on the camps:** On 18 March, the Odhav camp in Ahmedabad was approached by a group of people who started throwing stones and petrol bombs within its confines.

2. **Terrorizing the displaced:** The displaced persons inside the camps had reportedly to live in a state of terror. It has also been reported that in the Vatwa camps in Ahmedabad, audio cassettes containing the cries like 'maro maro' (kill, kill) had been repeatedly played at night on loudspeakers to frighten the camp dwellers.

3. **Selective targeting:** By all accounts, the minority community was 'selectively targeted' in the sense the attacks were directed against them and in 'the city of Ahmedabad and throughout the state, homes and shops belonging to the Muslims were destroyed, but neighbouring shops were unharmed.'

4. **Discriminatory behaviour** on the part of the government authorities: The few camps in Ahmedabad which were housing victims from the majority community (for example, the one in Kankaria) had received more visits from the government authorities and more regular rations. Even the National Human Rights Commission commented: '... during the course of its visit, many of the largest camps, including Shah-e-Alam in Ahmedabad, had not received visits at a high political or administrative level till the visit of the Chairperson of this Commission.'

5. **Inadequacy of relief:** Most of the reports make a mention of the poor quality and inadequate quantity of rations. Sanitation facilities were so poor that in some cases there was only one toilet for people. Outbreaks of gastro-enteritis and other kinds of infectious diseases were reported to be very common. In most of the camps, there was no trauma care facility. The National Human Rights Commission regretted the poor facilities in the camps and pointed out that 'particular care must be taken of the needs of the women, for whom special facilities should be provided.' The report of the Committee constituted by the National Commission for Women noted with concern that 'there was no special provision for the comfort of pregnant women.' It also called for 'privacy and a sense of safety for women while bathing and going to toilets' and describes it as the 'bare minimum'.

6. **Incomplete enumeration:** Not all those who live in camps were properly identified, listed or recorded by the government authorities. Some form of registration is essential for those who live in camps as well as in private accommodation in order to help them prove their identity and residence. Most of them had already lost all the official papers of their identity in course of their displacement.

7. **Family reunification:** The government authorities, according to Amnesty International, 'are reportedly not assisting in the task'. It is reported that at least 2,500 persons are currently missing since the violence broke out in Gujarat on 27 February 2002. Amnesty International was 'concerned to learn that government authorities have completely [failed] to establish the whereabouts of these people.'

8. **Right to move in and out of the camps:** In many cases. the survivors are reportedly not allowed to leave or move about freely, even to obtain basic necessities.

9. **Forcible return:** The camps inhabited by the Muslims but located in Hindu-dominated areas became a problem for the representatives of the government who basically keep their eyes on their electoral prospects. Running such camps could be construed by his/her electors as a policy of Muslim appeasement and this fear has actually made many of them ask for shutting or shifting of these camps from 'their' areas. The National Human Rights Commission took note of such perverse pleas and advised against them. In view of the *Gram Panchayat* elections, at many places, the victims were pressurized to return to their respective places so that they could cast their votes. In some cases, government also set forth deadlines for their return. It was reported that on 15 March several Muslim families that had been taking shelter in Chartoda Kabrastan, Ahmedabad went back to what remained of their houses. They rushed back to a relief camp during the night after people shouted intimidating slogans to them.[54] Sahmat in its report has likened the camps to the 'Nazi concentration camps'.[55]

10. **Disruption in academic calendar:** In most cases, the children or youth studying in educational institutions have had to lose their academic year. In fact, the fear was so great that the National Commission for Women was informed that many Muslim students could not appear for the Board examinations for, in such cases, they would have to cross through the Hindu localities.[56]

We may conclude this section by making a comparison between the two scenarios in Kashmir and Gujarat: First, the 40-day violence in Gujarat led to the eviction of more than 100,000 people mostly of the minority community of Muslims. In contrast to this, displacement in Kashmir has been the result of a more protracted violence mainly in the valley particularly since the year 1990. While militancy took a toll in the form of displacement of the Kashmiri Pundits living deep in the valley, the border-related displacement affected the people on the borders, mostly the Muslims and the other nomadic communities, like the Gujjars, for whom cattle-raising is the only means of livelihood. Second, by all accounts, the flight of Kashmiri Pundits was propelled by a deep sense of fear sometimes exacerbated by the administration. In simple terms, although casualties in the form of loss of lives were not altogether unknown, the communal frenzy in Kashmir never acquired the form of an actual genocide against them. It remains a matter of conjecture whether this could have happened in the valley, had they decided to continue to live in the valley. As a result, the brutality and barbarism associated with the killings in Gujarat have not been witnessed in Kashmir. It mostly took the form of individual assassinations, surprise attacks on targeted families, etc. Third, the relief camps meant for Kashmiri Pundits whether in Jammu or in such places as Delhi might have been running with inadequate rations and poor health and hygienic conditions; however, unlike Gujarat, since the IDPs were outside the epicentre of violence, there was hardly any news of attacks on these camps. Moreover, these camps have been, for whatever reasons, receiving regular visits by the high officials. It is alleged that Kashmir has since already received high diplomatic and governmental attention.

THE CASE OF WEST BENGAL

It is important to note that displacement in West Bengal is not very significant in terms of its magnitude. Nor has it become part of Bengal's public agenda. But it has acquired some significance because of its complexity. The complexity of internal displacement may be attributed to a plurality of factors, two of which may be mentioned in this connection: One, the environment-related cluster accounts for a very significant percentage of displacement in West Bengal. But, it has never acquired the kind of alarming proportions as it has elsewhere. But the problem is that the shifting of the course of the main river—the Ganges—and the erosion of river banks particularly along the Bengal side have been contributing to an almost continuous process of displacement, pointing to an inevitable natural and human disaster in the near future. Moreover, since it has been well spaced over a long period of time, it remains invisible. The rapid displacement of population has the advantage of sensitizing the public to the humanitarian crisis by sounding the alarm bells. We have the tendency of ignoring the early warnings. Two, it is true that industrial expansion in the state is slow compared to many other states in India. But, the plans for industrial expansion have already led to displacement in some parts of the state. Kolkata remains the main urban centre that continues to attract migrants from outside. Their unplanned and haphazard settlement in some parts of the city has already become a cause for concern for the authorities. Eviction drives are taken almost on a routine manner causing displacement of population. In short, the magnitude of displacement may not be all that great but the sources are multifarious, making it an interesting case study.

West Bengal, particularly Kolkata, was the largest recipient of migrants, immediately after Independence and the Partition of the subcontinent, from the then East Pakistan.[57] Although the government, whether at the centre or at the state level, tried its best to accommodate them into India's fledgling nationhood, the city has never been able to successfully grapple with the problem. As a result, many of them and their descendants are still associated with the small and informal sector of the economy and, most importantly, with the hawking of mainly ready-made garments on the sidewalks of the busy thoroughfares (a phenomenon known popularly as, *hawkery*). A sample survey, for example, points out that 68 per cent of the hawkers in Kolkata happen to be people of East Pakistani origins.[58] In 1999 when the government of West Bengal decided to evict the hawkers from such places as Gariahat, Esplanade, Shyambazar, Maniktala, Moulali, etc., through an operation code-named 'Operation Sunshine', the returnees from East Pakistan were subjected to another round of displacement— this time from their means of livelihood. The same survey also points out that 46 per cent of the hawkers coming from East Pakistan were neither the owners nor the licensees of the land on which they hawked their wares. 'Operation Sunshine' in 1996 evicted about 24,000 hawkers.[59] The survey also points out that the hawkers who were most adversely affected as a result of eviction were those whose income level was extremely meagre. Of those evicted 68 per cent had an income range between Rs 500 and Rs 1,000 per month, 75 per cent were not served with any prior notice and 18 per cent of the sample simply did not know of the actual date of eviction. The impact of eviction was manifold: First of all, the hawkers were deprived of their means of livelihood. Although, on the surface, it implies a displacement from the workplace, the hawkers found it difficult to continue to live in the city. Many of them, according to Shaktiman Ghosh, an important hawker leader, committed suicide.[60] Second, in most cases, the evicted hawkers were not rehabilitated in other parts of the city. Justice Vinod Kumar Gupta of Calcutta High Court issued an injunction on the process of eviction and observed that although the court did not have the authority to stop the government order in this connection, the government ought to be involved in eviction through 'an integrated planning'.[61] The inadequacy of rehabilitation has been one of the major problems. While 24,000 hawkers were evicted, the government could provide for the arrangement of only 2,962 stalls.[62] In desperation many of them have returned to their old places, this time without the temporary, makeshift shanties, but under the open sky. The government did not choose to be harsh towards them allegedly on the ground that their eviction would not hold out favourable electoral prospects for the ruling party.[63] It only shows how rehabilitation varies with the fluctuating prospects of elections in a democracy where elections are considered as the be-all and end-all of public life.

Eviction from 'habitual residence' as part of urban planning in Kolkata has assumed serious proportions in recent years. *Manthan Samayikee*—a Bengali 'little magazine'—conducted a survey of 553 persons belonging to as many as 130 households who were under the threat of being evicted as a result of the government's proposal for widening Beliaghata Circular Canal in order to facilitate free flow of water, sewage and waste, and save Kolkata from periodic floods. The survey also provided identity cards to the respondents and found that only 280 amongst them were actually working persons. Most of them were handcart pullers, maidservants, fixed zone hawkers, mobile vendors, daily-wage earners, factory workers, drivers and from such other professions. A People's Court was convened with Justice Rajinder Sachar, Moloy Sengupta, Piyus Som, Dunu Ray, Maitreyee Chatterjee, Samar Bagchi, Sanjay Parekh, Colin Gonsalves and Monideep Chatterjee to deliberate on the affected people and make some recommendations to the government. It conducted hearing with the people and NGOs from Kulpi, Chandmani, Falta, Rajarhat, Chandannagar, Beliaghata, Naya Patty, Sarberia, Jammudweep, Birbhum, Tollygunge, Dhakuria railway colony, Tolly's Nulla, Udayachal and Shaktigarh. It called for making the potential oustees participate in the process of making decisions concerning eviction and argued that eviction is an outcome of development projects. The persons to be evicted needed to be rehabilitated near their homes and habitual residence. Force and coercion could not be applied while evicting them. It also recommended that eviction drives were not to be conducted in times of bad and inclement weather. The tribal land would have to be restored to the tribals. It called for humanitarian treatment in matters of eviction and rehabilitation of victims.[64] The same thing happened when about 700 families were evicted from their homes as a measure of constructing the Park Circus Connector. Formerly they were assured of being given a one-time compensation of Rs. 1,500 per household while in actuality, a survey revealed that none of them had received it.[65] The 'New Town' project of Rajarhat, which is proposed to be made a satellite of Kolkata, has evicted about 1,31,000 persons. Of them 6,170, 2,105 and 4,605 are marginal, small and landless farmers, respectively, while 4,000 happen to be fishermen.[66]

In a country of dams, about 3,000 big and medium-sized dams have already been constructed in West Bengal while 700 are still under construction. A scheme of 300 more dams is now under active consideration.[67] An area-wise profile of losses incurred as a result of floods is available in the reports of the National Flood Commission.[68] Inspired by the Tennessee Valley Corporation, the dams of the Damodar Valley Corporation were constructed as early as 1950s. The dams, to say the least, have not been effective in controlling the floods for which they were primarily constructed. Residents claim that over the years the intensity of floods in the lower Damodar area has increased. They attribute this to the fact that water from the dams is released during the peak monsoon periods. The Damodar Bachao Andolan (Save Damodar Movement) is actually modelled on the Narmada Bachao Andolan. Although work is ongoing in order to generate some data on the extent and nature of displacement, at the moment there is nothing other than the sporadic reports in the newspapers.

The erosion of the Ganges has continued unabated for the last three decades. Such areas as Shantipur, Ranaghat and Chakda have been the worst affected. Many large villages like Beharia, Boyra-Malipota, Pujalia, Brittir Char, Jaal Nagar under the Shantipur police station simply do not exist today.[69] The entire 174 km stretch along the Ganges, from Bhutni in Malda to Jalangi in Murshidabad, has been facing erosion. In 2001 alone, about 2,500 families were rendered homeless in Malda. Two school buildings, with a student population of 500, are now under water. About 191.41 sq. km and 356 sq. km. of land in the districts of Malda and Murshidabad respectively have been eroded between 1931 and 1999. The thickly populated downtown of Dhuliyan in Murshidabad is now under threat. The District Planning Board estimated the loss in April 2000, as six high schools, one police station, three banks, one panchayat (local government) office and at least 42 primary schools, all of which are now completely under water. The problem is that erosion does not always inundate the homes and residential places. But remaining at homes without the basic conditions of life is as good as losing homes. In 1994, three-fourths of Jalangi town in Murshidabad district was submerged in the Ganges as a result of erosion. About 3,00,000 people of three blocks of Malda and eight blocks of Murshidabad faced the threat of being displaced. About 600,000 persons have been displaced in these two districts. Many have lost their cultivable lands.[70] Moreover the number of times the same family has been displaced ranges from an average of four to 16 times.[71] It means that the displaced families have nowhere to go but to move within the unsafe and threatened areas.

Some broad trends in the internal displacement in West Bengal are easily discernible: First, unlike in Gujarat where a particular community irrespective of the classes its members belonged to, was reportedly targeted in the 2002 communal riots, in West Bengal the environment-related displacement or displacement caused by urban planning has adversely affected the weaker and poorer sections of the people. This is in conformity with the general trend all over India. While the tribals form only 7 per cent of the country's population, they account for almost 40 per cent of the country's displaced population.[72] Although a minority, the Scheduled Castes have had to similarly bear the brunt of the problem. Second, since displace-ment is slow and distributed between not only spatially scattered villages but also diverse clusters and types, no clear overall picture emerges from the surveys sporadically conducted by some voluntary organizations. The data, pieced together, point to a definite human disaster in the near future. Of course, one does not have to unnecessarily panics. The point is that it is always advisable to make early preparations. West Bengal represents a case where, probably, timely and appropriate interventions might save us from the tragedy that we seem to be heading for. Third, the fact that environ-ment-related displacement has its ramifications for the relations between India and Bangladesh, and even between two or more states of the Indian Union, is evident from the internal displacement in West Bengal. As one part of the Ganges gets eroded, newer chars are created on the other bank and these areas become a bone of contention between the concerned po-litical units. As those who are rendered homeless look for homes at the other side all on their own, they sometimes face the bullets of Bangladeshi Rifles (BDR) or draw the flak of the government of Jharkhand. The People's Convention held at the Nayabazar High School of Panchanandapur, Malda on 2 September 2001, for example, argued that the newly acquired 191.41 sq. km of land on the western bank of the Ganges 'belongs beyond any doubt to the district of Malda' but is presently under Jharkhand administra-tion. It demanded the 'settlement of the problem without any delay'.

The Legal Regime

We have already said that the need for a separate legislation on the problem of IDPs has been more deeply felt since the end of the 1980s. The Working Group on Internal Displacement attached to Lokayan, New Delhi, prepared the first draft. While it provided the point of departure, it continues to be debated and discussed even now. New Delhi, for example, contended for a long time that rights related in the Guiding Principles are also covered by the Indian Constitution and that there are courts and procedures in place to address the rights of the displaced. A noticeable change has occurred in the attitude of the government and, in this context, a reference may be made to the draft National Resettlement and Rehabilitation (R & R) Policy prepared in 1998 by the then Ministry of Rural Development (MoRD), which is the first state-led attempt in this direction. In the draft National Policy, the 'family' includes every adult member, his (her) spouse, along with minor children. A single adult is treated as half a family, thus eliminating some of the biases inherent in existing R & R policies. Its primary objectives are to ensure minimum displacement, help resettled people enjoy a better standard of life than before displacement and finally enable displaced people to enjoy benefits on the same scale as the beneficiaries of the developmental project. The draft policy treated as owners of land, for purposes of R & R, those people residing for more than five years before the date of acquisition, who are otherwise termed as 'encroachers', on common land. Similarly, forest dwellers residing in forest areas prior to 30 September 1980 shall be considered as the owners. Also, provisions for compensation were made for non-owners, such as tenants, sharecroppers, etc. Other significant features of the draft policy are community consultation for R & R package, open public hearings, publishing of the R & R plan, fixing of the R & R cost at 10 per cent of project cost, and linking compensation with gross productivity. It seems that government is planning to promulgate a National Policy on internal displacement.

Whatever be the shape of laws to come, we may conclude that a separate legal regime in India is necessary not simply for compiling the existing provisions but also for plugging their loopholes. First of all, the problem of displacement requires to be treated in a sensitive and discriminatory manner. The same set of laws cannot be applied to all sorts of displacement. The draft laws in this regard show a definite bias in favour of the development-related displacement. Although a significant percentage falls under this category, ethnicity-related displacement has acquired a certain momentum in recent years. In this connection, it is also necessary to provide for the punishment of the guilty. A penal system has also to be a part of any legal instrument in this manner. Second, it is also necessary to treat the displaced person as a legal person. While the state is under the obligation of providing them with legal recognition, the individual per se does not seem to enjoy the right to legal recognition. Unless the individual is granted such a right and identity is established prior to displacement, any displacement will not be simply a spatial displacement but a displacement of identity of the one who is displaced. The pre-displacement identity will have to be fully established so that the individual can enjoy the rights that pertain to him/her. Third, laws have a tendency to respond to sensational and episodic displacements while the case of West Bengal tells us that displacement can be slow, tacit and dispersed over time and space. The displacement of the hawkers does not amount to a displacement from homes or habitual residences. But the displacement from livelihood has the potential of developing into a fully blown crisis of internal displacement in future. These situations are likely to cause humanitarian crises in future. The legal provisions must be geared to the development of databank on displacement in this connection. This will make forecasting and prediction possible and help us in avoiding displacement in the future.

NOTES

(All translations from non-English sources are by the author.)

1. National Working Group on Displacement, 'A Draft National Policy on Developmental Displacement of Project-Affected People', in Walter Fernandes and Enakshi Ganguly Thukral (eds), *Development, Displacement and Rehabilitation* (New Delhi: Indian Social Institute, 1989), 104–34.

2. See, 'Introductory Note by the Representative of the Secretary-General on Internally Displaced Persons: Mr. Francis Deng', in *Guiding Principles on Internal Displacement* (OCHA, February 2000).

3. David A. Korn, *Exodus within Borders: An Introduction to the Crisis of Internal Displacement* (Washington, DC: Brookings Institution Press, 1999), 90.

4. Kalin Walter, *Guiding Principles on Internal Displacement: Annotations*, Studies in Transnational Legal Policy: No. 32 (Washington, DC: The American Society of International Law, 2000), vi. I quote from the 'Preface' by Francis Deng.

5. Ibid., v.

6. Roberta Cohen and Francis Deng, 'Exodus within Borders: The Uprooted who Never Left Home', *Foreign Affairs* (July–August 1998): 14.

7. Ibid., 2.

8. See Subir Bhaumik's chapter in the present book. Also, Samir Kumar Das, 'Population Displacement in Northeastern India: A Critical Review,' in Girin Phukon (ed.), *Political Dynamics of Northeast India* (New Delhi: South Asian, 2000): 88–105.
9. Ibid., 2.
10. Samir Das, Sabyasachi Basu Roy Chaudhury and Tapan Bose, 'Forced Migration in South Asia: A Critical Review', *Refugee Survey Quarterly* 19, no. 2 (2000): 51–52.
11. Nancy Gaekwad and Ganesh S. Nochur (eds), *National Conference on Development, Displacement and Rehabilitation: Policies and Strategies: A Report* (Mumbai: Tata Institute of Social Science Resaerch and NAPM, 1995).
12. S. Parasuraman, 'The Anti-Dam Movement and Rehabilitation Policy,' in Jean Dreze, Meera Samson and Satyajit Singh (eds), *The Dam and the Nation: Displacement and Resettlement in the Narmada Valley* (Delhi: OUP, 1997), 33.
13. Mohan Sahay, 'Massacre in Bhagalpur', *The Statesman* (Calcutta), 25 November 1989.
14. Jiten Nandy (ed.), *Benche Othar Tukdo Katha* (Calcutta: Manthan, 2002). This source is in Bengali. The title translates as 'Snippets on living up.' It is a report from the lanes of Kasai and Ghasiram in Gujarat.
15. I have discussed this phenomenon in 'Democracy as the Mainstream or De-Mainstreaming Democracy? A Review of the Democratic Institutions and Practices in Contemporary Northeastern India' (2002, mimeo.).
16. Roberta Cohen and Francis Deng, op. cit., 15.
17. Seminar on 'Breaking the Silence: Women and Kashmir' organized by WISCOMP in New Delhi on 9 December 2000.
18. Tapan Kumar Chattopadhyay, *India and the Ecology Question: Confrontation and Reconstruction* (Calcutta: Ekushe, 1999), 31.
19. Paramjit Singh Judge, 'Response to Dams and Displacement in Two Indian States,' *Asian Survey* (September 1997): 840–51.
20. Ibid.
21. Madhab Gadgil and Ramachandra Guha, *Ecology and Equity: The Use and Abuse of Nature in Contemporary India* (New Delhi: Penguin, 1995), 71.
22. There is rich and growing body of literature on this. See, for example, Stuart Corbridge and John Harriss, *Liberalization, Hindu Nationalism and Popular Democracy* (New Delhi: OUP, 2000).
23. Quoted in Shyam Koul, 'From Refugees to Bonded Labour', *Kashmir Sentinnel* (1 September–15 October 1998).
24. Pankaj Mishra, 'The Unending War', in *The New York Review of Books* (19 October 2000).
25. V.M. Tarkunde, Rajinder Sachar, Amrik Singh, Balraj Puri, Inder Mohan, Ranjan Dwivedi, N.D. Pancholi and T.S. Ahuja on behalf of Peoples' Union for Civil Liberties, Citizens' for Democracy, Radical Humanist Association and Manav Ekta Abhiyan, 'Report on Kashmir Situation,' 22 April 1990.
26. Hiram Ruiz, 2000, *Report on Kashmir*, Washington, DC: US Committee for Refugees.
27. Report by Charles Sanctuary, BBC, 15 June 1999.
28. ICRC, 'ICRC Aid for the Internally Displaced in Jammu and Kashmir,' Press Release, 1 February 2002.
29. Anuradha Bhasin Jamwal, 'Walking into the Death Trap,' *Newsline,* February 2000.
30. Panun Kashmir memorandum to Secretary-General of the United Nations presented through the Head of the United Nations Military Observer Group for India and Pakistan at Jammu, 11 September 2000.

31. Ajay Chrangoo, 'Minorities in J & K Evolve a "Doctrine of Survival"', 1–31 March 1999.
32. Pankaj Mishra, op. cit.
33. Amnesty International, 'India: The State Must Ensure Redress for the Victims. A Memorandum to the Government of Gujarat on its Duties in the Aftermath of the Violence', (28 March 2002), 1.
34. Communalism Combat, 2002, *Genocide 2002*. Report released to the media by Sahmat on 25 April 2002.
35. Mahasweta Devi, 'Rammandir Nirmanarthe Nirbachita Bali,' in Ashok Dasgupta (ed.), *Gujarat Dichchhe Daak* (Calcutta: Aajkal, 2002), 15.
    This source is in Bengali. The title of the article translates as 'Select sacrifices for the construction of Ram temple'. The title of the book translates as 'Gujarat is calling'.
36. Fact-finding by a Women's Panel, 'Sexual Violence against Women,' in Suranjan Das (ed.), *Communalism Condemned: Gujarat Genocide 2002* (Calcutta: Netaji Institute of Asian Studies, 2002), 173, 175.
37. Salman Rushdie, 'Slaughter in the Name of God', *Other Voice* (March 2002), 193.
38. Citizens' Initiative, 'How has the Gujarat Affected Minority Women', (Ahmedabad, 16 April 2002).
39. Priyanka Kakodkar, 'Sleep and the Innocent,' *Outlook*, 13 May 2002.
40. Sanskritik Morcha, Bhopal; People's Union for Democratic Rights, Delhi, *The Bhopal Riots: A Report* (Delhi: PUCL, 1993), 16–17.
41. Asghar Ali Engineer, 'Gujrat Carnage: Implications Secularism', *Secular Perspective*, V, no.11 (June 2002), 1–2.
42. Harsh Mander, 'The Police could have stopped the riots had they wanted it,' in Asok Dasgupta (ed.), *Gujarat Dichchhe Daak* (Calcutta: Aajkal, 2002), 91.
43. Sahmat, 'Genocide in Ahmedabad,' *Other Voice* (March 2002), 222–23.
44. Dipankar Chakrabarty, 'Aamra Kothai Chalechhi,' Rhdradeb Mitra (ed.), *Gujarat: Naramedh Yagna* (Calcutta: Pratibhas, July 2002), 103.
    This is a Bengali article, the title of which translates as 'Where are we going.' The title of the book translates as 'Gujarat: The Burning of Human Beings'.
45. Teesta Setalvad, 'Cry, the Beloved Country: Reflections on the Gujarat Massacre', *Other Voice* (March 2002), 228.
46. Citizens' Initiative, op. cit.
47. Mr Narendra Modi, the Chief Minister of Gujarat, for example, invoked Newton's third law to argue that the riots were only a reaction to the event of Godhra.
48. Sahmat, op. cit., 215.
49. *Karsevaks* are the devotees who were going over to Ayodhya where a 400-year old mosque was demolished in December 1992, with a vow to reconstruct the Rama temple in its place.
50. The role of digital and electronic media in fanning communal passions has been detailed in Aakar Patel, Dileep Padgaonkar and B. G. Verghese (eds), *Rights and Wrongs: Ordeal by Fire in the Killing Fields of Gujarat*, Editors' Guild Fact Finding Report (New Delhi: Editors' Guild, 3 May 2002).
51. Asok Dasgupta, 'Gujarat Dichchhe Daak,' in Asok Dasgupta (ed.), *Gujarat Dichchhe Daak* (Calcutta: Aajkal, 2002), 103. Also, Harsh Mander, 'Ei Glani Aami Aar Bahan Korte Parchhi Na,' in Rudradeb Mitra (ed.), op. cit. Harsh Mander's article too is in Bengali. This title translates as 'I Cannot Bear This Slight Anymore.'

52. For a history of communal riots in Godhra before 2002, see, Siddhartha Guha Ray, 'Ainer Sasan, Ganatantra o Rashtra,' *Other Voice* (March 2002). This is a Bengali source and the title translates as 'The Rule of Law, Democracy and State'.
53. Ibid., 1.
54. Paraphrased from Amnesty International, op. cit.
55. Sahmat, 'Genocide in Ahmedabad', 224.
56. Report of the Committee constituted by the National Commission for Women to assess the status and situation of women and girl children in Gujarat in the wake of the communal disturbance, 22 April 2002.
57. For a review of the problem, see, Pradip Kumar Bose, *Refugees of West Bengal: Institutional Practices and Contested Identities* (Kolkata: Calcutta Research Group, 2000).
58. Soumili Biswas, 'Kolkatay Hawker Uccheder Prasangikata Ebang Uccheder Prabhab', unpublished M. A. dissertation (Kolkata: Department of Political Science, University of Calcutta, 1999).
    This is a Bengali source and the title translates as 'The Relevance and Impact of Eviction of Hawkers in Calcutta'.
59. Murad Hussain, the Secretary of the Hawker Sangram Committee disclosed the data. See, ibid. The term 'sangram' may be translated as 'struggle'.
60. Soumili Biswas, op. cit.
61. *Ananda Bazar Patrika*, 23 November 1996.
62. Soumili Biswas, op. cit.
63. Santosh Bhattacharya, 'Kolkatar Hawker Punarbashaner Arthaneeti-Rajneeti'. (mimeo).
64. *Jara Khalpade Basa Bendhechhilo* (Kolkata: Manthan Samaiyakee, December 2002).
    This is a Bengali source. The title translates as 'Those Who Established Houses by the Canal'.
65. Keya Dasgupt, 'Eviction in West Bengal: A Note' (mimeo), 7.
66. Ibid.
67. Sitangshu Sekhar Ganguly, 'Bandh Bitarka,' *Uttaran*, West Bengal State Engineers Association, Platinum Jubilee Special Number (1995), 18.
    This is a Bengali source and the title translates as 'Dam Controversy'.
68. Piyus Basu, 'Prasanga: Banya Niyantran Neet', in ibid., 172–73.
    This is a Bengali source and the title translates as 'The Context: Flood Control Policy'.
69. 'Ganga-Bhangon', *Bipanna Paribesh*, Nagarik Mancha, (January 2000), 95.
    This is a Bengali report and the title translates as 'Erosion of the Ganges.'
70. Kalyan Rudra, *Ganga–Bhangon Katha* (Calcutta: Mrittika, 2002), 5–6.
71. Kalyan Rudra, 'Maldahe Gangar Bhangon Pratirodh: Bikalpa Bhabna', *Ekhan Bisambad* 3, no. 2 (October 1999): 1.
    This is a Bengali article and the title translates as 'Stopping the Erosion in Malda: An Alternative Perspective'.
72. Walter Fernandes and Enakshi Ganguly Thukral, 'Introduction: Development, Displacement and Rehabilitation', op. cit., 5.

CHAPTER 4

INDIA'S NORTHEAST: NOBODY'S PEOPLE IN NO-MAN'S-LAND

Subir Bhaumik

I ndia's northeast, sandwiched between China, Bhutan, Bangladesh and Burma, is where India looks less and less India and more and more like the highlands of Southeast Asia. This is where two of Asia's great civilizations—the Indo-Gangetic and the Southeast Asian—meet. Often described as India's 'Mongoloid fringe',[1] this is one area of post-colonial India that came to be incorporated into a centralized subcontinental empire only during British rule. All previous attempts, by other pre-British empires of mainland India, to take over areas that currently constitute the country's northeast had failed. Even the mighty Mughals had to retreat from Assam after losing the battle of Saraighat to the legendary Ahom general Lachit Barphukan. That victory inspires present-day Assamese separatists who argue that 'they were never part of India' and that they 'are capable of throwing out the Indian occupation forces'.[2] That is possibly being too optimistic, but the memory of being independent until as late as the advent of British rule in the nineteenth century has fuelled powerful separatist movements in the 225,000 sq. km region. The separatist groups often argue that when India won independence from the British, they should have got theirs as well.[3]

The feeling of being different from the rest of India—and from each other—has not only reinforced secessionist tendencies but also created conditions for sustained ethnic strife. Religious differences often exacerbated the conflicts, though religious similarities largely failed to prevent them. The fact that Nagas and Kukis are both predominantly Christian have done little to stop their militia groups from attacking each other. Northeast India is a post-colonial construct that emerged out of the hasty process of British withdrawal from the subcontinent. Though many population groups in the region can be loosely clubbed as Mongoloid races, they often share memories of conflict and domination. The Reang tribes in Tripura resent the oppression by the Tripuri rulers and the aristocracy and look back at the history of their failed rebellions with some nostalgia. So when the Tripuri-dominated political groups, who while resenting Bengali domination, try to enforce their Kokborok language and Borok tribal identity on all tribes in Tripura, the Reangs—or at least, many of them—oppose the effort.[4]

The Nagas have as little in common with the Assamese as the Tripuris have with the Bengali migrants, and the Meiteis have very little to share with the Nagas and the Kukis but for their language which is spoken by large number of Nagas and Kukis who live in Manipur. But that does not prevent these tribes from fighting for their own imagined homelands. The ethnic diversity has prevented, despite occasional attempts, the emergence of a united front of separatist groups fighting against Indian federal rule. The Indo-Burma Revolutionary Front (IBRF) was a non-starter—and that it had to use 'India' and 'Burma' to signpost the organization goes to indicate the lack of common focus and unity among the separatist groups themselves. This contrasts with neighbouring Myanmar, where the National Democratic Front and its successor organization, Democratic Alliance of Burma (DAB) existed for quite a while and was only undermined after several ethnic rebel armies signed ceasefire agreements with the ruling military junta at Yangon in the late 1990s.

India's northeast is as ethnically diverse as the rest of the country. Of the 5,633 communities listed by the 'People of India' project sponsored by Anthropological Survey of India in the last decade, 635 were categorized as tribals, of which 213 were found to be living in northeast India. This project also listed 325 languages—of which 175 belonging to the Tibeto-Burman group and the Mon-Khmer group were spoken in northeast India. While Hinduism, Islam and Christianity are practised extensively in the region, large numbers of tribes still adhere to their animistic beliefs—even after they have formally converted to one of these three major religions. And when some tribes in Arunachal Pradesh try to institutionalize their animism and nature worship into a formal cult like Donyi Polo, the stage is set for conflict with those tribals who have converted to Christianity and aggressively practise it.

The British refrained from directly administering the whole area—only Assam, with its oilfields and tea plantations, was integrated into the Empire. The two princely kingdoms of Tripura and Manipur, once they had accepted British suzerainty, were left alone, though British political residents closely monitored the activities of the native rulers. And a large sprawling hill region, populated by fierce warlike tribes, was left to be administered by indigenous chiefs. Inner Line Regulations were promulgated to ensure that this hill region between Bengal and Burma was beyond the scope of settlement for people from other parts of India. By such measures, the unique demography of the hills of what is now northeast India was protected. And with the exception of what is now Arunachal Pradesh, this whole hill region witnessed massive conversion to Christianity. States like Nagaland, Mizoram and Meghalaya are now almost wholly Christian—all within a century or a little more.

But though the hills of the region were largely protected from large-scale influx of outsiders, Assam and, later, Tripura were not. Both were subjected to continuous influx from the erstwhile East Bengal (now Bangladesh). While Bengalis had already come to constitute the majority in Tripura in the years after India became independent, Hindus and Muslims of Bengali descent account for more than 40 per cent of the population of Assam. These demographic changes have provoked fierce ethnic conflict leading to large-scale displacement of populations. On the other hand, tribes with competing homeland demands have not only found themselves pitted in conflict against the central government but militias claiming to represent them have also fought bloody internecine feuds among themselves.

The sustained deployment of government forces, the violent activities of the separatist armies and the fighting between the militia factions, often representing different ethnicities but sometimes competing for the loyalty of the same tribe or ethnic group, have led to continuous violence and bloodletting in the region. The militarization has impeded the emergence of civil society and restricted the space in which it could thrive. Large-scale violations of human rights, ethnic cleansing, extra-judicial killings and rampant use of terror have all contributed to internal displacement in India's northeast. Sometimes, the displacement has been visible, sometimes not. The displacement of the Adivasis (central Indian tribes settled in Assam by the British) from Bodo-dominated areas is visible—the steady displacement of the Bengalis from all over northeast India is rarely visible but tens of thousands of Bengalis from the region have silently moved away to West Bengal in the past two decades, pushing up land prices in and around Kolkata. Many of them moved away after the area they resided in the northeast was hit by violence. Many others reacted in panic and moved out, often selling their property at throwaway prices. After periodic outbreak of anti-Bengali violence in

Shillong, capital of Meghalaya, during the 1980s and the 1990s, thousands of Bengalis have moved out of the city. Meghalaya papers like *Shillong Times* still carry lots of advertisements regarding distress sales of properties owned by Bengalis.

While these conflicts have regularly led to considerable internal displacement of population, mostly later migrants who are perceived as outsiders or infiltrators, development projects undertaken by central and state governments have also displaced a good number of people, mostly belonging to indigenous tribes and economically weaker sections. The development-induced displacement has often contributed to deterioration of ethnic relations and has exacerbated the process of conflict. The Dumbur hydroelectric project in Tripura's south district uprooted thousands of ethnic tribes, but it benefited both migrant Bengali fishermen (who got fishing opportunities in the reservoir lake) and urban dwellers (who got electricity from it). Large numbers of tribal insurgents in Tripura hail from those families that were ousted by the Dumbur project. In neighbouring Meghalaya, Khasi and Jaintia tribespeople have stridently opposed uranium mining by Indian government agencies in the state's Domiosiat and Wakkhaji region because they apprehend health hazards. Any attempt to mine uranium forcibly may turn these tribes against other Indian communities.

PATTERNS OF DISPLACEMENT AND THE NUMBERS GAME

In northeast, internal displacement has been caused by (a) development projects; (b) violent conflicts; (c) counter-insurgency operations of security forces; (d) natural disasters like floods; and (e) takeover of land by migrating communities. Reliable data on displacement caused by floods and takeover of land by migrating communities are not available either with the government or with the non-governmental organizations (NGOs) that have worked on the issues, and estimates made by some researchers are difficult to verify. Data on displacement caused by counter-insurgency operations are also not very reliable. Only in Mizoram, where the army pushed through 'village regrouping' as part of its counter-insurgency operations, can a reasonably accurate assessment about the extent of displacement be made. Displacement caused by development projects is available in certain specific cases, as is the case with displacements caused by violent conflicts. It is not possible for a study based on available data to quantify the extent of displacement caused by natural disasters and take-over of land by migrating communities.

This chapter will (a) focus on the patterns and conditions of internal displacement in northeast India in the backdrop of the conflicts and the major development projects; (b) examine the relevance and applicability of the Deng principles to the problem of internal displacement specific to the northeast; and (c) finally, explore possible remedies. The concept of 'internal displacement' is rarely used in the popular domain in northeast India; media reports and official correspondences refer to those internally displaced as 'refugees'. So Tripura newspapers talk of 'Reang refugees' (Reangs displaced from Mizoram and now living in Tripura) in the same way as they talk of 'Chakma refugees' (Chakmas who fled into Tripura from Bangladesh after large-scale fighting broke out between Bangladeshi security forces and Shanti Bahini guerrillas in the Chittagong Hill Tracts during the 1980s and the 1990s). Government reports also make no distinction between those 'internally displaced' and those who have come in to take refuge from other countries. Camps sheltering internally displaced persons (IDPs) are also called 'refugee camps' in government reports and official correspondences. Only some non-governmental groups with exposure to the global discourse on refugees and internal displacement tend to make this distinction.

The northeast accounts for almost half of India's conflict-induced internally displaced persons—if not more than half of it. The Global IDP survey, first published in 1998, estimated the number of conflict-induced IDPs in India at 390,000. But this survey gave wrong data about the IDPs in Assam, where thousands of Santhals, Mundas and Oraons have been displaced due to violence by guerrillas belonging to the Bodos. It said: 'While the majority of Adivasis (Santhals, Mundas and Oraons) numbering about 80,000 has returned home, about 70,000 of them remain in relief camps'.[5] But the Assam government says that the process of return only started in August 2002 and is very slow because of sporadic violence between the warring ethnic groups. Until August 2002, a total of 37,677 families (237,768 people) were staying in makeshift camps in three districts of western Assam—Kokrakjhar, Bongaigaon and Dhubri.[6]

So, it is obvious that the Global IDP survey has got wrong statistics about the IDPs in Assam at the time it was published. The statistics about IDPs elsewhere in the region provided in the survey is also inaccurate. In March 2001, during the budget session of the Tripura Legislative Assembly, it was pointed out that 'there are about 37,000 Reangs displaced from Mizoram, staying in north Tripura.'[7] So, it is not correct to keep the number of Reang IDPs in Tripura at 15,000. With 33,672 Reangs displaced from Mizoram still in camps in Tripura (about 6,000 have melted away amongst ethnic kinsmen in the Kanchanpur subdivision of north Tripura), with more than 200,000 Adivasis and Bodos still in camps in western Assam and between 50,000 to 60,000 Bengalis displaced by tribal guerrilla violence from various parts of Tripura, the total number of conflict-induced IDPs is close to 300,000 in northeast India alone. So the country's total conflict-induced IDP population would be well over half a million. The World Refugee Survey (2001) is more accurate in its estimates of IDPs in India, when it says there are at least 507,000 IDPs in India, besides 290,000 refugees from other countries.

THE ETHNIC CAULDRON: CONFLICT AND DISPLACEMENT

India's northeast has witnessed seven major cases of conflict-induced internal displacement in recent years:

1. displacement of Bengali Hindus and Muslims from and within Assam;
2. displacement of Adivasis (also called Tea Tribes on account of their representation in the workforce of the plantation industry) and Bodos within and from western Assam;
3. displacement of the Bengalis from Meghalaya, particularly from Shillong;
4. displacement of the Bengalis from and within Tripura;
5. displacement of the Nagas, Kukis and Paites in Manipur;
6. displacement of the Reangs from Mizoram;
7. displacement of the Chakmas from Arunachal Pradesh and Mizoram.

The first major displacement in post-colonial northeast India was reported from Assam, where religious riots displaced around 100,000 Muslims in post-Partition riots. There has been the displacement of 60,000 from Goalpara district, 20,000 from Kamrup district, 14,000 from Cachar district and 6,000 from Darrang district. But almost the entire displaced population that migrated to the then East Pakistan returned to Assam after the Nehru–Liaquat Pact in 1950.[8] It would be better to categorize this displacement as a refugee situation, because it was not 'internal' to

Indian territory, as the displaced Muslims had left for Pakistan and then returned to India after an agreement between the two nations. But since the displacement had started due to violence that preceded the Partition, there is also that 'internal-ness' to the displacement that cannot be over-looked.

After the Partition riots, the first major ethnic conflagration in Assam occurred during the language movement in 1960. As the Assam government decided to make Assamese the official language of the province, the Bengalis protested because they feared loss of job opportunities. As the Bengali-dominated Barak valley erupted in agitation and there was a spate of police firings, Assamese mobs started attacking Bengali settlements in the Assamese-dominated Brahmaputra valley. During the worst phase of the violence in July–September 1960, nearly 50,000 Bengalis, almost wholly Hindu, crossed over to West Bengal, seeking shelter. The West Bengal chief minister Dr B.C. Roy, wrote to Prime Minister Jawaharlal Nehru:

> The exodus has taken place in three distinct waves. The first lot of 4,000 came between 5th and 11th July. These were the real fugitives from the fury of the Assamese. Between the 12th and 20th July, there was a small trickle of 447 people who may not have all been victims of violence. From the 31st of July, however, the floodgates have really opened.[9]

Dr Roy in a subsequent letter said 45,000 displaced Bengalis had taken shelter in West Bengal: 'We have no more space for them. In spite of all the Assam government has done recently, more than a thousand people are coming away to West Bengal, most of whom are not direct victims of violence, but are migrating for fear of disturbances.'[10]

The violence was most intense in 25 villages in Goreswar in Kamrup district and a one-man Enquiry Commission under Justice Gopalji Mehrotra was set up in November 1960. The Commission's report observed that 4,019 huts and 58 houses of Bengalis were vandalized and destroyed in the 25 villages. Nine Bengalis were killed and more than one hundred injured and there was at least one instance of attack on women. But this was certainly not the first time that the Bengalis had been attacked. The *Bangal Kheda* (drive away Bengalis) movement started in 1948 with the looting of Bengali shops in Guwahati. Widespread disturbances took place in the district of Goalpara during the visit of the States Reorganization Commission. But the 1960 disturbances sparked off an exodus of Bengalis to West Bengal and to other Bengali-dominated areas of northeast India like Tripura and Barak valley of Assam. While 45,000 left for West Bengal, almost twice as many Bengalis relocated themselves in other Bengali-dominated areas of Assam and Tripura. Fresh language riots erupted in 1972 and large-scale violence was again reported throughout the Brahmaputra valley. Again Bengali Hindus were the main target because they were at the forefront of the agitation to prevent imposition of Assamese. More than 14,000 Bengalis were displaced during the 1972–73 language disturbances and fled to West Bengal and elsewhere in northeast.[11]

But the real extent of Bengali displacement from Assam is far more than these figures would suggest. While only those who fled during the disturbances and took refuge in camps in West Bengal were accounted for in government records, thousands who took shelter with relatives or just relocated themselves by buying up property in West Bengal after selling off their possessions in Assam escaped government or media notice. And those who continued to leave Assam after the riots had ended for fear of future attacks were not taken into account. But if the Bengali Muslims largely escaped attacks by the Assamese during the language riots because they had mostly accepted the Assamese language, they also faced substantial displacement during the war with Pakistan in 1965:

Instead of sealing off the border with Pakistan and preventing possible infiltration from there, the government in Assam launched a massive and rapid action manhunt for the Pakistani nationals in Assam. The operation of the Prevention of Infiltration from Pakistan (PIP) scheme terrorized the defenceless and virtually unorganized rural Muslim peasantry.[12]

Assam's late chief minister, Hiteswar Saikia, later admitted that between 1961 and 1969, 192,079 Muslims of Bengali descent were deported to East Pakistan.[13] While this cannot be categorized as 'internal displacement' and would rank as a case of outright pushback, it is not clear how many Muslims relocated themselves elsewhere in India or in the northeast. There is some indication that many did; but since none of them went to government camps for fear of detection and possible pushback, there are absolutely no statistics available on their displacement.

During the six-year-long anti-foreigners' agitation in Assam (1979–85), there was substantial internal displacement of both Hindus and Muslims of Bengali descent. The displacement took place in two phases:

(a) the initial phase of the movement was in 1979–80; and (b) the second phase was after the massive violence that rocked Assam in February–March 1983 during the Assembly polls. During the initial phase of the movement, attacks were reported on Bengali Hindu and Muslim settlements throughout the Brahmaputra valley. Incidents such as the killing of a Bengali technical officer, Rabi Mitra, at the Oil India's headquarters in Duliajan in Upper Assam led to panic amongst the Bengalis. But while at least 7,000 Bengali Hindus crossed into West Bengal in 1979–80, the Muslim peasantry of Bengali descent stayed put. They became targets of massive attacks by the supporters of the agitation in February–March 1983, when at least 1,200 of them were butchered in Nellie, 70 km from Guwahati. This was described as one of the worst pogroms a minority community had ever faced in post-Partition India. But the Muslim peasantry of Nellie, as indeed of many other places in Brahmaputra valley who had become targets of the agitationists and their zealous supporters, returned to their lands within a few days of the massacre. As marginal peasants whose ancestors had left East Bengal in search of some land and survival, they had nowhere to go and very little to lose.

But even those who braved the attacks were displaced under sustained pressure from the administration that was dominated by the Assamese. In 1985, the new regional party Asom Gana Parishad (AGP) came to power. Those who had led the Assam agitation composed the AGP almost entirely—and their supporters backed by the administration went about hunting for 'foreigners'. Thousands of Bengali Hindus and Muslims fled to Barak valley and West Bengal and many Muslim and lower-caste Bengali Hindu peasants vacated their cultivable lands and went further deep into forest areas. Nearly 50,000 were allowed to settle down in the disputed border region of Assam and Nagaland. The administration that was hounding them out from elsewhere in Assam was willing to allow the Muslims to settle down in the disputed border region.

It is after the Assam agitation that the Muslims of Bengali origin started entering Nagaland. In July 2002 a Naga rebel group, National Socialist Council of Nagaland (NSCN)-Khaplang faction asked 'all Muslims in Nagaland to take work permits' from its offices or face 'dire consequences'.[14] Nagaland government sources say that the Semiyas (so called because Muslims are referred to as Miyas in the region and they have mostly inter married with the Semas in Nagaland) now number at least 80,000 to 100,000—though some intelligence agencies place their number at between 250,000 and 300,000.[15] It is difficult to say whether all of them have migrated from Assam or have used Assam as a corridor to reach

Nagaland. Intelligence reports indicate that most of the Muslims in Nagaland are of East Bengali extraction and are second-or third-generation settlers in India and have come out of Assam to settle down in Nagaland.[16] Even accepting the intelligence version that many of these Muslims of Bengali extraction are recent infiltrators, it would be reasonable to accept that tens of thousands of them moved to Nagaland after displacement from Assam during the violence of the early 1980s.

The Bengali Hindus and Muslims from Assam however quickly settled down wherever they relocated themselves. About 25,000, who were displaced in attacks by the guerrillas of the Bodo tribe in western Assam during the 1993–94 violence either returned to their lands or quickly settled down in the place of their relocation. But the Adivasis who were displaced in attacks by the Bodos in western Assam have remained in makeshift camps in large numbers. Many Bodos, also displaced during clashes with the Adivasis, have remained in camps. In 1987, the Bodo organizations intensified their movement for a separate state. Large-scale violence, including explosions in trains, buses and rail tracks, started. For six years, western and central Assam was ravaged by violence. But at this stage of their movement, the Bodos did not attack non-Bodo population, though many were killed in explosions set off by them. The Bodos targeted government property and security forces. The Assam government, then run by the regional party, Asom Gana Parishad, alleged that central intelligence agencies were propping up the Bodo militants to bring down their government.[17]

In 1993, the Indian government and the state government, then run by the Congress party, finally agreed to set up an autonomous council for the Bodo tribe and an agreement was signed with the agitating Bodo groups. But the agreement proved to be a non-starter. The Assam government refused to hand over a huge area, comprising 2,570 villages and some townships, to the Bodoland Autonomous Territorial Council, saying that it would 'be unfair to the non-Bodos who were a majority in many areas of the proposed Bodoland Council'.[18] The Bodo leaders who had signed the agreement stood discredited. The separatist National Democratic Front of Bodoland (NDFB), which had opposed the agreement, was vindicated and many Bodo militants who had decided to return to normal life returned to the jungles. Since the Assam government refused to hand over those areas to the Bodoland Autonomous Territorial Council where non-Bodos were in majority, Bodo hardliners argued 'that majorities would have to be created over the area that historically belongs to the Bodos if that is the way to secure an independent homeland'.[19] Even moderate

Bodo groups, discredited by their failure to get the autonomy arrangement working on ground, said that the area demanded by the Council was their 'historic homeland' and if the Bodos had become a minority in some areas, it was because governments in Assam had failed to stop 'illegal infiltration into those areas'.[20]

The stage was clearly set for a fierce ethnic conflagration. And it started within a few months of the Bodo Accord. In October 1993, Bodo militants started large-scale attacks on Muslims of Bengali descent. These migrants, mostly of the peasant stock, had taken over land throughout Assam, initially causing displacement of ethnic Assamese and the tribal peasantry. In the 1980s they were targeted by the Assamese agitators. A decade later, they became targets of the Bodo militants. During the attacks in October 1993, more than 20,000 Muslims were displaced in Kokrajhar and Bongaigaon districts. The attacks continued in 1994, covering four western Assam districts of Barpeta, Bongaigaon, Dhubri and Kokrajhar. More than 60 villages were completely devastated. Casualty figures varied, government sources placing them at 300–400 dead, while Monirul Hussain, one of Assam's noted academics, says 1,000 Muslims, mostly women and children were killed.[21] Intelligence reports from the area suggest this estimate is on the higher side—the Assam Police Special Branch estimated around 400 Muslims dead.[22] The Bodo militants did not even spare camps set up for the displaced Muslims—one large camp at Banhbari was subjected to a night attack and nearly 90 camp inmates were massacred even as the police guards stood by as spectators, too frightened to take on the heavily-armed Bodos.

What started with specific attacks on Muslims of Bengali descent (also called Na-Asamiyas, because they had adopted Assamese as their language) slowly engulfed other non-Bodo communities like the Bengali Hindus and the Adivasis (also called Tea Tribes because their ancestors, who hailed from tribes of central India, were inducted into Assam at the turn of the nineteenth century to work in the tea gardens). Unlike in the case of some of the previous ethnic pogroms in Assam, this time the pattern of violence appeared to be very calculated. The Bodo militants first targeted the Muslims of Bengali descent in 1993–94. Then in 1995–96, they started attacking the Bengali Hindus. And finally in May–June 1996, they launched massive attacks on the Adivasis throughout western Assam. But unlike the Muslims, the Adivasis and the Bengali Hindus formed their own militant groups and started attacking Bodo villages.

The Adivasi Cobra Militants of Assam (ACMA) and the Bengali Liberation Tigers, a group formed by Bengali Hindus teamed up and attacked several Bodo villages after the massive Bodo-sponsored violence of May–June 1996. Besides large-scale displacement, the mushrooming of ethnic militias has created a Bosnia or a Lebanon-type situation, in which the central and state authorities were often seen as helpless spectators, merely capable of setting up camps for displaced persons but totally incapable of stopping the proliferation of militias and the violence they unleash to cause displacement. Assam government says more than 250,000 people were displaced, of which at least 237,668 people including 181,932 Adivasis and the rest of them Bodos were still staying in camps.[23]

After the first outbreak of Bodo–Adivasi violence in May–June 1996, the clashes between the two ethnic groups became a regular feature in western Assam. It started with the recovery of three dead bodies of Bodo girls at Satyapur under Gosaigaon police station. While the Bodos say that they were raped and killed by Adivasi militants, the ACMA alleges that they were prostitutes from the Bhutanese border town of Phuentsoling who were killed and left in a jungle to spark off the riots.[24] These murders sparked off fierce attacks by the Bodos but the Adivasis also retaliated, killing the kin of a Bodo legislator. Then it turned into a free-for-all.

In 1998, the violence intensified just when some of the displaced people were returning home. Thousands fled their villages again, exacerbating the displacement. The Assam government admitted that 1,213 people had died in the violence in 1996 and 1998—but since the militias continue to attack people of the rival communities, the casualty toll continues to mount. For instance, the National Democratic Front of Bodoland (NDFB), easily the best-armed and trained group in western Assam, has imposed a ban on tree felling and woodcutting in the area. More than 90 woodcutters from non-Bodo communities have so far died in NDFB attacks. The NDFB has also kidnapped and killed a number of non-Bodo businessmen and contractors when they failed to pay subscriptions. The ACMA has retaliated quite often.

The Assam government decided to keep the displaced in 47 relief camps, improving their security but not providing them with enough rations and medicines.[25] At the same time, both the Indian Union and the Assam state governments steadfastly opposed the entry of international organizations like Medicines Sans Frontiers (MSF) to work in the camps. Since it was not immediately possible for sending the displaced people back to their villages as long as the militants were at large, the Assam government decided to initiate extensive counter-insurgency operations in the area. The split in the Bodo underground movement, with the

Bodoland Liberation Tigers Force (BLTF) coming out openly against the NDFB, the government found it convenient to quell the pitch of the Bodo insurgency. While it started negotiations with the BLTF and got it to scale down its demands of a separate Bodo state within India, the NDFB remained the target of the counter-insurgency operations since it maintained that it would fight on until an independent Bodo homeland was established.

In August 2002, the Assam government finally started sending back the Adivasis and the Bodos to their villages from the makeshift camps. The government has drawn up a detailed plan to rehabilitate these displaced people in four phases—beginning with the resettlement of 16,783 families in the first phase. But during a visit to western Assam, it was found that only 348 families from the Align Bazar relief camp, 58 families from Dhanpur Karigaon relief camp and 15 families from the Bishumuri relief camp in Kokrajhar district have actually gone back from the camps. Kokrajhar deputy commissioner A.K. Bhutani told *The Times of India* that the process of rehabilitation would be slow because the situation in the area was still far from normal.[26] Even as the displaced persons were beginning to go back after being in camps for eight years, the threat of fresh violence was hanging heavy in the area. Nine Adivasis were killed by suspected NDFB rebels in the same week. The Adivasi Cobra militants then started some retaliatory counter-attacks on Bodo villages.

Following the accord that the government has signed with the BLTF, the non-Bodos say they fear loss of land rights and sustained ethnic cleansing once the Bodo leadership takes over full power in the Bodoland Territorial Council. The non-Bodo communities in western Assam—the Bengalis, Assamese, Adivasis, the Hindi-speaking and the Muslims—have formed an organization called the Sanmilito Janoghostiya Sangram Samity (SJSS) or United Nationalities Struggle Committee. The SJSS organized a strike on 15 August 2002, to coincide with the Indian Independence Day, to protest against the proposed formation of the Bodoland Territorial Council. The BLTF and other groups like the All Bodo Students Union and the Bodo Peoples Action Committee are upset with the stand of the SJSS and the activities of the Adivasi militants. The All Adivasi Students Association of Assam (AASAA) has even threatened an economic blockade of the Bodo areas if the council is created.[27] The BLTF spokesman Maino Daimary said in a recent interview: 'If the Bodos fail to get meaningful autonomy soon enough, relations between them and the other communities in the area will further worsen'.[28] If that happens, it would mean more conflict between the Bodos and the non-Bodos, with the threat of large-scale displacement.

BONGAL KHEDA SPREADS

Bongal Kheda as an organized campaign of ethnic cleansing originated in Assam but was not restricted to the state. In the early 1980s, it spread to Tripura and Meghalaya. In both states, tribal people attacked Bengalis, resenting their growing numbers or dominance in jobs and business or both. In Meghalaya, the mayhem was largely restricted to Shillong, the former capital of undivided Assam where the Bengalis dominated the bureaucracy and the professions. In 1980, a Bengali legislator was killed and many Bengali localities came under systematic attack. The pattern was repeated at regular intervals—mostly before or during the main Bengali Hindu festival Durga Puja. In the 1990s, Bengalis remained the prime target of tribal violence but other non-tribal communities like the Biharis (people of Bihar) and the Marwaris (people of Marwar, a region in Rajasthan) also came under attack. More than 50 people have died in these attacks during the last two decades—a small number compared to neighbouring Tripura or Assam—but scary enough to trigger a Bengali exodus. Since the early 1980s, an estimated 25,000–35,000 Bengalis have left Shillong and some other parts of Meghalaya and settled down in West Bengal and other states of India. In 1981, there were 119,571 Bengalis in Meghalaya—8.13 per cent of the state's total population. Ten years later, in 1991 it stood at 144,261—only 5.97 per cent of the population.[29]

But the attack on the Bengalis in neighbouring Tripura has been much more widespread than in Meghalaya, where it was restricted to urban areas like Shillong. Since Bengalis had taken over land on a large scale from the tribal people and reduced them to an ethnic minority in Tripura, ethnic hatred was much more intense and widespread. Land alienation and loss of political power due to the end of princely rule and the coming of a democratic dispensation, where numbers count, explains the continued intensity of the violence. It started with the fierce ethnic riots of June–July 1980 in which about 1,076 Bengalis and 278 tribals were killed. 327 Bengalis were butchered in the village of Mandai. During the June 1980 riots, 189,919 people, 80 per cent Bengalis and the remaining 20 per cent tribals, were displaced and took shelter in the 186 camps that were set up for them. Bengalis were sheltered in 141 camps while the tribals took refuge in 45 camps.[30]

Most of the displaced lot went back to their villages but after a while, the Bengalis relocated their villages closer to police outposts, semi-urban centres and roadside positions. Mandai is a classic example—the old Bengali part of the settlement has now been largely taken over by the tribals and the Bengalis have moved away to 'New Mandai', a new fledgling semi-urban location guarded by a paramilitary camp. In fact, most new Bengali settlements came up near the camps set up by the security forces where they had taken their shelter. The villages they had lived in earlier were abandoned and in most cases taken over by the tribals. Many Bengali farmers tried to cultivate their landholdings from their new locations and often became victims of sneak attacks by rebel tribesmen. On the other hand, the tribals who were displaced returned to their ancestral villages though many of their young men, implicated in rioting cases and hunted by the police, left for the hills and joined the Tribal National Volunteers (TNV) and the All Tripura Peoples Liberation Organization (ATPLO), the two rebel groups that emerged at that time. The ATPLO surrendered in 1983 and was disbanded but the TNV continued its depredations after the June 1980 riots until they gave up insurgency in 1988.

More than 600 of them died in the TNV raids between 1982 and 1988–more than 100 of them in the two months preceding the 1988 state elections. But though the TNV gave up the path of insurgency, the two rebel groups, the All Tripura Tiger Force (ATTF) and the National Liberation Front of Tripura (NLFT) emerged with the same agenda of driving the Bengali migrants away from Tripura. These two rebel groups adopted a new tactic. Instead of just launching TNV-style night attacks on Bengali villages and killing scores of Bengalis, they also started en masse kidnapping of Bengalis—officials, businessmen, just about anybody with some capacity to pay up. Between March 1992 and March 2002, the rebels killed 823 Bengalis but 3,312 were kidnapped. About one-seventh of those kidnapped did not return.[31] Abductions are often not reported to the police and the families pay up quietly; the actual number of abductions of Bengalis would be much more (the average of almost one abduction a day). Most of the families that had someone abducted have been rendered penniless by the rebels as they squeeze out every bit of family property before releasing the victim. The NLFT and the ATTF have periodically issued 'quit Tripura notices' to the Bengalis who entered Tripura after the state merged with the Indian Union on 15 October 1949. Bengali settlements have been regularly attacked and subjected to systematic massacres.

In the past 22 years since the first major ethnic riots in the state, more than 1,00,000 Bengalis have been displaced. During the particularly violent phases of the rebel depredations, camps were opened in violence affected areas like Khowai but were quickly closed down, unlike in Assam. In Khowai alone, 2,600 families, almost totally Bengalis, were displaced by the NLFT and the ATTF attacks between 1998 and 2001. Some of these displaced Bengalis even went over to Bangladesh from where they had come to Tripura in the 1960s and 1970s. In other parts of West Tripura district (in areas under Sadar and Bishalgarh subdivision), another 2,400 families were displaced between 1998 and 2001 alone. Government officials said the total displacement of Bengalis in Khowai, Sadar and Bishalgarh subdivision between 1995 and 2002 would be more than 7,000 families—between 40,000 to 50,000 people in all. This is corroborated by collation of data between the two Censuses (1991 and 2001), which indicate change of residence by nearly 50,000 people in these three subdivisions.

Throughout the hills of Tripura, a silent exodus has taken place. Bengali peasants and small traders from the hills have fled to the roadside locations or crowded into the outskirts of the towns situated on Tripura's western border with Bangladesh and are largely dominated by the Bengalis. In March 2002, a large number of Bengalis displaced from Takarjala, Jampuijhala and Gabardi on the outskirts of Agartala crowded into the city and took over the town's main cultural hall, Rabindra Bhavan. The ruling Marxists said the Opposition Congress was provoking them to embarrass the government; but, the displaced Bengalis said they were agitating to highlight their problems before an 'insensitive government'.[32] In fact, two distinct trends of Bengali out-migration caused by violence in Assam has also been seen in Tripura—a good percentage of those who left the state and relocated in West Bengal had not suffered direct attacks but fled more in anticipation of violence, while many left after their settlements had been attacked. The number of those fleeing in anticipation of attacks rather than having suffered one was larger than those who fled after suffering attacks.

In both Assam and Tripura, which has accounted for the bulk of the internally displaced population in northeast India, the situation remains fluid. Fresh conflicts cannot be ruled out and the threat of large-scale displacement remains a distinct possibility in both these states. Rampant migration that alters the demographic balance of these states and threatens to reduce, or actually reduces, the indigenous groups to a minority has provoked nativist violence, often degenerating into insurgencies.

Competition for jobs, business opportunities, land and political power has pitted the Assamese, Bodos and Tripuris against the migrant Bengalis and other communities from the Indian mainland. In the last two months of 2000, suspected guerrillas of the United Liberation Front of Assam (ULFA) launched a series of attacks against Hindi-speaking settlers throughout Assam, killing 118 of them. The ULFA formally denied the charge but the Assam police and intelligence insisted that no other organization could have unleashed such terror over such a wide area in Assam other than the ULFA. Following the attacks, there was an exodus of Marwari and Bihari settlers from upper and central Assam. However, no definitive estimate of this displacement has been possible so far, because the Marwaris, like the richer section of Bengali Hindus, moved over to West Bengal or other Indian states that provided business opportunities. The Biharis are believed to have moved to 'safer areas' in Assam or back to some of the Hindi-speaking states or to northern Bengal. The Hindi-speaking settlers are also being displaced in some numbers in Karbi Anglong and North Cachar Hill districts, where rebels of the United Peoples Democratic Solidarity (UPDS) and Dimasa Halam Dago (DHD) are attacking them at regular intervals.

TRIBAL WELFARE OR ETHNIC CLEANSING

The situation may not be as critical in other northeastern states as in Assam and Tripura, but tense relations between battling ethnicities and tribes and counter-insurgency operations have led to substantial internal displacement in Manipur, Mizoram and Arunachal Pradesh. These states that straddle the border with Burma have been spared the kind of rampant migration from across the border that has upset the demographic balance of states like Assam and Tripura—but various tribes that have entered these states in medieval times entertain conflicting homeland demands that have often led to conflicts and have created substantial internal displacement. After Partition, the Indian government kept the northeast outside the purview of the linguistic reorganization process. In the rest of the country, states were created around population groups largely speaking one language. But since the northeast was diverse, this principle was not extended to the region. An exception to this was made in 1963, when Nagaland was created as a separate state. This was done to take the steam out of the powerful Naga insurrection and provide the moderates with some political space to manoeuvre. But the moment the

Nagas got a state, other ethnic groups began to demand theirs. In 1972, the northeast was politically reorganized when a new tribal state, that is Meghalaya, was created. Later Mizoram and Arunachal Pradesh also got full statehood in 1987. This spurred many ethnic groups to demand homelands and even adopt armed militancy as the tactic to achieve them. These armed groups often attack settler communities or rival tribes as part of their strategy of ethnic cleansing to achieve ethnically compact homelands. But often they hit soft targets to pressurize the government to concede to their demands.

Manipur has witnessed substantial internal displacement and ethnic relocation in the wake of the Naga–Kuki and the Kuki–Paite feuds in the 1990s that led to nearly 1,700 deaths and destruction of property worth millions of rupees. There were also riots between the Hindu Meiteis and the ethnic Manipuri Pangal Muslims in 1993. The National Socialist Council of Nagaland (NSCN)'s vision of an independent homeland—Nagalim, includes all but one of the five hill districts of Manipur. Churachandpur, where Kukis hold more than 95 per cent of the landholdings, has never been part of their Nagalim demand. The United Naga Council (UNC) of Manipur, which has close relations with the NSCN's Issac–Muivah faction, that is active in Manipur and is the stronger of the two NSCN factions, issued a 'quit notice' to all Kukis who lived in the state. A new militia, Naga Lim Guards, formed by Nagas of Manipur as a back-up force to the NSCN, came into existence and they started rampant attacks against the Kukis. The worst carnage occurred at Zopui, a remote hill village north of the state's capital Imphal, where 87 Kuki males were beheaded one night. The NSCN alleged that the Kuki National Front (KNF) and some other Kuki militant groups enjoyed support of the Indian Army and were, in fact, helping them curb the NSCN.[33]

The Kuki militias also retaliated but only in a few areas that they controlled. Soon Manipur was gripped by a fierce spiral of tribal feud that threatened to spin out of control. The Indian government, and that of the state of Manipur, increased the presence of security forces but did little else to control the violence. Delhi appeared keener on using the issue to discredit the NSCN at international forums. The Naga human rights groups had been active at international forums since the early 1980s with regular documentation of human rights violation by Indian security forces. The Indian agencies are beating the NSCN with the same stick. The Kuki Inpi—the tribe's most representative body—submitted a series of memorandums to the Indian and the Manipur governments, demanding more security and restoration of their lands to the Kuki owners. Only in 1998, six years after the violence had started, did the Indian government formally react and the Home Ministry formally asked the Manipur government to furnish details and comment on the charges made by the Kuki Inpi.[34] By then, Delhi had started negotiations with the NSCN (Issac–Muivah faction). But the Kukis remain apprehensive over the demand for 'Greater Nagaland' which the NSCN has not given up. Though they are more numerous than the Nagas in Manipur, the latter have a longer tradition of guerrilla warfare against the Indian state and are much better organized for armed conflict.

The violence was finally controlled after the Baptist Church intervened and got leaders of both the Naga and Kuki communities to accept a ceasefire that would be binding on their militant elements. The Paites who are the ethnic cousins of the Kukis but had developed close ties with the Nagas were also involved in a bitter feud that led to hundreds of deaths. A similar agreement between the leaders of the Zomi Council and the Kuki-Inpi brought an end to the Kuki–Paite feud. Peace has thereafter reigned in the violence-ravaged hills of Manipur but the two agreements are barely two years old and it is too early to say that we have seen the last of these bitter tribal feuds that ravaged Manipur. But the displacement was limited because neither the Nagas nor the Kukis nor the Paites remained in camps for too long. They returned to their ancestral villages at the first opportunity—at worst they relocated their villages in safer areas but did not give up control over land as far as possible.

The Manipur government says that not more than 15,000 Nagas and Kukis have been permanently displaced. In mixed Naga–Kuki districts like Senapati, Tamenglong and Chandel, where the violence was fierce and sustained, the Nagas and the Kukis stuck to their lands and homesteads in most cases. Only in districts where one ethnic group was in total dominance did the other find their position untenable and was forced to move. For instance, the town of Moreh (with a population of about 15,000 people) that sits on the lucrative drug route on the border with Burma, does not have a single Naga living there now. In February, when this writer visited Moreh, the vehicle in which we were travelling was halted by Kuki vigilantes who were checking for Nagas. Three Buddhist women from Arunachal Pradesh who perhaps resembled Nagas were dragged out of the vehicle forcing this writer to intervene. Only when the women produced their Indian voters' identity cards that gave their places of residence as Arunachal Pradesh did the Kukis relent and let them off.

At least 600 villages were burnt down during the Naga–Kuki feud, in which nearly 10,000 houses were destroyed. The Nagas killed 898 Kukis during the eight-year-old feud, and 312 Nagas were killed by the Kukis. The Paites killed 210 Kukis in clashes and lost 298 of their own tribesmen during the feud. Three thousand houses in 47 villages were destroyed and 22,000 Kukis and Paites were displaced. During riots between the Meiteis and the Pangals, more than 100 were killed in which 196 houses in nine villages were destroyed.[35]

In June 2001, the Indian government extended the ceasefire with the NSCN to Manipur and the rest of the country. This provoked fierce protests in the Imphal valley and angry Meiteis burnt down the State Assembly building, offices of political parties and houses of senior politicians. Nearly 20 Meiteis were killed in police firing. The agitation created panic amongst the Nagas—and though it goes to show the political maturity of the organizations leading the agitation that not a single Naga was attacked anywhere in the Imphal valley, more than 10,000 Nagas left the plains and moved into the hill districts or to neighbouring Nagaland. Most of them have not returned. Some of these Nagas interviewed by this writer said that they feared a massive backlash against the Nagas if any part of Manipur was included in a settlement between the Indian government and the NSCN. Therefore, they do not find it safe in the Imphal valley.[36]

In neighbouring Mizoram, the majority Christian Mizos had reportedly unleashed a wave of terror against the minority Reangs in 1998. From October that year, hundreds of Reangs started fleeing into neighbouring Tripura complaining of persecution. The refugees spoke of 'villages burnt down, Reang women raped and men beaten up and killed'.[37] The Reang militant group, which calls itself the Bru National Liberation Front or the BNLF started attacking Mizoram police and that further provoked the Mizos to commit atrocities on the Reangs who straddle Mizoram's western border with Tripura. The Tripura government says that 30,690 Reangs belonging to 6,859 families have fled into Tripura during the last three years. But the Mizoram government refuses to accept them. They say that the Tripura government has not given details of residence of 10,435 people belonging to 2,075 families— therefore their claim to be residents of Mizoram is untenable. Mizoram chief minister Zoramthanga told this writer in an interview that the 'Reangs are from Tripura and if they are not happy in Mizoram, they are welcome to go back to Tripura'.[38] The chief minister also alleged that the Reangs would try to come back with more of their ethnic kinsmen and that must be stopped. In an attitude reminiscent of the Bhutanese authorities, who are unwilling to take back the refugees of Nepalese origin, the Mizoram government is trying to stall the return of the Reangs. The Union Home Ministry's efforts of ethnic persecution of smaller tribes in Mizoram are not new. The Chakmas have always faced discrimination and pressure from the Mizos, not the least because the Chakma rebel group, Shanti Bahini, which fought the Bangladesh security forces in the neighbouring Chittagong Hill Tracts, attacked Mizo rebel bases in that area at the behest of the Indian government between 1978–85. The Mizo National Front, which fought the Indian forces, had several bases in the Chittagong Hill Tracts. When the MNF returned to normal life after signing an accord with the Indian government in 1986, it became a legitimate political party and now rules Mizoram. Zoramthanga, now chief minister, ran the MNF bases in the Chittagong Hill Tracts. Immediately after the 1986 Accord, the MNF put pressure on the Indian government to abrogate the Chakma Autonomous District Council, but the Indian government did not agree. Rajiv Gandhi told a rally in Aizawl: 'If the Mizos expect justice from India as a small minority, they must safeguard the interest of their own minorities like the Chakmas'. But Mizo officials have deleted names of Chakma electors from the voter's list at random—so much so that even a former Chakma legislator, S.P. Dewan, had his name recently struck off the rolls. Besides the Chakmas, there are two other autonomous district councils in Mizoram meant for the smaller Mara and Lai tribes. They want to join hands with the Chakmas and turn the territory of the three district councils into a centrally administered area that is called Union Territory in India.[39] If that movement picks up, Mizoram police and administration will try to curb it and the possibility of fresh displacement cannot be ruled out.

The Mizos themselves were victims of large-scale displacement in the late 1960s when the Indian Army started Malaysia and Vietnam-style village regrouping to contain the MNF rebels. Nearly 45,000 Mizos from 109 villages were herded into 18 group centres guarded by a military company (120 soldiers) in the first phase of the regrouping. In the second phase, another 87,000 Mizos were grouped in 84 Regrouping Centres. The regrouping forced the Mizo farmer away from his lands, as he was forced to settle in roadside locations guarded by the army. This was meant to denude population cover and food support for the rebels—but, according to Amrita Rangaswami, it ended up destroying Mizoram's rural economy. Almost half of the population of the Mizo hills was affected by this displacement engineered by the army. The final phase of the regrouping could not be carried out due to a stay order issued by the Guwahati High Court, the only High Court in northeast India.[40]

Unlike in Mizoram and Manipur, the conflict between the indigenous tribes of Arunachal Pradesh, the Chakma and Hajong refugees has been simmering but has not exploded into a bloody feud. The Chakmas and the Hajongs fled from what was then East Pakistan to escape persecution and displacement in the mid-1960s. Nearly 15,000 of them belonging to 2,748 families were settled over 10,799 acres of land in Lohit, Subansiri and Tirap districts of Arunachal Pradesh (which was then centrally administered as North East Frontier Agency or NEFA). The indigenous tribes like the Adis and the Nishis resent the settlement of the Chakmas and the Hajongs who now number around 65,000. In the last few years, groups such as the All-Arunachal Pradesh Students' Union (AAPSU) have periodically organized economic blockades in areas inhabited by the Chakmas. Many villages have been attacked and some houses set on fire. The indigenous tribes are upset with the Supreme Court order in January 1996 that directs the state government to forward applications of the refugees for grant of citizenship to the federal government. The AAPSU and other local groups argue they have no objection if the Chakmas and the Hajongs are granted citizenship so long as they are shifted elsewhere in India, because they fear that in a sparsely populated state like Arunachal Pradesh with a population of less than half a million, the grant of citizenship to so many settlers would upset the power equations and make the Chakmas and Hajongs a decisive factor in the legislative politics of the state.

Organizations like the World Chakma Organization (WCO) allege that more than 5,000 Chakmas have already left Arunachal Pradesh, unable to bear the persecution as they continue to remain stateless and have great difficulty in securing education, jobs and businesses. Many have come to Assam, though in 1994 the Assam government issued shoot-at-sight orders along the border with Arunachal Pradesh. Some have gone to Tripura where the Chakmas do not face the wrath of the local tribesmen like in Mizoram and Arunachal Pradesh. The WCO and other Chakma human rights groups say that unless the Chakmas and the Hajongs are granted citizenship and provided full protection, they will be forced to look for some other place to settle. A human rights activist describes the condition of the Chakmas and the Hajongs as 'stifling, because they live in the constant dread of pogroms, economic blockade and large-scale displacement'.[41] On the other hand, some bureaucrats in the region have argued that if the Chakmas and the Hajongs are provided with citizenship and then allowed to stay in Arunachal Pradesh, that may lead to large-scale violence like in other northeastern Indian states. Here is obviously a crisis in the making and only a dubiously maintained status quo (in which even the Supreme Court order has not been implemented) has perhaps prevented an explosion.

DEVELOPMENT AND DISPLACEMENT

Development-induced displacement has been a widespread phenomenon in northeast India, like elsewhere in the country. Development projects like dams, oil and gas fields, mines and industrial projects have displaced thousands of people in the northeastern states. Among development projects, dams have so far been the single largest source of displacement in northeast India. The Dumbur dam of the Gumti hydel project in South Tripura district, intended to generate a meagre 8.60 MW of power, displaced a total of 5,845 tribal families—between 35,000 to 40,000 people in all. This writer has argued that this displacement aggravated the degenerating ethnic relations between Bengali migrants and ethnic tribespeople because while the urban Bengalis got power from the project and the rural Bengali fishermen got a huge reservoir to fish from, the tribespeople lost their land and, with it, their only source of livelihood. And so it is incumbent on the state government, dominated by the Bengalis as it is, to undo that historical injustice by decommissioning the Dumbur dam since Tripura has now discovered huge natural gas reserves and several large gas-based thermal projects are on the pipeline, more than capable of taking care of the state's power needs. The Loktak hydel project in Manipur displaced around 20,000 people as their villages went under water.

The Pagladia dam in Assam, predominantly an irrigation and flood control project, is likely to displace nearly 150,000 people when completed in 2007 and a people's committee to resist work on the dam has already come about. The Tipaimukh dam, which will generate 1,500 MW, is also likely to displace 40,000 people. Besides displacing so many people, the Tipaimukh dam, like the Dumbur dam, also has the potential to exacerbate the hills–plains conflict because it will submerge lands of the hill people in Manipur and benefit the Barak valley districts of Assam, which are Bengali-dominated. Another 20,000 to 25,000 tribespeople are likely to be displaced in Arunachal Pradesh, if the three large dams at Pugging in Upper Siang district, Ranging in East Siang district and Payum in West Siang district are commissioned. These three dams will have a combined generation capacity of 23,000 MW.

Various oil and gas fields when drilled and commissioned have displaced up to 15,000 farmers in Assam and Tripura. The tribals have resisted displacement in Domiosiat and Wakkhaji in Meghalaya's west Khasi Hills district where a huge uranium deposit has been struck. They fear radiation hazards. But if the government pursues mining of uranium, the level of panic prevalent in the area will force nearly 7,000–8,000 Khasi tribesmen to flee the area. Paper mills in Assam and Nagaland and other industrial projects, including the yet-to-be-implemented Reliance Gas Cracker project at Lepetkata, have displaced nearly 10,000 people. Even the setting up of the Indian Institute of Technology on the outskirts of Guwahati, capital of Assam, has displaced up to 600 families, around 35,000 people. These numbers may not appear big by the standards of displacement that projects like Narmada Dam may bring about; but in ethnically-sensitive northeast India, even small levels of displacement can produce bitterness and conflict if one community benefits from the projects and the others suffer. And such conflicts may produce more displacement than those caused by development projects. Displacement caused by the takeover of tribal lands by migrants has invariably led to continuous ethnic conflict and can lead to more.

ARE THE DENG PRINCIPLES THE WAY OUT?

If large-scale displacement in conflict-prone regions like northeast India has to be avoided, the government must adopt certain measures at the policy level. They are as follows:

- Illegal migration into the region from Bangladesh, Nepal and Burma must be stopped. Resources are scarce and the region's agrarian economy cannot take any further load of population. Any major inflow of population is bound to create ethnic or religious backlash, or both. For example, for purely economic reasons, the Mizos, who are ethnic cousins of the Chins from Burma, resent when the latter tend to settle down in large numbers in Mizoram.

- Rampant migration from other Indian states into the region should also be discouraged. There must be a strict national labour policy of protecting the interests of indigenous populations. Only if higher skills are not locally available, should people from other states be allowed to work in the northeast. That surely contradicts provisions of the Indian Constitution and any executive order designed to protect the interests of local labour is likely to be challenged in the courts but keeping social temperatures down is a sure way of avoiding conflict—a better proposition than handling or containing it when it explodes.

- Protection of land of indigenous peoples is a must because land alienation is one of the major sources of ethnic conflict in areas such as northeast India. If tribals lose land in a large measure, insurgency is likely and that would then lead to large-scale displacement.

- Extensive autonomy should be provided to the tribal regions before they resort to violence while demanding it.

- Having recommended autonomy for indigenous peoples and protection for their land and share of scarce resources, it is important to work out a multi-ethnic ethos of governance. No province can be totally homogenous in ethnic or religious terms and minorities are bound to be around. Even if the minorities happen to be illegal migrants who had entered the region at some stage, their present generation cannot be faulted for the decision of their ancestors. Empowerment of indigenous populations should not restrict a tough policy towards insurgents who resort to ethnic cleansing and violent militancy. There is no reason why such groups should be legitimized or unnecessarily placated as that encourages such other groups to surface when they know violence can be politically rewarding.

- Once displacement has taken place, it is important to provide security to the affected population and organize their return to ancestral villages as soon as possible. Delay in rehabilitation may create problems, like in the case of the Adivasis, who have stayed in makeshift camps in large numbers and rued the experience; the younger elements have got round and formed a militia because they had no faith left in the ability of the state to defend them. One ethnic militia which has resorted to attacks is bad enough; if they have rivals and competitors that will reply in the language of the gun, a civil war situation is bound to develop. And that would mean periodic large-scale displacement with accompanying de-humanization and miniaturization of the area.

- In India, where internal displacement is a frequent phenomenon— and one that is no longer restricted to Kashmir or the northeastern states, what with Gujarat riots of 2002—and lack of funds often impairs rehabilitation, it is necessary to develop a national rehabilitation fund which can take care of the displaced persons. The fund should be managed at the centre.

Having laid down some policy measures, it is necessary to take a look at the relevance of the Deng Principles in situations that obtain in northeast India. The General Principles (1–5) are important because they emphasize the Union government's responsibility for providing protection and humanitarian assistance. In the northeast, the Union government has generally tended to overlook this responsibility and left it to the state governments to provide protection and assistance. Even when it has provided funds, Delhi has rarely pressurized state governments to expedite protection and assistance to the internally displaced. Principle 3 (1) is most significant because it clearly says national authorities have the primary duty and responsibility to provide protection and humanitarian assistance to internally displaced persons within their jurisdiction.

Since law and order is a state subject in India and ethnic conflict is seen as a local law and order issue, rehabilitation of the victims is mostly left to the state governments. Only when two state governments are involved in a problem relating to the displacement—like the Reangs from Mizoram who are sheltered in Tripura, which wants to send them back soonest—does the centre gets involved. About two year have passed and central intervention has failed to solve the problem.

If India accepts the Deng Principles, it would have to accept that any large-scale displacement caused by conflict or development project (such as the proposed dams in Arunachal Pradesh which will give the whole country a lot of electricity) would be Delhi's responsibility. That would mean (a) a commitment to deploy central forces in such conflicts to protect the displaced persons and (b) commitment to provide funds for rehabilitation. That, in turn, would mean better care and protection and the prospects of speedy return home for those displaced. Principle 3(1) is the most relevant principle for the kind of displacement scenario existing in northeast India because it would make displacement a national problem rather than a festering local one.

Principle 1 (1) is also crucial because it would mean equal rights for the Reangs in Tripura or the Bengalis in Tripura and Assam, protecting them from confinement in camps against their wishes and scope to seek out some additional sources of livelihood to supplant any limited monetary help they may have secured access to. Principle 2 makes it obligatory for insurgent groups and other non-state actors to accept the basic humanitarian principles. Since these groups (that are so often the major source of violence leading to displacement), value global acceptability, it would be useful to bind them to some mandatory observance of humanitarian principles, flouting of which will only make them global pariahs. Principle 4 (6) that seeks to prevent discrimination is important in the northeast where majority ethnic groups controlling the state administration—like the Assamese in Assam,—often institutionalize discrimination against a displaced community, forcing them to relocate outside the state.

The Principles 5 and 6 relating to protection against displacement are the most relevant to the northeast because they explicitly bar ethnic cleansing as an option and clearly state that displacement shall not last longer than required by circumstances. That brings us to the key issue—the need to undo displacement as soon as possible, to avoid further worsening of ethnic relations, emergence of new ethnic militias born of and reinforced by a memory of pogroms and displacement, and reminding the authorities of an obligation to end displacement. Principles 7–9 are also very relevant for northeast India. They seek to prevent development-induced displacement, talk of the need for other feasible alternatives that can avoid displacement and the need to secure the free and informed consent of those displaced. This would constitute useful guarantees against displacement, if accepted. Principle 9 is particularly significant to the northeast because it reminds states of a 'particular obligation' to protect indigenous peoples, peasants, pastoralists and minorities against displacement. Indigenous peoples and minorities are two categories. One cannot underestimate the importance of Principles 10–23 that deal with protection during displacement because in northeast India this is a phase when many displaced persons fall victim to killings. Since ethnic cleansing as a tactic to promote homeland demands has been adopted by ethnic militias, their guerrillas have regularly attacked men, women and children of target communities and massacred them. Inherent right to life in Principle 10 (1) is crucial to protection of non-combatants of all warring communities who become targets of attack by the guerrillas. In 1992, Naga Lim Guards lined 87 Kuki males and beheaded them. The Lim Guards were the militia created and backed by the National Socialist Council of Nagaland (NSCN), which is now negotiating with Delhi for a settlement of the Naga insurgency. The Deng Principles, if accepted and considered binding on all combatants, state and non-state groups, would deter the armed groups and the state from perpetrating extra-judicial executions and massacres. In short, there would be pressure on both state and non-state actors to shun violence.

Principle 11 can protect women and children. The National Liberation Front of Tripura, for instance, has resorted to a large number of rapes on both tribal and non-tribal women. The non-tribals were raped when their villages refused to pay subscription to the rebels. The tribal women were raped when their menfolk refused to convert to Christianity or join the NLFT or performed Hindu rites like pujas, overruling the dictate of the rebel group. Since the NLFT has also resorted to large number of kidnappings, Principle 12 can protect the victims because it lays down that no internally displaced person can be taken hostage. Principle 13 is important because it can stop recruitment of child soldiers—a frequent practice with the newly-established rebel groups in the region. Principle 14 can however be a source of a problem: if internally displaced persons are allowed to move freely and choose their residence that can create problems for their security and make it difficult for the government to protect them. For instance, the displaced Muslims and Hindus of Bengali descent in western Assam have been attacked whenever they have entered the forests for woodcutting banned by the Bodo rebels who want to protect the forests in their area.

Principle 16 places additional responsibility on the government because it would have to inform the relatives of the missing displaced persons about their whereabouts—a commitment generally given a pass by the authorities in massacres in Mandai or Nellie. Principle 17 calls for reuniting families, which is crucial for undoing the trauma of displacement and for the initiation of a process that would reverse the displacement itself. Principles 18–23 take care of basic needs of displaced persons, guarantees medical treatment, protection of property and the right to secure documents to enjoy legal rights during displacement. Since in northeast India, as perhaps elsewhere in the country, the ethnic militias who target other communities want to displace them and take control of the properties, protection of property and handing it back is the key to undoing displacement. Principle 24 would be important in northeast India because it seeks to prevent diversion of humanitarian assistance for political or military reasons. It can prevent Mizoram-style village regrouping and displacement—or could at least guarantee assistance to those displaced by such acts. Principle 25 is important because it reiterates that the primary duty and responsibility for providing humanitarian assistance to internally displaced persons lies with national authorities. That would mean victims of internal displacement would no longer be at the mercy of provincial authorities who often represent majoritarian ethnic or religious interests and are responsible for encouraging the displacement of minorities, if not causing them. Though national authorities, particularly regimes which are sovereignty-conscious in the extreme, may be upset by Principle 25(2) which speaks of a role for the international humanitarian organizations and 'other appropriate actors' to offer services to the internally displaced, the primacy of national authorities should assuage such regimes.

But national governments may not accept the principles related to return, resettlement and reintegration of the internally displaced persons. Security and financial considerations would lead governments to deny the full participation of the internally displaced persons in planning and management of their return. Principle 28(2) would thus not be easy to accept in the context of northeast India because allowing the displaced to plan and manage their return could easily lead to more strife between battling ethnicities. And no sovereignty-conscious government would agree to Principle 30,[42] particularly in an era when the United States is seeking to find ever-new ways to legitimize intervention for pushing forward its hegemonic agenda on an evolving unipolar world order.

NOTES

1. Nandita Haksar says: 'The northeast is very distinct from the rest of India essentially because of race.' See Haksar, 'Movement of Self-Assertion in the Northeast,' in Madhusree Dutta, Flavia Agnes and Neera Adarkar (eds), *The Nation, The State and Indian Identity* (Stree, Calcutta, 1996).

2. Paresh Barua, commander-in-chief, United Liberation Front of Assam (ULFA). As stated during an interview with the author, broadcast on the BBC World Service, 21 April 1994.

3. Thuingaleng Muivah, general secretary, National Socialist Council of Nagaland (NSCN). As stated during an interview with the author, published in *Sunday*, Calcutta, 16–22 June 1996.

4. Dhananjoy Reang, founder-chairman of National Liberation Front of Tripura (NLFT). As stated during an interview with author, broadcast on BBC Bengali Service, 17 January 1998.

5. Omprakash Mishra, P.V. Unnikrishnan and Maxmillian Martin, 'India,' *Internally Displaced People— A Global Survey*, Global IDP Survey Project (Norway: Norwegian Refugee Council, 2000).

6. A.K. Bhutani, Deputy Commissioner, Kokrajhar district, western Assam, quoted in *The Times of India*, 22 August 2002.

7. Retired Lieutenant General A.K. Seth, Budget Speech in the Tripura Legislative Assembly, March 2001.

8. Monirul Hussain, 'Post-Colonial State, Identity Movements and Internal Displacement in Northeast India,' Paper presented to International Conference on Forced Migration in South Asian Region, organized by the Centre for Refugee Studies, Jadavpur University, 20–22 April 2000.

9. Former West Bengal Chief Minister Bidhan Chandra Roy's letter to Prime Minister Jawaharlal Nehru, dated 23 August 1960, quoted in full in Saroj Chakrabarty, *The Upheaval Years in Northeast India* (Kolkata: Saraswati Press, 1984).

10. Dr. B.C. Roy's letter to Jawaharlal Nehru dated 30 August 1960, in Chakrabarty, ibid.
11. Chakrabarty, ibid.
12. Monirul Hussain, op. cit.
13. Saikia, quoted in Hussain , ibid.
14. NSCN–Khaplang faction's order dated 26 July 2002, reported in BBC World Service, 29 July 2002.
15. Subsidiary Intelligence Bureau, Monthly Summary of Information from Kohima Branch Office, March 2002
16. Ibid.
17. Prafulla Kumar Mahanta, Assam Chief Minister, quoted in Reuter's report, 12 April 1989.
18. Hiteswar Saikia, chief minister of Assam in press conference at Guwahati, 29 September 1993.
19. Ranjan Daimary alias D.R. Nabla, chairman of the National Democratic Front of Bodoland (previously Bodo Security Force). As stated during an interview with the author, quoted in Reuter's report, 21 January 1994.
20. Press statement of Bodo Peoples' Action Committee, 12 October 1993.
21. Monirul Hussain, op. cit.
22. Assam Police Special Branch report dated 4 November 1993.
23. Figures quoted in Assam government's rehabilitation plan for displaced persons in western Assam in 2002. Made available to the author by A.K. Bhutani, deputy commissioner, Kokrajhar district and cross-checked from the camps by local journalist Shib Shankar Chatterji. In 2004, around 200,000 people are still in the camps.
24. Adivasi Cobra Militant of Assam (ACMA) memorandum to Assam Chief Minister Tarun Gogoi dated 5 February 2002.
25. ACMA, ibid.
26. A.K. Bhutani, Deputy Commissioner, Kokrajhar district, western Assam, quoted in The Times of India, 22 August 2002.
27. Justin Lakra, President, All Adivasi Students of Assam, quoted in The Times of India, 3 October 2002.
28. Maino Daimary, Central Publicity Secretary, Bodoland Liberation Tigers Force (BLTF). As stated during an interview with the author, broadcast on BBC World Service, 12 August 2002.
29. Meghalaya Census Reports, 1981 and 1991.
30. Dinesh Singh Committee report into the disturbances of June 1980 in Tripura.
31. Compiled from Monthly Crime Summaries of Tripura Police, April 1996 to June 2002.
32. Dainik Sambad, 11 April 2002.
33. NSCN press note dated 23 November 1993.
34. Haokip, 'Ethnic Conflicts and Internal Displacement in Manipur,' in C.J. Thomas (ed.), Dimensions of Displaced People in Northeast India (Delhi: Regency Publications, 2002).
35. Ibid.
36. Twenty-five Nagas who fled from Imphal were interviewed in Ukhrul and Senapati by this author during February 2002.
37. This author interviewed the first batch of 38 Reang families who crossed over from Phuldungsei in Mizoram to Kanchanpur subdivision in North Tripura district in October 1998. The BBC broadcast the story on 23 October 1998 in its World Today programme.
38. Zoramthanga, as stated during an interview with the author and broadcast on BBC World Service on 14 May 2001.

39. Joint memorandum by the Chakma, Lai and Mara district councils to the Indian government submitted to Home Minister L.K. Advani on 13 December 2000 in Delhi.
40. Lianzela, 'Internally Displaced Persons in Mizoram', in Thomas, 2002, op. cit.
41. Interview with Mrinal Kanti Chakma of the Japan Committee on Chittagong Hill Tracts.
42. Prnciple 30: 'Grant and facilitate rapid and unimpeded access to international humanitarian organizations' for handling internal displacement.

CHAPTER 5

BANGLADESH: DISPLACED AND DISPOSSESSED

Meghna Guhathakurta and Suraiya Begum

While in both national and international law a distinction is usually made between internal and external displacement, from the perspective of the displaced persons these terms only serve to confuse the issue. For example, the formation of ethno-national communities within the state of Bangladesh, like the Chakmas or Rakhains, has been the result of migration patterns which go back to the remote past, before even the formation of nation states in the region. Hence their identity politics or their claims to fundamental rights are often disregarded by the modern nation state. For example, the Garos of the plains of Bangladesh call themselves 'Achiks' which means hill people. This is with reference to the Garo hills, which lies north of Bangladesh on the Indian side of the border. From the Garo perception therefore, their land extends from the Garo hills to where they now reside in the plains of Bangladesh. This naturally creates a problem for both Bangladesh and India. The Partition of Bengal in 1947 helped to complicate matters. What was once one socio-economic region became divided on the basis of religion. Religion therefore was used time and again as a defence of the boundaries, which divided the two Bengals. The narrow definitions of the nation state adopted by the Bangladesh government makes it reluctant to define the political movement of the Chittagong Hill Tracts (CHT) as an indigenous movement. This is because 'indigenous' is defined as being internal or external to political boundaries of the nation state as opposed to a cultural definition of the indigenous. The narrow conceptual boundaries of the nation state therefore give rise to a kind of cultural hegemony where groups such as the ones mentioned above are excluded or marginalized. It was precisely such processes of exclusion by the Pakistani military bureaucratic oligarchy, which gave rise to the demand for a new independent state of Bangladesh. The Liberation War of 1971 had not only caused millions of people to flee across the border but had also displaced people from their natal homes, towns and villages. People took refuge wherever they could; in jungles, neighbouring villages, districts, homes of relatives, friends and even with strangers. It was said then that once you're out on the road, the road itself should find you a friend. Next to the memories of displacement by river erosion this represents perhaps the most widespread memories of displacement experienced by Bangladeshis. But the very logic of cultural hegemony did not disappear with the advent of a new state. It developed its own hegemonic cultural values, which excluded 'other' ethnic, religious groups. Some of these will be dealt with in a later section.

The Constitution of the Peoples Republic of Bangladesh is the reservoir of the principles of fundamental rights in the country. Bangladesh as a member of most UN agencies is bound by their mandates. Thus most writ petitions have to draw largely from the fundamental rights enunciated in the Constitution from Article 26 to Article 43. Articles 26 and 27 lay down the general principle that no laws of the state should be against the general principles of the fundamental rights stated in this section of the Constitution. Article 28 states that no law or policy of the state should discriminate against its citizens on the basis of religion, caste, creed or gender. The section of fundamental rights also ensures the right to defend oneself in court as well as the right to mobility, right to assemble, right to organize, right to freedom of thought and conscience, right to freedom of profession and occupation, right to practise one's own religion, right to property, right to secure one's household and self against arbitrary entry, search or arrest. Bangladesh as a signatory of UN Convention of Human Rights is also bound to abide by their mandate. In addition to being a member of UNHCR, it is bound to abide by its mandate as well as take on board the Guiding Principles relating to the IDPs. However, the above legal conditions are often violated by the Bangladeshi state, given its nature and political climate.

The Constitution of Bangladesh has undergone qualitative changes from its first draft since the principles of socialism and secularism were modified. Two hegemonic discourses dominated the text: linguistic and religious. The unitary nature of the Constitution privileges Bengali language and culture over other cultural and linguistic groups and the declaration of Islam as a state religion marginalizes non-Muslims from the ideological mainstream, notwithstanding the equality clause (all citizens are to be treated as equal regardless of class, caste, religion, creed and belief). The political movements for autonomy in the Chittagong Hill

Tracts and the violence against the minorities in the aftermath of the elections in October 2001 are both examples of such marginalization. Incidents like these have given rise to certain debates dominating civil society discourses, for example, (a) the problematization of religion and politics and (b) the acceptance by the state of the modernization paradigm in development.

CONDITIONS AND PATTERNS OF DISPLACEMENT: FIVE BROAD CATEGORIES

The following five categories depict the multifaceted nature of internal displacement taking place within Bangladesh today. We deal with them case by case.

Internal Displacement by River Erosion

Bangladesh is a deltoid land criss-crossed by several major rivers. River erosion is one of the most significant forces changing the physical landscape of Bangladesh and with it the lives of millions of people. The social impact of this erosion is incalculable. According to stricter definitions of IDPs, their displacement may not be considered as politically sensitive as that caused by aggression, occupation, or civil war. However we think it is a phenomenon which is very central to the memories of displacement in Bengal and hence essential to the specific perception and understanding of the phenomenon in the Bangladesh context.

Some of the more serious incidences of river bank erosion have occurred along the banks of the Jamuna, the youngest of the rivers entering Bangladesh from the north. Many environmentally displaced persons in the erosion-prone zone of Kazipur Union in the Sirajganj district bordering on the Jamuna have become *uthalis*, that is landless, partially dependent on the generosity of people. In our study area, the location of Kazipur proper has been totally eroded away in the period 1980–84. During 1984–87, a total loss of 969 m of bank line in the Meghai village of Kazipur was encountered.[1]

In Kazipur, 23 per cent of its total area was eroded during the early 1980s. About 46 per cent of population experienced displacement during 1980–86 and 42.9 per cent of those displaced experienced dislocation for more than four times.[2] Kazipur thana has now been relocated 75 miles northwest of Dhaka in a 138 square mile area near the village of Meghai.

The population of this thana has been formed mainly by the displaced people. Meghai is a village of Kazipur thana situated near the Jamuna. Seven to eight years ago, this village was situated two or three miles from the river bank. In the last few years, these villages were completely washed away. Water and Power Development Authority (WAPDA) has built an earth filled dam, encircling the village. Those who have lost their homes have rebuilt their homes on the slopes of the dam.

After talking to several families we found that after being made homeless three or four times, they had finally settled on the slopes of the dam. The houses were small and simple but the tin roofs were new. They claimed that they had mainly bought the roofs with their hard-earned savings although some said that they received some help from the Union Parishad Chairman. It was later known that the tin roofs would be made available, as part of the government relief fund but the Union Parishad members would extort money from the poor villagers in exchange for this benefit. Not many people could afford to pay this amount. People therefore make an effort to save, often by forgoing food, to buy the tin roof in the market as it saves from repairing their houses every year. On top of this, in the event their houses are washed away again, they can take the roof with them and set up house elsewhere. Almost all the settlers on the dam said that the land was not government property but belonged to relatives or kin who let them stay. Later we were informed by some lawyers that when a government institution acquires land to build an embankment, it buys up land both on the site of the embankment as well as surrounding areas. So the land the people had built their houses on was very much government property. They had denied it out of fear that if they admitted to this fact they would be evicted.

The main source of income for uthalis was cultivation of crops. Rice was the staple crop grown in the area for six months of the year. The Jamuna floods the land the rest of the year. The uthalis informed us that very few of their children go to school. As one old man told us rather sadly, after getting an education, the children leave home for the town and they do not look after their elders, or those left behind, so it is better that they do not receive education in the first place. It was noticed that though time and again the river ravages their homes and lives, uthalis generally tended to build their homes by the bank of the river. They do that in the hope that when new *chars* (new land formed by sedimentation of the river) rise in the river, they would perhaps get some of their lost land back. Many however said that they have yet to see their forefathers' land rising from the river.

Because of continuous erosion of land, uthalis fail to settle in a one particular place. They have little or no certainty in their lives and all they can think of is how to get food the next day. In the village of Meghai, they are relatively stable because a spur has been built which would give protection against further erosion. Their local MP, who was the home minister in the Awami League government that was in office from June 1996 to June 2001 and held considerable power, accomplished this. But despite this there is yet to develop any standard of living among the uthalis. Access to basic healthcare facilities is often not available. One respondent said that his son had died for lack of proper medical treatment. The communication system was worse several years ago. Now there is a metalled road. An indigenously designed vehicle locally called *bhotbhoti* serves most of the communication needs of the area. It is a three-wheeler run by the motor engine of a shallow tube well. But it will not be true to say that all uthalis are poor. Some, over the years, have done well for themselves. One such example is Abdul Aziz.

Abdul Aziz lives in the newly acquired land of Kazipara thana (police station). After being displaced for about four or five times, he has finally settled in Kazipara since the last 13 years or so. He works in a construction company situated near Dhaka. His sons and daughters are educated. Aziz told us that uthalis usually settle where they have relatives or neighbours. Those like him who owned sizeable land in the char lands, would scout around to buy land in higher grounds once they sensed that their lands will be washed away. He, for example, had bought six decimals of land in Kazipara. The land price of Kazipara however has rocketed sky high over the last five years. This was both because of the protective spur on the river as well as the construction of the Jamuna bridge. As a result of the bridge, the currents were slower on this side but it was affecting land on the other shore. Abdul Aziz thought that the area had benefited from having a powerful minister as a local MP during the tenure of the Awami League government from June 1996 to June 2001. He could get things done. But after the change of government, he feared that the area may be victimized by the current regime, the Bangladesh Nationalist Party with the Jamaat-e-Islami that came to power in October 2001.

Internal Displacement due to Armed Conflict: The Chittagong Hill Tracts

Internal displacement in the Chittagong Hill Tracts occurred during the armed conflict from the mid-1970s to 1997. The violent conflict in the

Chittagong Hill Tracts between the 13 different ethnic groups and the Bengalis of the plains has been the root cause of one of the largest occurrences of internal displacement in Bangladesh. This spanned over three decades until an accord was reached between the armed wing, the Jana Samhati Samiti (JSS), demanding autonomy of the *jumma* (slash and burn cultivators), and the Bangladesh government in 1997. A Government Task Force estimated that as of July 2000, 128,000 families were internally displaced in this region.[3] The three decades of forced evictions, terrorization as part of counter-insurgency techniques and planned settlements of plains land Bengalis in the CHT have caused havoc in the life of people who refused to flee to India. After the accord many refugees have come back to find their land taken away and occupied by Bengali settlers and military. They now join the ranks of the internally displaced.

Background of the Armed Conflict

The CHT occupies an area of 5,093 square miles or 13,295 sq. km constituting 10 per cent of the total land area of Bangladesh. The CHT has long been a problematic region of Bangladesh, because of its strategic location between India and Burma.[4] Prior to the creation of Bangladesh as a state 33 years ago, the population in the CHT was mainly composed of 13 different indigenous tribes, commonly called the Jumma people.[5] The indigenous population is predominantly Buddhist and their culture and social customs differ from the rest of the Bangladesh population. Until the 1960s, the CHT enjoyed a high degree of autonomy with little interference from the ruling governments.[6] Conflict over land together with the pressure for assimilation into the majority culture of Bangladesh constituted the background to the armed conflict.[7] Among the ethnic groups, the Chakmas, Marmas and Tripuras constitute the majority. Non-indigenous hill people, that is Bengalis who are predominantly Muslims also at present live in the CHT.

According to the 1991 Census, the total population is 974,465 out of which 501,145 (that is 51 per cent) are from different ethnic groups. About 49 per cent are Bengalis. It is to be noted that about 70,000 refugees who were in the Indian state of Tripura from 1986 to 1998, are not included in this census report. Out of the total land of the CHT, only about 3.1 per cent is suitable for agricultural cultivation, 18.7 per cent for horticulture and the rest 72 per cent for forestry.[8] Apart from the land issue, militarization, the transfer of population from plains districts and the control of administration by non-inhabitants of the CHT, the discrimination, deprivation and exploitation in social, cultural, economic and political fields and the programme of assimilation of the indigenous hill people into the majority Bengali population are concerns which have attracted attention, national and international.

Since the 1960s, and particularly after the creation of Bangladesh, the government resettled the landless, poor, Muslim Bengali peasants from the densely populated and land-scarce delta region, in the CHT. Often, the local tribal population was evicted from their land. An armed indigenous group, Shanti Bahini, waged a low-level conflict in the CHT from the early 1970s. The government responded by forcefully imposing its strategy of 'Bengalizing' the CHT until a peace agreement came into effect in December 1997.[9] In addition to a fast-growing military presence in the region, Bengali settlers were also mobilized against the indigenous population. During this period, the demography of the CHT changed drastically: from constituting only 9 per cent of the population in the CHT in 1947, the non-tribal propertion increased to almost 50 per cent in the Census of 1991.[10]

Information about uprooting of the indigenous population varies. Amnesty International states that more than 50 per cent of the indigenous population were forced to leave or fled massacres, arbitrary detention, torture and extra-judicial executions,[11] while the U.S. Committee for Refugees (USCR) more carefully estimates that some 64,000 Jumma people sought refuge in India while more than 60,000 others became internally displaced.[12] After more than two decades of armed conflict, a Peace Accord was signed in 1997 between the government of Bangladesh and the main organization of the indigenous people, PCJSS. Since then, the Bangladesh government has maintained that virtually all problems in the CHT have been solved.[13] However, although the Accord paved the way for the return of Jummas who had sought refuge in India, it did not resolve the problem of internal displacement in the CHT. The land issue remains at the core of the problem of internal displacement. While property rights of the tribal population have been regulated by local traditions and not registered in public records, the Bengali settlers obtained official documents certifying their ownership of the land. After the Peace Accord, the Bengali settlers were dispossessed of land previously belonging to returning Jumma refugees and their papers were considered invalid. Many Bengali settlers were therefore relocated several times upon return of the Jumma refugees, and in some cases made landless. According to figures from the government CHT Task Force, some 38,000 Bengalis had become internally displaced in 2000.[14] However, PCJSS does not consider non-tribal people as internally displaced and demands that they be relocated outside the CHT.[15]

Not surprisingly, many Bengali settlers, backed by the military and the main opposition party in Bangladesh, refused to give up the land to the returning Jumma refugees. Based on available figures, it may be suggested that about 30,000 persons have not been able to regain possession of their land—thus making them internally displaced upon return to the CHT.[16] For the estimated 60,000 Jumma people who remained internally displaced within the CHT during the conflict, the situation is still unresolved. While at least half of the refugees got their land back upon return from India, the large majority of the internally displaced are waiting for their cases to be solved by a land commission that was created as part of the Peace Accord. The work of the land commission has not yet started. The internally displaced are therefore left in the same situation as when the Accord was signed seven years ago.

Apart from the land question, other parts of the Accord remain to be implemented, the most serious being that most of the non-permanent army camps have not been closed down. The tribal population is reportedly still victim of human rights abuses by Bangladesh security forces.[17] Furthermore, the Peace Accord is heavily criticized from different sides. Groups within the Jumma society say that the agreement does not provide enough autonomy. The Bangladesh National Party, the winner of the national elections in October 2001, says that the Accord discriminates against the Bengali population in the CHT.[18]

Very limited information is available regarding the current situation of the internally displaced in the CHT. Although the conflict in the CHT caught the attention of the international community and the Peace Accord was generally well received, the presence of international actors on the ground is limited. While humanitarian access has improved and the government launched a rehabilitation package for the internally displaced, no information has been found on assistance activities specifically targeting this group. A study from one area claimed that the internally displaced population suffered from starvation and diseases.[19] Most of the internally displaced live scattered in the remote and inhospitable hill and forest areas with limited livelihood and with no access to healthcare facilities.[20]

Causes and Patterns of Internal Displacement Caused by Conflict

The displacement of indigenous people of the CHT started in the then East Pakistan on the completion of a dam at Kaptai near Rangamati between 1957 and 1963.

At least 54,000 acres of settled cultivable land, mostly farmed by the Chakma tribe, were lost in 1957 when the government began the construction of the Karnaphuli hydroelectric project. Over 400 square miles of land were submerged with far-reaching effects on the economy and lifestyle of the tribal people there. Some 100,000 people (18,000 families) lost their homes and prime agricultural lands. Compensation for lost land was inadequate and over 40,000 Chakma tribals crossed the border into India where the majority has sought Indian citizenship.[21] During construction, the dam flooded an area of some 655 km, which included about 22,000 ha of cultivable land—40 per cent of all such land in the CHT.

The issue of resettlement of the displaced people was handled poorly because of a number of reasons. First, there was a general lack of understanding of the tribal culture by the government of Pakistan and the donor agencies (the dam was funded by the USAID). They thought that these were 'nomadic' people and it was unnecessary to design a permanent resettlement programme for them. In reality, the tribal people did move from hill to hill but they had a long cycle of jhum cultivation. Before the inundation of the Karnafuli valley, the average cycle of jhum cultivation was 7 to 10 years, and in some cases 15–20 years. After the flooding that took away 40 per cent of the fertile agricultural land, this cycle became reduced to only 3–5 years due to the loss of soil fertility caused by intensive agriculture.

But the main period of displacement was during the more than two decades of armed conflict in the form of insurgency and counter-insurgency operations in the Chittagong Hill Tracts. During the conflicting period, at least 12 massacres upon the hill peoples were committed by Bangladesh armed forces. As a result of this conflict, a kind of centrifugal and centripetal tendency of population displacement was observed. Just to avoid the conflict and atrocities of the military, some groups of hill people silently moved towards the small towns and administrative centres while others moved toward the deep forests and were compelled to live a kind of nomadic existence. In 1986 at the height of the conflict, 60,000 of them had become refugees in Tripura state of India.[22]

People displaced between August 1975 and August 1992 are considered as IDPs. Some 60,000 tribal people were internally displaced during this period though estimates have varied. They included people whose villages were attacked, whose neighbours were massacred and whose homes were burnt during army operations.

Case Study: Kabita Chakma

Kabita Chakma, president of Hill Women's Federation, writes her story of displacement. Kabita Chakma came from a large family of six. Her father was a primary school teacher. She remembers the terror of army raids when she was in classes one and two. All the grown boys and men used to run away. Her mother used to take a sickle in her hand and pretend to work in the field clearing the jungles with the little ones by her side. Women also went to the market instead of boys, since boys were often suspected and caught. Women were harassed on the streets as well, but even that seemed a lesser price to pay than if their boys were caught or murdered. The army used to come and steal or demand chickens for themselves. Her father was a village headman. He was responsible for head counts, which the army often demanded. Any missing persons or guests had to be reported. If there were anyone missing then they would beat up the persons present.

When she was in class eight, they gathered all the villagers to interrogate them on what they knew about Shanti Bahinis. She saw them threatening to kill people unless they told the truth. She saw one boy being beaten as he was suspected. An army camp was next to her village. Hence their raids were frequent. They did not seem to bother a Marma village nearby however. Therefore the Chakmas suffered the most. Neighbouring Bengalis would attack them sometimes, sometimes along with Marmas. After the Panchchari battle of 1986–87, Shanti Bahini became divided. Then the raids became very frequent. Everyone took shelter in the hills. They could hardly take their meals properly. One night they had to flee while they were eating their evening meal. Because her father was the Karbari (village headman) he had to return to the village. The target was the school teacher's house. The army noticed her father and chased him into the jungles. Her father managed to escape but was badly scathed and bruised by thorny bushes. Once they were put on a list drawn up by the JSS to go to Tripura, India. Usually the JSS would give the green signal to say who could go. But because her father was headman, the village would suffer if he left, so they did not go. Her father was caught one day as he went to report the guests in the village. He was imprisoned for several months. He was tortured; needles were pierced through his fingers, his arms smashed by bricks. The army then declared the houses in the village should be dismantled and cleared. People were to tear down their own houses and go elsewhere within one month. Most people left for India. Kabita's family left for their aunt's place. They saw their neighbours tearing their houses and storehouses and granaries with their own hands. They did the same. Her mother who had been a simple housewife took up a job as school teacher. She used to run after people, officials, so that her husband would be released. Kabita remembers going to see her father once. He was almost mad. He kept asking for money from other prisoners. He was released after 9–10 months. After a while her aunt too became a refugee. Then Kabita went to stay at her married sister's house for a while. She could not attend her classes regularly and had to drop a year. She remembers a *daroga* (a Bengali police officer) who used to visit their house regularly. Her mother used him to do *tadbir* (lobby) to release her father. But the daroga started liking Kabita and wanted to talk to her. Kabita found it repulsive and demeaning but would be scolded by her mother if she did not talk or be nice to him. She therefore used to run away when she sensed him coming. After her father was released on bail, they rented a house. They bought some land there. It was in this village that Kabita came in touch with some women activists of Pahari Nari Shomiti. They inspired her to work as well. They used to meet in a library set up by a group of young students. She used to sit there quietly listening to others discussing the problems of the day. She described herself as very shy. Her shyness was such that when after school she used to pass the boys' college, her knees would melt into water. But the group treated her affectionately. They used to go to *gono* picnics (peoples' picnic) and special festivals. They were involved in active welfare type of work, for example supplying water during Kothin Chibar Dan festival. Girls who went to study in Chittagong were active. But it was not until 1990–91 that the Hill Women's Federation emerged as a force (Meghna Guhathakurta, 2002).[23]

Estimates of the Internally Displaced Population in the CHT

The Government Task Force on CHT, set up just after the Accord, concluded that by the end of 1999 a total number of 128,000 families were internally displaced. The government CHT Task Force finalized figures for internally displaced at the end of 1999 at 90,208 tribal and 38,156 non-tribal internally displaced families. The Chittagong Hill Tracts Commission says that about 500,000 people are internally displaced. The chairman of the Task Force says that IDPs are too scattered to be contacted easily and thus to be named in the list of the IDPs. Unknown source estimates that 250,000 people were internally displaced at the peak of the conflict. The Task Force has sent to the Ministry a list of 128,364 families (or approximately 500,000 individuals) of internally displaced persons to be rehabilitated, comprising 90,208 Jumma families and 38,156 non-permanent settler families. The number of internally displaced refugees identified by the Task Force is huge if one takes into consideration the total population of roughly 600,000 Jummas and 500,000 Bengalis in the CHT. This means that about half of the population of the CHT has been designated as displaced by the 25-year-long conflict.[24]

Table 1
Statistics of Refugees in the Greater Chittagong Hill Tracts

District	Tribal families	Non-tribal families	Total
Khagrachari Hill district	8,126	876	9,102
	11,189	3,858	15,047
	3,541	2,755	6,296
	8,096	1,800	9,896
	1,925	3,122	5,047
	6,249	7,802	14,051
	4,659	1,036	5,695
	2,085	121	2,206
	700	1,001	1,701
	46,570	22,371	68,941
Tribal families	46,570		
Non-tribal families	22,371		
Total families	68,941		

District	Tribal families	Non-tribal families	Total
Bandarban Hill district	1,906	0	1,906
	1,648	2	1,650
	1,800	10	1,810
	90	0	90
	591	176	767
	1,153	81	1,234
	378	0	378
	477	0	477
	8,043	269	8,312
Tribal families	8,043		
Non-tribal families	269		
Total families	8,312		

Table 1 contd.

Table 1 contd.

District	Tribal families	Non-tribal families	Total
Rangamati Hill District	304	0	304
	3,723	0	3,723
	297	12	309
	4,553	0	4,553
	2,598	2,568	5,166
	6,439	1,281	7,720
	165	59	224
	7,253	7,463	14,716
	1,659	203	1,862
	2,895	1,636	4,531
	5,709	2,294	8,003
	35,595	15,516	51,111
Tribal families	35,595		
Non-tribal families	15,516		
Total families	51,111		

Source: Norwegian Refugee Council/Global IDP Project, 2001.

The government CHT Task Force includes Bengali settlers who had to leave the land upon return by the indigenous population. USCR and Amnesty International estimate more than 60,000 internally displaced, but these figures do not include the tribal population. Hill people and the government disagree on the definition of internally displaced in the CHT (2000). According to the Peace Accord, the internally displaced refugees were to be rehabilitated by the Task Force. One of the most contentious issues in connection with the rehabilitation of these internally displaced refugees was over the role of the Task Force. A major conflict erupted between the government and the JSS leadership over the mandate of the Task Force, or more concretely over the question of whether Bengali settlers should also be considered internally displaced people. The Task Force had sent to the ministry a list of 128,364 families (or approximately 500,000 individuals) of internally displaced persons to be rehabilitated, comprising 90,208 Jumma families and 38,156 non-permanent settler families. The Task Force chairman Dipankar Talukdar (Jumma MP for Rangamati district) had given instruction to include Bengali settlers, but the JSS vehemently opposed this, fearing that this could lead to the legal recognition of settlers as residents of the CHT and thereby as legal owners of the land.[25] Even in 2004, many people who were rehabilitated claimed that they could not reclaim their lands nor did they get the compensation due to them.

Systemic Internal Displacement in a Majoritarian Democracy: Post-Election Violence and Religious Minorities

Whilst communal violence has been a regular feature of politics during the Pakistan era, the establishment of an independent Bangladesh on the basis of secular ideals had offered to the polity a sense of citizenship as opposed to that of religious sectarianism. Even though the word secularism had been omitted from the 1975 Constitution, a non-sectarian concept of citizenship was something quite acceptable in the Bangladesh polity until recently. As regional and global politics became more and more influenced by religious fundamentalism, sectarian identities of Hindu and Muslim re-emerged in the arena of politics. That by itself would not have unleashed the violence against the Hindu minorities, such as on 2 October 2001. Rather the incident was the result of machinations of vested interests who saw it to their advantage both politically and economically to use sectarianism as political vendetta against the Awami League. The increasing communalization of politics in Bangladesh has been marked by a significant rise in the exodus of Hindus to India. But there are still many among the Hindu community who do not consider it as a first option. For such people frequent internal displacement has become almost a way of coping with contemporary political realities.

Discrimination against Hindus

As a minority community in Bangladesh sharing a language and religion with the Indian population of West Bengal, Hindus have been subjected by Muslim groups in Bangladesh to discriminatory practices and attacks. No government in Bangladesh since independence has taken any decisive steps to protect Hindus in the face of potential threats, including during the current attacks. The wave of attacks against the Hindu community in Bangladesh began before the general elections of 1 October 2001 when Hindus were reportedly warned by members of the Bangladesh National Party-led alliance not to vote, as it was believed that Hindus would cast their votes for the Awami League, their key adversary. The backlash after the elections was systematic and severe. Reports indicate that the worst-affected areas were in Barisal, Bhola, parts of Pirojpur, Khulna, Satkhira, Gopalganj, Bagerhat, Jessore, Comilla and Norsingdi. Attackers reportedly entered Hindu homes, beat up members of the family, looted their property and, in some cases, raped Hindu women. One of the affected villages was Ziodhara. Fear of backlash created a severe atmosphere of tension in the village. Several hundred Hindu villagers left for fear of being attacked and Hindu children would not attend schools. In another village, Deuatala Bazaar, gangs of young men wielding sharp weapons reportedly went from door to door telling Hindus to 'go away'. Hundreds of Hindu villagers reportedly left the village. In the village of Daspara in Mirersarai *upazila* (sub-district), a gang of about 25 youths reportedly attacked homes of Hindus around midnight on 5 November 2001. One person, Sunil Das Sandhu, 28, was reportedly hacked to death and 16 others were injured, some seriously. They ransacked houses, looted them, dragged family members out of their homes and beat them. Police reportedly arrested 12 persons in connection with this attack, but it is not known if they were charged.

Hundreds of Hindu families have fled across the border into India because they have been attacked or threatened. They have been trickling into India reportedly either by paying bribes or crossing along the remote, unmanned border areas. According to *Agence France-Presse* of 29 October 2001 they have either ended up in camps or gone to their distant relatives. Hindus interviewed by journalists have said they have been targeted because they were thought to have been supporters of the defeated Awami League. Some Hindu places of worship have also been attacked, including one in Chandaikona Bazaar in Royganj area in Sirajganj on 22 October 2001 by a group of youths who damaged Hindu idols and looted the place. Human rights organizations in Bangladesh believe that over 100 women may have been subjected to rape. Reports persistently allege that the perpetrators have been mainly members of the BNP or its coalition partner Jamaat-e-Islami. Rape victims are often reluctant to disclose their ordeal. What follows is a sample of the available information. A college student was reportedly raped in front of her mother at her home in Azimnagar, Faridpur. The attackers reportedly entered her home on 6 October 2001 at about 9 p.m., ransacked the house, looted valuables and raped the student before leaving the house. A school girl was reportedly gang-raped in Delua village in Sirajganj sub-district on 8 October. Attackers entered her home, ill-treated members of her family, took her outside the house and raped her. Two Hindu women were reportedly raped in front of their husbands on 11 October in Khanzapur upazila in Gournadi, Barisal. The attackers reportedly came at night, knocked at the door, and told the family that they should leave the area because they had voted for the Awami League.

A number of Hindu girls were reportedly abducted. It is not known whether or not they have returned to their families. A gang of armed men reportedly abducted three Hindu girls at the village of Nohata in Magura district on 11 October 2001. The men reportedly entered their home at midnight and took the girls away. Another girl was reportedly abducted from her home at Razarchor in Barisal district after the attackers were not paid a large sum of money which they had demanded for leaving the family alone. They also molested the girl's mother and her aunt. There are fears that all of these girls may have been subjected to rape.[26] Following a petition filed by a Bangladeshi legal aid organization, Ain-o-Salish Kendra, the High Court ordered the government on 26 November to explain why it had not done more to protect the country's Hindu religious minority. The court gave the government one month to respond. The following case study depicts the long term effects of the atrocities committed and especially how families have become internally displaced in the process.

Case Study: Bhola

It was slightly more than three months that certain villages in Bhola had witnessed one of the worst forms of violence against the Hindu minority community in the post-electoral violence beginning 2 October 2001. A team of Ain-o-Salish field investigation unit visited the area. The purpose was to follow up the situation in Bhola, both at the grass-roots as well as with the local administration and look into prospects for developing individual cases as well as offering legal aid to victims. Two villages were visited: Annoda Proshad at Lalmohan Upozila where victims from the neighbouring Fatemabad village also came, as well as Char Kumari in Bhola Sadar Thana. In addition, efforts were made to talk with local police officers, commissioners and the superintendent of police, and district commissioner of Bhola.

It is interesting to note that although the two villages we visited were about 65 to 70 km apart, victims in both villages reported almost the same time of the first attack, that is the evening after election day. This was unlike normal communal uprisings where an incident in one place will be followed in another and hence spread like wildfire. It can be assumed therefore that there must have been a common source. Also interesting to note is that despite what the district commissioner told us about the unanticipated nature of the incident ('it took us all by surprise'), victims especially in the first village told us that they had been fearing such an attack. In fact, in the latter village, some had taken precautions to send the women in their family to secure stations. Many daughters-in-law were sent to their natal villages for security. The reason for their fear stemmed from the threats they had been receiving from BNP cadres before and during the elections. They were told not to cast their vote. Many did not go to vote, but one or two who did were beaten back from the polling station.

The attack on the Hindu minority on 2 October was conducted in both cases by men linked with the victorious party in the national elections of 2001, the BNP. In one village, the attackers were recognized as being men residing in and around the area who supported the BNP. In another village the men who attacked had their faces covered, but some of them declared that they 'did BNP'. Some Muslim villagers who themselves claimed to be supporters of BNP but had given shelter to Hindu women and children, had complained to BNP local leaders that their houses had been looted. In return they were scorned for giving shelter to Hindus and were told that was not a sign of being a 'Mussalman' or a supporter of BNP.

Looting of Hindu households and sometimes Muslim households which sheltered Hindus took place throughout the night and in waves, since most householders had fled in terror and their houses were left unguarded. No distinction was made between rich and poor households. Some of the victims said that even babies' clothes were stolen. Although men were terrorized as well, it was women and children who had to bear the brunt of the attack. Once they saw the attackers the women came out and begged for mercy or begged to have their husbands spared. The attackers then turned on the women, sometimes asking one woman to fetch another one by name, or else attempting to drag the women by hand. When a 12-year old girl refused to call her mother she herself was raped.

That night everyone had to hide in the rice fields, fending off water-leeches from their hands and legs and that of their babies and children. Some women also had to climb trees in order to rescue themselves. But the fear of more attacks prompted many to stay away from their own houses for more than a week, sometimes two weeks. In the second village we visited a mother who claimed that for 15 days her sons were forced to live in the betel nut orchards (*supari bagan*). Sometimes she would try to take food down to them, but the sons would hardly be able to eat due to sheer terror. If they could afford to do so, individual couples rented apartments in the nearest town for several months before returning to their homes. In the villages it was poor women who were hit most hard, since they earned their living through labouring in the land and they could no longer do that due to physical insecurity. Among the Hindu community there were a few female-headed households where the men were working in India. Their security was especially endangered. One such woman who lived with relatives found security by cooking for the emergency police force which was stationed there after the incident. No local NGOs had come to their rescue with programmes of relief. Organizations from Dhaka that had visited these villages to investigate the situation proved to be their only hope for salvation and relief. There were some cases of exodus into India, but only for those households that already had someone living there. But in many cases the victims said that they were too poor to take that option. In other cases where families came from the landed class, they still had too much at stake here to flee without preparation. Their exact words were: 'What shall we eat in India? We have to resort to begging'.

Although some steps were taken by the administration to arrest some of the more obvious culprits in one of the worst-hit places and an emergency police force was stationed in the vicinity of Annoda Proshad village, the systematic denial of these incidents nationwide prevented sterner measures being taken by local administration. People felt intimidated by the fact that some of the culprits were still roaming free and that those who had been arrested were being released on bail. Many culprits were reported as saying: 'So what if we had to go to prison, it was temporary, almost like going to one's in-laws' place for dinner.' The role of the administration from local to district level was at best dubious. Apart from the setting up of the police camp in the vicinity of Annoda Proshad there was little indication that the administration was taking positive steps to file charges or find and bring the culprits to justice. The people in Char Kumari complained that the police had not filled in specific charge sheets for weeks after the incident. There was a definite lapse of time (a few days) before the police even arrived at the scene to investigate. There were also reports of attempting to cover up complaints which had been made. For example, in the village of Annoda Proshad, a woman had wanted to file a case regarding her husband who was missing. But the local level leaders tried to coax her into believing that he had gone to India and had even produced a letter which was read out to her since she was illiterate. But the odd thing was that the officer in charge (OC) when asked about the incident repeated this story and he too gave the same excuse as to why a case could not be lodged regarding this 'disappearance'. The district commissioner on the other hand seemed more sympathetic and was keen to maintain peace but also did not want to take any action that would displease local elites.

Locally it was only the media which reported faithfully the incidents and followed them up regularly. The role of the politicians however has been wanting. Local MPs have either reportedly been inciting the attackers or indirectly supporting them by protecting the culprits from law-enforcing agencies. The minister for Religious Affairs elected from this area was sympathetic but was too far away in the capital to be able to monitor the day-to-day events. The centralization of power within the party structure has been paralleled by a geographic centralization in the capital. Thus a large number of MPs who win seats in parliament are occasional visitors in their constituencies and normally reside only within the limits of the capital city. Hence much of their political control over their constituencies is handed over to their local henchmen, who in turn exercise control over local administration as well (not unlike absentee landlordism of past eras). When the time comes to distribute the booties of an electoral victory, there are obviously more candidates to satisfy than there are resources and hence leaders often turn a blind eye to consequent processes of extortion, which go on in the localities. One of the characteristics of the assaults of October 2001 was that most of them took place in rural areas. And in this kind of politics, characterized by techniques of 'char dokhol' or 'chandabaji', it is easier to justify extortion to their political leaders if the victims happen to be political opponents or their die-hard supporters, or in other words those outside the purview of state power. Indeed one even stood the chance of being offered the post of a minister or state minister as a reward for it!

The participation of religious minorities in mainstream politics has been largely marginalized with the establishment of a pro-Islamic ideology. Even so because of the specific historical connection of the Awami League with secularist ideas, the minorities have been identified as a substantive vote bank of Awami League. However, the existence of many structural discriminatory practices as well as the Vested Property Act which was for over three decades, until it was repealed by the previous Awami League government, which was in power from 1996 to 2001, responsible for systematic and pervasive eviction of Hindus from their homesteads. The nature of the party structure and leadership has contributed towards both the criminalization and communalization of politics. The issue of the assault on minorities is therefore enmeshed in a complex web of power relations, which characterizes the current nature of politics in Bangladesh. Many say it is a careful plan to reduce the number of Hindu voters and create a separate electorate for them so that they no longer become a vote bank for the Awami League. Others mention that this is due to the machinations of a powerful circle allied to the ruling party whose own petty interests often override the concerns of a national government.

Economic Displacement in a Globalizing World: Shrimp Cultivation

The southwestern region of Bangladesh consists of the southern lowlands of the present districts of Bagerhat, Khulna and Satkhira. It is a coastal area constituted by the fresh waters of the innumerable rivers and distributaries, which end up in the saline waters of the Bay of Bengal. It is a region which houses part of the world's largest mangrove forests, the Sundarbans. According to the Gazette of 1978, the area covered by the Sundarbans was recorded as 2,316 square miles. The Sunderbans is an area traditionally well known for its biodiversity but gradually succumbing to the mono-culture of shrimp cultivation. Shrimp cultivation is not only using up agricultural land but also *khas* or government-owned land, which by law is to be distributed by the local government to the landless. Another important deprivation is the loss of grazing land. Lack of fodder also prevents poor people from raising goats and poultry as income-generation activities. This has often left only one opening for income generation in the area and that is fishing for small fries in the numerous rivers of the locality. All this is affecting not only the poor in the region, but more specifically the women. They are victims of the socio-economic transformation described above. Most women are either divorced, or deserted by their husbands. The husbands are forced to leave because of the lack of means of livelihood in the area. Shrimp cultivators do not use local labour for their farms; instead they bring in labourers from other regions for this kind of seasonal work. As a double curse for the destitute and deserted women, many of these men enter into relationship and marry them only to desert them again when the season is over. We thus see internal displacement taking place directly, through people being evicted from their agricultural land due to pressure exerted by powerful shrimp farmers, as well as indirectly, by people changing their professions, from dependence on land to dependence on the market for survival.

Structural transformation is evident in changing class hierarchies within the region. For example, during and after the Partition of 1947, the area was mostly Hindu dominated with the Hindu zamindars controlling the lion's share of the landholding. It was also an area, which had yielded a great variety of crops along with the staple rice and where the adjacent

Sundarbans forests and the intertwining of the multitudinal rivers provided employment opportunities of a wide variety. Hence a stratified system of caste-specific hierarchies was also predominant which evolved
round particular occupations, for example, *kolus* (those who grind oil from
mustard seeds), *rishis* (trading in leather and leather products), *moualis*
and *bawalis* (thriving on the forests), and weavers and fishermen. Traditional subsistence agriculture also included subsidiary activities like cattle
rearing and poultry farming, all of which are endangered due to the environmental degradation resulting from shrimp cultivation. All these
activities, as well as the position of those whose subsistence depended
on these activities, are undergoing change. For some, the cash economy
being introduced with the advent of the shrimp industry has proved to be
a blessing, especially those who could adapt their skills to the changing
scenario. For example, the landless labourers who could switch to fishing
for fries in the rivers are assured of a steady income, which was no longer
haunted by the scourges of *Mora Kartik* (the lean season of Bengal when
spectres of famine loom large). Or even those like the *Kolus* who used to
grind mustard seeds to produce oil for the market have merely changed
into petty traders buying from the oil mills and selling the oil in the local
bazaars, thus transforming a productive community into a trading one.
The caste-oriented professional boundaries are also undergoing change.
Previously, many of these communities were looked down upon as their
work was not considered clean by the upper-caste Hindus. But currently
many of these professions which have proved lucrative are being taken
over by peasants and landless labourers outside the traditional caste boundaries. The injection of the cash economy, therefore, is eroding traditional
caste boundaries and in certain cases, a certain upward mobility among
the poor can be noticed. For example, those who catch fries mention they
can get 50 to 60 taka per day for an average catch. This is ready cash in
hand, whilst as daily labourers, cash payment would be uncertain and
their payment would partially be in kind, for example one meal a day.

But there is another side to the picture. Not everyone is benefiting
from this transformation. Many among the poor still hold onto their lands
and are used to tilling the land. They somehow do not possess the apti-
tude to do any other kind of work. They are the ones who feel intimidated
by the changes taking place. They also feel that the shrimp industry is
aggravating the difference between the rich and the poor. Thus we see
that structural changes are taking place in two ways. First, those who
have a lot of land are benefiting from a windfall gain in profits reaped
from leasing their land to shrimp farms. This is turning a class of

hardworking farmers into a rural-based intermediate class. However, they admit that there is a certain degree of risk involved since the payments promised may not be as forthcoming from the *gher* owner if a virus affects the crop. Second, it is also creating a class of poor who are not left with any other alternative work except to work for the industry through collecting and selling fries or work in the farms or leasing their lands to them. Environmental degradation has succeeded in displacing agricultural and agriculture-related work and activities like rearing of cattle and poultry. It has also proletariatized a class that previously could depend on the economy of a stable agricultural household. Now everything is bought and sold in the market. There is no stock of rice available for handouts in the lean season any more.

Case Study

Women of the area particularly are victims of the socio-economic transformation described above. When I visited a local group of 18 women who were members of local NGO, Sushilan, they all turned out to be married but without husbands. Three were widowed, their husbands killed by tigers in the forests while foraging for their living. The rest of the women were either divorced or deserted by their husband due to lack of agricultural land. The picture of shrimp farm areas or *ghers* as they are locally known are areas of social conflict and tension. The common source of these conflicts is the issue of land usage since shrimp cultivation has brought radical changes in land use patterns (Ghafur et al., 1999).[27] The state manifests itself in these conflicts at different levels. The government of Bangladesh supports shrimp cultivation since it is supposed to bring in much coveted foreign exchange into the economy. Processed shrimp, they maintain, comprises the largest export commodity of these newly-generated employment opportunities. Since the 1980s, the government of Bangladesh has been offering incentives to businessmen based in cities to enter into this profitable business. It has extended support by way of administrative backup and bank loans. There are supposed to be regulations such as the condition that voluntary consent of 85 per cent of local landowners must be had before taking over land for shrimp cultivation. But the entry point of businessmen who were outsiders to the area had been ensured through the use of locally hired musclemen together with political support, especially by local authorities. As case after case showed, it is this configuration which has been at the root of most of violence in the area.

In a report on the socio-economic and environmental impact of shrimp culture in southwestern Bangladesh by Ghafur et al. (1999), the authors list the principal sources of social conflict in the *gher* areas:

1. forced or false contractual agreement on leasing of land
2. non-or partial payment of lease-money called Hari
3. dispute over *khas* land
4. insecurity owing to physical torture and molestation of women
5. fear generated by environmental impact
6. semi-intensive mode of shrimp culture
7. deteriorating health
8. state patronization for farm-owners

Some of the violence took the form of murder or attempted murder, grievous bodily harm or infliction of deliberate injuries. Abductions also take place in connection with shrimp-related controversies. Setting ablaze of farms has also been known to happen to put pressure on the opponent. Implicating opponents in false cases is a very common tactic. In all this, the state mechanism plays a vital role. The government policy, law and its implementation all go in favour of the rich shrimp farmer and turn a blind eye to the interest of the landless peasant and marginal farmer. Social tension arises from the insecurity of food and lack of work opportunities for a large number of coastal people. Shrimp cultivation brings in rich and powerful outsiders who often control the areas at gun-point, and their hired hooligans play havoc in the areas.[28]

Local authorities, especially, play an intermediary role in this situation. Charges against hooligans and musclemen are often not framed and the labyrinth of time-consuming legal procedures more often than not deters victims from seeking justice. Even when a case is being tried, local musclemen are active in preventing any eyewitnesses from giving evidence in court, as well as bribing local level officials so that they ignore or twist that evidence. In one case where a criminal case had been filed against hooligans who beat up a poor farmer, it was reported that the officer in charge of the particular police station had dropped the names of the main accused from the charge sheet. The trial was still on but the local people were sceptical of its outcome or effectiveness. In another case of double murder, allegation of partiality was brought against the Assistant Police Superintendent of the Criminal Investigation Department (CID) Khulna who after a long investigation was to submit a charge sheet regarding the double murders committed over the control of Bidyar

Bahan Gher. CID Headquarters rejected the memorandum of evidence and the case was transferred to the Jessore zone.[29] In other incidents where cases have been filed by the 'shrimp lords' themselves, especially against poor landless farmers, the police were quick in their arrests, and their hyperactivity came under suspicion.[30]

Poor women in the shrimp areas were concerned primarily with their security. In many cases they were held hostage to the tyranny of the shrimp lords. Their insecurity was enhanced by the fact that they did not feel that the local authorities were there to protect them but rather added to their worries. Poor landless women spoke of various instances when they were allegedly apprehended by the police and charged of smuggling sarees across the border. Women caught by the police were often trafficked across the border to be sold as housemaids and prostitutes in India, Pakistan and the Middle East. Therefore women were always on the alert not to fall into such a trap. Among the most common type of insecurity that women faced in these areas were rape, threat, false cases, cattle lifting, physical torture. Verbal abuse, forced marriages, fear of theft, dacoity and terrorism were also not uncommon. The triggering condition for all insecurities however was the scarcity of food and cash.[31] With the state playing such a restrictive and negative role for the poor in general and women in particular, it is not surprising therefore to witness the outburst of many resistance movements in the area and the active participation of women. One of the more popular stories of resistance is around the killing of Karunamayee Sarder in Polder 22.

Karunamayee Sarder, of village Bigordana under the Deluti Union of Paikgacha thana, was a leader of landless women's group and member of the Bittyahin Shamabai Samiti. The local people and Karunamayee's family alleged that mercenaries of the shrimp lord Wazed Ali Biswas killed her ruthlessly. Wazed was planning to set up a shrimp farm forcefully and illegally over two thousand *bighas* of land in the village of Horinkhola of Polder 22. For this, he wanted to get a lease agreement from a few absentee owners. But most of the inhabitants, mainly landless and marginal peasants, were strongly opposed to shrimp farming because of the hazards it brought with it. From the experience of neighbouring polders they were alerted that the whole area may be affected by salinity and the ecosystem would be destroyed. Health hazards accompanied the salinity and land would then be unfit for cattle grazing. Polder 22 covers an area inhabited by 10,000 people from 14 villages. The area consists of about 11,000 bighas. A 17-km long embankment was made to protect the crops from saline water. Under financial assistance from the government of Netherlands, a project was undertaken to ensure the development of the polder area agriculturally and socially. An NGO called Nijera Kori and the subsequently-formed local Bittyahin Shamabai Samiti was given responsibility for this project. So the movement was spearheaded by these organizations. On 7 November 1990 at about 10.00 a.m. five trawlers carrying cadres of Wazed Ali came to Horinkhola to cut the embankment in order to set up a shrimp farm. Hearing the news, members of the Bittyahin Shamabai Samiti brought out a peaceful procession, chanting slogans in protest against the shrimp farm. Wazed's men attacked the innocent people ruthlessly with guns, bombs and sharp instruments. Karunamoyee who was leading the procession died instantly, part of her skull severed from her body. Twenty more people were seriously wounded. The 7th of November is observed every year in memory of the late Karunamoyee, who is still regarded as a martyr in the locality.[32]

The death of one Zahida Bibi and the movement which it led to was yet another event which caused much uproar in the area. The year was 1998. Here too the root cause was a group of influential and powerful people who in collaboration with local government officials and the police sought to forcefully evict thousands of landless families and acquire several hundred acres of land for shrimp farming. It was illegally done through the bribing of local officials and producing false documents. The landless then organized themselves together and started petitioning the local leaders and MPs. Despite the mobilization, when the district magistrate ordered the police to occupy the land in question, the landless organized a protest march and confronted the police. It was at this time when Zahida Bibi, a landless woman carrying a child in one arm and a broom in another as a symbol of her protest at being made homeless, broke through the police barricade and marched towards the district magistrate. This took the officials by surprise and they gave the order to shoot. Zahida Bibi and her child were mowed to the ground by bullets. Many people were injured. It took several hundred angry demonstrators to keep the pressure on the government to take effective measures against the officials.[33]

Displacement due to Forced Eviction by the State

The city of Dhaka has a population of over 11 million today and it is estimated to be growing at 4.7 per cent per annum. Of this population, it is estimated that 46.7 per cent are living in abject poverty with about half of this group categorized as living in object poverty. Landlessness, natural calamities, river erosion and lack of income-earning opportunities push the rural poor to urban areas, indicating a process of urbanization of poverty. This process is manifested by the sprawling growth of slum and squatter settlements especially in the capital city of Dhaka. The slum-dwellers constitute a floating population who are driven from one slum to another. Although the poor are an integral part of the city, their right to live in the city is not recognized by the authorities including the central government agencies and local government. There is the school of thought that the urban poor should be taken back to the villages and resettled there and indeed such a programme is currently being implemented. The National Housing Policy, 1993 (revised in 1999) recognizes that slum settlements should be upgraded with security of tenure. However, successive governments have been resorting to violent evictions and sometimes using subtle methods. On 11 August 1999, when the Bangladesh government decided to evict several city slums, several thousand slum-dwellers faced the prospect of being made homeless again. At the same time, the slum-dwellers with the civil society raised their voice in protest. From 8 to 10 August 1999, the slums of Kamalapur, Titipara, Balur Math, Gopibag, Doyaganj, Gandaria and Juraine were cleared. The people living in these slums were very poor and when the government evicted them in the name of rehabilitation and various training programmes, they became internally displaced in the real sense of the term.

When the government declared its eviction policy in August 1999, several NGOs started protesting from the very beginning. On 11 August 1999, Ain-o-Salish Kendra and Bangladesh Legal Aid and Services along with two slum-dwellers named Ismat Ara Dipu and Rohima filed a writ petition in the High Court. This writ was filed on the basis of fundamental rights described in the Constitution. The petition read:

> ...the petitioners being committed to protection and promotion of human rights and the rule of law and conscious of their constitutional obligation and the law to maintain discipline to perform public duties are concerned about the recent cases involving basti (slum) people who are now exposed to the imminent threat of illegal eviction and demolition of their residences without assigning any reason or issuance of notices as has already been suffered by many basti dwellers in different parts of the city which subverts the rule of law and undermines the protection of laws guaranteed by the Constitution and also the serious tension and fear of eviction and demolition of properties of the basti people.[34]

The Division Bench of the Court ordered the government to postpone the slum eviction programme until the hearing on this writ petition began. On 19 August the slum-dwellers started residing with their families on the premises of the Supreme Court and in the National Idgah Maidan. They also settled in the pavement outside Dr Kamal Hossain's house in Baily Road. In the context of this situation, the bench of the High Court Division consisting of Judge Asgar Khan and Judge Fazlul Karim advised the government to clear the slum through a step-by-step rehabilitation and they ordered the removal of the slums in front of the Supreme Court and in front of Dr Kamal Hossain's house in 24 hours. But even after the judgement, slum eviction has been continuing.

Ironically during the period of the caretaker government (July to October 2001), over 12,000 families were evicted in the name of cleaning up the city of criminal elements. The Report of the Fact-finding Mission of the Asian Coalition for Housing Rights (ACHR) and Centre for Housing Rights and Evictions (COHRE) of 2000, documents in detail the situation faced by the poor of Dhaka. Since the publication of this report, the caretaker government commenced evictions under the pretext of cleaning up the city before the general elections. During the month of August 2001 large-scale demolitions and evictions were carried out by Rajdhani Unnayan Kartripakkha (RAJUK) and other government organizations. The worst affected by these evictions were women garment workers who came back to their sleeping shacks after their shift to find them demolished. Rough counts made by NGOs indicated that about 12,000 families were affected. Ironically settlements upgraded under the UNICEF's Urban Basic Services Programme were also demolished. Coalition for Urban Poor (CUP) organized a protest rally, prayers and a high-level seminar to stop the evictions. NGOs also organized the communities who were threatened with eviction, to resist. Under tremendous pressure from organs of civil society and the resistance from the communities the government then stopped the evictions.

Case Study: Urban Cleansing of Agargoan

The area known as Agargoan is the location of some of the new office blocks of government and international organizations. The view from these modern offices is the sprawling slums down below. These slums have been in existence for over 20 years although the lands have been allocated to different departments for the construction of offices. In January 2002, an eviction order was issued by the ministry of Housing and Public Works to the inhabitants of the Amotoli Bustee. Ain-o-Shalish Kendra (ASK), a human rights NGO, filed a case in the High Court against this order. On 9 February 2002 the High Court issued a 'show cause' notice to the ministry of Housing and Public Works and the Police. The ruling of the High Court was that alternative accommodation must be provided. This Court ruling was seen as a great victory for the poor people of Agargoan and to the NGO community working with them. Sadly this was not to be. Since the Court order made evictions illegal, authorities devised new tactics of eviction. The new strategy takes the form of the police raiding the houses in the night and arresting men and at the same time *mastans* (hooligans) move into the settlements—looting, harassing and raping women. They carry on these activities for a few days consecutively and the poor people have no choice but to leave the settlement. Only a very few of the people are arrested on charges like possession of drugs or illegal arms, and rest are arrested and released after a few days. None of the women have come forward to make a complaint because of the police involvement in the actions. NGOs working with the people stated that this action is well organized and that it has been carried out systematically with a similar pattern in each case. Coalition for Urban Poor and their affiliated NGOs have been gathering information regarding the movement of families out of the Agargoan slums. The information reveals that in July 2001, 13,613 families were living in the bustees in this area and by 10 March 2002 only 4,620 still remained. People have moved out into other settlements in the outskirts of the city towards the river bank. Rents in other slums have gone up 3,000 taka per month, as a result of the sudden demand. This method of eviction is a violation of all forms of human dignity and the fundamental rights of the poor. This form of 'urban cleansing' can be compared only to ethnic cleansing. It is about time that the international human rights organizations paid attention to plight of the poor in Dhaka.

The process of displacement through slum eviction can be understood through the following case study: Raushon Ara came to Dhaka 12 years ago to visit her sister and got married to a rickshaw-puller. After getting married she started living in the slum of Balur Ghat area where there were almost 500 small huts with four to five persons living in each of them. All the huts in the slum were made of mud. They formed a union in the slum and the procedure of renting and leasing home in the slum was done through this union. On 8 August 1999, the government demolished the Balur Ghat slum by a bulldozer. Raushon Ara informed us that they were not provided with any notice from the government before the demolition. The authorities ordered the slum-dwellers to leave the slums on the spot. Though they did not get any notice, they did hear rumours that such a move may take place some days prior to the eviction. At the time of eviction Raushon Ara was unable to shift her house as her husband was out to work. The houses were looted at the time of eviction. After this, Raushon Ara had no other option but stay under the open skies for three days with her family. Then she rented a house in Mugdapara on a higher rent and she didn't get any compensation for her loss in the eviction. And she knows for sure that she never will.[35]

To know more about the legal basis of slum eviction, we talked to two people from ASK. They told us that ASK had filed a writ petition against the slum eviction on the basis of fundamental rights according to the Constitution. The right to liberty and the right to protection is described thoroughly in Articles 27, 28, 31, 32 of the Constitution. There is no existing law in Bangladesh concerning the right of the landless to live on public land. So ASK petitioned on the basis of fundamental rights. There was no direction, but observation in the judgement that was announced in this case. But in the case of removing slums from the Supreme Court grounds and from Dr Kamal Hossain's house, there was a definite direction as the involved area was not fallow and some activities were going on there. The United Nations Commission on Human Rights and Regulation 1991/92 clearly declare that 'forced eviction constitutes a gross violation of human rights, in particular the right to adequate housing and urge governments to undertake immediate measures at all levels aimed at eliminating the practice of forced eviction.'[36]

Case Study: Forced Eviction of Sex Workers from Brothel

The brothel of Tanbazaar situated in Narayanganj near Dhaka was one of the biggest brothels in Bangladesh. This brothel was started at the time of the British colonial period. At that time, Narayanganj was one of the largest duty-free ports in Asia. After their arrival, the British gathered together women from around the villages through coercive measures for the purpose of entertainment. Later these women were socially boycotted. These internally displaced women from different villages were gathered here in Tanbazaar and eventually a brothel was formed. Several attempts were made in the past to evict the residents of this brothel. At last, on 24 July of 1999, the sex workers of Tanbazaar and Nimtoli were evicted with the help of the government, arrested and sent to vagabond centres in order to be rehabilitated. This incident created different responses in society. On 25 June 1999, a committee consisting of 51 members under the local MP Shameem Osman was formed to end prostitution and to rehabilitate the sex workers. On 29 June, 13 out of 16 house owners in the brothel agreed to leave this profession willingly. On the night of 30 June, the police conducted a raid in the brothel arresting 16 clients. The sex workers panicked when this happened. Early next morning, a sex worker named Jasmine was murdered and the situation in the area deteriorated. A large number of police was posted on guard both inside and outside the Tanbazaar area. On 3 July it was announced in a public meeting that the sex workers would not be evicted but rehabilitated. The then Prime Minister Sheikh Hasina announced a grant of taka two crore for their rehabilitation. On the other hand, as tension spread in the area, the clients stopped coming and the sex workers began to disperse from the brothel. On 14 July various leaders of the brothel convened a press conference and urged the government not to evict them from Tanbazaar and Nimtoli. In this press conference, the sex workers were helped by several women organizations like Naripokkho, Care Bangladesh, Nari Moitri, Bangladesh Women Health Coalition and their own organizations of sex workers like Durjoy, Mukti Nari Shongho, etc. But on 24 July at 3 p.m., police attacked the area of Tanbazaar and Nimtoli. Sex workers were picked up in a police van by force. Their leader, Shathi, was also arrested by the police. The rest evacuated their homes leaving everything behind, for fear of being arrested by the police. The number of sex workers sent to the vagrant centre in Gazipur, was 267. There were approximately 5,000 sex workers at that time in Tanbazaar, and 34 magistrates and 140 police personnel participated in this raid.

The sex workers were kept in inhuman conditions in the vagrant centre of Gazipur. They were physically tortured. Reporters and journalists were not allowed inside the centre. They were not supplied with adequate food or medicine and many of them tried to run away from the centre. The government decided to give credit and technical training to the sex workers. Fifty-nine organizations together formed a human rights front named Shonghoti to protest the eviction and human rights violation of the sex workers. But protesters were attacked by a group of thugs. On 1 August 'Volunteer Association—59' filed a writ in High Court against constitutional rights' violation. On 14 March 2000 the High Court pronounced the judgement of this case. This was as follows:

The High Court Division of the Supreme Court has declared that the profession of sex workers was not illegal, but that they had a right to fend for their living in any way possible. Their evictions from Nimtoli and Tanbazaar brothels and putting them into vagrant homes were unlawful.

The Court observed that the profession of sex workers was not illegal since they were in it to earn their livelihood, like any other profession. The right to life as guaranteed by the Constitution under Article 31 could be treated as a right to livelihood which is a fundamental right that cannot be taken away except in accordance with the process of law. The right to livelihood of the sex workers is enforceable as a fundamental right. This verdict of the High Court is the recognition to the right to movement and right to choice of the sex workers. Later, on 30 March 2000 the Apellate Division of the Supreme Court stayed the High Court judgement till 30 April 2000.

We talked directly to some evicted sex workers named Shilpi, Maya and others from Tanbazaar on 10 May 2002. Shilpi was one of the leaders of the sex workers and had attended several press conferences before. She was also taken to the vagrant home in Gazipur. While describing the situation of the vagrant home, she told us that they were given two pieces of bread with molasses each morning and only softened rice both for lunch and dinner. As they were brought all of a sudden they could not bring any extra clothes, nor were they supplied with any clothes from the centre. Many a time they had to wear gunny bags. Their life in the centre was inhumane. Though the government promised that each sex worker would be given 7,000 taka each, with a sewing machine, this was not properly distributed. On the other hand, the guard inside the centre who was known as jomadar sexually harassed them. Shilpi herself could only leave the vagrant home after providing sex to the guard. Shilpi was in the vagrant home for about a year and then she saw that the only help offered to them in the centre was providing the sex workers in the home with medical treatment. Shilpi told us that she had been displaced as a result of the eviction. Before she had a roof over her head. After escaping from the vagrant centre she started to live on the streets and worked as a floating sex worker. One night at about 10 p.m. police beat her in front of everyone as they recognized her to be a leader from Tanbazaar area who had given a speech in one of the meetings. While beating her, the police said that she was polluting the area. After this she started living on another street. Now she is living in Kamrangir Char area, a squatter settlement by the river, but as a working place she chose the Shangshad Bhavan area. She had a son. When he was six-month-old she left him by the side of

Science Laboratory road and went to entertain a client. When she came back, she saw that her son had been brutally kicked by the police, and he died soon after. Now she has a girl aged one-and-a-half. She comes to work leaving her alone at home. She also said if her girl does not get accustomed to this, it will be impossible for her to work. Shilpi told us that the amount they earned in Tanbazaar had severely decreased after they were evicted. Moreover she had to share her earnings with the local hooligans, police and middlemen. She informed us that she and others had not wanted to continue in this profession, but the lack of government assistance and the insecurity of their future had compelled them to choose this profession.

RECOMMENDATIONS

In this section we try to summarize some of the lessons learnt from the above cases in the form of recommendations and strategies for the government, non-government agencies and international bodies. We do this keeping in mind the UN Guiding Principles on IDPs. First we point out the general characteristics, which we saw in the review of the cases of displacement. Then we go step by step into recommendations to be taken: (a) protection from displacement; (b) protection during displacement; and (c) resettlement and reintegration of displaced people.

General Characteristics

Internally displaced people in Bangladesh do not enjoy equal rights as citizens and have been discriminated on the basis of one or more of these categories: ethnicity, religion, sex, social status (by virtue of being poor) and property. Displacement in the Chittagong Hill Tracts was an obvious case of ethnic discrimination and the assault on mostly Hindu minorities in the post-2001 election by ruling party cadres was definitely strategized on the basis of religious constituencies. The forced and illegal eviction of sex workers from the Tanbazaar brothel hinted at sexual discrimination and exploitation, but this along with other cases of eviction such as that by river erosion, the forced eviction of slum-dwellers and landless peasants was based on poverty; that is, the vulnerability of the displaced people was based on their lack of property and access to resources. In most cases we have seen that their legal status was affected, that is their displacement was proved to be a violation of the fundamental rights as upheld by the Constitution of Bangladesh. In all cases of displacement discussed we have seen that women and children have been specifically affected, but no cognizance has been taken of this fact except in the case of sex workers and that too in a negative way. Furthermore, in cases of forced displacement by the state, displacement has taken place as result of an executive order and not empowered through proper legal processes as in the case of the settlement of Bengali settlers in the Hill Tracts or the sex workers of Tanbazaar.

Protection from Displacement

- Since river erosion is a systemic occurrence in Bangladesh, there should be some kind of local level planning to take care of the issue, keeping in mind the environmental implications. A central policy like the Flood Action Plan once conceived by the government was heavily criticized due to its environment unfriendly nature but more long-term local level planning is suggested instead of leaving it to ad hoc solutions which is the present situation. For example, the people in Sirajganj thana feel protected only because steps were taken to prevent river erosion by a ruling party MP who incidentally happened to be home minister between 1996 and 2001.
- The distinct cultural and national identities of the indigenous Jumma peoples of the Chittagong Hill Tracts, and the implementation of effective measures to protect and promote them through organs of regional autonomy, should be guaranteed through constitutional safeguards.
- The customary rights of the Jumma people to use and control the land and the natural resources of the Chittagong Hill Tracts should be recognized and safeguarded.
- The Chittagong Hill Tracts should in all practicality be considered as a demilitarized zone.
- An administrative region with organs of self-government, having powers that are constitutionally guaranteed so that no modification thereof is possible without a constitutional amendment and without informed agreement by the representative bodies of the indigenous Jumma peoples of the Chittagong Hill Tracts should be recognized. The regional council, elected democratically by the indigenous Jumma people and containing safeguards for the representation of all the indigenous Jumma peoples of the Chittagong Hill Tracts, women, and minority residents of the Chittagong Hill Tracts, should

have real political powers including budgetary powers to make and execute decisions.

- *Khas* land should not be distributed to *gher* (shrimp farm) owners as it overwrites the directive that local authorities are empowered to distribute it to the poor and needy.
- As land is taken up in river erosion, it is very much necessary to keep extensive records to avoid unpleasant situations occurring in *char* lands (embankments) and shrimp farm areas.
- Despite the existence of a National Housing Policy (1993), there is still a dire need to provide adequate accommodation and necessary sanitation facilities for the urban poor. Therefore it is just as necessary in the case of slum eviction to establish the constitutional rights of slum-dwellers and give them proper rehabilitation. Long-term plans should be made because slum eviction is a continuous process in Bangladesh. When a slum or brothel is demolished from one place, it starts building up in another as a result of lack of rehabilitation.
- The government of Bangladesh has neither admitted nor identified the post-election violence in October 2001 on the minority communities to be a problem. That this is an ideological problem and its roots are deep inside the society, should be admitted as a fact. A problem cannot be overcome unless it is identified as a problem. The same thing goes for brothel eviction.
- A more humane practice of law enforcement is suggested and excesses of the law enforcement agencies should be given exemplary punishment.
- If decision for displacement is legally taken by the state then full information should be provided and proper rehabilitation measures undertaken.

Protection during Displacement

- In cases of displacement due to river erosion, slum eviction, etc., children's education is severely disrupted. In this respect the government should have a continuous and long-term planning
- In all cases of displacement, pillage of property and goods is common and people are financially ruined. To stop this tendency, adequate protection of lives and property should be ensured.
- Murder, rape and torture are a common feature in all the above-mentioned cases which is a violation of human rights. Various

organizations, especially women's organization should raise their voices on this issue.

- Poor Bengali settlers in clustered villages in the Hill Tracts have often been used as a 'human shield' for army camps during armed conflict in the Hill Tracts. These people should be given right of mobility and other freedoms.
- The right to freedom of thought, religion, beliefs and opinion should be ensured even during the period of displacement.
- The right to employment should not be affected when a person is displaced from his regular habitat. If necessary, service rules should make allowances for employees affected by flood, river erosion or other such natural or man-made disasters, which cause them to be temporarily dislocated.
- In the ultimate case where the displaced persons seek to migrate elsewhere either outside the country or in any other region within the country, they should be allowed to do so.

Return, Resettlement, Reintegration

- An end to the government-sponsored movement of settlers into the CHT should be effected and agreement reached by the parties on a programme for their systematic withdrawal from the CHT. Such a programme should respect the human rights of all concerned, and could include financial incentives or compensation for the persons who are being relocated.
- Illegal eviction of returnees from transit camps must be prevented. In cases where state parties are involved in such eviction practices (see special report on eviction of returnee refugees from transit camps at Dighinala), civil society pressure should be exerted at local and national levels.
- Cluster villages of the Jummas need to be dismantled and an invitation extended to the Representative of the United Nations Secretary-General on Internally Displaced People to study the full problem of internal displacement of Jumma people within the Chittagong Hill Tracts.
- Resettlement, as well as maintenance of freedom and security, is necessary for minorities affected by post-election violence as well as those forcefully evicted from their lands and slums.
- A mechanism should be built which would ensure the return of plundered property and goods of returnees.

- No documentation has been found on aid specifically for internally displaced persons. Rehabilitative programmes need to take cognizance of the UN Guiding Principles for IDPs in a more serious and systematic way.
- Rehabilitation centres should be made more humane places where displaced people may be given long-term training in skills which would prepare them for the competitive job market. International monitoring of these agencies should be permitted.

CONCLUSION

Many of the above recommendations hinge on the existence of a pluralist, secular, transparent and accountable state, a description which Bangladesh fails to fit into given the above narration of its political development. To be that kind of state Bangladesh must ensure:

- respect for human rights, including the rights of women as stipulated in the UN convention on all forms of discrimination against women;
- the practice of secularism in society and state. This practice can be established through the parliament and educational system. National politics should be related with international politics in such a way that it does not play any acute role on the people;
- to establish the fundamental rights of the citizens as inscribed by the Constitution;
- to establish transparency and accountability of all state and non-state institutions.

One therefore has to address the issue of IDPs in Bangladesh within this broader perspective. To make a transition from the existing situation to an ideal one, it is not only the policies and practices of the government which should undergo change, but the media, civil society and its institutions too must have a role in facilitating such change both at the level of the state and within its own institutions. It has been noticed that the media and civil society have a major role to play in preventing cases like ethnic cleansing, post-election violence and slum and brothel eviction. Freedom of thought and speech should be maintained at all costs in the society and the state. The community affairs of different races, religions and ethnic groups should be practised nationally so that people retain faith in a pluralist and multicultural ideology despite the fact that Bangladesh is a Muslim majority state. On the other hand, state should protect the right of practising the religious festivals of different religions. But most of all, with regard to the specific case of internally displaced persons, awareness raising programmes based on the principles of the UN Guiding Principles on IDPs should be designed for all state bodies, NGOs and other voluntary and civil society groups working within Bangladesh.

NOTES

1. M. Mafizuddin, 'The Characteristics of Riverbank Erosion: Kazipur Case Study,' in K.M. Elahi, K.S. Ahmed and M. Mafizuddin (eds) *Riverbank Erosion, Flood and Population Displacement in Bangladesh*, Savar: Jahangirnagar University, 1991.
2. Ibid.
3. Chittagong Hill Tracts Commission (CHTC) Report, 2000. '"Life is Not Ours"—Land and Human Rights in the Chittagong Hill Tracts, Bangladesh'.
4. Thomas Feeny, 'The Fragility of Peace in the Chittagong Hill Tracts, Bangladesh,' *Forced Migration Review* (October 2001), http://www.fmreview.org/fmr119.htm
5. Unrepresented Nations and Peoples Organisation (UNPO), 1998, Chittagong Hill Tracts, http://www.unpo.org/member/chitta/chitta.html
6. Amnesty International (AI), Human Rights in the Chittagong Hill Tracts, Bangladesh, February 2000. http://www.web.amnesty.org/ai.nsf/Index/ASA130012000? Open Document&of=COUNTRIES\BANGLADESH
7. Ibid.
8. Norwegian Refugee Council/Global IDP Project, Profile of Internal Displacement: Bangladesh. 2001. As of 28 November 2001, compilation of the information available in the Global IDP Database of the Norwegian Refugee Council, http://www.idpproject.org
9. AI, February 2000, op. cit.
10. UNPO, 1998, op. cit.
11. AI, 2000, Annual Report 2000, http://www.web.amnesty.org/web/ar2000web.nsf/countries/7ea2b2a68ae6360a802568f200552902?OpenDocument
12. US Committee for Refugees (USCR), Country Report for Bangladesh, 2000, http://www.refugees.org/world/countryrpt/scasia/bangladesh.htm
13. United Nations Committee on the Elimination of Racial Discrimination (UNCERD), 'Eleventh Periodic Reports of States Parties due in 2000, Addendum Bangladesh,' 30 May 2000, (UN ref. CERD/C/379/Add.1), http://www.unhchr.ch/tbs/doc.nsf/(Symbol)/CERD.C.379.Add.1.En?Opendocument
14. International Federation of the Red Cross (IFRC), 'Humanitarian Assistance, Appeal no. 01.22/2000, Situation Report no.1, Covering Period January–June 2000', July 2000. http://www.ifrc.org/cgi/pdf_appeals.pl?emerg00/01220001.pdf
15. Netherlands Development Assistance Research Council (RAWOO), 'Mobilizing Knowledge for Post-Conflict Management and Development at the Local Level', Advisory Report, no. 19, May 2000, http://www.nuffic.nl:3500/rawoo/19.pdf
16. AI, February 2000, op. cit.

17. United Nations Committee on the Elimination of Racial Discrimination (UNCERD), 'Concluding Observations of the Committee on the Elimination of Racial Discrimination: Bangladesh (Concluding Observations/Comments)', 22 March 2001, (UN ref: CERD/C/58/Misc.26/Rev.3), http://www.unhchr.ch/tbs/doc.nsf/(Symbol)/CERD.C.58.Misc.26.Rev.3.En?Opendocument

18. AI, February 2000, op. cit.

19. 'Displaced People in CHT in Bad Shape,' *Daily Star News*, 16 February 1999. http://www.dailystarnews.com/199902/16/n9021601.htm#BODY5

20. USCR, 2000, op. cit.

21. AI, February 2000, op. cit.

22. Mrinal Kanti Chakma, 'Empowering the Internally Displaced Peoples,' Paper presented to The Regional Conference on Internal Displacement in Asia, Bangkok, Thailand, February 2000, http://www.thirdculture.com/jpa/jcc/editorial/idps.htm

23. Guhathakurta, 'The Nature of the Bangladesh State', in Hameeda Hossain (ed.), *Human Rights in Bangladesh 2001* (Dhaka: Ain-o-Salish Kendra, 2002), 19–34.

24. CHTC, 2000, op. cit.

25. Ibid., 48.

26. AI, 2000, Annual Report 2000, http://www.web.amnesty.org/web/ar2000web.nsf/countries/7ea2b2a68ae6360a802568f200552902?OpenDocument

27. A. Ghafur, Mesbah Kamal, Matiur Rahman Dhaly and Sayema Khatun, 'A Final Report on the Socio-Economic and Environmental Impact of Shrimp Culture in South-western Bangladesh: An Integrated Approach, (Dhaka: RDC, 1999), 52.

28. Ibid., 52.

29. Ibid., 60.

30. Ibid., 64.

31. Ibid., 87.

32. Ibid., 63–64.

33. Mridha, Kanailal Mridha, 'Nirjatito Bhumiheen o Shahid Zahidar Hottyar Kobita,' in Saydia Gulrukh and Manosh Chowdhury (eds), *Kortar Shongshar: Naribadi Rochona Shonkolon* (Dhaka: Rupantor, 2001).

'Nirjatito Bhumiheen o Shahid Zahidar Hottyar Kobita' is a poem about the oppressed landless and the killing of Zahida. The title of the book, *Kortar Shongshar: Naribadi Rochona Shonkolon*, which contains the poem, translates as 'The Master's World: A Collection of Feminist Works'.

34. Supreme Court of Bangladesh, High Court Division (Special Original Jurisdiction), Writ Petition No. 3034 1999, ASK and others vs. Govt. of Bangladesh and others, 1999).

35. Refugee and Migratory Movements Research Units (RMMRU), Eviction of Status, Role of the State, Civil Society, Dhaka, July 2001.

36. UN Conference on Human Settlements, Report of the Habitat, Vancouver (1976).

CHAPTER 6

BURMA: ESCAPE TO ORDEAL*

Sabyasachi Basu Ray Chaudhury

This chapter is about the nature and magnitude of contemporary internal displacement in Myanmar. Myanmar is a country, which was virtually under British colonial rule for more than one hundred years and very briefly came under Japanese occupation during World War II. The post-colonial existence of Myanmar has largely been influenced by military rule and the problems of ethnic nationalities, insurgencies organized by the aggrieved minorities and tough counter-insurgency measures of the military junta. In that sense, Myanmar has a past that would find very few comparable counterparts elsewhere in the world. The problem of internal displacement in Myanmar has to be looked into against this complex backdrop of the country's socio-political situation. Under the circumstances, it may not be possible to go into a detailed analysis of the varied experiences of the internally displaced people in Myanmar. Instead, I will concentrate mainly on a narrative history of the situation of the IDPs in Myanmar. I will briefly analyse the conditions and patterns of displacement in this context. Looking back to that recent past, I will attempt to analyse the legal situation in Myanmar in the light of the UN Guiding Principles on Internal Displacement (1998) and in the broader context of human rights. I will also deal with the contemporary political climate in which these mechanisms have to operate. Finally, there will be a brief analysis of the available remedies and deficiencies in arrangements or absences thereof.

---

*Officially Burma is now considered Myanmar. But different ethnic groups residing in Myanmar are not in favour of this name. For this reason, many western news agencies still use 'Burma' instead of 'Myanmar'. Considering this, I have used 'Burma' at least to refer to the colonial period of the country.

LOCATION AND THE COLONIAL LEGACY

Myanmar lies between 92 degrees and 102 degrees east longitudes, and 10 degrees and 28 degrees north latitudes. It has a total area of about 230,800 square miles. As modern Myanmar is situated on the borderland of different cultures, Mongoloid and Indian, people belonging to competing cultures and civilizations have often fought each other on the soil of this not-so-big country. The country with huge rice fields, varieties of flowers and fruits, and monasteries and pagodas, is located between the contemporary constructs of South and Southeast Asia. In other words, due to the unique geographical location of Myanmar, the people living there have frequently found themselves caught in the crossfire. The Irrawaddy, Salween and Chindwin rivers encircle the rice-producing flatland in the country, and the Irrawaddy delta offers fertile agricultural land. While Bangladesh and India lie southwest to Myanmar, China is in the north, and Laos and Thailand have borders with Myanmar in the east. To the south and southwest lies the sea. A variety of large and small ethnic groups reside in Myanmar. Major among them are: Burmans, Karens, Mons, Arakanese (or Rakhaines), Chins, Kachins, Karennis (or Kayahs), Nagas, Pa'os, Palaungs and Was. In the pre-colonial period, the rulers in the lower Burmese kingdoms often claimed suzerainty over surrounding mountainous areas. Some kind of patron–client relationship was also found between these kingdoms and people in the mountains. The local chiefs and princes used to send tributes to the kings in the lowland.

The British merchants first entered Burmese waters in the early Seventeenth century. In 1824, the British captured the Tenasserim and Arakan regions and finally annexed lower Burma in 1852–53 and central and northern Burma in 1885–86.[1] In a way, Burma was under the British colonial rule for more than one hundred years. If the competition and rivalry among the Burmese ethnic groups were in a way postponed for an uncertain future, then their conflicts began to resurface with more complications with the outbreak of the World War II and became crucial once it was understood that the colonial masters were about to leave the country. With the disappearance of the common enemy, that is, the British, the mask of unity among some of the local inhabitants quickly peeled off.

The erstwhile feudal society of colonial Burma was, in no time, adversely affected by the post-colonial conflicts emerging or re-emerging with the modern political concepts and ideologies. As the Burmans were going to be handed over power after de-colonization, their leaders were keen to map the nation in order to fit it in the proposed Union of Burma. As a consequence, the 'frontier areas' with hilly terrain and sparse population were to be 'included' in the new state. The autonomy they enjoyed earlier was soon to be replaced with the centralization of power in the hands of the Burmans. Perhaps one exception was General Aung San, the person leading the pre-independence executive council. He selected several non-Burmans for several high-ranking jobs in the government, visited the ethnic nationality areas, and organized a multi-ethnic conference at Panglong, Shan town. This conference aimed to frame a political structure acceptable both to the Burmans and non-Burman ethnic minority groups. The concept of a federal union was accepted at Panglong although all the major ethnic groups did not participate in the conference. The Karens, for instance, attended the conference as observers. The Kachins, Shans and Chins, however, participated in it.[2]

Originally, four ethnic states were to be created. The Karenni and Shan states were even accorded the right to secede after 10 years if they were not happy with their status in the union. The Kachin state was not allowed to secede as it consisted partly of the territory which had been under Burman control in the past. The Chins did not ask for a state. However, the Mons and Arakanese were not allowed to have their own states. Nevertheless, a provision was included for the possible formation of more new states in future.[3] Within most of the ethnic groups living in the mountains and border areas there were people who were willing to join the new union, as well as people who were adamantly opposed to it. So, as the drafting of new constitution drew a lot of attention of the Burmans, groups of Karens, Karennis, Mons, Buddhist Arakanese and Muslims in the Arakan territory prepared themselves for armed struggle.[4] So the clouds of violence and disturbance loomed large on the Burmese horizon.

De-colonization and the Beginning of Militarization

Burma was de-colonized on 4 January 1948. Despite armed struggle of the communists in the country, semblance of democratic order was visible in the first decade of Myanmar's post-colonial existence. But after September 1958, when General Ne Win and his associates took power, Myanmar started to drift away to authoritarian rule. After the 1962 coup, General Ne Win and his Revolutionary Council imposed complete military rule in the country that lasted almost uninterrupted until 1988.

The contemporary phenomenon of large-scale displacement of people in Myanmar has turned into a matter of acute concern in the last one and a half decades. Since 1988, the military rulers (who subsequently renamed the government as the State Peace and Development Council or SPDC in 1997) more than doubled its military strength, and troops were deployed throughout the ethnic states. The army, in fact, has expanded from 175,000 to more than 400,000 soldiers since 1988. The civilians in Myanmar soon started to become internally displaced as the military rulers intensified their efforts to control areas populated by the ethnic minority groups since the late 1980s. In other words, the displacement of the civilian population accelerated after the crackdown, by the army, of the democratic movement in 1988. Conflict-induced internal displacement in ethnic minority areas became a major issue during the 1990s when the military rulers intensified their campaign to gain control over ethnic insurgency groups in the previously autonomous border areas. The army of the ruling SPDC, at present, controls most of the ethnic minority areas, but at a heavy cost. Although several ceasefire agreements have been signed between insurgency groups and the government, fighting continues in the Shan, Karen (Kayin) and Karenni (Kayah) states, displacing thousands of civilians.

From Militarization to Displacement

The growing militarization of Myanmar, in view of the growing conflicts between the government forces and the opposition, and between the majority Burman-dominated administration and the rebel groups constituted by the aggrieved ethnic minorities created a backdrop for the large-scale violation of human rights and large-scale displacement of civilians and non-combatants. Whereas some displaced civilians could take shelter in countries on the other side of the border, mainly in Thailand, and sometimes in India, the rest could not or did not cross the international border and became internally displaced persons (IDPs). As we know, according to the Guiding Principles on Internal Displacement, the IDPs are those persons or groups of persons who have been forced or obliged to flee or leave their homes or places of habitual residence, in particular to avoid the effects of armed conflict, situations of generalized violence, violations of human rights or natural or human-made disasters, and who have not crossed an internationally recognized state border. Moreover, there was continuing deprivation in many of the resettlement villages and satellite new towns, which the State Law and Order Restoration

Council (SLORC) accelerated on a massive scale after 1988.[5] The relocations were ordered in two major contexts—either in urban development schemes or in rural counter-insurgency sweeps. Difficult living conditions were exacerbated by the widespread use of forced labour, which was also increased under the SLORC. In short, these civilians got displaced either in anticipation of forced relocation when the government troops ordered them to relocate, or they fled when the human rights abuses or military threats became absolutely intolerable for them. In fact, the human rights situation in the border areas of Myanmar is among the worst in the world, and includes, as has already been indicated, counter-insurgency operations directly targeting civilians, forced labour, restrictions on farmers and land confiscation. There are regular reports of torture, arbitrary executions, sexual violence and indiscriminate use of landmines to make areas uninhabitable and forced recruitment by both the government troops and armed opposition groups.

Apart from the insurgencies conducted by the rebel ethnic groups and the counter-insurgency operations on the part of the military junta, the widespread use of forced labour in Burma has also been a major cause for displacement. The International Labour Organization (ILO) has already indicated how forced labour is both directly linked to military operations (for example, civilians are forced to act as porters and labourers during the construction of military camps) and public infrastructure projects. The ILO governing body also expressed concern about the limited impact of new legislation introduced by the military rulers to stop this practice.[6] It is a matter of serious concern that, in recent years, a large number of civilians evaded moving to the resettlement sites by seeking refuge in the jungle or host communities outside the reach of the SPDC troops. Some hid in areas close to their villages and sometimes tried to continue some cultivation of food crops.

In the sites of relocation, the government does not usually provide the minimum means of survival as required by the UN Guiding Principles on Internal Displacement. The sites are often just empty stretches of land where the relocated people have to erect their own makeshift shelters. These relocated people normally have to be satisfied with restricted freedom of movement and have to live in poor living conditions with minimum of health and sanitation facilities and very limited access to food. If the displaced people decide to hide in jungles, they have to cope with extremely harsh conditions where cultivation of food coops is difficult and hunting and gathering of food are largely restricted due to the presence of government troops in the nearby areas. Lack of physical security is another major problem facing both the IDPs in hiding and those residing in relocation camps. The absence of independent observers in the areas of displacement makes IDPs extremely vulnerable. People in the relocation sites are being used by the SPDC troops as porters for carrying military supplies as well as to build and maintain army camps.[7] The government has forcibly recruited large numbers of the IDPs as labour for road and other construction projects. There are also reports of killings of people searching for food outside their relocation areas. The fact that the border areas are fitted with landmines adds to the risk. Several international organizations have also raised the issue of inadequate protection of refugees repatriated both from Bangladesh and Thailand.

It should be remembered that the forced relocation of thousands of villages is a product of counter-insurgency operations carried out by the *Tatmadaw*. The residents of the relocated sites are subject to extortion and they are compelled to work for the government infrastructure projects. Therefore, many people tend to avoid the sites of their relocation and take shelter in the jungles and comparatively inaccessible areas of the country. But the Tatmadaw regularly launches missions to find out those absconding IDPs and destroy their temporary shelters and food supplies. It is interesting to note that the people forced to move to relocation sites are the majority among the IDPs.

Since the late 1960s, counter-insurgency operations became quite common in view of the civil war in Myanmar. This strategy was known as the Four Cuts policy or *Pya Ley Pya* in Burmese. Faced with ethnic-based armed uprisings against its repressive rule from all over the country, in the early 1970s the SLORC implemented the Four Cuts policy that is still in effect today. This strategy was aimed at undermining insurgent activities by targeting their civilian support base. There are four cuts altogether in this strategy. First of all, there is an attempt to cut off the supply of the recruits. Then there is an attempt to cut off their access to food, finance and intelligence. The aim is to turn the 'black' (rebel-held) zone into the 'brown' (contested) one. After turning the rebel-infested areas into 'brown' zones, the attempt would be to turn them into 'white' (fully controlled by the government forces) zones. According to this policy, Tatmadaw units issue orders to villages in 'black' and 'brown' zones to relocate to the government-controlled areas with hardly any advance warning. This policy has virtually reached the heights of ethnic cleansing in several instances. The villagers refusing to move to the relocation sites face severe violation of human rights including death. At the least, the reluctant villagers forego their rights to get medicines and similar other basic amenities and are forced to assist the government armed forces without any remuneration whatsoever. In this manner vast areas of the countryside have been depopulated. The Four Cuts policy, in fact, aims to cut the supplies of food, funds, recruits and information to resistance groups by systematically terrorizing, controlling, and impoverishing the civilian population in resistance areas so that they have neither the opportunity nor the means to provide any form of support to the opposition. The main pillars of the Four Cuts policy are: (a) detention, torture and execution of villagers and village elders perceived as having any contact whatsoever with the resistance; (b) systematic extortion and pillage of the villagers' crops, food supplies, livestock, cash and valuables; (c) forced labour to get the civilians working for the army and deprive them of time to do anything else; and (d) forced relocation to sites and villages directly under the control of the SPDC military troops.

Many villages now being burnt by SPDC troops were first burned in 1975 when the Four Cuts policy was first implemented, and some villagers speak of having been on the run from the Myanmarese troops since 1975. But even these villagers say that since the late 1990s, the situation has become even worse. The direct attacks on the civilian population, characterized by mass forced relocations, the destruction of villages and the village economies, and completely unsustainable levels of forced labour, have now become the central pillar of SPDC policy in non-Burman rural areas of Myanmar. Where, in the past, two or three villages were destroyed at a time, now 100 villages are destroyed at a time.[8] The Myanmar army now occupies large territories formerly under insurgent control and the few remaining traces of insurgence are being eliminated through the already mentioned Four Cuts policy. The cleansing process is thorough and systematic and leaves the population completely terrorized and impoverished. The condition of the displaced people hiding in the jungle or living at relocation sites is so poor that their primary concern is simply survival. The government agencies, however, do not hesitate to mount military offensives in these areas, to forcibly relocate all villages to sites under direct Myanmar army control, to use the relocated villagers and others as forced labour, to move more army units in and use the villagers as forced labour to build bases along the access roads. The army then allows the villagers back into their villages, where they are now under complete military control and can be used as a rotating source of extortion money and forced labour, to consolidate control through 'development' projects and forced labour farming for the army. In case of resistance on the part of these hapless people, retaliation is carried out against villagers by executing village elders, burning houses and other violent means.

These relocations have often been accompanied with other forms of human rights abuses. Villagers are told that they will not be permitted to go home until the opposition groups have capitulated.[9] After relocation orders have been issued and people have been expelled from their homes, SPDC declares vast areas as free-fire zones—anyone who tries to remain in their homes can be shot at sight. In such a situation, the ethnic minority women are, in particular, victims of the army's counter-insurgency strategy. Six per cent of the rape incidents took place actually within the relocation sites, where villagers are supposed to be 'safe' if they obey the orders of the Myanmarese military. The military personnel did not even need a pretext of 'punishment' to commit rape. The proximity of most of the relocation sites to the Myanmarese military bases thus increased the vulnerability of the relocated villagers to rape and other forms of violence.[10]

Burma has one of the highest numbers of children within governmental armed forces in the world, and the orphans and street children are particularly vulnerable to forced recruitment. Reports of teenage boys fleeing to avoid conscription are quite common. Both the governmental armed forces and armed opposition groups have recruited children, voluntarily and forcibly. Although reliable and objective information is difficult to obtain in the case of Myanmar, it is clear that the country has one of the highest numbers of children within governmental armed forces in the world, including those under 15. Some are recruited voluntarily, attracted by the prestige or financial reward of a military career or hoping to protect their family from harassment by the SPDC, but many others are forced to join. According to an ILO Commission of Inquiry on Burma, there is regular forced recruitment throughout Myanmar, including children, into the Tatmadaw and various militia groups. This recruitment does not appear pursuant to any compulsory military service laws, but is essentially arbitrary. Each district and village in Myanmar is required to provide the armed forces with a certain number of recruits, with quotas being given to the local authorities. The local authorities that fail to achieve their quota may be fined, while a reward of a similar amount is provided for each recruit provided in excess of the quota. This procedure has resulted in many men and teenage boys either being forcibly recruited or fleeing to avoid conscription. Indeed, the village or ward authorities are known to hold lotteries to decide who should go and this commonly results in the forced conscription of children.

According to the ILO Commission of Inquiry, children, some as young as 10, are forced to carry materials for the military. Men are preferred for this role but as they sometimes run away, the troops resort to women and children. A refusal to do the carrying job is systematically met with the physical punishment or fines. According to the local reports, in Northern Rakhaine state nearly all of the men and boys of a village (between the ages of 7 and 35) perform up to 10 days per month of labour in the military, and are reportedly required to carry food and ammunition to the border. The ILO Commission of Inquiry also reported on other kinds of extremely hazardous work carried out by children for the armed forces. Civilians, including children, are used as human shields and minesweepers. In potential conflict areas, civilians, including women and children, were often forced to sweep roads with tree branches or brooms to detect or detonate mines.

Since the 1980s, the Tatmadaw has implemented the Four Cuts policy along with the policy of forced labour. In July 1988, an ILO Commission of Inquiry reported how the government and army of the country treat the civilian population as an unlimited pool of unpaid forced labourers and servants at their disposal. The people affected in this manner include large numbers of old and infirm, apart from women and children. These unpaid forced labourers are denied food and medical treatment. In case of unwillingness on their part, these hapless people are physically abused, tortured, beaten, raped and even murdered. If the villagers can bribe the local commanders of the Tatmadaw, they may be let off.[11] It must be remembered that the SPDC has implemented the Four Cuts policy more systematically and brutally than did its predecessors. Army columns of 50 to 300 men move from village to village. On arrival near a village, the troops first shell it with mortars from the adjacent hills, then enter the village firing at anything that moves and proceed to burn every house, farm, hut and shelter they find in the area. Paddy storage barns are especially sought out and burnt in order to destroy the villagers' food supply. Any villagers seen in the villages, forests, or fields are shot on sight with no questions asked.

Widespread forcible relocation and forced labour have caused major disruption to many ethnic minorities' traditional ways of life. Those who have been forcibly relocated have lost their farms, their livelihoods, and their ancestral attachment to their land. The result of frequent forced labour has often been that many ethnic minorities can no longer earn their living as farmers because they are too busy working for the military to tend their fields. In this regard, ethnic minorities are denied not only their civil and political rights, but also their economic, social and cultural rights. These rights are guaranteed in the United Nations International Covenant on Economic, Social and Cultural Rights. Article 1, part 2 states *inter alia*: 'in no case may a people be deprived of its own means of subsistence'. It may be noted in this context that the forcibly relocated people constitute a subcategory of IDPs according to the UN Guiding Principles on Internal Displacement. According to these Principles, they have been obliged to flee or to leave their homes or places of habitual residence. Without hiding in the jungles or seeking refuge across the international boundary, these people have complied with the relocation orders. That does not mean that they have voluntarily shifted to another place. The application or the threat of force compels these people to follow official orders. In other words, the site of forced relocation is an area of settlement where residence is virtually a product of coercion rather than free choice. People in Myanmar become displaced either as they are forced by the army to relocate in the anticipation of forced relocation or they flee as human rights abuses or military threats become intolerable, including counter-insurgency operations, forced labour, restrictions on farmers and land confiscation. In urban areas, massive forced relocation has reportedly taken place for purposes of land development planning and other urban works.

If not moving to the relocation sites set up by the army, the displaced trek to neighbouring rural areas or hide in the jungle. Many of the Myanmarese refugees lived as internally displaced before they crossed the border. The living conditions at the relocation camps are difficult: access to health facilities is minimal, if any, the food provided by the army is scarce and the IDPs have to shelter in makeshift huts. The IDPs hiding in the jungle also face extremely difficult conditions, especially with regard to food, as they are often not in a position to cultivate their own crop. It has been reported that SPDC troops are not only confiscating food from the villagers, but they are also taking their land and forcing them to grow food for the army. Since the end of the rainy season in October 2000, the SPDC intensified its counter-insurgency campaign and their efforts to destroy the crops and food supplies which the displaced villagers need to survive. SPDC campaigns often targeting the civilian population with almost no attempts made to seek out the armed resistance groups or engage them in battle. Villagers are forced to move to the army-controlled sites further west for use as forced labour constructing and maintaining more army posts, but many flee before the arrival of the military troops.

Since 1999 more and more troops have been sent into the hills to hunt out the villagers trying to hide near their villages. The villagers are shot in the fields at harvest time, crops are trampled upon or burned, and fields and abandoned villages have been landmined. The situation of the internally displaced is desperate. In the SPDC garrisoned villages, things are a little better, as the army's constant demands for forced labour, money, food and materials and its arbitrary torture of village elders and others drives people to flee into the hills and become displaced themselves. The situation for all of the villagers in the region is becoming increasingly desperate, but there is no sign of any decrease in armed resistance activity and going by the current trend it is difficult to imagine that the torture will end in near future.

Apart from such conflict-induced displacement, the cases of development-induced displacement remain another area of major concern. The villagers displaced from the highly militarized pipeline corridor claimed in May 2000 that violence and forced labour in the pipeline region was continuing. Since the early 1990s, a terrible drama has been unfolding in Myanmar. Three western oil companies—Total, Premier, and Unocal—bent on exploiting natural gas, entered into partnerships with the brutal Burmese military regime to build the Yadana and Yetagun pipelines. Determined to overcome any obstacle, the regime created a highly militarized pipeline corridor in what had previously been a relatively peaceful area. The results, predictable to anyone familiar with the recent history of Burma, were violent suppression of dissent, environmental destruction, forced labour and carrying of goods for the army units, forced relocations, torture, rape, and summary executions.

In July 1996, the Earth Rights International and the Southeast Asian Information Network (SAIN) released *Total Denial*, a report that exposed the human rights and environmental problems associated with the Yadana pipeline. Since the publication of this report, the violence and forced labour in the pipeline region have continued unabated. It may be noted that the development-induced displaced people in Burma have very limited access to the basic amenities in life. In fact, these people have largely been displaced due to the construction of dams and other infrastructural projects in their traditional homeland.

MAGNITUDE OF THE PROBLEM

In terms of displacement, the worst affected are the border areas in the east and, in particular, the Karen, Karenni and Mon ethnic groups. But the Muslim Rohingya people and other minority groups in border areas towards Bangladesh and India have also become victims of the military campaign. It is very difficult to make an estimate of the number of IDPs in Myanmar. After all, in Myanmar, the government does not even officially acknowledge the problem of internal displacement.[12] Reliable figures are not available as, normally, the junta does not even provide access to the international humanitarian agencies in the country. Independent monitoring or assistance to internally displaced persons has so far not been authorized and it is thus not possible to verify the number of IDPs in Myanmar. Tens of thousands of villagers in the contested zones remain in forced relocation sites or are internally displaced within the region.

Most of the information about the IDPs in Myanmar comes from the unpublished field reports of different humanitarian agencies working around the border areas of Myanmar. Available figures suggest that there were between 600,000 and 1 million internally displaced persons by the beginning of 2002. People have in addition been internally displaced from urban areas in central Myanmar.[13] According to another estimate, the military junta's repression of minority ethnic groups and political opponents is estimated to have created between 500,000 and 1 million IDPs.[14] By the end of 2000, a minimum of 600,000 IDPs were in the border areas of Thailand. According to one estimate, about 1 million people living in Myanmar adjacent to Thailand have been displaced since 1996. At least 150,000 of them have fled as refugees or joined the huge number of 'illegal immigrants' moving to Thailand. At present, about 600,000 people are internally displaced in Myanmar. They are either in hiding in jungles, mountainous areas and comparatively inaccessible parts of the country or have been taken to about 175 forced relocation sites by the military junta in Myanmar. The distribution of the IDPs who are in hiding or in temporary settlements is as follows— about 100,000 in the Karen state, about 75,000 in the Shan state, about 50,000 in the Karenni state, about 40,000 in the Mon state, and about 6,600 in Tenasserim. The maximum number of people displaced in relocated sites is in the Shan state—about 200,000. About 100,000 and 60,000 people are displaced in the relocated sites of the Karen state and Tenasserim, respectively. The number of affected villages is also highest in the Shan state, approximately 1,500. In the Karen state, at least 700 villages have been similarly affected. Internal displacement has in particular affected ethnic minority groups and gross violations of international human rights and humanitarian law continue in the war-affected areas of Myanmar. Among the ethnic minority groups, the Shan, Karen, Karenni and Rohingya, in particular, continue to be the target of indiscriminate violence whether they are civilians or insurgents.

In areas of Myanmar such as the Karen, Karenni (Kayah) and Shan states where opposition groups continue to fight, the SPDC's current tactic is massive forced relocations of the civilian population. Forced relocation was used as a military tactic in the past, but only on a localized scale. In 1996, however, the junta began delineating regions of resistance and forcing hundreds of villages at a time to move to army-controlled sites along main roads or to camps near major towns. In hill villages throughout Karen state, residents are now being ordered to move into the centre of their villages, implying that they are only to go to their fields between dawn and dusk under threat of being shot if they violate curfew. This restriction disrupts the entire crop cycle because villagers are used to staying in field huts far from the village for much of the growing season. Many of them find that they can no longer produce enough food for themselves.

In order to undermine the access by the insurgent groups to intelligence, supplies and new recruits, the government troops have practised forced village relocation in a systematic manner. In 2001, in the Shan state alone, a total of 1,400 villages were relocated.[15] Similarly, a substantial number of Karenni and Karen villages were emptied. In the Tenasserim division, the civilians were forced to leave their villages to create a 'security corridor' on both sides of the proposed gas pipeline to reduce threats from the armed insurgents. Usually, the villagers are given about one week's notice to leave their villages and the government troops thereafter loot remaining belongings and destroy buildings and food crops to discourage return. Even the civilians have to organize their own means of transport for their journey to the proposed sites of relocation. For instance, about 120,000 Karen civilians were reported to be in hiding or on the move away from government troops in 2001. Even the refugees from Burma endured several years of internal displacement before crossing the border to take shelter in neighbouring Thailand. Becoming a refugee in Thailand is most often considered a final option chosen only when the alternatives for protection inside Burma have been exhausted. After all, the Thai government implements a strict asylum policy and only offers protection to refugees fleeing direct fighting.[16]

During the last three years, the situation in Arakan state deteriorated further. The aftermath of the September 11 attack and the global anti-terrorist campaign have had a strong impact on the Muslim communities of Myanmar, in general, and on the Rohingya Muslim population of northern Arakan, in particular.[17] In fact, on 1 August 2002, the SPDC signed the United States–ASEAN Joint Declaration of Cooperation to Combat International Terrorism. Against this backdrop, the ethnic cleansing policies against the Rohingya Muslims now appear to have been newly consecrated as an 'anti-terrorist campaign'.

In order to understand the situation of displaced Karens, one needs to note that, at least four political identities have emerged over the years among the 20 Karen speaking subgroups.[18] They are Karen (Kayin), Karenni, Kayan (Padaung) and Pao (Taungthu). In 1952, when a separate Karen state was created within Myanmar in the mountainous border land of Thailand, it did not include even one-fourth of the total Karen population in the country. In fact, more than 1 million Karens live in the Irrawaddy delta region, where they do not have any ethnopolitical representation. Decades of warfare have left a devastating legacy in many Karen communities around the Thai–Myanmarese border. When peace talks between the KNU (Karen National Union) and SLORC failed during 1995–96 and fighting between the two forces then resumed, a large number of Karens got displaced. According to the community leaders, about 300,000 inhabitants of the Karen state are displaced now.[19] The Karens were once again affected in the 1990s, when the Yadana gas pipeline was built across the Karen-inhabited areas of the Tenasserim division.[20]

Similarly, Karenni is the collective term for a dozen Karen-speaking groups whose name comes from the traditional colour of clothing of the largest subgroup of the Kayahs.[21] Like the Shan state, the Karenni state was granted the right of secession in the 1947 Constitution. Accordingly, local administrative powers were temporarily left to the traditional leaders for the next 10 years. In fact, the Karenni state was recognized as separate from Myanmar during the colonial period, although it was eventually ruled like the other frontier areas.[22] After the British had taken control of lower Burma in the mid-1850s, the British and King Mindon signed an agreement recognizing Karenni territory's independence in order to maintain a buffer between the British and Mindon's kingdom.[23] Many of the state's inhabitants, numbering around 250,000 have been displaced due to fighting between the government forces and the rebel soldiers. This includes 12,000 villagers relocated by the government in 1992 and another 25,000 during 1995–96.[24]

The ongoing conflict between the state and non-state armed groups has led to the large-scale displacement of Karenni civilians. Patterns of their conflict-induced displacement include displacement into state-controlled areas such as relocation sites, displacement into hills and forests surrounding the village, either to avoid threats or actual violence due to the presence of both state and non-state armies or to avoid relocation orders into state-controlled areas, displacement into other areas where lesser hostilities mean less harassment and generalized violence, displacement within non-state-controlled areas apart from the displacement into Thailand.[25]

The Mon nationalists took up arms in 1949, but the Mon state was ultimately created in 1974 under the BSPP. Local aid workers estimate that there are around 20,000 internally displaced Mons in armed opposition areas near the border.[26]

The modern Shan state has witnessed more than five decades of armed conflict, which, according to some observers, is comparable to those of Lebanon and Afghanistan in its complexity.[27] Under the 1947 Constitution, the Shan state was reformed as one, with the important right to secede in recognition of its past traditions of independence.[28] By 2002, it was estimated that as many as 300,000 villagers had been displaced from their homes.[29]

In order to consolidate Myanmar's border with Bangladesh and to protect the country from infiltration by Islamic extremist militants and to further control the activities and movements of Rohingya in Arakan, the military junta is implementing new policies. Two recent developments in this regard include military consolidation and expansion, and the establishment of new model villages, both resulting in a higher demand for forced labour, in addition to land confiscation. In 2002, the villages were deprived from their daily income on account of compulsory labour. Such compulsory labour again increased with more frequent sentry duty and the building of a new army camp in Kha Moung Seik and two 'model villages' for the Buddhist settlers in Maungdaw township. Other forced labour such as brick baking, shrimp farm maintenance, bamboo and wood-cutting are producing commercial benefits for the army and the NaSaKa. This was a particular issue of concern to the ILO on its field visit in Northern Arakan state in January 2003.[30] In other words, the establishment of new army bases such as the new NaSaKa camp in Kha Moung Seik, north of Maungdaw made it necessary for villagers to provide building material as well as their labour during the monsoon of 2002 when farmers were busy in their fields. Women were also grabbed to participate in this camp construction, which is otherwise unusual among the Rohingya community.

The outcome of General Khin Nyunt's visit to northern Arakan state in early 2002 has been the establishment of new 'model villages' to resettle Buddhists in Muslim areas, a move apparently aimed at further securing the border with Bangladesh. There were already 26 such model villages of about 100 houses each in the Muslim part of Arakan. Since May 2002, a fresh drive in setting up additional ones has emerged. Two such new villages of the settlers of about 50 houses each were constructed during the rainy season with extensive forced labour of the local Rohingya. Pratheit, near Maungdaw town, was set up to rehabilitate a group of more than 220 members (and their families) of a breakaway faction of the Arakan army (a militant Rakhaine Buddhist outfit) that surrendered to the SPDC in April 2002. Nga Yan Chaung, in the far north of Maungdaw township and very close to the Bangladesh border, was built with forced labour and during the second half of October 2002, new settlers were brought in. They included 13 families from central Burma, and 33 members with their families of a Kachin ceasefire group, possibly for use as paramilitary forces for border surveillance. In addition to forced labour, the construction of these model villages also resulted in land confiscation, and has exacerbated inter-communal tension. Forced labour also seems to be connected with ethnicity as Rohingyas claim that they are forced to serve as porters while nearby villages of Buddhist Burmans are exempt.

In 2000, the Committee for Internally Displaced Karen People (CIDKP) estimated that there are around 3,00,000 internally displaced Karens hiding in parts of Irrawaddy delta and in areas adjacent to the Thai–Burmese border in the southeast part of the country. They were displaced either for political reasons, economic reasons or due to military operations in their areas. The Burmese government forces have either destroyed their homes and villages or forced them to flee, or both. The jungle areas where these displaced people normally take shelter are ridden will malaria, diarrhoea, measles and pneumonia. Toungoo, Nyauglabin, Thaton, Papun, Pa'an and Duplaya districts are the worst affected in this regard. The Mon state has about 40,000 IDPs which does not include the refugees repatriated from Thailand. Similarly, the Karenni state has about 50,000 IDPs.

It may be recalled that, according to the UN Committee responsible for monitoring the 1966 Covenant on Economic, Social and Cultural Rights, forced eviction implies permanent or temporary removal against the will of the individuals, families and/or communities from the homes and/or land which they occupy, without the provision of, and access to, appropriate forms of legal and other protection. In the case of Burma, for instance, the Wa relocation sites in southern Shan state are crude examples of human rights violations. Such forced relocation sites are also found in the states of Shan, Karenni, Karen and Mon, and Tenasserim division adjacent to the Burmese–Thai border, and also in Arakan and Chin states.

Since 1997, the SPDC has been involved in an intensive campaign to consolidate control over the rugged hills and river valleys of Papun and Nyaunglebin districts in northern Karen state and eastern Pegu division. The entire campaign has targeted the civilian population rather than the armed resistance. In order to undermine any possibility of resistance and gain complete control over the subsistence Karen farmers who inhabit the region, the SPDC has destroyed over 200 villages, driven thousands of villagers out of the hills to garrison villages, and continues to hunt and kill the villagers who have fled into the hills to hide from the forced relocations. Over 40 battalions have been sent in, new roads have been established, and all of the villagers now living under SPDC control must do forced labour to support these battalions.

The key element in this SPDC campaign for control is that it almost solely targets the civilian population. In the hills of northern Papun district and eastern Nyaunglebin district, at least 200 villages have been destroyed or abandoned in the past five years and tens of thousands of villagers are still in hiding in the forest. Where the SPDC has partial control in western Dweh Loh township of Papun district, the military has intensified relocations of hill villages to army-controlled villages. The nearby Bu Tho township and the eastern portion of Dweh Loh township are well into the cycle of relocation, return, and repeated relocation, as the SPDC progressively increases its control. Furthest to the west, the plains of the Sittaung river are under the strongest SPDC control. The villagers there faced a wave of forced relocations and were compelled to construct roads in 1998–99 and most of them are either still in the SPDC-controlled relocation sites or have fled eastward into the hills to join the internally displaced.

The SPDC began its 2001–02 dry season offensive operations with a three-pronged push in Papun district and eastern Nyaunglebin district. This has been followed by moves into northern Papun district and along the Salween river where it forms the border with Thailand. The main attacks came at the beginning of the rice harvest season, forcing villagers to leave much of their crop in the fields where some was eaten and the rest destroyed by the SPDC soldiers. Most villagers had little left from the previous year's harvest and these new attacks almost guaranteed that they did not have enough rice to see them through to the next harvest at the end of 2002.

From 9 November 2001, five battalions of SPDC Light Infantry Division 33 came down from K'Baw Tu Army camp in Ler Doh township of eastern Nyaunglebin district and moved into south-central Lu Thaw township of Papun district. The five battalions split into two columns which moved east into Kheh Pa, Yeh Mu Plaw and Pay Kay village tracts of Lu Thaw township, an area along the border of Nyaunglebin and Papun districts which had become a tenuous safe area for displaced villagers who fled from further west in 2000 and early 2001 when SPDC columns entered, burned and land-mined their villages in Ler Doh and northern Hsaw Tee townships of Nyaunglebin district. In November 2001 these already displaced villagers found themselves under attack and on the run again, along with local villagers of the Kheh Pa and Yeh Mu Plaw areas. The soldiers destroyed any possessions, school supplies, crops or food caches that they came across. One of the columns burnt Lay Wah, Thay Koh Der and Maw Thay Der villages in southeastern Lu Thaw township. However, most of the villages were not burned. Some in the area have speculated that this is because the SPDC does not want burned villages to be photographed and used internationally as evidence against them. Instead, some of the unburned villages have been land-mined, which still makes them uninhabitable for the villagers. The two SPDC columns reunited and crossed back to the west side of the Bilin river on 27 November 2001, then went back west into Nyaunglebin district. Many of the villagers who had fled the columns later returned to their villages or other makeshift shelters. Schools reopened and the villagers tried to gather what paddy remained in the fields. However, the situation remained unstable. In fact, one column of troops did return to the Lay Wah area in early March 2002, forcing the villagers in the area to flee once more.

The situation of displacement, landmines, and extra-judicial killings is most acute in Papun district in Kayin state and Nyaunglebin district in Pegu division. Many of those interviewed by Amnesty International said that there were some KNU soldiers in their vicinity, but these soldiers usually moved through areas and did not maintain any fixed bases. The KNU occasionally asked for rice, but in general did not harass Karen civilians and sometimes acted as guides or provided intelligence about the Tatmadaw's movements to villagers. However, the KNU is essentially unable to protect Karen civilians in Papun and Nyaunglebin districts from the wide variety of human rights violations, which the SPDC inflicts on them. Karen civilians, particularly those in 'black' areas, are considered as enemies by the Tatmadaw and suffer terribly. Areas distant from the Thai border are difficult to reach for the groups and individuals providing unofficial assistance. Attempts have been made to reach distant IDP groups through mobile medical trips.[31]

Finally, the situation of displacement in the Chin state is not well known, but estimates by the Chin population reflect large-scale displacement. In the Sagaing division, the Naga have suffered significant conflict-related displacement in recent years. In addition to conflict-induced displacement, people have been forcibly resettled through the border area development programmes. The situation in Chin state is not yet well documented except in one report.[32] Therefore, the scale of the problem is not always known. The estimates by the Chins themselves reflect large-scale displacement of population, and it is believed that about 40,000–50,000 people have been displaced from their homes.[33]

INTERNATIONAL RESPONSE

International organizations are not permitted access to the displaced people. They are neither allowed to assess the situation nor provide humanitarian assistance to the affected people. The operational assistance by the UN organizations inside Burma consists mainly of social development projects targeting the poor in the government-controlled areas, including the southern Shan state, Chin and Kachin states. International NGOs operating inside Burma face restricted freedom of movement. Only some unofficial international support reaches the displaced people across the border from Thailand and enables local support groups to provide people in hiding with some medical and food assistance. But the blatant human rights abuses in Burma are regularly condemned through resolutions passed in different international fora. The government's extensive use of forced labour has created strong international reactions. In 2000, following an exhaustive 1998 report by the International Labour Organization (ILO) Special Commission of Inquiry into Forced Labour in Burma, several unprecedented steps were taken to address the widespread and systematic use of forced labour in the country.

In June 2000, the ILO Conference suspended Burma, barring it from receiving ILO technical assistance or attending ILO meetings, due to the government's 'flagrant and persistent failure to comply' with Convention 29 on forced labour. On 16 November 2000, the ILO Governing Body voted to apply sanctions requesting ILO members to review their relationship with Burma and take appropriate measures to ensure that those relations do not perpetuate the system of forced labour. The sanctions also require the ILO to advise international organizations working in the country to reconsider any enterprise that they may be engaged in within Burma and to cease any activity that could have the effect of abetting the practice of forced or compulsory labour.

Although the UN Special Rapporteur obtained authorization to visit Burma for the first time in April 2001, access to provide humanitarian relief to the internally displaced is still largely denied. The operational assistance by UN organizations inside Burma consists mainly of social development projects targeting the poor in government-controlled areas. International NGOs operating inside Burma face restricted freedom of movement and ICRC (International Committee for Red Cross) is the only international organization with access to detainees and selected villages in the Shan, Karen and Mon states. There have been several calls for improved coordination and concerted action among UN agencies to assess the needs of internally displaced in Burma.

In Shan state, a pilot health promotion project implemented by the Danish Red Cross since 1999 has continued. The emphasis was on community-based primary healthcare, mainly preventive measures and immunization programmes, and on providing access to safe water. Community health workers and auxiliary midwives were also trained. Contacts with various interlocutors helped the ICRC to improve its knowledge about IDPs in Shan state. Several field trips in the eastern Shan state enabled the ICRC to gain a better understanding of the living conditions of the civilian population in particular, and the humanitarian environment in general.[34]

The international response to the issues of displacement in Burma has remained limited and uncoordinated within the country. International agencies like UNICEF, FAO or WHO have not confronted the government over rights of access and NGOs have not gained unimpeded access to the displaced in contested areas. Cross-border initiatives to reach internally displaced people from neighbouring countries have proved effective and significant in terms of relief assistance. Some UN agencies and international NGOs are present in Burma but the Burmese regime restricts their activities, which limits their ability to serve internally displaced persons. Nevertheless, these agencies, along with local NGOs and ethnic-based groups, succeed in providing some assistance though some critics have charged that the government siphons off much of the aid. On the whole, international response to the issues of displacement in Burma has not influenced the government either to recognize or address the problems of displacement. In some cases, the intergovernmental agencies have inadvertently supported the relocation of population and, in particular, of the ethnic minorities.

On the basis of the brief discussion above, for a better understanding of the problem one can categorize the IDPs in Burma according to the roots of their displacement. These are: conflict-induced displacement, development-induced displacement and displacement through forcible relocation of habitual residence. One may also add another category, that of the potentially displaced persons (PDPs), which holds true in any situation of displacement. The PDPs refer to those who are invalid or infirm, or people suffering from terminal ailments, orphaned children or widowed women who are basically too weak to move to a new place. A significant percentage of them are too poor to meet the minimum costs of migration. They are in a displaced-like situation and ironically are far less fortunate than those who can migrate to safe and secure areas.[35] The preceding typology may help one deal with the problem of internal displacement in Burma in a larger scale.

GENERAL OBSERVATIONS AND RECOMMENDATIONS

The present system of military-ruled governance cannot provide relief to the citizens of the country belonging to different ethnic groups. The problem of ethnic minorities is likely to be more complex in the face of a policy of growing repression by the Tatmadaw. The insurgency and counter-insurgency operations have put the civilians in the line of fire and have violated their human rights. The conflict-induced displacement, therefore, has become a regular phenomenon in contemporary Burma. Over and above this, relocation of people by the military junta in order to contain insurgencies, and in the name of development programmes, has made the life of the common people vulnerable. The policy of forced labour has added insult to the injury.

In order to deal with this acute and complicated problem of internal displacement in Burma, it is necessary to remember that all IDPs are potential refugees. This is one more reason why the world outside should seriously look into the problems of the IDPs in Burma and try to put an end to the ordeal of these invisible sufferers without any further delay. In order to provide relief to these people on the run, one has to consider the resolution of the ethnic conflict and the restoration in Burma apart from finding ways to provide immediate humanitarian relief to the affected persons. To deal with the problem of internal displacement in a country like Burma, a few urgent measures may be considered:

1. The recruitment and use of forced labour should be stopped immediately.
2. Forcible confiscation of land, food and other basic items of civilians should be stopped.
3. All citizens of the country should be treated equally, irrespective of their ethnic and religious identities.

4. Burma has already ratified ILO Convention 29 on Forced Labour and 87 on Freedom of Association. They should be respected.
5. The forcible recruitment of children into the *Tatmadaw* should be stopped.
6. The Universal Declaration of Human Rights, 1949, Geneva Conventions on the Laws of War, the Convention on the Rights of Child and other international human rights instruments should be given due importance.
7. All the IDPs should be treated as human beings and provided with basic amenities.
8. The military junta should start negotiations with the democratic opposition and the representatives of the major ethnic groups to restore peace and stability in the country. This would minimize the chances of creating IDPs in Burma in the long run.
9. The international agencies should encourage the government to respect the international human rights mechanisms.
10. The global civil society should encourage the government to start negotiations with the democratic opposition and ethnic representatives to bring the country back to peace.
11. The UN Guiding Principles on Internal Displacement should be given due importance by the government of Burma.
12. Following Principle 30 of the UN Guiding Principles on Internal Displacement, all authorities concerned should grant and facilitate international humanitarian organizations and other appropriate actors to gain rapid and unimpeding access to the IDPs to assist in their return or resettlement and reintegration. Special initiatives should be taken to ensure the full participation of the IDPs in the planning and management of their return, resettlement and reintegration.

NOTES

1. David I. Steinberg, *Burma: A Socialist Nation of Southeast Asia* (Boulder, Colorado: Westview Press, 1982), 24–34.
2. Christina Fink, *Living Silence: Burma under Military Rule* (London: Zed Books, 2001), 22.
3. Ibid., 23.
4. Ibid.
5. Martin Smith, *Burma: Insurgency and the Politics of Ethnicity* (London: Zed Books, 2nd edition, 1999), 427; also see, Martin Smith, *Ethnic Groups in Burma: Development, Democracy and Human Rights* (London: Anti-Slavery International, 1994), 78–84.

6. ILO, 'Developments Concerning the Question of the Observance by the Government of Myanmar of the Forced Labour Convention, 1930' (No. 29), March 2002, Geneva http://www.ilo.org/public/english/standards/relm/gb/docs
7. Karen Human Rights Group, 'Exiled at Home: Continued Forced Relocations and Displacement in Shan State', Chiang Mai, April 2000.
8. National Coalition Government of the Union of Burma (NCGUB), July 1999, *Human Rights Yearbook 1998–99: Forced Relocation and Internally Displaced Persons*, Washington DC, 121.
9. NCGUB, *Human Rights Yearbook Burma 1999–2000*, 2000, 130.
10. The Shan Human Rights Foundation and Shan Women's Action Network, *Licence to Rape: The Burmese Military Regime's Use of Sexual Violence in the Ongoing War in Shan State, Burma*, Chiang Mai, 2002, 18.
11. For more details on Four Cuts policy, see Martin Smith, op. cit., 1999, 258–65.
12. David A. Korn, *Exodus within Borders: An Introduction to the Crisis of Internal Displacement* (Washington, DC: Brookings Institution Press, 1999), 56.
13. Burma Ethnic Research Group (BERG), 'Internal Displacement in Burma', in *Disasters*, 24(3), 228–39.
14. David A. Korn, op. cit., 1999, 28.
15. Amnesty International, 'Myanmar: Ethnic Minorities, Targets of Repression', 13 June 2001, AI ref: ASA 16/014/2001, http://web.amnesty.org/ai.nsf
16. See Burmese Border Consortium (BBC), 'Relief Programme: July to December 2001', Bangkok, 2002.
17. Chris Lewa, 'Overview on the Bangladesh-Burma Border: Briefing Notes Presented at the CCSDPT Meeting, Bangkok', Bangkok, 11 December 2002.
18. Martin Smith, *Burma (Myanmar): The Time for Change* (London: Minority Rights Group International, 2002), 16–17.
19. See Burma Ethnic Research Group (BERG), *Forgotten Victims of a Hidden War: Internally Displaced Karen in Burma* (Chiang Mai: Nopburee Press, 1998); Amnesty International, *Myanmar: The Kayin (Karen) State: Militarization and Human Rights*, London, 1999; and BBC, *BBC Relief Programme: July to December 2001*, Bangkok, 2002.
20. See Karen National Union (KNU), *Report of the Facts: The Yadana Gas Pipeline Construction in Tavoy District*, Mergui-Tavoy, 1996.
21. Martin Smith, op. cit., 2002, 17.
22. Christina Fink, op. cit., 2001, 22.
23. Ibid., 258.
24. V. Bamforth, S. Lanjouw and G. Mortimer, *Conflict and Displacement in Karenni: The Need for Considered Responses* (Chiang Mai: BERG, 2000), 49–50.
25. Ibid., 49.
26. Martin Smith, *Burma (Myanmar): The Time for Change* (London: Minority Rights Group international, 2002), 18.
27. Ibid., 19.
28. Christina Fink, op. cit., 22.
29. See Amnesty International, *Myanmar: Exodus from the Shan State*, London, 2000; also see Shan Human Rights Foundation, *Uprooting the Shan*, Chiang Mai, 1996.
30. http://www.antislavery.org/archive/submission/submission2003-CHRBurma.htm
31. BERG and Friedrich Naumann Stiftung, 'Forgotten Victims of a Hidden War: Internally Displaced Karen in Burma' (Bangkok, 1999).
32. Images Asia, *All Quiet on the Western Front? The Situation in Chin State and Sagaing Division, Burma* (Chiang Mai, 1998).

33. For details, see ibid.
34. International Committee of the Red Cross (ICRC), *Myanmar—Field Activities in January 2002*, 15 March 2002.
35. In this context, it may be helpful to refer to the typology of internal displacement in South Asia in general, and India in particular, that was developed a few years ago by Samir Kumar Das, Sabyasachi Basu Ray Chaudhury and Tapan Bose, 'Forced Migration in South Asia: A Critical Review', *Refugee Survey Quarterly*, 19(2), 2000, 51–52.

CHAPTER 7

NEPAL: A PROBLEM UNPREPARED FOR

Manesh Sreshtha and Bishnu Adhikari

When one talks about the internally displaced in Nepal, it is about one of three categories: (*a*) the development-induced internally displaced; (*b*) the Kamaiyas (who form a category) who were formerly bonded labourers in the houses of landlords; and (*c*) internally displaced due to conflict between government forces and the armed insurgents of the Communist Party of Nepal (Maoist).[1] There has not been a huge number of internally displaced due to development projects.[2] Whatever internal displacement there has been due to development has been because of the building of dams and establishment of wildlife and national parks. The internally displaced due to conflict has been a matter of concern since the ultra-left Communist Party of Nepal (Maoists) began their so-called People's War in 1996. The Kamaiyas hold a unique position since they have not had a home of their own to speak of since they have been living as bonded labourers serving their masters for generations. This chapter will look at the situation of the internally displaced in Nepal and the government's response to them. This chapter will also present an analysis of Nepal's policy, or lack of it, vis-à-vis the Guiding Principles.

DEVELOPMENT-RELATED DISPLACEMENT

In Nepal populations have been displaced for roads, irrigation schemes, airports, promulgation of national parks, and watershed management projects. However, the extent and history of these displacements have been mostly forgotten.[3] There exist no records of how people were compensated for the land acquired by the earlier projects and there are no figures for how many people were affected. In the Trishuli hydropower project of the 1960s, for example, land was acquired without any coherent plan.[4]

Rara National Park

Based on his field enquiries in Chisapani in western Nepal, Harka Gurung concludes that 331 households were affected and paid compensation when the area around Rara lake in northwestern Nepal was gazetted as a National Park.[5] The affected households were compensated with land in the terai plains in the south and additionally provided with facilities like food for a certain period, timber for construction of houses and there were provisions for tube wells in the newly resettled lands and also schools for the children. From the original location the displaced households moved to another location where they complained of poor soil and lack of irrigation. These households moved to yet another location and the government continued to support the activities at the new location including provision of water supply. As of 1987 the 331 households had 373.2 hectares of land, though 222 households had not had land registration done. In 1989 Gurung found that those displaced from the area around the Rara lake were better off economically at their new location. The government support provided was multisectoral.

Kulekhani Hydroelectric Project[6]

The Kulekhani hydro electric project (1977–82) affected a population of 3,000 from 450 households. Those affected were given the option of cash compensation or land elsewhere. Most of the IDPs opted for the former. Compensation was also given for 450 houses and 50 water mills but trees and bushes were not considered. A socio-economic survey indicated that the compensation was not at prevailing market price nor was the permanent loss of potential resources and the loss of production taken into consideration.

The immediate effect of the cash inflow was the increase in land prices by four to five times in irrigated lands. Gurung makes three observations from the Kulekhani experience. Those with large cash compensation gained most as they could establish new enterprises and those who received little compensation were adversely affected. Second, the land-for-land option was not seriously considered either by the project authorities or by the affected households. Third, the majority of the affected households had become poorer than before.

Marsyangdi Hydroelectric Project[7]

The Marsyangdi hyrdoelectric project acquired 60.5 hectares of land and displaced 222 households with a population of about 1,800. Compensation was given only in cash and the rates of compensation were close to the market price. The majority had no knowledge of their legal right. No land had been acquired through negotiation despite there being such a legal provision. The project consultants had earlier recommended 15 per cent disturbance allowance, special assistance to hardship cases, priority for employment on the project work and assistance to increase production on remaining land. But none of these was implemented by the project.

THE KAMAIYAS

The second example of 'internally displaced' is the case of the Kamaiyas who have been 'obliged to ... leave ... places of habitual residence'.[8] Kamaiyas are traditionally bonded labourers who served and lived in the households or fields of landlords from whom the Kamaiyas' forefathers had taken loans which had not been repaid. In July 2000 the government of Nepal declared the Kamaiyas 'free' and all their loans were arbitrarily written off. They left their landlords' homes and lands—their places of habitual residence —and went elsewhere.

Depending on whom you ask, there were 50,000 to 200,000 Kamaiyas freed through the government decree of July 2000. These internally displaced have had, by and large, to fend for themselves and that is what they were doing as late as February 2003. The government did promise relief and in the early days of their freedom donor agencies and the civil society did come together to distribute among them such things as plastic sheets to roof their dwellings, blankets and food, but there never was any concerted effort to integrate them into the society. The Kamaiyas lived in forest clearings and public lands in town, as they searched for work and livelihood. To be sure the government did form a committee within the Ministry of Land Reforms to distribute land to the Kamaiyas and rehabilitate them but with frequent changes in the committee members and the ongoing insurgency little has been done for the sake of the Kamaiyas. There are newspaper reports from time to time that land has been distributed to Kamaiyas and they are given title deeds by ministers and senior bureaucrats with a lot of fanfare; however, more often than not, the land mentioned in their deeds does not exist on the ground. This is not to say that no one has received land; some have, but the percentage of those who have is very small.

CONFLICT-RELATED DISPLACEMENT

Starting from February 1996, the Communist Party of Nepal (Maoist) has been waging a 'People's War' in Nepal. The war started in a few districts in the mid-western hills. This is a region characterized by extreme poverty and with an economy that has for long been sustained by remittances of males who have migrated to India for work, a fact recognized by the Nepal Human Development Report 1998, which lists all the hill and mountain districts of western Nepal as scraping the bottom of the socio-economic barrel.[9] An understanding of the causes behind the armed conflict in Nepal would be helpful to understand the nature of conflict-related internal displacement in Nepal.

The Origins of Conflict[10]

The Unity Centre (a grouping of the four different communist factions that came together after the restoration of democracy in 1990) held its first conference in 1991 in which the proposal for a 'protracted armed struggle on the route to a new democratic revolution' was discussed and accepted. It was also decided that the Unity Centre would go underground although, in practice, it remained semi-underground. The undivided Unity Centre participated in the 1991 general elections and emerged as the third largest group with nine seats in the 205-strong House of Representatives.

When the Nepali Congress won an outright majority in the House of Representatives, the traditional distrust between the centrist Nepali Cogress and the Left parties took an ugly turn as Left activists in outlying districts began to face harassment at the hands of the local administration at the instigation of local Congress politicians. This happened most prominently in the western hill districts of Rukum and Rolpa where the United People's Front, the political wing of the Unity Centre, had a very good showing, winning both the parliamentary seats in Rolpa and faring very well in Rukum.

By the time the 1994 mid-term elections came around, Unity Centre had been divided into two, both called Unity Centre. One was led by

Prachanda, the nom de guerre of Pushpa Kamal Dahal, the supremo of Maoists. The Prachanda-led Unity Centre boycotted the 1994 mid-term elections. In March 1995, Prachanda's Unity Centre held its 'Third Plenum', during which they foreswore elections and decided to take up arms. It was during that meeting that the Unity Centre led by Prachanda was renamed Communist Party of Nepal (Maoist). In September 1995, the party's central committee adopted a plan for the historical initiation of the people's war, which stated that the protracted people's war would be based on the strategy of encircling the city from the countryside according to the specificities of the country. The party reiterated its eternal commitment to the theory of people's war developed by Mao as the universal and invincible Marxist theory of war.

The abuse of state power continued, meanwhile. Not to be cowed down, and in line with their stated aim of armed struggle, in 1995, the Maoists (and the United People's Front—UPF, the political wing of the undivided Unity Centre)—began a campaign to propagate the Maoist ideology. In the words of one who took part in the programme, it consisted of training, after which the cadres went back and practised what they had learnt. The purpose was to arouse the masses and heighten political consciousness. The teams of leaders worked with the masses, building roads and bridges, and doing farming.

The Maoists continued to clash with the Nepali Congress workers and also with the Communist Party of Nepal (United Marxist–Lenninist)—CPN-UML—the mainstream communist party, which had won 69 seats in the 1991 general elections (Nepali Congress had won 110). Although the CPN-UML and the UPF had worked out seat adjustments for the 1991 elections, the strong showing by the UPF in the western hills seems to have alarmed the CPN-UML into viewing the UPF as a potential competitor for left-minded party workers as well as voters. Meanwhile, the response of the Nepali Congress government was a police operation codenamed Romeo to 'win the heart and minds' of the people. The result, in the words of a top Maoist leader, was a reign of terror against the poor peasants... indiscriminate ransacking and looting of properties of common people by the ruling party hoodlums under the protection of the police force. More than 10,000 rural youth, out of a population of 200,000 for the whole district, were forced to flee their homes and take shelter in remote jungles. The INSEC Human Rights Yearbook 1995 reports:

The government initiated...suppressive operations to a degree of state terror. Especially, the workers of United People's Front were brutally suppressed. Under the direct leadership of ruling party workers of the locality, police searched, tortured and arrested, without arrest warrants, in 11 villages of the district. Nearly 6,000 locals had left the villages due to the police operation. One hundred and thirty-two people were arrested without serving any warrants. Among the arrested included elderly people above 75 years of age. All the detained were subjected to torture.

On 4 February 1996, the CPN (Maoist) presented the Nepali Congress-led coalition government of Sher Bahadur Deuba with a list of 40 demands related to nationalism, democracy and livelihood. These included abrogation of both the 1950 and the Mahakali treaties with India (one on 'peace and friendship' and the other on the sharing of the water on the western frontier river); introducing work permits for foreign (that is Indian) workers in Nepal; curtailing all privileges of the royal family; drafting of a new Constitution through a Constituent Assembly; nationalizing the property of comprador and bureaucratic capitalists; declaring Nepal a secular nation; other details such as providing villages with roads, drinking water and electricity; and the complete guarantee of freedom of speech and publication. Incidentally, these demands were not much different from the points outlined in the 1991 election manifesto of the above-ground UPF. The covering letter with the demands contained an ultimatum that unless the government initiated positive steps towards fulfilling those demands by 17 February 1996, 'we will be forced to embark on an armed struggle against the existing state.' Prime Minister Sher Bahadur Deuba was on a state visit to India when the Maoists struck in six districts on 13 February, four days before the deadline had even expired.

Categories of Violence-related IDPs

Based on field studies and the available literature, the conflict-related IDPs can be categorized into two broad groups.

The Wealthy and Political IDPs

There are a large number of the internally displaced people who are aligned to the Nepali Congress. They are targets of the Maoist violence because of the traditional rivalry between them and the Maoists. These IDPs have been the ones to instigate security forces to harass the supporters of the former UPF and since 1996, the CPN (Maoists). The pro-Nepali Congress displaced group comprised of the elected representatives. They are now displaced in district headquarters, regional centres like Nepalganj and Dang or even Kathmandu. According to the officials of the Association for the Sufferers of Maoists in Kathmandu, 90 per cent of the 900 associated with the association are aligned to the Nepali Congress. In addition to the supporters of the Rastriya Prajatantry Party, there are also people from the right of centre political party made up of the former *panchas* (the rulers before the restoration of multi-party democracy). These IDPs can be included in the category of the wealthy and politically affiliated. Also included in this category are the cadres of the CPN (UML) who have been targets of Maoist violence. Before the imposition of emergency in November 2001, and the escalation of hostilities, this group formed the majority of the internally displaced.

Youth and the Poor

A large number of men have migrated to India since the imposition of the emergency. Those that are migrating to India may not be 'internally' displaced in the strict sense of the term. But it needs to be noted that the border between India and Nepal being open, this group of migrants would be usually called refugees since they cross an international border. However, they have been labelled internally displaced for the purposes of this study.

Seasonal migration to India has been a traditional phenomenon in the Nepali hills, especially in western and far-western Nepal. There are no data available on the exact scale of seasonal migration but studies conducted in villages in the western region have shown that between 60 to 80 per cent of the male population are away from home during the winter.[11] In spite of taking seasonal migration patterns to India into consideration, there is ample proof that the number of displaced has increased dramatically after the escalation of hostilities between the security and rebel forces since November 2001. According to district government officials and development workers in Nepalganj (one of the main crossing points to India), very few people returned home during the monsoons of 2002.[12] Seasonal migrants have traditionally returned home during the monsoon to plant rice. Maghe Sankrati, a festival in mid-January is another occasion when seasonal migrants return home. But in 2003, the migrants were going in the other direction towards India.[13] According to the records at the border at Gaddachauki in Kanchanpur district in far-western Nepal in the 30 days between 14 December 2002 and 14 January 2003, 40,000 Nepalis crossed over to India.[14] Following the increase in the flow of human traffic, the Indian border police post at Banbasa started keeping records according to which, between mid-September 2002 and mid-January 2003, more than 100,000 Nepalis crossed over to India.[15] Due to the lack of any data from previous years, one can only assume the extent of 'internally displaced' Nepalis in India. High school students have also been migrating to India to avoid the forced conscription by Maoists in their 'People's Liberation Army'. 'I have reached here (Rupediya, an Indian border town near Nepalganj) having run away from the Maoists who had been forcing me to join their ranks', said Pradip Bahadur Shahi, a tenth grade student from Dailekh.[16]

In June 2002, 700 people of a total population of 1,300 from Kholagaun Village Development Committee (VDC) of Rolpa district left for Uttaranchal and Uttar Pradesh in India in search of work after the Maoists attacked a police post in Ghartigaun. The group was led by the VDC vice-chairman.[17]

In one week in early December 2002 some 8,000 people crossed over to India at Nepalganj, according to the records at the Jamunaha police post at the border.[18] This is the first time in its history that the police post kept records on its own initiative rather than because of any government directive. Yet another proof that the number of those entering India is higher than usual are the number of buses leaving for Delhi, Haridwar and Shimla from Rupedhia, which is now 12 a day and is higher than the usual eight.[19]

Recent government directives require that people leaving their homes must get a letter of approval from their area police post. This directive has been issued ostensibly to ensure that Maoist fighters or workers are not leaving. This could have been a good way to record the number of people being displaced but records of the number of people to whom such approval letters are issued are not maintained.

A Question of Numbers

There has not been an extensive survey on the displacement caused by Maoist violence. Nor are there any camps that have been set up for the IDPs. There have been a few small-scale studies published in 2002 and series of newspaper reports on the cases of displacement. Based on these reports it can be said that the number of the internally displaced persons rose rapidly with the deterioration of the security situation in November 2001 when the state of emergency was declared. But based on interviews with the internally displaced, it can be said that conflict-related displacement began in Nepal with the launch of the People's War by the CPN (Maoist). In the beginning, elected representatives from the Nepali Congress were forced to flee their homes in the villages of Rukum and Rolpa, the two districts that were worst affected by the violence. These are the same districts where the Maoists are considered the strongest.

For obvious reasons it is next to impossible to quantify the number of the internally displaced due to conflict in Nepal. For example, there is no way of ascertaining how many of the migrants to India can be considered internally displaced. Not everyone who has been displaced registers themselves with the disrtict administration offices or the regional administration offices. The government began to register IDPs in August 1998 and others have collected their own information on the number of those displaced. The numbers vary considerably depending on who collects the information. For example, according to the district administration offices in eight districts (Syangja, Gorkha, Gulmi, Humla, Kalikot, Surkhet, Pachthar and Doti) there are a total of 342 internally displaced; however, according to a survey carried out by the Nepal Red Cross Society (NCRS) in these eight districts in June 2002 there were a total of 922 IDPs. The government registers one person per family but the NCRS counted individuals.

According to government statistics, last updated in September 2002, the number of displaced stands at 2,514 people.[20] Since the government registers only one person per family, even going by this number, the actual figure could be much higher. But the fact is that for every person displaced all his/her family members may not be displaced because they could be continuing to live in their homes tending the fields and looking after the animals, and this needs to be considered as well.

Table 1
District-wise Breakdown of the Internally-displaced as of August 2002

	District	No. of IDPs
1.	Taplejung	0
2.	Panchthar	33
3.	Ilam	24
4.	Jhapa	20
5.	Sankhushaba	71
6.	Dhankuta	15
7.	Terathum	8
8.	Bhojpur	3
9.	Sunsari	1
10.	Morang	16
11.	Solukhumbu	159

Table 1 contd.

Table 1 contd.

	District	No. of IDPs
12.	Okhaldunga	75
13.	Khotang	19
14.	Udaypur	26
15.	Saptari	0
16.	Siraha	7
17.	Dolakha	11
18.	Ramechhap	52
19.	Sindhuli	60
20.	Sarlahi	11
21.	Dhanusa	5
22.	Mahottari	2
23.	Rasuwa	2
24.	Nuwakot	17
25.	Kavrepalanchowk	52
26.	Sindhupalanchowk	10
27.	Kathmandu	0
28.	Bhaktapur	0
29.	Lalitpur	215
30.	Dhading	54
31.	Bara	0
32.	Parsa	0
33.	Rautahat	46
34.	Makwanpur	0
35.	Chitwan	15
36.	Manang	0
37.	Kaski	3
38.	Lamjung	101
39.	Syangja	23
40.	Tanahun	39
41.	Gorkha	72
42.	Parbat	9
43.	Myagdi	47
44.	Baglung	96
45.	Mustang	0
46.	Nawalparasi	4
47.	Rupandehi	1
48.	Kapilvastu	1
49.	Gulmi	29
50.	Arghakanchi	3
51.	Palpa	0
52.	Rolpa	0
53.	Rukum	0
54.	Salyan	64
55.	Pyuthan	35
56.	Dang	87
57.	Banke	7
58.	Baridiya	101
59.	Dailekh	124

Table 1 contd.

Table 1 contd.

	District	No. of IDPs
60.	Surkhet	147
61.	Jajarkot	60
62.	Jumla	61
63.	Humla	9
64.	Kalikot	117
65.	Mugu	18
66.	Dolpa	2
67.	Achham	19
68.	Doti	32
69.	Kailali	14
70.	Bajhang	21
71.	Bajura	17
72.	Kanchanpur	22
73.	Darchula	22
74.	Dadeldhura	45
75.	Baitadi	33
	Total	**2,514**

Source: Home Ministry, Government of Nepal.

If the number of people crossing the border into India is taken into consideration and if human rights activists are to be believed or if one goes according to the statistics of the Nepal Maobadi Pidit Sangh (Association for the Sufferers of Maoists, ASMA, Nepal) the number is definitely much higher. According to ASMA there are 2,250 registered displaced in Kathmandu, but only 215 have received government allowance in Kathmandu. What makes the government statistics doubtful is the fact that this number is low compared to reality. Yet another reason to doubt the accuracy of the above government statistics is that there are no registered displaced in Rukum and Rolpa districts, the two districts which are worst affected by the Maoist violence. However, ASMA members estimate that about 450 families are displaced in the headquarters of Rolpa district. According to the human rights organization, INSEC, 100 elected officials, 500 political activists and 20,000 youths have been displaced in Rukum district.[21] According to those displaced from Rukum and presently living in Kathmandu, there are about 300 families displaced in the district headquarters.

Women and Children

Based on government statistics, newspaper reports and interviews with the displaced, it can be concluded that the majority of those displaced are men. However, women are also displaced, though very few are registered with the government.[22] Most of the women displaced have migrated to India with their families. Women who stay back home are also sufferers of the conflict. Emigration and recruitment of men into Maoist cadres or security forces as well as the killing of the male members of the family by Maoists and security forces have increased the burden on women. Some of the tasks that men traditionally performed have fallen upon the women who have become the head of households.[23]

According to a report by Child Workers in Nepal, it is estimated that 4,000 children have been displaced by the conflict.[24] There is no way that this can be verified independently. When men leave their homes, their children naturally suffer in the absence of the father, both emotionally as well as because the main earner is absent.

Reasons for Displacement

1. Political Target
People from the political and wealthy groups have mostly fled their villages because of fear of being Maoist targets. This was gathered from conversations with those displaced by the conflict. When the conflict began in 1996, it was initially just the cadres of political parties, in particular those of the Nepali Congress, who were displaced. Most of them moved to the district headquarters or to towns like Nepalganj, Dang Surkhet in west Nepal or even Kathmandu, depending on the support for them in these places by their relatives. As the conflict intensified and spread to other parts of the country, the number of those displaced because of fear of being political targets of the Maoists grew.

2. Human Shield and Forced Recruitment
As the conflict intensified and especially after the imposition of emergency in November 2001, Maoists started recruiting people, especially the youth, to join their 'people's militia' and the hardcore fighting group. In August 2001 recruitment policy of Maoists began at the rate of one per family. This forced many to flee their homes. Again there are no statistics on the number of people fleeing for this reason. An idea of the extent of displacement because of this reason may be gathered from a newspaper report that of a population of 75,000 in Jumla district, an estimated 35,000 had fled.[25]

It has been reported that Maoists have also recruited villagers to join them so that they can be made human shields when armed Maoist fighters attack police posts and military barracks. These 'human shields' are the first to be shot at in any counter-attack by the security forces. In a survey conducted among 83 internally displaced people in Kathmandu in May–June 2002, 34 per cent said that this was the reason they fled their homes,[26] to escape being made human shields.

3. Forced Donation Collection

A large number of the displaced have fled their homes because of forced donation collection by the Maoists. This forced collection is in the form of cash or kind. Maoist fighters and cadres show up in the homes of villagers who are forced to feed them. Unable to bear the additional expenses due to this, villagers leave their homes.

4. Harassment by Security Forces

There is more than one reason why people have been displaced. Most of the non-political groups that have fled become targets of harassment by the security forces. The security forces ask villagers to tell them where Maoists are and there have been cases of security forces killing innocent villagers.

Case Studies[27]

1. Govinda Shahi, 45-year-old, Former Vice-Chairman, Khagankot VDC, Jajarkot

Govinda Shahi was elected vice chairman of the Khagankot VDC representing the Nepali Congress in the local elections held in November 1997. Since the Maoists had called for a boycott of the local elections, Shahi had been away from home for most of the time since then, fearing for his life. If he did go back to his village it was with the police or where there were policemen stationed. In December 2000 he stopped going to the village altogether after the police posts in the villages in the districts were shifted to the district headquarters of Khalanga for security reasons. The Maoist forces were attacking police posts about then. Finally in August 2001 he returned home after the government and Maoists declared a ceasefire. Meanwhile in June 2001 the Maoists had held elections for the Village People's Government, VPG (in place of the state's village development committee). To Shahi's dismay, a person who had a grudge against Shahi had been elected the chairman of the VPG.

After Shahi returned in August 2001, the Maoists sent for him. He went and they framed charges against him. They kept him for a few days and told him that he would not be let off until his family members paid a ransom of Nepali Rs 100,000. When asked what the charges against him were, he was told that he was charged with corruption. Shahi claimed that he hardly signed any papers as the VDC vice chairman and so he could not be possibly accused of corruption. The Maoists then asserted that he had been corrupt during his tenure as the chairman of the consumer group in the village. They then reduced the fine to Nepali Rs 50,000. Many times in the discussions he heard the Nepali word '*chalan*' (literally means dispatch). Shahi had heard that this was a euphemism for death sentence by the Maoists. He feared that he would be killed. But a message was sent to his family for the ransom and they brought the money. When they did, the Maoists took only Nepali Rs 35,000. Shahih's family had to sell gold and borrow money. He had to also pay Rs 10,000 to a neighbour and so he tried to sell his land. The Maoists heard of this and told him that he could not sell his own land. The Maoists said he had to first submit an application to the Maoist VPG. Soon afterwards fearing for his life and that of his family, he moved with his family to the district headquarters and later to Kathmandu.

2. Jagat Bista, 23-year-old, Kotwada VDC, Kalikot District

Jagat Bista was a district president of the Nepali Congress-aligned Nepal Students' Union. In January 1998 the Maoists attacked his home, looted and burnt it. They wanted Bista to quit the Nepal Students' Union and join the Maoists. Two months later he left home and moved to the district headquarters to live there, never to return. He also joined college there. While he was away his family got threatening letters from the Maoists. In May 2000 his father came to the headquarters to visit him, returning home a few days later. Four days after return, his father was kidnapped and killed by the Maoists. Two days later, the Maoists put up a notice in the village saying that he was killed on charges of corruption. His father's body was never found.

After his father was killed there were threats to the rest of his family. In July 2000 all 11 members of his extended family were forced to flee their village. They are now in the district headquarters but have not got any relief from the authorities because of lack of papers. According to Bista, 296 families from different villages in the district have been displaced to the district headquarters.[28] Prices of essential commodities are extremely high. Rice that would cost Rs 12 in normal times costs Rs 32 per kilo and kerosene, the price of which has been fixed at Rs 17 by the government for all over the country, costs Rs 75 per litre. Families survive by brewing and selling illicit liquor.

3. Laxman K.C., 22-year-old, Pipal VDC, Rukum District

Laxman K.C. has been in Kathmandu for the last three years. He was a student but later got displaced. After the ceasefire in August 2001, he had gone to his home in Pipal VDC, Rukum district. While he was in his village, his uncle fell ill and had to be taken to the hospital. The Maoists threatened him because he was using the state's services. The Maoists do not want the people to use the services provided by the government like the land records office, the courts, the postal system or the hospital. One day when he was in his fields his mother came there saying the Maoists were looking for him. Without even going home he fled to Kathmandu and has not gone back since.

4. Krishna Raut, Suikot VDC, Salyan District, presently at Kohalpur

Krishna Raut's father Kul Bahadur Raut was the VDC chairman and was aligned to the Rastriya Prajatantra Party. They had a cloth shop in Suikot VDC as well as a rice mill. Maoists had been harassing them asking for donations and also threatening them since 1997. In May 1999 they came and looted the shop and took away goods worth Rs 1,50,000. His grandfather and uncle were beaten up. His father has stopped going to the village since then and now lives in Kohalpur, where he has built a house to be near his relatives.

5. Bharat Bahadur Thapa, Farmer from Ward no. 2, Narayan Nagarpalika, Headquarters of Dailekh District

On the night of 2 June 2002 Bharat Bahadur Thapar had come out of his house when the army started shooting at him in the dark without warning. Only after the shooting did the soldiers ask questions. When they saw him hit, they administered some preliminary first aid and brought him to Nepalganj hospital. The cost of treatment is being borne by the district administration office and he has also received Rs 5,000. According to him, families of security forces (police and army) from his village have come to the district headquarters because of lack of security from Maoists in their village.

6. Khadga Bahadur Pun, Baniyabhar VDC of Bardia District

On 1 September 2002 Khadga Bahadur Pun was on his way to plough his landlord's land, but the Maoists got hold of him along with four others. The Maoist killed one of them, beat up three people and broke Pun's leg, accusing him of spying for security forces. He is in the Bheri zonal hospital and has no intention of returning to the village.

7. Giri Bahadur G.C., Pyuthan District

Giri Bahadur with his wife and three children—two daughters and one son—shifted to Nepalganj after he was beaten up for not attending mass meetings organized by Maoists. He has been given an assistance of Nepali Rs 2,000 in total since coming to Nepalganj in June 2002.

8. Gore Bhandari, 73-year-old, Chairman of Bijeswari VDC from Nepali Congress, Rukum District

Goe Bhandari has been living in Nepalganj for the last three years. He came to Nepalganj because the Maoists harassed him for money and planting paddy on his fields and harvesting it. He lives in a hotel in Nepalganj on his own resources. Party leaders asked him to go back to the village after the elections were announced. His wife, son, daughter-in-law and two grandchildren are at home in the village. One other son and daughter-in-law are working in Lucknow, India.

RESPONSE OF THE AUTHORITIES

The government began to help the conflict-related IDPs informally and on an adhoc basis since 1996 when the Maoists launched their people's war. According to the IDP records in the district administration office in Nepalganj, the oldest record is from January 1997.

The Association of Maoist Victims, Nepal (ASMAN) has been instrumental in lobbying with the government for formal and legal assistance for the displaced. ASMAN has been informally active since March 1999 and got itself registered as an NGO in December 1999. The government made a decision in November 1999 to provide relief to those who have been displaced by the conflict.[29] It decided to provide Rs 100 per day per person for a family of three members, and if a family had more than three members to provide Rs 100 to two members of that family. A maximum of two members of a family can receive the relief allowance. According to the home ministry actual disbursement began in the fiscal year 2001/2002.[30]

For a displaced person to be eligible for this relief amount, s/he has to be registered at one of three places: the district administration office, the regional registration office or the capital, Kathmandu. The person is registered only after the security committee of the district verifies that s/he has been genuinely displaced. The security committee consists of the chief district officer as chairman, the local development officer, chief of the district police and the head of the district branch of the government financial controller's office as members. They in turn need papers from the concerned village development committee to authenticate a person's claim of being displaced. Since VDC offices have moved to the district headquarters in many Maoist-affected districts, the displaced do not need to go to the VDCs. IDPs receive the relief amount only from the time they are registered, not retrospectively. In the regional administration office in Nepalganj, which looks after 15 districts, till September 2002 there were 84 IDPs registered, of whom one was a woman. Fifty of them were registered as IDPs in 2002. Thirty-four more have applied but have not been registered because of lack of papers.[31]

In November 2001 the central government released Rs 90,000 to be distributed as relief to those registered as IDPs in Nepalganj. The central government also released Rs 50,000 to each of the districts in the mid-western region.[32] These amounts are clearly not sufficient for the relief allowance at the rate the government has established. In other districts too, the allowance is not provided regularly according to the officials of ASMAN. In such cases whatever is released from the centre is distributed to the IDPs on the basis of need rather than at the rate of Rs 100 per day. Some are given Rs 2,000, some Rs 3,000, and some Rs 5,000 in no systematic way. According to the latest statistics of the home ministry of February 2003 a total of Rs 15,070,000 has been disbursed to the various districts for IDPs—Rs 4,220,000 in the fiscal year 2001/2002 and, Rs 10,850,000 in the fiscal year 2002/2003.

Another problem, according to the IDPs, is that the relief allowance is sometimes disbursed in the centre, and sometimes in the district or regional centre. This depends on the political climate prevailing at the time and according to the wishes of the home minister. When the government announced the relief package in November 1999, the relief could be collected from the centre (no money had been disbursed to the districts at that time), then the minister changed and the new minister directed that the relief amount be distributed from the districts. Later when there was a different home minister he changed the policy so that displaced people would have to collect the relief amount from the centre. After the government announced general elections the same minister changed the policy again and said the relief would be distributed only from the districts so that the political cadres could return to the districts and work for the elections.

THE GUIDING PRINCIPLES

Given the open border between Nepal and India, an arrangement which probably does not exist between any other two countries in the world, the definition of IDPs, in the case of Nepal, must include the tens of thousands, or even hundreds of thousands, of migrants who have gone to India since the conflict started in 1996, and in particular after the escalation of hostilities between government forces and the Maoist rebels in November 2001. For decades now, the poor from the western hills of Nepal have been going to India. Thus, it is no doubt difficult to ascertain who are economic migrants and who are IDPs. However, as we have seen, the number of those crossing the open border to India after November 2001 has been higher than in the past.

Another case that is unique to Nepal is that of the Kamaiyas. The Kamaiyas have been, by definition, 'obliged to leave or flee their homes or places of habitual residence' because of a government decree.

The Kamaiyas and the Development-related IDPs

The Kamaiyas were freed from their status of bonded labourers by a government decree of 17 July 2000. But little has been done by the authorities for their rehabilitation or other rights as laid down by the Guiding Principles. There has not been a coherent plan by the authorities to relocate them. By and large they have been left to fend for themselves. The Kamaiyas do not have access to essential food and potable water, basic shelter and housing, appropriate clothing and medical care. Also, they have not been registered as permanent residents anywhere, thereby affecting their legal rights to vote, file legal cases or be considered a person before the law. Many have not been given citizenship certificates. From time to time, the government has made promises to provide land to the Kamaiyas, training for employment and education for their children, but this has not been turned to reality. With the government focusing on fighting Maoists and seeking a solution to the armed conflict in the country, the problems of Kamaiyas have taken a back seat for the moment. But questions remain about the government's sincerity given that there is not enough people advocating their case.

In cases of displacement because of building of dams, the full information on the reasons and procedures of displacement has not been provided to the IDPs or would-be IDPs.[33] Gurung notes that majority of those provided compensation during the building of the Marsyangdi Hydroelectric Project were not aware of their legal right to lodge a complaint.[34]

Conflict-related Displacement

Conflict-related IDPs in Nepal have not been resettled in alternative locations. Nor has there been a planned, integrated programme to provide them relief. The government response is mainly confined to providing the displaced Rs 100 per day. Given this situation, an analysis of the humanitarian assistance provided to them vis-à-vis the Guiding Principles on Internal Displacement is neither complete nor exhaustive. Also, with the hostilities between the government troops and the rebel forces continuing and with no settlement in sight, any agreement between the government and the rebel forces on who will return and how they might be resettled and reintegrated seems a far cry.

Are IDPs in Nepal by and large enjoying 'the same rights and freedoms ... as do other persons in their country'.[35] One cannot vouch for this in areas controlled by the Maoists. Other than in the district headquarters, the presence of security forces and by extension that of the government is minimal in many areas. Therefore, the situation of IDPs in the Maoist-controlled areas cannot be ascertained. To be sure, due to the atrocities committed against suspected Maoists and Maoist sympathizers there have been people who have been displaced because they fear the government troops. But one can assume that they have either migrated to India or have joined the Maoist forces.

The government is following some parts of the Guiding Principles since IDPs are enjoying their rights of movement, freedom and association, but the same cannot be said of the Maoist forces. According to those displaced by the Maoist violence, many have not registered themselves as IDPs in district headquarters because of the fear of Maoist reprisals.[36] The government assistance (that is Rs 100 per day for a family up to three and Rs 200 for a family of more than three members) is not sufficient to make ends meet. Most of the internally displaced therefore are living on their own resources. The poor have either migrated to India or are looking for other sources of income. According to a journalist, the displaced in the district headquarters of Rukum brew illicit liquor and sell it to make ends meet. Although there has not been any discrimination based on colour, race, sex, language, religion or belief, IDPs have claimed that it is difficult to get the papers required to register themselves as IDPs.[37]

In Nepal's situation of conflict, it is not possible for the government to 'ensure' that the displaced get proper accommodation with satisfactory conditions of safety, nutrition and health.[38] This is mainly because there isn't a proper rehabilitation policy for the displaced and the only government provision is the Rs 100 a day. Also family members are being separated since in most cases it is only the men who are displaced and not women. Women often stay back to look after the fields. Only when the situation for the family members also becomes risky do whole families flee their homes.

Again since conflict-related IDPs are not concentrated in certain areas like camps, it is difficult to ascertain the extent to which the Principles relating to the protection during displacement have been adhered to. Maoist forces have used people as human shields but there have been no evidence of the use of IDPs for this purpose. Although it seems that by and large the IDPs are fairly secure, a study among 83 IDPs in Kathmandu found that 69 per cent feel only partially secure at the place of displacement, 19 per cent do not feel secure at all and only 7 per cent feel fully secure.[39]

Although the border between Nepal and India is open and a Nepali can freely walk into India, recent government directives require that persons leaving the country need a paper of clearance from their VDCs without which they are not allowed to go past the border. But VDCs do not have records of how many have been given such a clearance.[40] This is being done apparently to check Maoists leaving the country.

There have not been cases of missing IDPs in Nepal.[41] Without the provision of camps or a planned rehabilitation programmes for IDPs, there has not been a case of family being forced to live apart. If there are families living apart, it is mainly because of economic reasons. Families have been separated because they do not have the resources for survival in a new location.[42] With regard to medical facilities, special provisions have not been made, whereby they can be given special concessions or free medical check-ups.[43] But the Ministry of Home has a provision to provide medical assistance to political sufferers, whether they are IDPs or not. The records of how many have availed themselves of this facility are not available.

There is no evidence if the property of the IDPs is being protected. There have been many cases of Maoists destroying the property of IDPs. Given that the political targets who have been displaced are 'class enemies' as far as the Maoists are concerned, it is justifiable for them to destroy the property of such 'enemies'. The exact extent of such destruction has not been determined and, given Nepal government's archaic data collection mechanism, it is hardly possible for it to be done. But there is provision by the government to provide compensation for the damage to property by the Maoists. The government does not discriminate against the IDPs in this regard but approval from the chief district officer (CDO) is necessary and the process of getting compensation could take months. Only politically well-connected people have managed to access these resources, including the home minister himself.[44]

The government is providing assistance of Rs 10,000 to Rs 20,000 a year for the education of the children of those deceased in the conflict but not for the internally displaced. Except in the case of a few districts, there is no provision for compulsory education in Nepal.[45] Although an amount of Rs 100 per day is to be made available to IDPs as per government provision, the disbursement of such funds has been irregular at best. IDPs have to visit the district administration office regularly to avail themselves of this facility. For example, although there are 84 IDPs in Banke district, only Rs 90,000 had been disbursed by September 2002. According to officials of ASMAN and of the district administration office at Nepalganj, the central government does not release the amount regularly, citing resource constraints. International relief and humanitarian agencies have not been involved in assisting IDPs. The US and British governments have pledged humanitarian support, but it is not clear for whom this support will be used, for the families of the deceased, for the general population in the district affected by violence or for the IDPs. The pledged support comes in the same package as the support for military hardware and in such a scenario, the smooth distribution of the relief will be doubtful as the rebels may not allow it and also because there exist no mechanisms in place for the distribution of such relief.

CONCLUSION AND RECOMMENDATIONS

It is clear that the government of Nepal does not have any fixed policy on IDPs but is dealing with it on an ad hoc basis. Development-related displacement is and will be a regular feature in Nepal, given that the country has a big potential for water resources development. In the absence of any other major economic resource to speak of, Nepal will take this on in a big way in the future. To what extent this will create IDPs depends on the policy the government will take vis-à-vis water resources development—small, medium or large scale projects. It needs to be noted here that the Land Acquisition Act of 1977 states that it is not mandatory for the government to compensate according to market price for the land acquired for government projects/institutions. This provision disregards the very concept of human rights. The act needs to be reformulated or amended.[46] Another issue is that of bringing the affected groups into the decision-making process regarding compensation and rehabilitation.[47] The policy on this will also depend on the policies of donor agencies like the World Bank and the Asian Development Bank. This is because the loans from these sources are provided with certain conditions.

On the question of Kamaiyas too, the government has been procrastinating in its rehabilitation efforts (if what the government has done so far can, in fact, be labelled rehabilitation). Again a clear-cut long-term policy on this, like providing enough land for subsistence, training to gain skills and employment opportunities is necessary for a long-term solution to this humanitarian problem. We say this not to undermine the government's decision to free the Kamaiyas in July 2000.

On the issue of conflict-related IDPs, the government is too busy concentrating its resources fighting the Maoist rebels to give any serious thought to the plight of the displaced. With the border between Nepal and India open, the potential problem of 'internal displacement' has found a safety valve. If it were not for that open border, Nepal would have been beset with a humanitarian crisis. Where would all the internally displaced have gone? What kind of protection, or non-protection would there be in store for them? The open border is not a solution; it is just a fortunate convenience. What Nepal needs in the long term is a concrete policy on IDPs. What if India starts guarding the borders tomorrow? What would happen if tomorrow jobs are not made available to Nepalis in India?

Since the potential problems of IDPs have been diverted for the moment, humanitarian assistance from international relief agencies has not been sought nor have there been concrete offers from such agencies to help the IDPs. In case such a need arises, the government must not accept any humanitarian assistance which comes attached with military assistance. Only then would humanitarian agencies gain access to rebel-controlled territory without interference.[48] Also there would be less chance of such assistance being diverted for military or political purposes.[49]

Till the second ceasefire was declared by the government and the Maoists in early February 2003, there were no signs of a long-term policy decision by the government regarding the displaced. But once the ceasefire happened it was hoped that things would change. However, even that hope has disappeared from the horizon. Among the Maoist-affected political class, there are doubts about the sincerity of the rebels. 'As long as they have the gun, they will have the upper hand', said one of them. 'The reality in the capital is different than the reality in the village in the mid-western hills of Nepal'.

The rehabilitation of the IDPs does not seem to be in sight. For the IDPs to return, security conditions must be congenial enough so that displaced persons can return home voluntarily and with dignity.[50] This means that the Maoists too will have to 'endeavour to facilitate the reintegration of returned or resettled displaced persons'[51] since it is largely because of fear generated by them that many displacements have taken place. This is an agenda that must be included in the imminent talks between the government and Maoists. The government and the Maoists also need to take measures to compensate for the loss of property and possessions after the rehabilitation of the IDPs. If the general public and the Maoist-affected are to have complete faith in the peace that will, hopefully, follow the talks and by extension on the sincerity of the government towards their plight, the government must make the process of getting compensation a swift one and not a long-drawn-out process.[52] If the assistance of humanitarian agencies is needed they should be sought and they should be allowed to work unimpeded. [53]

NOTES

1. Kamaiyas were set free by a government decree on 17 July 2000.
2. It is difficult to ascertain the exact number of IDPs from development projects. The estimate would be less than 10,000. This estimate is based on Gurung, 1989.
3. Ajay Dixit, 'Water Projects in Nepal: Lessons from Displacement and Rehabilitation', *Water Nepal*, Vol. 4, No. 1 (Kathmandu, 1994).
4. Ibid.
5. Harka Gurung, 'Review of Policy and Experiences of Project Related Resettlement in Nepal', *Water Nepal*, Vol. 1, No. 4 (3) (Kathmandu, 1989).
6. Ibid.
7. Ibid.
8. Guiding Principles on Internal Displacement, 2000.
9. Esperanza Martinez, 'Conflict-related Displacement', Kathmandu, 2002. Unpublished report.
10. Deepak Thapa, 'The Killing Terraces', *Himal South Asian* (May 2001).
11. Esperanza Martinez, 2002.
12. Ibid.
13. *Himal Khabarpatrika*, 15–29 January 2003.
14. Ibid.
15. Ibid.
16. *Himal Khabarpatrika*, 16–30 December 2002.
17. Based on field enquiries in Nepalganj in August 2002.
18. *Himal Khabarpatrika*, 16–30 December 2002.
19. Ibid.
20. Statistics provided by the Home Ministry. See Table 1 for the district-wise breakdown of the number of internally displaced. These numbers may not be the number of displaced in a particular district but the number of IDPs registered in that particular district. For example, the 215 displaced in Lalitpur means that 215 people are getting relief from the district administration office in Lalitpur district.
21. INSEC, 'Internal Displacement a Glaring Problem in Nepal', Kathmandu: INSEC, 2002.
22. Of the 84 registered displaced at the regional administration office in Nepalganj, in western Nepal, only one was found to be woman in August 2002.

23. Esperanza Martinez, 2002.

24. *Nepalma Baladhikarko Sthiti*, 2003. This is a Nepali source and translates as 'Child Workers in Nepal.'

25. *The Observer*, London, 2 February 2003.

26. Pradeep Adhikari and Sunil Pokhrel, 'Internal Displacement of People as a Result of Maoist Insurgency in Nepal', Kathmandu, 2002. Unpublished report.

27. Based on field visit to Nepalganj in September 2002 and interviews in Kathmandu in February 2003.

28. According to government statistics last updated in August 2002, there are 60 IDPs in Jajarkot district.

29. In a partisan dispensation, it may be interesting to note that the government then was of the Nepali Congress and 90 per cent of those associated with the ASMAN are members of the Nepali Congress or supporters of the party.

30. The fiscal year in Nepal is from mid-July to mid-July.

31. Data made available by the District Administration Office, Nepalganj.

32. Data made available by the District Administration Office, Nepalganj.

33. Principle 7, Guiding Principles on Internal Displacement.

34. Ibid.

35. Principle 2, Guiding Principles on Internal Displacement.

36. Principle 3, Guiding Principles on Internal Displacement.

37. Principle 4, Guiding Principles on Internal Displacement.

38. Principle 7, Guiding Principles on Internal Displacement.

39. Adhikari and Sunil, 2002.

40. Principle 15, Guiding Principles on Internal Displacement.

41. Principle 16, Guiding Principles on Internal Displacement.

42. Principle 17, Guiding Principles on Internal Displacement.

43. Principle 19, Guiding Principles on Internal Displacement.

44. Esperanza Martinez, 2002.

45. Principle 23, Guiding Principles on Internal Displacement.

46. Ajay Dixit, 1994.

47. Ibid.

48. Principles 25 and 26, Guiding Principles on Internal Displacement.

49. Principle 24, Guiding Principles on Internal Displacement.

50. Principle 28, Guiding Principles on Internal Displacement.

51. Principle 28, Guiding Principles on Internal Displacement.

52. Principle 29, Guiding Principles on Internal Displacement.

53. Principle 30, Guiding Principles on Internal Displacement.

CHAPTER 8

SRI LANKA: A PROFILE OF VULNERABILITY

Joe William

INTRODUCTION

The armed conflict in Sri Lanka has caused immense suffering to hundreds of thousands of its citizens. Men, women and children have been uprooted, dispossessed, deprived of their means of livelihood and thrown into exile as refugees or became internally displaced persons (IDPs) as a result. As in all internal conflicts, civilians are the biggest casualties in this conflict. Loss of lives, including that of breadwinners, severe and permanent disability, destruction of personal and productive assets, loss of income, psychological trauma, accompanied by alienation and isolation along with enduring sense of uncertainty—the scars of war, particularly in relation to IDPs, go deep to produce a sociological reality and complexity that is staggering in its social, economic and psychological dimensions. To compound the crisis, fundamental human rights, democratic freedoms and economic and social development are gravely compromised and insecurity has become rampant.

According to government of Sri Lanka (GOSL) sources,[1] by conservative statistics, there are 800,000–1,000,000 IDPs from the north and east, and the figure may not adequately cover those having been displaced by the war in the areas of Mullaitivu, Kilinochchi and Mannar. This represents 200,000–250,000 families looking to resettle and rebuild their lives.

NARRATIVE HISTORY OF SITUATION OF IDPs IN SRI LANKA

Initial displacement of persons in Sri Lanka was a result of anti-Tamil conflicts in the southern parts of Sri Lanka in the years 1958, 1977 and

1978. These conflicts pressured many Tamil people to leave their homes in the Sinhala-dominated parts of the country and move to the north and east. In the aftermath of waves of attacks against Tamil people in the plantation areas in the late 1970s, many of these people from the central highlands of Sri Lanka settled in the Northern and Eastern Provinces.

Sri Lanka's ethnic conflict has displaced hundreds of thousands since it escalated in the early 1980s. Since 1983 when the military conflict between the Sri Lankan security forces and the Tamil militant groups became the order of the day, we have witnessed a never-ending saga of people forced into nomadic existence fleeing the areas of active conflict in search of a more secure and settled existence. Even though the majority of displaced persons are Tamils, Muslim and Sinhalese people living in Tamil majority areas have also been forced to leave due to threats against them.

CATEGORIES OF INTERNALLY DISPLACED PERSONS

IDPs can be categorized under different headings to get a clearer under-standing of the problem. The armed confrontation since 1983 has caused multiple displacements often following military operations. In many cases, communities and families have become separated and widely dispersed within Sri Lanka and overseas. To understand the situation of IDPs in Sri Lanka it would be useful to look at the period before the signing of the Ceasefire Agreement (CFA) in February 2002. At that time IDPs issues could have been categorized broadly under the headings detailed below.

Internally Displaced Persons Living in Government-Controlled Areas in the North and the East

Jaffna Peninsula

In the northeast the war escalated to unprecedented heights from April 1995. Although the government promised a quick and decisive victory over the LTTE, events proved otherwise. The intensified military operation against the LTTE witnessed the government forces capturing Jaffna town in December 1995, claiming their writ over an area considered to be the heart of the separatist movement. The most serious displacement of persons from the Jaffna town and its environs took place then, which was a huge, and largely unacknowledged, crisis for the northern Tamils. It was reported that victory was a hollow one since the LTTE ordered civilians to leave, turning the city into a ghost town. This created a new displacement of 400,000 persons of whom, approximately 170,000 stayed behind in the eastern part of Jaffna peninsula while 230,000 persons crossed to LTTE-controlled Wanni region. In May 1996 another 30,000–50,000 persons were displaced when the military took control over the whole of Jaffna peninsula. By mid-June 1996 many of the displaced in the military-controlled peninsula returned to their homes, but those in the Wanni were largely stuck there, mainly because of restrictions on civilian movements imposed by both the LTTE and the government.

From November 1999 to April 2000 the LTTE achieved massive military gains beginning with the capture of key military installations in the Wanni, overrunning the strategic Elephant Pass complex, reaching the outskirts of Jaffna town and coming within range to shell the military base in Palali and Kankesanthurai port. The fighting in Jaffna peninsula in May and June 2000 displaced an estimated 165,000 persons. Many families were separated during the displacement, between GOSL and LTTE-controlled areas. Civilians living in LTTE-controlled areas were reported to have taken shelter in underground bunkers due to shelling and bombing. Shortages were reported in essential food supplies. Schooling was disrupted as the displaced persons occupied a number of schools.

An area of critical strategic importance, the Jaffna peninsula has been subjected to major military incursions and waves of large-scale displacement. The present population of around 500,000 is thought to be about half the original number of inhabitants and many people have fled elsewhere on the island or overseas. The peninsula is now under government control and certain high security areas remain out of bounds for civilians. Overall, the region is heavily contaminated with landmines and unexploded ordnance (UXOs). A significant number of people in Jaffna have now returned to their original homes and agricultural production and farming is gradually recovering in some areas. People who remain in camps in Jaffna tend to be those who came from high security zones presently controlled by the Sri Lankan military. The possibility that they will return to their villages within the foreseeable future is very slim.

The East

The strategic and political importance of the east has meant large-scale militarization of the area, which in 1990 saw the dislodging of the LTTE from towns and major trunk roads. The east has thus remained a shifting patchwork of 'cleared' and 'uncleared' areas where the general situation has been very unstable. The LTTE after their loss of control of Jaffna and other areas in the north continued to be strong and effective in the east, and even now control most of the territory north of Trincomalee to the south of Batticaloa. The area is so large that the armed forces were stretched to even protect the roads during the day.

The other factor, which creates specificity for the conflict in the east, is its ethnic mix. The eastern province, particularly the Batticaloa region continues to be extremely volatile, with tensions running high between the LTTE, Tamil civilians and the Muslim community.

Vavuniya—The Gateway to the North

With the capture of Jaffna and Kilinochchi and the link-up to Mannar from Vavuniya, the town of Vavuniya as the gateway to the north, became a hub of many activities. Civilians leaving LTTE-controlled areas of Mullaitivu and Kilinochchi wishing to travel to Jaffna or to other parts of the island have to transit through Vavuniya. There has been a permanent displaced population since 1990. The first welfare centres were created in 1992 to accommodate refugee returnees from India. Among the displaced population in the region many are hill country Tamils who originally came from estates in the central highlands of Sri Lanka. In addition thousands of civilians who crossed over from Jaffna and the Wanni to Vavuniya following military operations from 1994–96 had been 'interned' in transit camps. Those who crossed over to Vavuniya were not all destitute but people with their own means of livelihood. However, everyone was made to suffer many indignities. They wanted freedom to move to the homes of their relatives in Vavuniya or to proceed to places like Colombo. Their fundamental freedom of movement was violated. One example of how the movements of the displaced were controlled can be gauged from an incident that took place in November 1999. There was a growing panic in Vavuniya as the LTTE ordered the 60,000 people living in the town to go to areas designated by them. Thousands of people were stranded on the roadside under trees. The military was also accused of attempting to use civilians as human shields when refugees in Vavuniya camps were denied permission to leave. People returned to Vavuniya when LTTE gave assurances that Vavuniya would not be attacked. Medicens Sans Frontieres (MSF) declared that the Sri Lankan Army and the LTTE had placed civilians at risk and restrictions on access of the population to humanitarian assistance sharply reduced the level of assistance provided to civilians in the north. Vavuniya is now largely under the control of the Sri Lankan armed forces, who maintain a heavy presence in the area.

Internally Displaced Tamils living in the North and the East in Territories Held by the Militants

In the Vanni and other contested areas in the north and east described by the Sri Lankan military as 'uncleared areas' the government maintained a skeleton administration and provided basic services. The LTTE had established a de facto parallel administration, which increasingly organized and controlled civil and economic life. The civilian population in LTTE-controlled areas endured years of economic blockade since 1990, briefly lifted during the peace talks in late 1994 and early 1995 but re-imposed after the breakdown of talks on 19 April 1995. These restrictions were relaxed beginning December 2001, which resulted in the free movement of civilians and goods.

'Operation Jayasikuri' (Victory Assured), the biggest military operation of the Sri Lankan security forces against the LTTE was launched on 13 May 1997. The main aim of the operation was to establish a land-based Main Supply Route (MSR), a 75-km stretch linking Vavuniya to Kilinochchi along A 9 highway to Jaffna. Only about two-thirds of the stretch was re-captured in nearly 18 months when the operation was called off. The operation cost more than $850 million a year, deployed more than 100,000 troops in the battle against the LTTE and displaced thousands of civilians from villages along the MSR.

The lack of regular and efficient transport facilities in these areas coupled with the restriction on fuel, medicines, building materials and other necessary amenities of life placed a serious impediment on this category of displaced population. The economic embargo enacted by the government and the lack of electricity has caused serious problems related to education and employment. Towns like Vavuniya and Batticaloa were heavily fortified with bunkers, barricades and sentry posts, looking more like fortresses, but the scenario 10 km away into LTTE held territory was entirely different. In LTTE-controlled areas, civilians moved freely even late in the night.

Another battle with regard to relief supplies was also waged during that time. Even though dry rations relief should have been given to 400,000 people, the Commissioner General of Essential Services (CGES) had statistics of his own. According to the statistics of the CGES, the dry ration relief had been given only to 295,000 people who were categorized as displaced, till 30 June 1998. Following the cut by the CGES only 193,163 people benefited from the ration relief. It was reported that the reduction in supplies meant that whatever was received was shared among all the displaced with the beneficiaries receiving only half of the allocated quantities.

Internally Displaced Muslims from the North

The Muslims of the northern province were also profoundly affected as a result of the conflict. The LTTE forced an estimated 100,000 Muslims living in the north to leave the area within 48 hours in October 1990. While some have returned to their original places of residence, many still remain in welfare centres more than a decade later—for a variety of reasons including security guarantees.

Internally Displaced Persons from Border Villages

The rise of Tamil nationalism had its impact on the areas bordering the north and the east. Internal displacement affected the Sinhalese as well. Although small in numbers, the Sinhalese living within or in border villages in the east and northwestern provinces claimed by the LTTE as being part of Tamil Eelam fled in fear when some of these villages were attacked and became victims of the ethnic warfare as well. The LTTE massacred civilians including children in several border villages heightening tensions in the non-conflict areas. Compared to other internally displaced persons, they were in a better position living in areas that have a regular system of transport and communication.

Internally Displaced Persons Living Outside Welfare Centres

Often local and international attention is paid to the displaced persons living in welfare centres. Less attention is paid to the 60 per cent of the total number of IDPs who continue to rely on the hospitality of relatives and friends. This constitutes a major relief operation by the communities themselves. The restrictions on providing accommodation for Tamils from the north and east in Colombo and other urban areas, security checks and other acts of intimidation under the cloak of Emergency Regulations or the Prevention of Terrorism Act often have eroded the traditional hospitality displaced civilians received in the past.

VULNERABLE PERSONS

Basic services and institutions in the uncleared areas providing food security, water, medical assistance, employment and education became progressively vulnerable and subject to collapse. The population of the north and east had suffered widespread psychological debility, physical illness, war-related injuries often nurturing a culture of dependency. Some specific vulnerable groups were:

Children

Children are for the most vulnerable, powerless and innocent victims of war. It was not a surprising fact that 50 per cent or more of the victims of conflict in Sri Lanka are children. Bombing and shelling can rarely identify civilians from combatants. Unrestrained attacks on communities provoked huge flights of survivors in search of sanctuary inside and outside of the country, the majority of victims were often children. The manipulation of food and relief supplies has often been a significant tactic of war, and Sri Lanka cannot, unfortunately, be entirely absolved in this respect. There was insufficient capacity to cater to the educational needs of displaced children. Among the displaced, one came across children, in particular, who for 10 years of their lives—a lifetime for many of them—had not known a settled existence, a home, a family, a village, a community. They felt no sense of belonging anywhere, whether it was a community or a group.

The widespread recruitment of young people less than 18 years of age from among IDPs as LTTE cadres for frontline duty appeared to be common practice endorsed by the movement's leadership. Although it appeared that most of these children were limited to battlefield support functions (that is, cooks, water-carriers, messengers, etc.), children have occasionally been discovered manning frontline (that is, combat) positions. This was despite the fact that in May 1998 the LTTE gave assurances to the Special Representative of the UN Secretary General for Children in Armed Conflict that they would not recruit children. Often children who lacked basic facilities and livelihood opportunities volunteered to join the LTTE.

Women

There is no doubt that women constituted a greater proportion than men among the IDPs. Internally displaced women also face serious security risks. Many have suffered from sexual violence and psychological and physical trauma. These included sexual harassment, rape, sexual favours for basic needs and forced prostitution, etc. Some had witnessed killings and atrocities and had lost close family members. Many internally displaced women have become the sole supporters of their families because they have lost their husbands. High numbers of female-headed households exist in the north and east. Such families are economically and psychologically vulnerable even in normal times. Reduction in the limited economic opportunities available, less paddy to harvest, less fish to process and slippage of various aspects of social safety net continues to cause extreme hardship to women.

The ways in which displacement affected women is multifaceted. In the first instance, the experience of leaving their homes and villages, the familiar environment and the support structures creates a vacuum in their lives, which is hard to replace. In the second instance, the experience of living in very crowded and cramped quarters with hundreds of strangers places them in an unfamiliar and very stressful new environment. The ways in which women have adapted to their new circumstances have had both their disturbing and exciting aspects; in some instances, the breakdown of family structures has had a disastrous impact on the lives of women, while in others, women have drawn on their latent resources to transform the most stressful of circumstances into something from which they can derive a sense of dignity for themselves. In welfare centres, one of the ways in which women have attempted to preserve their sense of themselves and of 'home', which is the focal point of their existence as they know it and define it, is to mark off their space within the camp in a clearly recognizable way; inside every welfare centre one found hundreds of small enclosures, spaces of 10 feet by 6 feet marked off with bricks, with cardboard boxes, with lengths of cloth, plastic and even jute.

One of the most tragic consequences of extended life in welfare centres on women in particular has been the breakdown of traditional and accepted forms and patterns of human and familiar relationships. The vacuum created by the absence of such patterns and norms has led to situations of conflict and tension affecting often the entire camp population. There have been reports of a large number of cases of extra-marital relationships; in some cases the relationships were those that would have been taboo in other, more 'normal' situations.

Men without Access to Regular Employment

Two areas of major male dominated economic activities, which have suffered as a result of the armed conflict, were farming and fishing. Restrictions placed on fertilizer inputs into LTTE-held areas, inaccessibility to farming lands in government-controlled areas have meant that many males lost their capacity to be gainfully employed. The ban on fishing in the north east coast, left thousands of fishermen and their families virtually destitute. A few who ventured to sail beyond the permitted distance from the coast often paid for it dearly with their lives.

The men were further victimized by being the main targets of arrest and harassment by the security forces both inside and outside the camp. This 'disempowering' of men, in the context of displacement, was a factor that very clearly led to a deep sense of frustration and tension within the men that then played out in various manifestations such as alcoholism, aggression and violence, primarily towards women and children in their families.

The Old and the Infirm

In the northern coastal belt as well as in the small islands in the north, and during the military takeover of the Jaffna peninsula, a fair section of people, particularly the handicapped, the sick and the elderly stayed behind in areas occupied by the armed forces. They stayed back because they could not join the others due to their physical inability or they were totally unprepared for such a situation. These people have remained cut off from their immediate family members. Even though they got assistance from the government in the cleared areas their day-to-day needs were often looked after by church-related organizations. The task of looking after this group of persons under the abysmal living conditions in LTTE-held areas was more difficult as they had to be moved from place to place along with the fleeing civilians.

The Sick

Internally displaced persons faced a number of medical problems not only during the process of displacement where healthcare was hardly available, but in camps where healthcare is limited. One very serious consequence of internal displacement was exhaustion and illness. Those among the displaced population who were most in need of urgent or regular medical care are frequently denied such assistance. Even in an insurrection to gain and hold territory, sick and displaced persons who live in areas that come under the control of the opposing non-state party to the conflict are entitled to medical care.

There appeared to be general unwillingness to permit adequate provision for north-eastern medical institutions to deal with injury, disease and sickness in accordance with internationally accepted standards of competence and compassion. This issue should have been addressed more from a medical angle than from a security one.

General

Tight security measures adopted by the military which led to physical checks at several barrier points, frequent combing operations, round ups, arbitrary and unfair arrest, prolonged detention, custodial rape and disappearance of young people, brought into focus gross violations of human rights that were committed following military reversals or acts of terror carried out by the LTTE. Many incidents of corruption such as stealing of aid given to IDPs, for personal use or for economic benefit, were also reported.

As will be seen from above, a large number of Sri Lankan families have been displaced for more than a decade. The vast majority of bread winners were fishermen, subsistence farmers and unskilled workers. What remained with them as financial resources were soon exhausted. One feature of internal displacement in Sri Lanka has been the multiple nature of the phenomenon, which was linked to particular military operations that were launched from time to time. The focus of these operations was at least twofold, to capture territory and to weaken the enemy. In the process of capturing territory those who suffered most were civilians who joined the ranks of IDPs in their hundreds of thousands. Another feature was that the capture of territory did not mean that civilians could return to their homes once the fighting was over, but had to languish in welfare centres or live with their friends or relatives for prolonged periods.

A BRIEF ANALYSIS OF THE POLITICAL CLIMATE IN WHICH THE MECHANISMS FUNCTION

The Sri Lankan government and the LTTE have a long history of repressing human rights. Despite its rhetoric, the government did not do enough to protect civilians caught up in the war. The humanitarian crisis was hidden not only from Sri Lankans but also from the international community. IDPs long remained pawns of the military dynamics of the Sri Lankan conflict. There were restrictions on their movement and on transport of essential supplies to areas under military control. An economic embargo in IDP camps close to military installations increased problems for them and these problems were further exacerbated by the use of civilians as human shields. The Guiding Principles on IDPs were often followed in Sri Lanka more in its breach than in its application. The ban on access for the media to the war zones benefited both sides of the conflict, as it prevented the outside world from learning the truth, which could have contributed to accelerating an end to the conflict.

Some other areas of concern to IDPs were the violation of the rights to adequate shelter, food security and medical provision. There is a need to sustain dignified life, to strengthen the efforts of local institutions to relieve suffering and build self-reliance; to widen the humanitarian space and seek humanitarian access to reach those in need on all sides of the conflict. In this respect human rights groups were not sufficiently active in the defence of IDPs, to disseminate knowledge of basic human rights norms in order to empower the displaced persons to understand their rights and help them articulate their concerns when they are violated.

Draconian security procedures have acted as a major constraint to humanitarian aid. Prior to the Ceasefire Agreement (CFA), most areas in the north and east were subject to curfew. Access to civilians had to be negotiated through the government, the Sri Lankan military and, in some places, the LTTE. The measures required to obtain clearances were also subject to regular change. For a long time the lives of dwellers in welfare centres, in Vavuniya, especially, were dogged by the pass system, there existing 15 different kinds of passes for a whole range of specific purposes. Children were even required to obtain permits to attend school.

Human rights policy in Sri Lanka remained largely uncoordinated and quickly marginalized when politically or militarily expedient to do so, and especially due to lack of strong implementation mechanisms. There was also a generally closed mind to constructive criticism, and the GOSL—at fora such as the UNCHR—continually failed to outline any concrete plan of action to rectify its human rights shortcomings. This, unfortunately, left both the international community and local human rights activists with very little to follow up on, or with which to productively engage the GOSL. Under such circumstances, those who subsequently adopted positions on human rights advocacy were most often construed by the GOSL as being hostile to them. The National Human Rights Commission continued its operations around the country. Saddled with a lack of resources and an irrationally sweeping mandate the Commission could yet become an effective instrument for the promotion and protection of human rights.

Following the CFA of February 2002, an improvement in the living conditions in the north and east and the prospects of a permanent settlement to the conflict, return of IDPs to their former places of residence began. Many returned spontaneously, with more contemplating doing so. Assisting them to do so continues to be an issue of critical impottance, particularly with regard to land and property issues. Besides landmines and UXOs that pose a serious physical danger, there are also issues of secondary occupation and restitution of property, occupation of land and property by the military, lost documents providing ownership, damage to housing, financial and other assistance to rebuild and restart livelihood, the situation of landless IDPs, land and property rights of women, legal redress and problems relating to the laws and institutional framework and capacity, and safe and dignified return of all IDPs who voluntarily choose to do so. Another matter of concern with regard to the return of IDPs is that of High Security Zones (HSZs). This is a serious problem, which has humanitarian, security and political implications and could well become a litmus test for the success of the peace process itself.

An Analysis of the Legal Situation in Terms of the Guiding Principles and in the Broader Context of Human Rights

Internally displaced persons shall enjoy, in full equality, the same rights and freedoms under international and domestic law as do other persons in their country. They shall not be discriminated against in the enjoyment of any rights and freedoms on the ground that they are internally displaced.[2]

IDPs have suffered restrictions on their freedom of movement and expression, access to water, basic healthcare and education. Many of the IDPs living in welfare centres have been living under difficult conditions. Due to the prolonged nature of displacement, many children born in welfare centres know no other kind of life. Conditions in welfare centres have led to a myriad of problems ranging from health and education issues and social problems. Conditions in these centres vary from location to location. Family life and economic activity have almost totally been destroyed. In some cases cultural identity and even their identity as a people was at risk. Restrictions placed on their movement were often senseless and counterproductive in respect of security objectives for which they were put in place. While their ability to participate in the political process was totally eliminated, they were often victims of partisan political manipulations. The embargo on 'war related' items, including medical equipment and drugs, infringed on the rights of IDPs in a variety of ways.

No ministry has overall responsibility for the welfare of IDPs nor are there comprehensive policies or guidelines on displacement. Various departments, ministries and aid agencies are responsible for various aspects of relief, protection and assistance. The allocation of ministerial areas of responsibility appears to be driven by political motives, such as securing a vote base. Administrative practices and departmental policies applied to IDPs are, on the one hand, subject to whimsical changes, while, on the other, not adopted to reflect the changing conflict situation. Thus, food entitlements were often arbitrarily cut, while the Rs 1,260 towards the dry food ration entitlement per month for a family of five has not been increased from 1993 to match the rise in the cost of living. Decisions taken at the level of the Ministry of Rehabilitation or the Ministry of Defence in Colombo were often ignored or altered by Local Area Army Commanders. There was also confusion with regard to the nature and scope of various aid agencies working in Sri Lanka who had to often work within the framework dictated by the government and the security forces.

The protection regimes afforded to IDPs include government assistance and international assistance from multiple donors, UN agencies and international and local NGOs. Despite this, many fundamental human rights concerns remain, which need arbitration and mediation. National instruments and institutions available for these were not made use of. 'The most worrying concern is the lack of governmental framework on displacement. State policy towards IDPs has been vague and constantly changing. There is an evident lack of policy and legal framework.'[3]

UNHCR has been playing a leading role in the promotion of the Guiding Principles on Internal Displacement (GPID) in Sri Lanka. Some of their initiatives in this regard carried out over the past few years are detailed below:[4]

- translation, printing and disseminating of the Guiding Principles into Sinhala and Tamil;
- the posting of translated versions on the global IDP Project web page;
- conducting training workshops on the GPID for the following groups:
  - implementing partners,
  - university students,
  - the military,
  - participants in human rights diploma courses,
  - government representatives,
  - welfare centre staff and residents,
  - lawyers and judges,
  - staff of the Human Rights Commission,
  - UNHCR staff in Sri Lanka;
- providing an access to justice programmes for IDPs and returnees based on the GPID through the Legal Aid Foundation of the Bar Association of Sri Lanka;

- launching a legal handbook for internally displaced persons (in English, Sinhala and Tamil) prepared under the LAF project;
- launching 'Remembering the Displaced' a pictorial promoting the GPID, in 2000, to coincide with the 50th anniversary of UNHCR;
- producing annually pocket calendar booklets with the key GPID and circulating them widely, especially amongst the military in the north and the east;
- introducing the GPID in RRR framework;
- developing a training toolkit on the GPID through an implementing partner (this toolkit is actually being used by the implementing partner);
- promoting the adoption of the GPID through the Eminent Persons Group in Sri Lanka.

A study was undertaken by the Consortium of Humanitarian Agencies (CHA), Centre for Policy Alternatives (CPA) and Law and Society Trust (LST) on *Internally Displaced Persons and Human Rights Commission* in 2001. The objective of the study was to generate a set of findings and recommendations that would assist the Human Rights Commission (HRC) in defining its role and guide the HRC to intervene in an effective man-ner to provide a framework for assistance and protection of IDPs. The study concluded that the Guiding Principles provided the best protection to be used in the Sri Lankan context by an institution such as the HRC. The study provided specific instances with key concepts and issues found in IDP situations as a basis to guide the involvement of the HRC to afford more focused protection for IDPs.

The study made two sets of recommendations on human rights viola-tions of IDPs and government policies. The first set of recommendations was specific to the HRC, while the second referred to recommendations the HRC could make to the government. The recommendations were made bearing in mind the mandate and the limitations within which the HRC functions. Among others, the study recommended that the HRC should, as per its functions, described in the Human Rights Commission of Sri Lanka Act, inquire and investigate all complaints of violations of fundamental rights from IDPs, including violence against women; strengthen existing HRC offices and establish new ones in places where there was no HRC presence. Where HRC recommendations had little or no impact, HRC should consider filing Fundamental Rights cases before the Supreme Court. With regard to HRC recommendations to the gov-ernment, the study recommended, among others, that the government should set up a central body on internal displacement and that the body should have authority over all actors involved in the welfare of IDPs. Its responsibilities would include: (*a*) framing a comprehensive policy on IDPs modelled on the UN Guiding Principles on Internal Displacement and SPHERE standards; (*b*) monitor the implementation of such policy by the different ministries responsible for the welfare of IDPs; (*c*) monitor all other policies and practices that affect IDPs, including those of the military forces; and (*d*) receive, forward or act upon complaints from IDPs.

According to Mario Gomez,[5] there has been an effort by the Human Rights Commission to respond to some of the recommendations contained in the study and build capacity within the institution to address the needs of IDPs. This process started initially with the recognition by the Commission that IDPs were a vulnerable group that required special intervention strategies. A study undertaken by the Sri Lankan HRC identified a lack of coherent government policy on displacement as a major gap. The Sri Lankan study also observed that modifying the national security laws so that they comply with international human rights norms was a task the Commission could undertake almost immediately.[6] As the Sri Lankan experience shows, national human rights commissions provide one way of responding to the concerns of IDPs. Their location within the government, their stature as a national institution, and the flexibility of the strategies they can potentially pursue, give them the possibility to make a difference in situations of internal displacement.[7] UNHCR, HRC and CPA have been independently studying land and property rights issues of IDPs, which was pushed centre stage as a result of recent developments following improvement of living conditions since the cessation of hostilities. Their reports were presented to a wider audience for discussions in February 2003. They highlighted restitution of property, access to land, defusion of landmines, assistance and legal redress as being some of the pressing challenges facing returnees, the government, the LTTE and the international community in their efforts towards restoring normalcy in the northeast.

A BRIEF ANALYSIS OF THE CONDITIONS AND PATTERNS OF DISPLACEMENT, AVAILABLE REMEDIES AND DEFICIENCIES IN ARRANGEMENTS OR ABSENCES THEREOF

In June 2002, GOSL adopted a National Framework for Relief, Rehabilitation and Reconciliation (Triple R), to provide a common strategy for needs assessment, joint planning and implementation of government assistance to the population with priority given to IDPs. UNHCR plays a key role in supporting the government's efforts to implement this strategy. The Triple R framework asserts,

> ...unlike in conflict situations in many other countries, the Government of Sri Lanka has from the start recognized its obligations to the conflict affected populations and is committed to providing humanitarian relief, essential services, rehabilitation and development support even while the conflict endured. These services were not limited to conflict affected persons living in secure areas, but through governmental civil administration structure which continued to function in all affected areas, food and medicine being provided by government agencies free of charge to all recognized displaced persons.[8]

While recognizing the operational hurdles and impediments in the delivery of humanitarian assistance, in carrying out rehabilitation projects, in reconstructing damaged and destroyed assets, the Triple R framework contends that no government can fully discharge its responsibilities under war conditions, when the prerequisites of relief, rehabilitation and development programmes are lacking. It adds,

> ...the government recognizes that relief and rehabilitation programmes have not been as effective as desired. In part, this was because of the dynamics of conflict and the confrontational attitudes it generated; in part operational obstacles arose from the persistent tension—and indeed contradictions—between rehabilitation objectives and security concerns. Understandably, the civilian administration and the military establishment, from their differing vantage points, did not always reach the same conclusions in assessing the needs of the populations living in the affected areas. With the present access and freedom of movement of persons and goods, this dichotomy in policy and operational approaches has largely been eliminated.[9]

The Triple R framework adopted the Guiding Principles on Internal Displacement as official policy for assisting IDPs affected by the conflict and commit concerned ministries to bring their policies and programmes into alignment with these principles.[10]

While mandating the HRC and the Legal Aid Commission to disseminate the Guiding Principles it recommended the review of the legal framework of laws relevant to the displaced using the Guiding Principles as the analytical instrument for identifying gaps in the national regime for the protection of the displaced.[11]

CONCLUSIONS

The achievements of GOSL and LTTE since the conclusion of the CFA in February 2002 greatly reduced tensions and large numbers of lives were saved and untold property damage avoided. With a focus on alleviating the hardships people have experienced during the years of war, GOSL and LTTE representatives during their round of negotiations in Thailand in September 2002 agreed to establish a joint task force for improving the living conditions of the people of all ethnic communities in the war affected areas of the north and east. Based on this decision and subsequent consultations in November 2002, the terms of reference for 'The Sub-Committee on Immediate Humanitarian and Rehabilitation Needs' (SIHRN) evolved. SIHRN was a short-term mechanism for responding to the immediate needs of the population of the conflict-affected regions in the north and east. SIHRN was meant to be a flexible and adaptable mechanism for meeting urgent needs of the population but it could barely become effective when the ceasefire ended. The role of SIHRN, among others, was meant to do the following: to identify humanitarian and re-construction needs of the population and prioritize implementation of activities to meet these needs. Priority was to be given to activities aimed at rehabilitation of IDPs, and to humanitarian action programmes and other activities supporting the return of IDPs to their original homes, such as reconstruction of roads, production infrastructure, health facilities, schools and similar issues. SIHRN also defined its own guiding principles for implementation of activities, which among others, included:

- the involvement of all ethnic communities so that their needs and aspirations would be considered.
- active consultation by the implementing agencies with the beneficiaries in planning and implementing of the activities.

The SIHRN secretariat located in Kilinochchi convened a meeting with NGOs and donors to introduce its 'Purpose and Activities' and also discuss modalities for co-ordination of initiatives within the development framework of the north and east. It transpired during the meeting jointly chaired by GOSL and LTTE representatives and the director of SIHRN that this joint GOSL/LTTE sub-committee would be time bound to look into immediate humanitarian needs and to co-ordinate resettlement of

IDPs on a priority basis. The North East Rehabilitation Fund (NERF) set up during earlier rounds of peace negotiations was expected to support the work of SIHRN, funding for which was to be under the custodianship of the World Bank.

It was also stressed that meeting humanitarian needs should go parallel to the political process. SIHRN was designed to serve all ethnic communities living in the north and east. Its two main priorities identified were: (a) humanitarian action; (b) accelerating resettlement of over 800,000 IDPs. The objectives were to identify humanitarian and rehabilitation needs, prioritise them, determine implementing agencies from among local NGOs and CBOs and allocate funds. Certain preconditions to be met included, respect for basic human rights, gender equality and the strengthening of democracy. Given that there is a multiplicity of government institutions dealing with IDP issues, SIHRN would be the prime body to co-ordinate activities. SIHRN's successful functioning would be pivotal to the success of the peace process itself.

As the peace process gains momentum, the focus on IDPs will undoubtedly shift from care and maintenance to durable solutions. Return to areas of origin is the optimal durable solution. Several thousand spontaneous returns that took place while the ceasefire was on is a good indicator of the perceptions of IDPs that conditions are changing for the better in the areas of return. While the will to return is obviously widespread, IDPs continue to be constrained by many pull factors not least of which is the present political situation. Among the other factors are:

- apprehension about whether the peace process would succeed and fear that it is premature to risk returning;
- the presence of landmines and UXOs and the inability to gain access to property and agricultural land;
- HSZs are under the occupation of the military;
- destruction of property and little or no resources to rebuild homes;
- occupation of lands and houses by others and the risk of being unable to reoccupy them;
- financial constraints of GOSL to provide adequate resettlement assistance and the lack of employment and income generating activities.

Finding a durable solution to the problems of IDPs is an essential element of the peace building process in Sri Lanka. As long as sizeable numbers of the population remain destitute and marginalized as a result of two decades of war, they will place the peace process at risk. It is the responsibility of GOSL and the LTTE to create conditions that will elimin-ate or substantially reduce this risk. Many believe that the peace process is going through a period of intense crisis. Present events portray that it was a misconception that the ceasefire has brought peace to the country. But peace can only be achieved through a hard and arduous process of negotiation. The groundswell of international support for the peace process can be harnessed and sustained if there is sufficient goodwill and political will within Sri Lanka to work resolutely to achieving peace which has eluded the island for two decades. Sri Lanka currently finds itself in a "no peace, no war" scenario. Some progress has been achieved during the six sessions of formal peace talks held to date, most notably the GoSL-LTTE agreement at the Oslo talks of December 2002. Since the breakdown of talks in April 2003, and the failure to establish an effective mechanism for the delivery of aid to conflict-affected areas, progress has been retarded to improve the lives and livelihoods of those most affected by the war. Approximately 400,000 people are still internally displaced, up to a million landmines remain scattered in some of the most heavily populated and fertile areas, and occupation of people's land in the High Security Zones continues. Human rights and human security issues deteriorated further and temporary displacements occurred following the breakaway of LTTE cadres loyal to the Eastern Commander in Batticoloa-Ampara districts. Distrust between GOSL and LTTE, fractious politics within the Sinhalese polity that have prevented the emergence of a coherent vision for peace and have rendered an already challenging task even more so. Unfortunately he present political situation can subvert the entire peace process. This would not only further delay finding a lasting solution for the displaced but also increase the potential for more waves of internal displacement.

Notes

1. Appeal submitted to the Pledging Conference in Oslo on 25 November 2002.
2. Guiding Principles on Internal Displacement.
3. 'Sri Lanka: State of Human Rights 2002', *Law & Society Trust Colombo*, October 2002, 19.
4. UNHCR, Colombo, February 2003.
5. Mario Gomez, 'National Human Rights Commissions and Internally Displaced Persons', *SAIS Project on Internal Displacement* (Washington, DC: The Brookings Institute, July 2002), 22.
6. Ibid., 32.
7. Ibid., 35.
8. 'National Framework for Relief, Rehabilitation and Reconciliation', *Development Form* (Colombo, June 2002), 5.
9. Ibid., 6.
10. Ibid., 18.
11. Ibid., 20–21

CHAPTER 9

RESISTING ERASURE:
WOMEN IDPS IN SOUTH ASIA

Paula Banerjee

The United Nations defines any conflict where there are more than
1,000 battlefield deaths as a major conflict.[1] According to this
definition, in 1965 there were 10 major conflicts. In 1992 the
number went up to 50, with another 84 lesser conflicts. In the post-cold
war era what became obvious was that most of these were 'civil or intra-
state' conflicts. The states were thus looking inwards and hence the
major casualties were from the civilian population. 'During World War I,
civilians made up fewer than 5 per cent of all casualties. Today, 75 per
cent or more of those killed or wounded in wars are non-combatants.'[2] In
the 1990s there was a growing realization that whether it was Kosovo,
Afghanistan, India or Sri Lanka, the major casualties of war were women
and children. The 1990s was also the time for the growth of another
interesting phenomenon all over South Asia, and that was that, while the
states were fighting wars against their own errant people they were also
creating mechanisms for the safeguard of the human rights of the people
who were being brutalized either due to conflict or development. Looking
at this phenomenon one observer remarked: 'It is unclear why some governments would create national institutions to implement international
norms that they routinely violate.'[3] Thus we have the birth of Human
Rights Commissions in most of South Asia in the 1990s. While these
were being set up, South Asia was emerging as one of the most conflict-
prone zones of the world with thousands killed and many more displaced
each year. Among the displaced were those who found refuge in other
countries; however, many more could not cross borders. They joined the
ranks of the internally displaced, were often forced to live within a system
that had displaced them in the first place and there was no treaty or any
institutional arrangement that interceded on their behalf.

The category of internally displaced people in South Asia acquired visibility with the escalation of conflict in Sri Lanka. By the end of 1995 more than 1 million people were displaced in Sri Lanka.[4] Around the same time, with increasing recognition that the internally displaced people (hereafter IDP) needed special attention, there were efforts to draft certain specific rules to guide their administration. It was recognized that no continent was spared the scourge of internal displacement or the cruelties associated with the phenomenon. It was also recognized that the women among the IDP population formed a special category by their sheer number. Therefore, unlike with the convention on refugees, when the Guiding Principles on the Internally Displaced Persons were drafted, attention was paid to the fact that 'overwhelming majority of the internally displaced are women and their dependent children.'[5]

In the Guiding Principles a concerted attempt was made to prioritize gender issues. For example, while discussing groups that needed special attention in Principle 4 it was stated that expectant mothers, mothers with young children and female heads of households, among others, are people who may need special attention. In Principle 7 it was stated that when displacement occurred due to reasons other than armed conflict authorities should involve women who are affected, in the planning and management of their relocation. Principle 9 upheld that IDPs should be protected in particular against '[r]ape, mutilation, torture, cruel, inhuman or degrading treatment or punishment, and other outrages upon personal dignity, such as acts of gender-specific violence, forced prostitution and any other form of indecent assault.' Special protection was also sought against sexual exploitation. Principle 18 stated that special efforts should be made to include women in planning and distribution of supplies. Principle 19 stated that attention should be given to the health needs of women and Principle 20 stated that both men and women had equal rights to obtain government documents in their own names.

Apart from the Guiding Principles, the 1979 Convention on the Elimination of All Forms of Discrimination against Women (hereafter CEDAW) and the 1999 Optional Protocol set out specific steps for states to become proactive in their efforts to eliminate discrimination against displaced women. Article 2 of CEDAW clearly states that public authorities, individuals, organizations and enterprises should refrain from discrimination against women. Article 3 reiterates women's right to get protection from sexual violence. Article 6 speaks against trafficking and sexual exploitation of women. Since most displaced women are particularly vulnerable to traffickers this article is of some importance to them. It must be noted that all the countries of South Asia are signatories to CEDAW with some reservations but not of the proportion that it negates the overarching principles, and therefore the onus of being gender sensitive in their attitude and programmes is on them. Apart from these there are other international provisions that protect women's human rights. Article 3 of the Geneva Conventions of 12 August 1949 calls for the halt of weapons against the civilian population and to protect all civilians, including children, women and persons belonging to ethnic and religious minorities from violations of humanitarian law. Article 29 of ILO 1930 Convention concerning forced or compulsory labour also impacts the situation of women. It calls for the end of violations of the human rights of women, in particular forced labour, abuse and torture of labourers including women.

In this chapter I will explore whether the countries of South Asia have successfully integrated gender sensitivity in their attitude towards, and programmes for, displaced communities. In my analysis I have included Myanmar because it shares borders with South Asia and reportedly has one of the worst cases of ethnic displacement in the region. Also, displacement in Myanmar has had serious consequences for South Asian countries that are often repositories where these displaced people eventually move to. This chapter also deals with two major categories of displacement: displacement due to conflict and displacement due to developmental projects. Displacement due to conflict may result from interstate or intrastate conflict. Among intrastate conflict we have state versus community and community versus community conflicts. Moreover, most of these conflicts are overlapping. Displacement due to developmental projects can be because of building dams, mining, shrimping, urban cleaning and other projects that allegedly bring in modernization. Our intention is to analyse how South Asian states have integrated gender concerns in their programmes for the displaced population. We will also critique whether gender specific violence has contributed in any way towards increasing displacement in the region. In South Asia there are numerous cases of displacement and our purpose is not to chronicle each and every one of them, but rather to show patterns of displacement and analyse the responses of the state, particularly towards women who are displaced and yet are forced to remain within the borders of their own country. We have to recognize that notwithstanding CEDAW, state power in South Asia is largely weighted against women and women are some of the worst victims of displacement. Yet to look at women as merely victims is to see only half of the story. It is imperative that we recognize how displaced women, even in their victimization, make efforts to organize and create movements to seek justice.

CONFLICT AND DISPLACEMENT:
THE SRI LANKAN SITUATION

Any discussion on IDPs in South Asia should necessarily begin with Sri Lanka since it was here that the phenomenon was first internationally recognized. Sri Lanka has been the scene of a brutal ethnic conflict since the 1980s. By 1990 about 10 per cent of Sri Lankan population were internally displaced.[6] The situation stabilized in the early 1990s with some displaced people being repatriated. But the situation worsened once again in October 1995 when the Sri Lankan armed forces launched an operation to wrest Jaffna from the control of the Liberation Tigers of Tamil Eelam (LTTE). Almost 90 per cent of the people from these areas became displaced. In 2000, LTTE launched a counter-offensive to retake Jaffna followed by a government offensive in 2001. In this protracted conflict civilian life was seriously affected. According to the estimates of UNHCR and Refugees International, by 2001 some 800,000 people were displaced. In February 2002, for the first time in seven years, the Sri Lankan government and the LTTE signed the first formal bilateral ceasefire between the two sides. This ceasefire is continuing even today.

In terms of social indicators the status of women in Sri Lanka was considered a marvel of South Asia before the ethnic conflict. Even today Sri Lanka has the highest literacy rate among women in South Asia. A high percentage (83 per cent) of Sri Lankan women are literate and their average life expectancy is 72 years. Maternal mortality is as low as 39.8 per 100,000 live births. Sri Lanka also has the singular distinction of electing the first woman prime minister in the world. Sri Lankan women have enjoyed adult franchise since 1931 and the country has ratified a series of international and pro-women treaties. It ratified the CEDAW without any reservation in 1981. It has also ratified the International Covenants of Civil and Political Rights and Economic, Social and Cultural Rights, the Convention on the Rights of the Child and the UN Convention against Torture and Other Cruel, Inhuman or Degrading Treatment or Punishment. However, it has not ratified the key ILO conventions regulating standards for women workers. As for internal mechanisms in Sri Lanka, the Penal Code (Amendment) Act Nos. 22 of 1995 and 29 of 1998, the Code of Criminal Procedure (Amendment) Act No.

28 of 1998 and the Judicature (Amendment) Act No. 27 of 1998, are all laws that have created a legal framework for more effective prosecution of alleged rapists. Among the changes in the penal code was the inclusion of a new provision recognizing the phenomena of rape in custody. However, even after ratifying all these international instruments and creating pro-women legal mechanisms it is interesting to note that women and children form the vast majority among the IDPs and their situation still worrying.

It has been stated from the beginning that although the government of Sri Lanka 'assumed some responsibility toward the displaced, its policy has been heavily influenced by security concerns that determined the extent and nature of the humanitarian response to be made towards the care of the displaced'.[7] In the conflict area often the armed forces enjoyed a certain amount of impunity, hence there were more cases of rape, torture and sexual violence against women leading to their displacement. As early as 1995 Francis Deng, the UN Special Representative on Internally Displaced Persons reported that some women had been raped prior to their displacement.[8] Human Rights observers from the Amnesty International repeatedly reported that security forces in conflict areas in Sri Lanka were raping women. In one such report, in April 2001, it was stated that: 'Two Tamil women who were taken into custody in the northwestern Mannar district by naval personnel were allegedly gang-raped by them on 19 March. Tamil politicians and the Catholic bishop of Mannar protested strongly and took the matter up with the authorities.'[9] In another report it was stated that two soldiers raped a 72-year-old internally displaced widow.[10] This is not exceptional but a typical report. The Amnesty International also reports that the figures showing the rapes committed by security forces also include 'many internally displaced women'.[11] In another comprehensive report it is stated that the 'risk of sexual violence for displaced women dramatically increases in the conditions immediately prior to, during and post flight.'[12] From such reports and other incidents of rape it is apparent that in Sri Lanka rape has been used as an instrument to displace women and among those who are displaced many have been victims of rape. Also when instruments of state such as members of the armed forces have perpetrated rape these people are hardly ever prosecuted.[13]

The process of displacement has proved to be extremely debilitating for women. Among the vast majority of displaced families were a number of women-headed households. Conflict in Sri Lanka resulted in the collapse of community and family structures. Many women had to leave their homes without any community support. This has rendered them more vulnerable to sexual violence. A large majority of the IDPs stayed with people known to them. Even while living with friends, women are expected to shoulder responsibilities for which they are often unprepared. In a recent CEDAW committee report it was stated that almost half of the female-headed households are in the hands of elderly women, many of whom are illiterate and devoid of adequate sources of income.[14] This has taken heavy toll on women's mental and physical health. Moreover, internally displaced women often lack easy access to healthcare facilities according to the UN Special Rapporteur on Violence Against Women.[15] As for women's mental health, this has not been considered an issue. In areas of conflict, one of the reasons why healthcare is such a problematic issue is that even though a range of international, national and local aid agencies provided assistance to the internally displaced the government restricts many relief supplies including medical provisions.

Among the IDPs who live in 348 government-run camps, as reported in 2001, the situation of women is extremely serious. Old saris and other pieces of rag often separate families from each other. There is a severe lack of privacy in these camps.[16] Often these camps, known as welfare centres, are heavily guarded and entry and exit are restricted. In such a situation young women are particularly vulnerable and, according to one social worker, there is an alarming increase of pregnancy among teenage girls in these camps.[17] It has been pointed out by one observer that the 'Sri Lankan experience shows that displaced women are more likely to seek work or engage in economic activity than men.'[18] The restrictions on entrance into and exit from camps affect these women who work outside of the camps. Also, Sri Lanka's non-ratification of ILO Conventions regulating standards for women workers has adversely affected women IDPs, who are now forced to take up jobs in the unorganized sectors. Further, according to reports of Jesuit Refugee Service, these camps are the recruiting grounds for agents who send these women to different countries to work as maids. Often they are victims of sexual abuse but because of the difficulty of finding employment in these camps, IDP women are forced to take up oversees assignments, which then drive them into abusive situations.

That, like most other South Asian states, the Sri Lankan state is often weighted against women becomes apparent when one considers that children of Sri Lankan women married to non-nationals were not granted Sri Lanka citizenship until 2003 and that even now (as of 2004) there is an aversion to granting visas to children and the spouses of Sri Lankan women married to non-nationals. Traditionally this has adversely affected the rights of single women of marriageable age who are displaced; they do not seek refugee status because in the prevailing situation, if they married a non-national, it would be difficult for them to return to Sri Lanka as their children are not granted citizenship. Considering the seriousness of the situation, particularly because after the Thailand Peace Talks in early 2003 Sri Lanka's displaced are being encouraged to return home, the Sri Lankan president, Chandrika Kumaratunga, signed a bill on 8 March 2003 allowing women to transfer citizenship to their children. However, it is still early days to understand how such an instrument has been translated into practice.

The Thailand Peace Talks have resulted in the formation of a Joint Task Force for Humanitarian and Reconstruction Activities. It has also resulted in the formation of a Joint Committee to address the return of IDPs to high security zones. Many women's rights organizations feel that they are not consulted by either of these groups. This can create problems because when in the early 1990s the political situation had improved and many women returned to their homes, they were then once again displaced and sometimes killed by either LTTE or the security forces. There is the well-known case of Ida Carmelita. She had returned to Sri Lanka from India in 1994 and was brutally raped and killed by security forces in 1999. This is not a solitary case. There are other women, such as Thambipillai Thanalakshmi, who were brutally raped after they returned to resettle.[19] Women are always the first to be repatriated because there is a fear that if men return they may be lured by the rebel groups or apprehended by security forces. In such a situation it is best to involve women's groups to explore whether it is safe for women to return to high security zones. The strip-searching of a Sinhalese woman in broad daylight in Sri Lanka on the suspicion that she was a Tamil suicide bomber shows that the situation of IDP women can be precarious.[20] Now that Sri Lanka is nebulously poised for peace any decision on IDPs should consider that a large part of that population consists of women and unless they are consulted on decisions about their future it will adversely impact the peace process.

CONFLICT AND DISPLACEMENT: THE SITUATION IN BURMA

Over 40 years of military rule in Burma has taken a heavy toll on the situation of women from ethnic minority groups. Burma until 1997 was ruled by a military junta calling itself the State Law and Order Restoration

Council (SLORC), which is now renamed the State Peace and Development Council (SDPC). The oppression and atrocities that pro-democracy Burmese women and ethnic minority women have been made to endure are becoming clearer each day. Despite Burma's ratification of the Convention on Elimination of all Forms of Discrimination against Women (CEDAW) in 1997, discrimination is apparent in virtually every facet of an ethnic minority woman's life. Since 1991 the UN General Assembly adopted annual resolutions concerning the appalling human rights situation in Burma. More recently in June 1999, the ILO announced that the Burmese authorities had not desisted in the least from carrying out or from condoning practices such as forced labour, arbitrary detention, torture and rape. In July, the ILO suspended Burma from participation until it reformed its forced labour practices. In October 1999, in a report to the UN General Assembly, Rajsoomer Lallah, the Commission's special rapporteur for Burma, concluded that the human rights situation in the country had deteriorated in 1998.[21] In January 1999 he gave a similar report to the UN Human Rights Commission.[22] There are recent indications that the international community is relaxing its pressure on the Burmese regime due to its apparent move towards political transition. But what has to be remembered is that there are an estimated 500,000 to 1 million IDPs in Burma who are largely from the ethnic minority community. Of the 1 million Burmese who have been 'internally displaced' by the war, around 80 per cent are known to be women and children. About 60 per cent of these displaced are women and girls escaping from threats to their lives and to their bodies from the Burmese army.[23] According to one observer, 'because of the diversity among Burma's 135 officially-recognized ethnic groups generalizing about them is risky. However, there clearly exists a countrywide pattern to the abuses suffered by Karen, Karenni, Mon, Shan, Kachin, Chin, Arakanese, Rohingya, and other ethnic women.'[24] The SDPC reportedly continues to target pro-democracy activists and ethnic minorities and rape is systematically used as a weapon to dislocate communities and displace women. Due to continuing lack of access and information the enormity of the situation is difficult to verify. But there are groups who have gone inside Burma and others who gather information from Burmese populations in Bangladesh, India and Thailand. The following section of my chapter is based largely on works of these research groups.

In one such work we hear the voice of Naing,[25] a young Burmese woman who works as a volunteer in a women's organization on the Thai–Burmese border. She shares her experiences in an article. According to Naing the regime 'issued a military law that states that all households must contribute to the building of railroad tracks connecting two villages. Each household in the area must contribute physical labour and/or 2,000 kyat (equivalent to US $20).' Naing says that women are favoured as workers for the junta's construction works, as their male supervisors feel that they can be easily controlled. The women, Naing notes, are forced to carry cement, bricks and other heavy materials. They are not given any choice of when or where to work, nor are they given any reprieve. Naing recalls the story of a young widow who went to her local administrative office to explain that as a widow with several children to support from her earnings as a seamstress, she could not contribute, whether in the form of manual labour or financially, to the construction of the tracks. 'The official seized the opportunity and gave her the option to contribute as mandated or to engage in sex with him,' she narrates. Having no other real choice, the widow had to do the latter. The official's demands were frequent, however, and also included that she clean house for him, cook and sew his clothes. She had to tolerate his sexual torture. Unable to tolerate her situation any longer, the widow made the painful choice of leaving her children and running away. She now lives in a refugee camp.[26] According to Naing this is not an exceptional story but one that is most common.

From the 1970s the regime has practised the forced relocation of ethnic minorities. The largest and most intensive forced relocation programme was carried out in 1996–97 in the central Shan state. Over 3,00,000 people from over 1,400 villages were forced from their homes into relocation sites where nothing was provided for them. Sexual violence against ethnic minority women has become commonplace, especially because of relocation. The context of civil war has given Burmese troops licence and impunity to practise sexual violence against local ethnic women. According to one report, 'Burmese military regime are systematically using rape as a weapon in their anti-insurgency campaigns against civilian population.'[27] In the same report it was stated that more than 25 per cent of women raped are killed. It was also stated that military officers committed 83 per cent of these rapes. The majority of these rapes documented (76 per cent) were in the areas where ethnic minority women were forcibly relocated. When villagers are relocated they are usually given a verbal or written order with a specified deadline with the threat that anyone found in the village after that time will be shot on sight. But often the military do not wait until the stipulated deadline to begin inflicting violence on the villagers, either immediately after the order is given or while the villagers are moving. Six per cent of the rape cases documented in the report occurred while the villagers were being forcibly relocated.[28] Rapes are reported even from within the relocation sites. In another report by Earthrights International, a human rights and environment organization dedicated to the needs of ethnic minorities and indigenous peoples, released its report entitled 'School of Rape'. This report focuses on the sexual violence experienced by Burmese and ethnic minority women during the Burmese civil war. The report estimates that nearly 1.3 million Burmese women and girls who have 'fled to camps or are in flight inside Burma's borders' are at high risk of rape by the military.[29] Thus, the Burmese army uses rape before, during and even after the process of displacement. Over 21 per cent of those raped reported the cases to local authorities but only in one instance has there been a conviction.

Another reason why displaced women become more vulnerable is because the Burmese army often recruit porters from these communities. This means that when troops arrive at a village the men run away, leaving women alone, lest they be conscripted. Once porters are conscripted they are in the service for years leaving their women back in the village. Often these women are raped when they are alone. War, migration, relocation and forced labour have all contributed to the increase of female-headed households among the displaced population. Typically relocation sites are in areas where land is unsuitable for cultivation. With very few opportunities for wage labour, women farmers must struggle to meet both their families' needs and the demands of the Burmese army for rations, taxes, and labour. The double burden of farm work and housework that most women bear takes a toll on their health. It is estimated that 40 per cent of the population is without access to health services of any kind. Poor healthcare, malnutrition, the stress of living in difficult conditions, and endemic diseases have led to high maternal mortality rates, estimated at 580 or more per 100,000 among some ethnic minority groups who are displaced.[30]

Although the Burmese government reports that 79 per cent of all women in Burma are literate there is an increasing illiteracy among women in relocated areas. Girls are discouraged from going to school out of fear that they may be molested on the way. Also, traditional gender attitudes dictate that when resources are scarce then boys are sent to schools rather than girls. Further, in most relocation sites there are hardly any schools for girl children. In these sites young women face further restrictions that increase their vulnerabilities. Measures like the 1997 order (enacted by the regional army command in eastern Shan state) prohibiting women aged 16 to 25 from travelling without a legal guardian actually increase the likelihood that women planning to migrate will enlist the help of traffickers, exposing them to greater risk of exploitation.[31] In a CEDAW meeting in January 2000 it was stated that the Burmese regime is forcibly trying to make the state more homogenous.[32] One way of doing so is by marrying off rape victims to the perpetrators, who are often Burmese soldiers. Their children are then registered as Burmese. Thus, the situation of ethnic minority and pro-democracy displaced women is extremely serious. There is a growing number of HIV-positive women among the internally displaced, which the SDPC denies. According to one observer among those women who are crossing the border and entering into India an overwhelming number of them are HIV-positive.[33] It is time for the international human rights community to intervene on behalf of the internally displaced women in Burma, otherwise any hope of peace in the region will prove to be a mirage.

CONFLICT AND DISPLACEMENT:
THE CASE OF THE LINE OF CONTROL

In the previous two cases we were looking at displacement due to intra-state conflict. The conflict over the Line of Control (LOC) between India and Pakistan is an interstate conflict that has resulted in severe dislocation and displacement of populations from both sides. The border between India and Pakistan has caused four wars (in 1948, 1965, 1971 and 1999) and many more near-war situations. The two countries fought over the fate of Kashmir. In the process Kashmir has been divided into three parts. Today the northern part is known as Azad Kashmir and it is under Pakistani control. The southern part forming largely the State of Jammu and Kashmir is under Indian control and the eastern part is under Chinese control. From 1989, in the Indian side of Kashmir there has been a raging state versus community conflict, which the Indian state has termed 'proxy war' by Pakistan. The rebels insist that their fight is a fight for freedom from Indian politics of homogenization and marginalization of valley Muslims. The state versus community conflict in Kashmir has resulted in the displacement of over 250,000 Kashmiri Pundits from the valley into Jammu and Delhi.

The National Commission for Women undertook a survey of displaced Kashmiri Pundit women. According to their report the policy of the Government of India (GOI) regarding these Kashmiris is premised on the idea that they will return to the valley whenever the situation is conducive for safe return. The displaced Pundits got some relief in terms of money and ration from the central government and the state government of Jammu and Kashmir. Compared to other displaced communities in South Asia their situation is slightly better because they do not face daily harassments from either the bureaucracy or the armed forces. Women of the Kashmiri Pundit community stated that they left Kashmir for fear of persecution in the hands of the Muslims. However, a 'majority of women said that they have heard about the victimization of women but personally they do not know.'[34] Most of the women questioned felt that the government did not have a specific rehabilitation policy for women. They felt that if there were policies that helped them to become economically independent they would be better off. Although most of them did not feel any threat to their person in this situation of displacement, they were sad because they found 'themselves completely excluded from this quest for a new Kashmiri identity.'[35]

The more recent IDPs in Kashmir have not been as fortunate as the Kashmiri Pundits. In 1999 India and Pakistan clashed over Kargil and although that war ended, there are intermittent skirmishes between the two armies periodically leading to enormous displacements. In 1999 itself in India between 60,000 to 100,000 people were displaced. The largest towns in the area, Kargil and Dras, were completely deserted. Most of the displaced fled due to heavy shelling.[36] The Indian military campaigns forced another 50,000 to be displaced from their homes in Jammu and Kashmir. After the 13 December 2001 attack on the Indian parliament there has been a steady build-up of troops near the border. Around the same time the Indian army ordered 20,000 people to evacuate from more than 40 border villages in Indian-administered Kashmir, while tanks, fighter jets and heavy artillery were moved into place.[37] By 2002 over 1,00,000 people were forced to migrate from the LOC alone.[38] Displacement also occurred in other bordering states such as Rajasthan. In a newspaper report the extent of displacement was described as follows:

In Sriganganagar, the hapless people plagued both by preparations for war and a devastating drought last year reportedly resented the Army presence in their neighbourhood. In Hindumalkot area which has 20 villages, a good number of families—ranging from 10 to 96 per cent in various villages—have moved out. Many hamlets have only the elderly who either refused to move out or are too weak to risk a journey. In Rohirawali village, an estimated 86 per cent of the people have left their homes while in 16 villages falling under Matili Rathan police station area, 25 to 93 per cent of the families have left. In the Anupgarh sector, 90 per cent of the inhabitants have left villages.[39]

The same report also maintained that among the first to be displaced were the women and children.

From the Pakistani side of the border there are reports that more than 45,000 people were displaced as of June 2002. Many of these are unable to return to their homes even temporarily because their villages have been mined in anticipation of an Indian ground attack. As on the Indian side of the border so on the Pakistani side the first to be displaced are women and children. They 'had to endure long exhausting mountain treks before finding shelter with relatives in nearby villages, in schools, government offices or temporary makeshift camps. Others would stay in their homes during daylight and seek shelter elsewhere during the nights when shelling became more intense.'[40] The shelling of villages had dire consequences for women. Many of them were injured and needed medical attention that was already scarce. In a report discussing the fate of one such woman who suffered leg injuries it was stated 'because of the pressure on beds she was moved from a bed with a fan (vital in the searing heat) to one that had no ventilation. Her son complained to the hospital authorities but with no success.'[41] Thus even in hospitals women are the last to be attended to.

According to observers, 'in the ultimate analysis the women of Kashmir have had to bear the end of the violence that has wracked the valley. It is they who as widows, half-widows, rape victims, victims of religious dictates, and victims of displacement have to ensure that the pattern of life continues as normally as possible even when the times are abnormal.'[42] Not only are they the first to be displaced but even in displacement they are pushed into sub-human lives. According to one eyewitness report the people relocated from the Indian side of the border were put in relief camps which were formerly storage sheds or condemned factories. In one such camp for the internally displaced due to war it was reported that 200 people including women and children were packed in a 1,800 sq. ft area. These camps had no heating facilities in the bitter cold winter. Due to unhygienic conditions and poor relief many of the inmates fell sick. On their arrival these people were given 5 kg of rice per head and 4 litres of cooking oil. They had no money to buy even wood fuel. 'Several women, old persons and children were suffering from cold, dysentery and influenza,' and they had almost no healthcare facilities. These displaced including women and children were dumped and forgotten.[43] The camps had no privacy for women and their lives in these camps were extremely harsh. Even an International Committee of the Red Cross (ICRC) report discussed the gravity of the situation faced by the internally displaced from villages near the LOC. It stated that these people were 'experiencing great difficulty in providing for themselves and their children, especially in the wintry conditions now prevailing in these mountainous areas.'[44] The UN Guiding Principles on the Internally Displaced Persons notwithstanding, the displaced women from the LOC face grave risks to their lives. Many of these women were maimed when they tried to return to their homes that were heavily mined. They are neither consulted nor conferred with before they are displaced. They are not allowed to carry personal items such as enough warm clothes with them because the trucks that transport them do not have enough room. [Even now many of these displaced women and children remain uprooted because their villages are full of landmines.] Although they are non-combatants they pay an enormous price for the vagaries of the two governments that have decided to continue their conflict no matter what the cost.

GENOCIDAL ACTS IN GUJARAT AND THE SITUATION OF DISPLACED WOMEN

For people in Gujarat, riots are not a new phenomenon. Beginning in 1969, communal violence of varying degrees occurred intermittently between 1985 and 1999. But the acts that took place in Gujarat from February 2002 onwards have been unprecedented in many ways. What was passed-off as riots were actually genocidal acts, where one community was slaughtered while the state machinery looked the other way. The cruelty and brutality witnessed in Gujarat was also of an unprecedented level. Few events of contemporary India have shaken the conscience of civil society as deeply as the Gujarat carnage of 2002. The events began with over 1,000 *Kar Sevaks* travelling from Ahmedabad to Ayodhya by Sabarmati Express on 22 February 2002.[45] On the way they reportedly harassed Muslim men and women in the train and in respective stations. While they were returning on 27 February reportedly there was again some altercation between the Kar Sevaks and Muslim vendors in Godhra station. Soon after, near Falia, it was discovered that a coach was on fire. As a result about 59 people died of whom 26 were women and 12 children. It is still not clear how the coach caught fire but the supporters of the Vishwa Hindu Parishad (VHP), the Bajrang Dal and the ruling Bharatiya Janata Party (BJP) made this an occasion to mount a massive attack against the Muslims in Gujarat leading to dislocation and displacement on an unprecedented scale. Soon violence spread across Gujarat. In Ahmedabad alone about 50,000 Muslims were displaced. Hundreds were killed in mob attacks. In Vadodara, Gandhinagar, Meghaningar, Sabarkantha, Himmatnagar, etc. many more were displaced. Reports kept coming that in Pandharvada village 70 people belonging to the minority community were burnt alive. In Mehsana, 28 farm labourers were murdered.[46] By April 2002 the government indicated that there were over 98,000 displaced people living in 100 relief camps.[47] In a citizens' report it was stated

> there are over 100 relief camps scattered all over Gujarat with over one lakh (100,000) victims. There is shortage of food, water and medical help. Most government functionaries, particularly Ministers, do not bother to visit most of the camps, as their only inmates are Muslims. There is urgent need to reach food, water and medical help to the victims.[48]

While the events were still unfolding it became clear that the attacks were not just against the minority community, but were particularly against women of the minority community as well as the women of the majority community, if they appeared errant. Among the first group of women to collect testimony of riot-affected women in Gujarat were members of the Vadodara PUCL and Shanti Abhiyan. They came out with a report on the basis of testimonies collected from women from 27 February until 26 March. They found out that between 28 February and 22 March more than 39 Muslim houses were gutted and 19 shops looted in Baranpura area alone. There were two police points close by and a fire brigade, which refused to come to the callers' aid. In Bahar colony when women asked police to help them 'the police refused to listen to them and in fact did lathi charge on them to drive them into their homes.[49] Among others an elderly woman Ameena Memon was badly hit in the lathi charge.'[50] In another incident Hamida Bano Ibrahim, a 40-year-old woman was hit by police so hard that her right hand was fractured in three places.[51] One of the recurrent themes of these reports is in fact the anger that women felt at the role played by the police and state machinery. The women were caught up in the reign of terror promoted by the police. Even women from the majority community were suffering from fear psychosis because they were constantly warned that the Muslims might attack them.

The Citizen's Initiative of Ahmedabad sponsored the first fact-finding visit by a women's panel. Between 27 March and 31 March the six-member team visited seven relief camps in both urban and rural Gujarat. These were in Ahmedabad, Kheda, Vadodara, Sabarkantha and Panchmahals districts. The team found compelling evidence of extreme sexual violence against women during the days of mayhem. In every case of mob violence there was evidence of pre-planned targeting of women. There were gruesome testimonies of how violence against women was used as an instrument to displace people. In one such testimony from Naroda Patia minor girls said that mobs started chasing them with burning tyres: 'We saw about 8-10 rapes. We saw them strip 16-year-old Mehrunissa. They were stripping themselves and beckoning to the girls. Then they raped them right there on the road.' In another camp a rape victim spoke of her experiences. She said that while running away from the mob she fell behind as she was carrying her young son, Faizan: 'The men caught me from behind and threw me on the ground. Faizan fell from my arms and started crying. My clothes were stripped off by the men and I was left stark naked. One by one the men raped me. All the while I could hear my son crying.' The fact-finding team also found evidence of police complicity in this carnage. Not only were women forced out of their homes and targeted in the streets but also the police helped the attackers. The report said that in the vast majority of the cases the police refused to lodge First Investigative Reports. When questioned about violence against women even the district collector of Panchmahals said, 'maintaining law and order is my primary concern. It is not possible for me to look into cases of sexual violence.' Women hid in the forests for three to four days before they could reach the safety of the camps. The report said the relief camps were organized by Muslim community leaders with hardly any help from the government. The report also stated that an

immediate impact of the violence is the creation of female-headed households. In many cases entire families have been killed. Women testified to having witnessed several members of their family dying. They were dealing not only with the trauma of this loss, but facing a future with their life's savings and livelihood sources destroyed.

Many women in the camps stated their fear of going back to their homes, where they might be targeted again.[52] Other groups such as Citizens Tribunal and All India Democratic Women's Association corroborated these evidences.[53]

There were other initiatives where women visited Gujarat to find out about the situation of the riot-affected women. Among the last to visit

Gujarat was a team set up by the National Commission for Women, which is mandated as the apex body for the protection of women's rights. This women's team visited Himmatnagar, Ahmedabad, Godhra, Kaiol and Vadodara between 10 and 12 April 2002. One of the members of this team wrote about her experiences of camp life. She said:

> How long could anyone stay in the camps? The temperature was already 43 degrees. In the next few weeks it would soar to 47 or 48 degrees. There were babies, infants and newborn under the canvas. There were pregnant mothers, the old, and the ailing. Water, sanitation and privacy were in short supply. There was no privacy during waking or sleeping hours, to feed the baby or change one's clothes. The situation was mired in pathos and humiliation.[54]

The National Commission for Women reported that many of the camps 'were not up to the mark' and they asked the government to carefully supervise relief. The team revealed that the camps organized by the government had no representation of women in the organizing committee. With several pregnant and lactating women and children they felt there should be adequate representation of women in these committees. They also felt that security arrangements for women and children were inadequate and both of these groups reported to feeling 'extremely insecure in the present circumstances'. There were no special provisions for pregnant women. The committee observed that, 'sanitary towels and other personal items of clothing such as undergarments, footwear, etc. also need to be provided.' They also observed that there was a lack of lady doctors and gynaecologists. More importantly there were no facilities for women and girls who have been widowed or orphaned to get any special training to earn their livelihood. No efforts were made to make women aware of the compensations that were promised to them. Although inadequate, these compensations could at least give some confidence to women who were traumatized by their own destitution.[55] What the members of the committee were most concerned about was that, 'no one seemed to have asked questions related to rehabilitation. What efforts were being made to make their homes and localities safe? Or to determine, in consultation with them, where the women without menfolk or children without parents would go?'[56] The displaced women in Gujarat were thus truly 'nowhere' people. Even today they remain in hostile environment, and as the evidence in the Best Bakery case[57] suggests, these women, if they seek justice, are displaced once again.

DEVELOPMENT-RELATED DISPLACEMENT:
DAMS AND DISPLACED WOMEN

India has one of the highest development-induced displacements in the world. There are, however, no reliable official statistics on the number of development-related internally displaced in India. According to official figures in 1994, about 15.5 million internally displaced people were in India and the government acknowledged that some 11.5 million were awaiting rehabilitation. But calculations, on the basis of the number of dams constructed in India and its associated displacement, show that the number of development-related displacement in India may be as high as 21 to 33 million people. Dam building is one of the most important causes for development-related displacement. According to one report,

> during the last fifty years, some 3,300 big dams have been constructed in India. Many of them have led to large-scale forced eviction of vulnerable groups. The situation of the tribal people is of special concern, as they constitute 40–50 per cent of the displaced population.[58]

As in any other kind of displacement women and children are also particularly vulnerable in development-related displacement. Usually displacement is forced upon communities who are already marginalized by systemic injustice, such as indigenous people.[59] 'Women as marginalized entities within marginalized communities are often forced to shoulder the ordeal of displacement far more intensely.'[60] The brutality of displacement due to the building of dams was dramatically highlighted during the agitation over the Sardar Sarovar Dam. It has been called 'India's most controversial dam project.'[61] A woman activist, Medha Patkar, spearheaded the anti-dam movement known as the Narmada Bachao Andolan. This movement for the first time systematically revealed how building dams can result in total dislocation of tribal societies. Whereas the beneficiaries of the dam are meant to be large landowners, tribal people are paying the price. In such situations it is common that women from these communities will be worst affected. As one observer points out,

> ... relief programmes tend to overlook women's crucial roles as producers, providers, and organisers, and have delivered assistance directly to male heads of households, whether it is food, seeds and tools, or training. This reduces women's influence over areas previously

controlled by them—such as the production and provision of food—undermining their position within the household and the community.[62]

Before discussing methods of eviction and forced relocation of tribal men and women in the Sardar Sarovar project, I will look into the building of another dam and then discuss the effects of forced relocation on women in the context of this other project. It is important to discuss this other project first because the National Commission for Women, for the first time, decided to undertake a study on the effects of development-related displacement on women specifically in the case of this other project. The project in question is the Tehri Dam. Before we discuss the case of the Tehri Dam we must first acknowledge that only recently has there been recognition of the fact that such development-related displacements may affect men and women differently.

The Tehri project is a multi-purpose irrigation and power project in the Ganges valley 250 km north of Delhi, located in the Tehri Garhwal district of Uttaranchal state. Initially in 1969 the Tehri Dam Project Organization (TDPO) estimated that about 13,413 persons would be affected by the construction of the dam. But a working group for the Environment Appraisal of Tehri Dam established in 1979 put the figure of expected internal displacement at 85,600 persons. According to the 1995 report of TDPO, out of 135 villages affected, 37 would be fully submerged once the dam was completed. The total land affected by the project is 13,000 hectares.[63] The National Commission for Women conducted a survey on displaced women in the Tehri project. They found that although the terms of rehabilitation were extremely modest, 'even this was not fully implemented.'[64] As for women who were displaced, most often they lost their share of livelihood and the area where they are relocated did not provide them with any possibilities of supplementary sources of income. Even the government had no programmes for their skill enhancement and so their chances of economic independence were severely restricted. Thus, displacement resulted in their disempowerment. According to the survey, these projects displaced people from their traditional habitat resulting in 'profound economic, psychological, environmental and cultural disruption.'[65] The women were severely affected because of breakdown of social units. Displacement resulted in mental trauma and loss of mobility because they were relocated forcibly to an unknown place. All this contributed to women's sense of powerlessness.[66]

Now, I return to the case of the Sardar Sarovar Dam project. The displacement and relocation process in the Tehri Dam project was not as violent as the Sardar Sarovar Dam project, which is a part of the Narmada Valley Development Project (NVDP). The NVDP is supposed to be the most ambitious river valley development project in the world. It envisages building 3,200 dams that will reconstitute the Narmada and her 419 tributaries into a series of step-reservoirs. Of these, 30 will be major dams, 135 medium and the rest small. Two of the major dams will be multi-purpose mega dams. The Sardar Sarovar in Gujarat and the Narmada Sagar in Madhya Pradesh, will, between them, hold more water than any other reservoir in the Indian subcontinent. The official figure indicates that about 42,000 families will be displaced but non-governmental organizations, such as the Narmada Bachao Andolan (NBA), put the figure at about 85,000 families or 500,000 people. They argue that the official figure has not counted people who will lose their livelihood as a result of these dams as project-affected families (PAFs). The official figure counts only families who will lose their land or homes as PAF. According to one report, 'the Narmada Valley Development Project will affect the lives of 25 million people who live in the valley and will alter the ecology of an entire river basin.' The first dam that was built as part of this project displaced 114,000 people but provided irrigation for only 5 per cent of the land that it was meant to irrigate.[67] According to one observer:

> Dams are built, people are uprooted, forests are submerged and then the project is simply abandoned. Canals are never completed... the benefits never accrue (except to the politicians, the bureaucrats and the contractors involved in the construction). The first dam that was built on the Narmada is a case in point—the Bargi Dam in Madhya Pradesh was completed in 1990. It cost ten times more than was budgeted and submerged three times more land than engineers said it would. To save the cost and effort of doing a survey, the government just filled the reservoir without warning anybody. Seventy thousand people from 101 villages were supposed to be displaced. Instead, 114,000 people from 162 villages were displaced. They were evicted from their homes by rising waters, chased out like rats, with no prior notice. There was no rehabilitation. Some got a meagre cash compensation. Most got nothing. Some died of starvation. Others moved to slums in Jabalpur. And all for what? Today, ten years after it was completed, the Bargi Dam produces some electricity, but irrigates only as much land as it submerged. Only 5 per cent of the land its planners claimed it would irrigate. The government says it has no money to make the

canals. Yet it has already begun work downstream, on the mammoth Narmada Sagar Dam and the Maheshwar Dam.[68]

The building of the Sardar Sarovar dam was stopped in 1995 when the NBA petitioned the Supreme Court that no further building of the dam could be undertaken without rehabilitation of those who had already been displaced. But in February 1999 the Indian Supreme Court through an interim order permitted the Gujarat government to resume the building.[69] Then again in October 2000, the Supreme Court gave a go-ahead for the construction of the dam. From that time the Gujarat government with increasing brutality has undertaken forcible eviction of the tribal people. One of the prime methods of eviction followed by the police is to enter a village and beat up women and children. This has been reported from most areas that have been cleared. In one such news item it was reported that,

> on 20 July 2002, about 400 police people entered the Man dam project affected village Khedi–Balwari (dist. Dhar, M.P.) and forcibly evicted the village using terror tactics. The women and even children were severely beaten up, the houses looted and the people were picked up and dumped at the so-called 'resettlement' site Kesur, 75 km away, where they remain under a virtual arrest with large number of police guarding them. The whole Khedi–Balwari village is now under the control of the police. [70]

Not only are women harassed and physically dumped in resettlement sites, which are totally unplanned, women face severe problems in these sites. These problems start from something as apparently small as no separate toilets for women, to bigger problems such as refusal to give women-headed households the status of PAF. Obviously, women are the worst sufferers in this process of displacement and relocation. Even when relief is given it is in the form of cash handed over to the male heads of households. Thus women are much less able to influence decisions as to how the money ought to be spent. If women protest, the police often physically abuse them. The lands that are handed over to them are often of very low quality and cannot be cultivated.[71] Sometimes, 'gender bias in resettlement is often manifested through non-recognition of women's ownership of land. For example, in Sardar Sarovar project, women with land titles (*patta*) were not given land for land.'[72] Often people are displaced multiple times and each time they are displaced they become poorer.[73] One observer clearly states,

> ... the most culpable aspect of state-induced impoverishment of displaced populations is the phenomenon of multiple displacement. It has been documented, for instance, that as a direct result of the lack of co-ordination between the multiplicity of irrigation, thermal power and coal-mining agencies ... most oustees have been displaced at least twice, and some three or four times in a matter of two or three decades and with each displacement the villagers were progressively pauperised.[74]

The dalit and adivasi women often do not have deeds to the land that they have lived on for years. Because of lack of deeds, these women and their families are not treated as PAF and so they cannot claim compensation. Often these women become destitute and easy prey for traffickers. Many of them end up in brothels. The government has no programmes for either their skill enhancement or for their protection. These are the women who are worst affected by development projects. The UN Guiding Principles have no meaning for them. Thus the processes of dam building in India have displaced not just thousands of people, mostly tribals, but have also caused severe disempowerment of women through displacement.

OTHER DISPLACEMENTS

What we have chronicled here are case studies of some of the more dramatic instances of displacement in South Asia. However, these are in no way exhaustive but rather symptomatic of the problem. By a conservative estimate India has over 500,000 conflict- induced displaced people, Pakistan has over 50,000 but many more refugees, and Bangladesh another 500,000 individuals or 128,364 displaced families in the Chittagong Hill Tracts.[75] Although almost no data are available on the situation of internally displaced in Nepal, it is quite safe to assume that the 'People's War', from 1996 onwards, has resulted in substantial displacement. In all these incidents it is apparent that women and children are some of the worst affected.

In the northeastern part of India there are close to 300,000 internally displaced people mostly due to conflict and sometimes due to developmental projects. In 1998, the US Committee for Refugees reported that there are 80,000 ethnic Santhals (and a small number of ethnic Nepalese) displaced in Assam; around 60,000 Bengalis are displaced in Assam; more than 20,000 ethnic Paite, Kuki, and Naga displaced in Manipur; 39,000 ethnic Reangs have been displaced from Mizoram to Tripura; 25,000

Bengalis are displaced in Tripura; and 3,000 ethnic Chakmas are displaced in Arunachal Pradesh.[76] These are largely conflict-induced displacements. Apart from these there are state-induced developmental projects such as Dumber Hydel Project in Tripura that displaced 5,000 tribal families. In Assam it was reported that 200,000 displaced families were living in 78 camps in Kokrajhar and Bongaigaon districts. Most of these people are leading a 'dehumanised life in makeshift unhygienic relief camps....The conditions of the relief camps are pathetic and inmates do not get adequate food. The displaced children are deprived of education for years together.'[77] Even in the northeast, among the displaced, women and children form the most vulnerable categories. For example, when Bodo militants attacked displaced people in Barpeta in July 1994, according to one analyst, 'about 1,000 persons mostly women and children were killed.' Even in the Nellie massacre of 1983 in Assam, women formed the largest group of casualty.[78] According to Gina Sangkham, a Naga woman activist in Manipur, among the displaced in the northeast there are sizeable numbers of women and children but no governmental agencies are looking into their conditions. In fact, the state governments insist that there are hardly any displacement-induced problems. Even when relief and rehabilitation is organized, according to Sangkham, women are hardly ever consulted although they are particularly suitable for rehabilitation work as the onus of care is traditionally on their shoulders.[79]

The situation of internally displaced women in the Chittagong Hill Tracts (CHT) is no better than that of their sisters in northeast India. The CHT was largely a tribal area and the tribes here were collectively called the Jumma people. A large number of Jumma people were for the first time displaced in 1961 following the construction of a hydroelectric project in Kaptai. The next stage of displacement of the same population began in the early 1980s following armed encounters between security forces of Bangladesh and the armed wing of the tribal people called Shanti Bahini. As a result of this conflict a large number of Jumma people crossed borders and those who stayed back became dispersed. Bengali settlers filled the areas that the Jummas evacuated. The state had a policy to displace tribals and encourage settlements of Bengalis in this area so that the demography would change in favour of the settlers. The state-sponsored reign of terror was particularly problematic for women who became victims of rape, abduction, kidnapping and forced marriages to the Bengali population. One researcher found that the overwhelming majority of internally displaced among the Jummas were women.[80] Displacement had tremendously adverse effects on women's mental and physical health. The government in no way aided these women. In fact, security forces rampantly raped and abducted women. One well-known case of abduction and killing was that of Kalpana Chakma in 1996, a leader of the Hill Women's Federation.[81] This created tremendous agitation among the hill women or the Jumma women but in no way did it stop repression from the security forces. When men were imprisoned, sexual violence was unleashed on women causing their displacement.[82] Even when the women identified the miscreants they were hardly ever brought to justice. The situation became so bad that women stopped wearing their traditional dresses so that they would not be easily identifiable as tribal people.[83] Although the CHT Peace Accord was signed in 1997, the majority of the IDPs still remain displaced, including the women. The Peace Accord stated that a Task Force would help the process of rehabilitation of displaced people. Much to the consternation of the Jumma people, the Task Force identified 90,208 Jumma families as displaced and 38,156 settlers as displaced, giving legal recognition to the settlers as residents.[84] The land situation in the CHT is such that it forecloses the possibility of easy rehabilitation and the present government is unwilling to bring perpetrators of violence in the CHT, including perpetrators of violence on women, to justice. Jumma people are still threatened by the security forces and they fear for their lives and dignity.[85] The Peace Accord seems to have changed very little of the situation and the plight of internally displaced people remains.

Displacement in Nepal is much less documented than that in the CHT. There are hardly any official statistics available although reports from human rights groups in the last five years have brought this issue into their discourse. An Amnesty International report stated that in the year 2002 alone, 66 people were said to have disappeared from police custody.[86] From such reports it is becoming clear that the People's War in Nepal is resulting in death and displacement of people from conflict areas. In one such report it was stated that, 'people living in the remote places of Taplejung district are leaving their houses behind and moving to the headquarters, Kathmandu or India.'[87] Such reports also mention that both the Maoists and the state are responsible for the displacement of people. They further highlight the harassment from the administration faced by the displaced people, who, because of the area they come from, are automatically labelled 'terrorists'.[88] These reports discuss violence against women such as rape and molestations in the conflict areas, but there are virtually no discussions on the situation of displaced women.[89]

'Women, who make up 51 per cent of the total population in Nepal, have a secondary status in the patriarchic [sic] Hindu structure.

Discriminated by the law and with the lack of awareness of rights and education, the majority of the women are socially oppressed,' says one report.[90] Throughout their lives, women face reduced opportunities and discrimination. Literacy rates and life expectancy are much lower for women than men. Women often face domestic violence and harassment, with no legal recourse, as paternalism and gender discrimination is deeply entrenched in society. Many laws are explicitly biased against women, especially those regarding property, citizenship and marriage.[91] Women are frequently prosecuted for having abortions, which were illegal until very recently.[92] Many rural women fall prey to the traffickers and trafficking of Nepali women has assumed horrifying proportions. Compounding these problems are the problems of women who are caught up in conflict. In villages men often disappear into the forests when there is war between the security forces and the CPN-Maoists. Either side may then descend on these women, harass them for food and often molest them. According to one observer, the security forces on the pretext of suppressing women from joining the Maoists, rape them.[93] Women caught in the crossfire very easily fall prey to the lures of traffickers or may join the Maoists and disappear from the villages or join the swelling ranks of internally displaced. An observer recounts the woes of one such woman. She says:

> A young woman with two children was forced to leave home in Rolpa because of police harassment…. Her husband was killed while he was working in the farm, her daughter murdered after being gang-raped by the police, her house burnt, crop destroyed and she was threatened with death if she stayed on in the village. She left the village with her children and started working as daily labourer in Surkhet where, being a young widow she was stigmatized. She faced greater threat as she was treated by society as a product of political conflict.[94]

However, there are almost no government-run camps for these IDP women. The warning bells have been sounded; now, is the time for the government to start listening.

DISPLACEMENT AND STATE RESPONSES

The cases that I have dealt with in this chapter are cases of displacement due either to conflict or developmental projects. The one category of displaced that I have omitted are calamity-induced displaced or those displaced as a result of natural disaster. One reason why I have considered only conflict-induced and development-induced displacement is because in both these forms of displacement the hand of state power is obvious. In most of these development and conflict-induced cases, state policies result directly in displacements. Even in displacement related to community versus community conflicts, the state can play a partisan role as is obvious from the situation in Gujarat. In perhaps all states of South Asia women are relegated to the margins of citizenship. They are hardly ever equal partners in the process of state formation. State machineries seek to create a 'unified' and 'national' citizenry that accepts the central role of the existing elite. This is done through privileging majoritarian, male and monolithic cultural values that deny space for difference. Such a denial has often led to the segregation of minorities, on the basis of caste, religion and gender, from the collective 'we'. Thus displaced women are often doubly marginalized since state policies are weighted against them both because they are women and also because often they are members of minority ethnic, religious and linguistic groups. In situations where the state is not an actor, the majority group imitates state behaviour thereby victimizing women as in the massacres by Bodo militants.

Women's bodies form the battleground for contests of male power. According to one observer in South Asia 'mystified notions of chastity' have guided attitude to women.[95] This has led to the acceptance that women in South Asia belong to their communities. Women as symbols of group honour are raped, molested and tortured so that men may be shamed. The media often plays up this concept of women's honour to incite one group of people against another. For example, after the Godhra incident there were false media reporting of the rape of Hindu women by Muslim men leading to the targeting of Muslim women in the riots. Another alarming trend is that there are increasing incidents of raped women being murdered after rape. In Burma more than 25 per cent of those who are raped are murdered and the same is true for rape victims from the riots in Gujarat. This is particularly true of violence sponsored by machineries of state, as is obvious from Burma and Gujarat.

That the states of South Asia at best patronize women and at worst abuse them will become obvious if one looks into their responses towards displaced women. When in the Indian parliament the issue of torture of women in Gujarat came up, the minister of defence commented that in civil war such things happen. In Sri Lanka, the unwillingness of the state, notwithstanding the UN Resolution 1325, to involve women's groups in talks for peace is another example of the male centrism of South Asian states. In Nepal, the apathy of the state to imposing anti-trafficking laws, again reveals the bias against women in state policies. Also, hardly any woman in Nepal has found a place in ceasefire negotiations that are on-going. When the state becomes an actor in displacing groups, violence against women reaches an unprecedented height because often the perpetrators enjoy impunity.

Notwithstanding the UN Guiding Principles or CEDAW, states in South Asia have no set policies for the internally displaced. They treat each case on an ad hoc basis. Therefore certain groups such as the Kashmiri Pundits, because of their proximity to state power, are able to get a certain amount of relief and rehabilitation packages; but the Muslims or the Santhals in Assam do not get even one-fourth of what is allotted for the Kashmiris.[96] When state policies result in displacement then getting any redress becomes even more problematic. Therefore often in development-induced displacement before rehabilitating the previously displaced the state moves on to displace even more people. In most South Asian societies women live under rigid patriarchies that control their mobility and value them only as symbols of group honour. In such situations women are often distanced from the public domain. Thus when state policies make them destitute they remain unprepared by their training to deal with the administration and thereby become further victimized by the system.

State policies refuse to accept that the displaced population is largely a feminine population and so often rehabilitation programmes are couched in gender-neutral terms thereby creating greater problems for women. Thus, even when camps are organized, there is a certain amount of apathy in considering the special needs of women. In many Sri Lankan camps, for example, the toilets for women are situated at the back of the camps, which make it hazardous for women to access them at night. When human rights groups criticize state policies regarding the displaced it becomes easy for the state machinery to invoke the rationale of national security thereby diverting attention from the plight of displaced women, as in the case of the displaced in the LOC between India and Pakistan. It is the state that has sought to manipulate and impose a particular national identity that marginalizes women. The state appropriates the right to define what national security is and in the process if tribal women or minority women suffer, they are asked to make sacrifices in the name of the nation. Thus, it is largely members, including female members, of minority groups who are displaced. In the case of India these are often tribal, adivasi and Muslim women; in the case of Bangladesh, the Jumma women; in the case of Burma, the ethnic minority women; in the case of

Nepal, the Tibeto–Burman women; and in the case of Sri Lanka, the Tamil women.

In most of the South Asian states, because they lack punitive power, the Human Rights Commissions are circumscribed. But in some cases they have effectively raised the question of displaced people. For example, in India the Human Rights Commission may not have done the job of protecting human rights properly or adequately; but it has at least taken up with the central government the question of persons displaced by dams and mega projects. The Commission wants New Delhi to amend the Land Acquisition Act in such a way that the rehabilitation of displaced persons becomes an integral part of the project. There can be no uprooting until the project makes arrangements for resettlement of the oustees. This is precisely what voluntary organizations have relentlessly demanded. Some among them have come together to even prepare model legislation, the Land Acquisition, Rehabilitation and Resettlement Bill, 2000, to incorporate the principle of settling before uprooting.[97] The government of India's Ministry of Rural Development (MoRD) is also considering a draft 'National Policy, Packages and Guidelines for Resettlement & Rehabilitation 1998'.

The draft policy treated as owners of land for the purpose of R&R, those people residing for more than five years before the date of acquisition, who are otherwise termed as 'encroachers' on common land. Similarly, forest dwellers residing in forest areas prior to 30 September 1980 shall be considered as the owners. Also, provisions for compensation were made for non-owners, such as tenants, sharecroppers, etc. Other significant features of the draft policy were, community consultation for R&R package, open public hearings, publishing of the R&R plan, fixing of R&R cost at 10 per cent of project cost and linking compensation with gross productivity.[98]

Women are however systematically ignored in resettlement processes and relief packages are usually handed over to the men. In an ICRC report of 2001 it is clearly stated that women are 'persistently excluded from decision-making process in peace-negotiations and peace-building.'[99] Female-heads of households are often stigmatized and ignored when relief is handed out. The government of India and other South Asian states should ensure that relief for the family should be handed over to the women, since they are responsible for the care of the family. Also any compensation for the loss of common resources should be distributed equally between men and women, as they, as women, are equally and sometimes even more dependent on those resources. Unless these concerns are incorporated into

R&R guidelines it may not serve its purpose. Also, women should be consulted in all steps of rehabilitation and it needs to begin with Sri Lanka. Further returnees, IDPs and other civilians face a serious lack of medical care in the northern part of Sri Lanka resulting from government restrictions and flight of qualified personnel. Many medical professionals and healthcare workers fled the area, causing a shortage of doctors, nurses and medical specialists. Also women have special medical needs and that is a concern that needs to be addressed. In Nepal, the government needs to face the fact that conflict-induced displacement often makes women easy targets for traffickers and unless the government has an alternate social and economic policy for these women the situation is going to get worse. But, above all, as long as the states of South Asia continue with their policies of treating women as less than equal citizens, women, either displaced or settled, will continue to be marginalized.

WOMEN'S RESPONSE AND THE STATE

That displaced women are much more than victims is apparent from their efforts to cope with their displacement. In camp life it is the women who are able to bring back some semblance of normalcy to family life. They concentrate 'all their efforts on bringing up their children in a safe and stable environment.'[100] As has been stated earlier in the case of Sri Lanka, while displaced, more women sought work than men. Women took up temporary labour to cope with material difficulties. Even in camps in Gujarat women were continuously looking for work.[101] It is the women who 'maintain cohesiveness within the family by consciously assessing the situation and deciding that their duty is to provide their dependents with financial and emotional security.'[102] Regarding the situation of women in Sri Lanka, one analyst has commented: 'displacement and camp life had also provided spaces for empowerment for several Tamil women who had taken on the role of head of household for various reasons'.[103]

Notwithstanding their personal loss and trauma, many a time displaced women organize movements for justice and peace. In the NBA, it is the women who volunteer to protest against state action even when they face severe human rights abuse and reprisals. One of the slogans used by women protesters is 'Nari Shakti, Narmada Shakti', (women power, Narmada power).[104] Often their protests stop labourers from doing the work that day. In the context of riots in Gujarat, it is the displaced women from the camps who organized and participated in huge rallies under the aegis of 'Women for Peace'. They were among the first to call for understanding and not revenge.

They organized a camp where women had blood tests showing to the communities that blood groups do not depend on either religion or caste.[105] On the Thailand–Burma border, women's groups aid incoming refugee women. It is these women who, even with tremendous threats to their lives, infiltrate and try to help women in conflict zones in Burma. Women organize a lot more than their family life. Protest movements are largely organized by them. Even at great personal cost they try to bring back normalcy and peace to their society. However, states often try to homogenize displaced women into the category of 'victims'. By transforming them into non-autonomous and dependent social category of victim the displaced women are often denied a voice in decision-making. Their individual identity is subsumed within the conflated identity of a victim. It should be recognized that even in their marginality, displaced women are never merely victims. Dislocation is a debilitating experience no doubt, but many exceptional women have transformed it into an empowering one. They have assumed newer roles as heads of households. Such experiences have increased their confidence, though at times it may have contributed to their trauma.

To formulate any programmes for displaced people, state and non-state actors should recognize the reality that responses to displacement can only be effective if women's concerns are incorporated in it. Such programmes should neither trivialize women's experiences nor club them into a nameless and faceless category of victim. When designing programmes for rehabilitation and resettlement any agency should consider that often displacement results in women's greater participation in public life. Thus, programmes need to accommodate this reality and enhance options for greater participation of women in the public domain. To improve women's participation in all spheres of life the state machineries should be committed to addressing questions regarding not just women's rights but also justice for reconciliation programmes. Women's voices should be heard and they should be made full partners in rehabilitation programmes.

Notions of displaced persons need to be gender-inclusive. Interventions should be targeted at both women and men. Women IDPs should be viewed as citizens with entitlement to the full realization of their human rights and then some, for the sake of justice. Women need to be made co-beneficiaries with men in any resettlement benefit packages. Female-headed households should be given special assistance prior to, during and after displacement. It should be realized that female heads of households with young children or with infirm family members are unable to seek outside employment. They should be aided with special programmes of income generation so that they can earn enough without leaving their homes. Attention should be given so that in no way is their authority undermined. Those vested with the responsibility of planning for resettlement and rehabilitation (R&R) should not consult only group leaders among the displaced in South Asia, as very often they are men, but also try to engage with women's networks. Also those in any stage of planning for IDPs should have women representatives in their groups. They should be aware and sensitive to local notions and understandings of equity. Often ignorance of customary law can undermine women's existing access over resources, as has been portrayed in the northeast of India. To make women's lives safer all countries in South Asia need to revise their penal codes so that no impunity is granted to members of armed forces if they have perpetrated rape. As the international community does, so should the states in South Asia treat rape as an offence against humanity. This is the only way that post-emergency rehabilitation interventions can address the potential for positive change to reduce gender disparities and promote greater equity in a reconstructed society.

It has to be recognized that the situation of women IDPs will change substantially only when states in South Asia identify women as equal partners in governance. We need to understand that in an already unequal context, disparities get further exacerbated. Thus, in the course of the developmental process in South Asia, it is often the indigenous people and the minority communities who get displaced. Among these communities, the more victimized such as women, children, old and the infirm get further abused and marginalized. Government and non-governmental agencies should consider addressing structural causes that discriminate against women. Programmes should be evolved that address questions of equity in sharing responsibility, resources and rights between women and men. Women should not be viewed only as victims because that negates women's experiences and agency. Only when women are accepted as agents of social change can the gamut of their lived experiences be considered crucial. Without such recognition any programme for women IDPs will only touch the surface and not make changes that are effective over longer periods of time.

NOTES

1. I need to thank Dr Roberta Cohen and Dr Ranabir Samaddar for their extremely helpful suggestions in writing this paper.
2. 'From Ashes of War: Women and Reconstruction', *Gender Reach Information Bulletin*, 30 November 1999, No. 6, 1.

3. Sonia Cardenas, 'Adaptive States: The Proliferation of National Human Rights Institutions,' Working Paper, Carr Center for Human Rights Policy (Harvard University, 2001).

4. In December 1995 there were 1,017,181 estimated internally displaced people in Sri Lanka, *Report, Ministry of Rehabilitation and Reconstruction/Commissioner General of Essential Services*, 2 January 2002.

5. David A. Korn, *Exodus within Borders: An Introduction to the Crisis of Internal Displacement* (Brookings Institution, Washington, DC, 1999), 14.

6. The figure is quoted in Kumudini Samuel, 'Foregrounding Women's Human Rights,' *Women in Action*, 30 June 1997, No. 2, 23.

7. Mario Gomez, 'National Human Rights Commission and Internally Displaced Persons: Illustrated by the Sri Lankan Experience,' An Occasional Paper, The Brookings-SIAS Project on Internal Displacement, July 2002, 10.

8. Report of the Representative of the UN Secretary General on Internally Displaced Persons, Francis M. Deng, *Internally Displaced Persons*, UN Document E/CN.4/1995/50, 2 February 1995, para. 30.

9. Amnesty International Report quoted in Christine Jayasinghe, 'Amnesty alleges security forces getting away with rape,' *India Abroad*, 13 April 2001, Vol. 31, No. 28, 12.

10. 'Sri Lanka: Rape in Custody,' Amnesty International, AI-index: ASA 37/001/2002, 28 January 2002, 6.

11. Amnesty International, AI-index: ASA 37/001/2002, 28 January 2002.

12. Sophia Elek, *Choosing Rice over Risk: Rights, Resettlement and Displaced Women*, Centre for the Study of Human Rights (University of Colombo, 2003).

13. Amnesty International, AI-index: ASA 37/001/2002, 28 January 2002, 8-9.

14. CEDAW 26th Session, CEDAW/C/2002/I/CRP.3/ADD.5, 30 January 2002, para 41.

15. Preliminary Report of Radhika Coomaraswamy, E/CN.4/1995/42, 22 November 1994.

16. Mario Gomez, 'National Human Rights Commission and Internally Displaced Persons: Illustrated by the Sri Lankan Experience,' an Occasional Paper, The Brookings-SAIS Project on Internal Displacement, July 2002, 12.

17. Interview of a social worker (who prefers to be anonymous) with the author in Trincomalee, 25 January 2000.

18. Mario Gomez, 2002, 12.

19. Amnesty International, AI-index: ASA 37/001/2002, 28 January 2002, 7.

20. Case reported by 'Women's Rights Watch Year Report 1999', in *Refugee Watch*, March 2000, 28.

21. General Assembly ref. A/54/440, dated 4 October 1999.

22. Ref. E/CN.4/1999/35 dated 21 January 1999.

23. Teena Amrit Gill, 'Rampant Rape in War,' *Women Envision*, 31 August 1998, No. 59-60, 5.

24. Brenda Belak, 'Double Jeopardy: Abuse of Ethnic Women's Human Rights in Burma,' *Cultural Survival Quarterly*, 31 October 2000, Vol. 24, No. 3, 24.

25. The proper names of individuals have been changed for the purpose of confidentiality.

26. Naing's interview in Luz Maria Martinez, 'Burma: Subdued but not Conquered,' *Women in Action*, 3, 30 September 1996, 78-79.

27. 'Licence to Rape: The Burmese Military Regime's Use of Sexual Violence in the Ongoing War in Shan State,' Shan Human Rights Foundation and the Shan Women's Network Action, May 2002, 8.

28. Ibid., 15.

29. Betsy Apple, 'School of Rape: A Report,' *Earthrights International*, 1996.

30. Brenda Belak, 'Double Jeopardy: Abuse of Ethnic Women's Human Rights in Burma,' *Cultural Survival Quarterly*, 31 October 2000, Vol. 24, No. 3, 25.

31. Author's interview with a member of Burma Border Consortium in Bangkok on 18 November 2002.

32. Images Asia , 'Alternative Perspectives, Other Voices: Assessing Gender Equality in Burma,' Submission to the 22nd Session of the Committee of the Convention on the Elimination of All Forms of Discrimination Against Women, December 1999.

33. This is an opinion given by Subir Bhowmick, BBC Correspondent, to the author on 6 March 2003, Colombo.

34. 'Kashmiri Migrants', in *Impact of Displacement on Women*, National Commission for Women, New Delhi, 2001, 95–96.

35. Asha Hans, 'Women Across Borders in Kashmir: The Continuum of Violence,' *Women in Conflict Zones*, Vol. 19, No. 4 (York University Publication, 2000), 79.

36. US Committee for Refugees (USCR), 2000, *World Refugee Survey 2000* (Washington, DC), 166.

37. 'Villagers Flee India–Pakistan Border,' BBC Report, 29 December 2001, http://news.bbc.co.uk/go/em/fr/-/1/hi/world/south_asia/1732865.stm

38. Displacement in Kashmir due to military tensions and armed clashes between India and Pakistan (1999–2002), www.idpproject.org

39. *The Hindu*, 6 January 2002, http://www.hinduonnet.com/2002/01/06/stories/2002010600661400.htm

40. *Profile of Internal Displacement: Pakistan*, Compilation of the information available in the Global IDP Database of the Norwegian Refugee Council, January 2003, 4.

41. 'Kashmir: Asian Sub-continent on the Brink of Catastrophe' (An eyewitness account from a socialist in Pakistani Occupied Kashmir), Committee for a Workers' International, May 2002, http://slp.at/cwi/infos_int/neu_0205_kash.html

42. Sumona Das Gupta and Ashima Kaul Bhatia, 'Women in Conflict Resolution: The Road Ahead in Kashmir,' http://www.ipcs.org/issues/newarticles/671-kas-sumona.html

43. Tapan K. Bose, 'A Kargil War Refugee Camp: Reporting from Gagangir,' *Refugee Watch*, No. 7 (September 1999), 7–9.

44. 1 February 2002 Press Release 02/09 ICRC aid for the internally displaced in Jammu and Kashmir, http://www.icrc.org/Web/eng/siteeng0.nsf/html/57JRKW? Open Document&style=custo_final

45. Kar sevaks are volunteers who raise money and work for extreme right wing organizations such as the VHP.

46. Teesta Setalvad, 'Communalism Combat,' in Basudeb Chattopadhay, Ashis Ranjan Guha and Ramkrishna Chatterjee (eds), *Communalism Condemned: Gujarat Genocide 2002* (Progressive Publishers, Kolkata, 2002), 3–16.

47. 'We have No Orders to Save You'—State Participation and Complicity in Communal Violence in Gujarat, *Human Rights Watch (HRW)*, April 2002, 6

48. Onlinevolunteers, 30 May 2002, www.idpproject.orgIndia

49. Lathi means baton.

50. 'Gujarat Carnage: Women's Perspectives on the Violence in Gujarat,' by PUCL Vadodara and Shanti Abhiyaan, Vadodara, 27 February–26 March, 7.

51. Ibid., 8.

52. Syeda Hameed, Ruth Manorama, Malini Ghosh, Sheba George, Farha Naqvi and Mari Thekaekara, *How has the Gujarat Massacre Affected Minority Women?: The Survivors Speak*, Fact-finding by a Women's Panel, Citizen's Initiative, Ahmedabad, 16 April 2002.

53. The concerned Citizens' Tribunal reported, 'A distinct, tragic and ghastly feature of the state-sponsored carnage unleashed against a section of the population, the Muslim minority in Gujarat, was the systematic sexual violence unleashed against young girls and women. Rape was used as an instrument for the subjugation and humiliation of a community. A chilling technique, absent in pogroms unleashed hitherto but very much in evidence this time in a large number of cases, was the deliberate destruction of evidence. Barring a few, in most instances of sexual violence, the women victims were stripped and paraded naked, then gang-raped, and thereafter quartered and burnt beyond recognition.' *An Inquiry into the Carnage in Gujarat* (Citizens for Justice and Peace, Gujarat, 2002). http://www.sabrang.com/tribunal/vol2/womenvio.html

54. Vasudha Dhagamwar, 'The Women in Gujarat's Camps—I', *The Hindu*, 22 May 2002 (online edition) http://www.hinduonnet.com/thehindu/2002/05/22/stories/2002052200351000.htm

55. 'Report of the Committee constituted by the National Commission for Women to Assess the Status and Situation of Women and Girl Children in Gujarat in the Wake of Communal Disturbance,' in *The Gujarat Pogrom: Indian Democracy in Danger*, Compilation of various reports, Indian Social Institute, New Delhi, June 2002, 48-56.

56. Dhagamwar, op. cit.

57. Ibid.

58. National development in post-colonial India based on mega-projects often displacing large numbers of rural population (1999-2002), www.idpproject.orgIndia

59. E. Thukral, *Big Dams, Displaced Peoples: Rivers of Sorrow, Rivers of Joy* (Sage, New Delhi, 1992).

60. Lyla Mehta and Bina Srinivasan, 'Balancing Pains and Gains: A Perspective Paper on Gender and Large Dams,' A Working Paper of the World Commission on Dams (unpublished), prepared for *Thematic Review*, Cape Town, South Africa, http://www.dams.org/

61. 'Narmada: A History of Controversy,' BBC News, 16 November 2000, http://news.bbc.co.uk/1/hi/world/south_asia/1026355.stm

62. Tehmina Rehman, 'Internal Displacement: Atrocities on Women in India,' *Gender Issues*, http://www.punjabilok.com/india_disaster_rep/issue_significance/gender_issues.htm

63. 'Tehri Dam Project,' in *Impact of Displacement on Women*, National Commission for Women, New Delhi, 2001, 1-2.

64. Ibid., 7.

65. Ibid.

66. Ibid., 1-25.

67. 'Development Induced Displacement in Narmada Valley (2000-01): A Case Study', www.idpproject.orgIndia

68. Arundhati Roy, 'Cost of Living,' *Frontline*, 4 June 1999, http://www.flonnet.com/fl1703/17030640.htm.

69. V. Venkatesan, 'A Triumph for Gujarat,' *Frontline*, Vo. 16, No. 6 (13-26 March 1999).

70. Alok Agarwal, 'Villages Evicted with Police Terror Tactics, Preparations on for Demolishing: Women, Children also Beaten Up: NBA Demands that Submergence should be Stopped Till Resettlement is Over,' NBA Press Release, 21 July 2002, www.narmada.org

71. Angana Chatterjee, 'Whither Democracy in India,' June 2002, www.narmada.org

72. Comment attributed to Chitroopa Palit (Silvy), in Mohammed Asif, Lyla Mehta and Harsh Mander, *Engendering Resettlement and Rehabilitation Policies and Programmes in India*, Report of the workshop held at the India International Centre on 12 and 13 September 2002 organized by the Institute of Development Studies and Action Aid, India with support from DFID, November 2002, 5.

73. Dilip D'Souza, *The Narmada Dammed: An Inquiry into the Politics of Development* (New Delhi: Penguin, 2002), 68–94.

74. 'Forced relocation is often traumatic to the local population and lack of co-ordination sometimes leads to multiple displacements (1999–2000),' www.idpproject.orgIndia

75. Data gathered from *Compilation of the information available in the Global IDP Database of the Norwegian Refugee Council*, www.idpproject.org

76. Subir Bhowmick, BBC Correspondent in India, is of the opinion that the number has been incorrectly reported in the report cited. He is of the opinion that the number of displaced is much more in this region, 6 March 2003, Colombo.

77. C. Joshua Thomas, 'Displacement of Affected People and Humanitarian Tasks in Northeast India,' in Samir Das and Paula Banerjee (eds), *Civil Society Dialogue on Human Rights and Peace in the Northeast* (Kolkata, Calcutta Research Group, 2001), 26.

78. Monirul Hussain, 'Displacing Identities, Displaced Identities: The North-East Today,' *Refugee Watch*, No. 13 (March 2001), 15.

79. Comment attributed to Gina Sangkham, in Samir Das and Paula Banerjee (eds), *Civil Society Dialogue on Human Rights and Peace in the Northeast* (Kolkata: Calcutta Research Group, 2001), 31.

80. Syeda Rozana Rashid, 'Coping Mechanism of Women in Stress Situations among Chakma IDPs and Rohingya Refugees: Brief Report,' research carried on in Refugee and Migratory Movements Research Unit (RMMRU), supported by Bangladesh Freedom Foundation under *Forum on Women in Security and International Affairs Project* (unpublished).

81. See Kabita Chakma, Ilira Dewan and Samari Chakma (eds), *Kalpana Chakmar Diary* (in Bengali) (Dhaka: Hill Women's Federation, 2001).

82. Meghna Guhathakurta, 'Women's Narratives from the Chittagong Hill Tracts', in Rita Manchanda (ed.), *Women, War and Peace in South Asia: Beyond Victimhood to Agency* (New Delhi: Sage, 2001).

83. *Life is not Ours: Land and Human Rights in the Chittagong Hill Tracts Bangladesh* (Update 4) (The Chittagong Hill Tracts Commission, CHT, 2000), 60.

84. Ibid., 48.

85. Ibid., 49–50.

86. Amnesty International, AI-index: ASA 31/076/2002, 19 December 2002.

87. 'People Displaced from Village,' *Human Rights Situation Report (INSEC)*, Year 10, no. 2 (1 August 2002), 23.

88. Ibid.

89. For reports on rape by security forces, refer to Amnesty International, AI-index: ASA 31/076/2002, 24 December 2002.

90. *Governance Planning with the People: A Report* (South Asia Partnership Nepal, Kathmandu, 2002), 21.

91. 'Discrimination in Nepal', in *Human Rights Feature*, 20 August 2001, http://www.hrdc.net/sahrdc

92. In 1999, 22 women were convicted for abortion; many more were killed when they went to unskilled people for abortion. *Nepal: Human Rights Yearbook 2002* (INSEC, Kathmandu, April 2002), 142.

93. Shobha Gautam, *Women and Children in the Periphery of People's War* (Institute of Human Rights Communications Nepal, Kathmandu, 2001), 110.

94. Meena Poudel, 'Feminine Faces of Conflict,' in *Quest for Peace* (SAP-Nepal, Kathmandu, July 2001), 138.

95. Samir Das, 'Ethnic Assertion and Women's Question in Northeastern-India,' in A.K. Jana (ed.), *Indian Politics at the Crossroads* (New Delhi: Commonwealth, 1998), 177.

96. C. Joshua Thomas, 'Displacement of Affected People and Humanitarian Tasks in Northeast India,' in Das and Banerjee, 2001, 28; 'No Refuge: The Plight of Conflict Induced Internally Displaced Persons in India,' *Human Rights Features*, 23 November 2002, http://www.hrdc.net/sahrdc/hrfeatures/HRF33.htm

97. Kuldip Nayar, 'Displaced and Deprived,' *The Hindu*, 30 April 2001, http://www.hinduonnet.com//2001/04/30/stories/05302523.htm)

98. N.C. Saxena in Mohammed Asif, Lyla Mehta and Harsh Mander, *Engendering Resettlement and Rehabilitation Policies and Programmes in India*, Report of the workshop held at the India International Centre on 12 and 13 September 2002 organized by the Institute of Development Studies and Action Aid, India with support from DFID, November 2002, 4.

99. 'Women Facing War,' ICRC Report, *Newsletter*, Issue 22, 28.

100. Gameela Samarasinghe, 'Stories of Coping,' in Sasanka Perera, *Stories of Survivors: Socio-Political Contexts of Female-headed Households in Post-Terror Southern Sri Lanka (Vol. 1)* (New Delhi: Vikas Publishing House, 1999), 113.

101. Comment attributed to Elaben Bhatt of SEWA in Vasudha Dhagamwar, 2002 (online edition), 1. http://www.hinduonnet.com/thehindu/2002/05/22/stories/2002052200351000.htm

102. Gameela Samarasinghe, 'Stories of Coping', in Perera, 1999, 118.

103. Dharini Rajasingham-Senanayake, 'Post Victimisation: Cultural Transformation and Women's Empowerment in War and Displacement,' in Selvy Thiruchandran (ed.), *Women, Narration and Nation: Collective Images and Multiple Identities* (New Delhi: Vikas Publishing House, 1999), 143.

104. D'Souza, 2002, 77.

105. Bela Bhatia, 'Women's Initiative for Peace,' *Frontline*, Vol. 19, Issue 15 (20 July–2 August 2002), 1–5.

EPILOGUE: INTERNATIONAL LAW ON THE INTERNALLY DISPLACED PERSONS

David Fisher

A s the foregoing chapters in this volume have plainly shown, internal displacement is nothing new in South Asia. This is equally true of nearly every other continent on the globe. However, it is only recently that the international community as a whole has begun to explore the question of internal displacement and what its role should be in addressing it. One of the most important milestones in that inquiry has been the development in 1998 of the Guiding Principles on Internal Displacement,[1] the first international instrument specifically dedicated to the rights of the internally displaced.

While they have not been formally endorsed by states in the manner of a treaty, the Guiding Principles are gaining growing recognition as shared norms at the international, regional and national levels. As such, they are of increasing value to governments designing policies on internal displacement, humanitarian organizations and agencies seeking to complement national efforts to provide assistance and protection, advocates for the internally displaced wishing to intervene with authorities on their behalf, and internally displaced persons themselves.

In this chapter, I will describe the background and development of the Guiding Principles, discuss their content in light of the examples discussed by the other authors in this volume, chart their growing acceptance and use worldwide, and reflect on the question of their authority in international law. I will conclude with brief suggestions as to how they might best be used by the various actors at whom they are targeted.

THE GENESIS OF THE GUIDING PRINCIPLES

The Guiding Principles sprang from a basic dilemma in the international community's response to forcible displacement. For persons forced to flee their homes who also cross international borders, international and regional refugee instruments[2] provide the special legal status of 'refugee' accompanied by rights specific to their situation, such as the rights not to be returned to persecution in their own countries ('non-refoulement'), access to public relief, freedom of movement and treatment equal to that of other migrants in areas such as work eligibility. A sizable United Nations agency, the High Commissioner for Refugees, is available to address refugee issues and the rationale, and the reality of international intervention on their behalf has become widely accepted. As High Commissioner Ogata explained in her 1994 'Note on International Protection':

> The reasons for the United Nations (meaning, in this context, not merely the institution but the community of nations assembled within it) to assume responsibility for the international protection of refugees seems clear: fundamental rights and freedoms are normally secured for the individual by his or her Government. Since refugees do not enjoy the effective protection of their own Government, this normal remedy is unavailable, and it falls to the international community as a whole to provide the 'international' protection necessary to secure to refugees the enjoyment of these rights.[3]

Persons forcibly displaced from their homes who, for whatever reason, do not or cannot cross borders are excluded from the international refugee law regime.[4] Yet internally displaced persons face conditions as bad as—and frequently much worse than—refugees.[5] Moreover, although they theoretically enjoy recourse to their own governments, for many millions of internally displaced persons this benefit is illusory as governments overwhelmed by conflict have proven unable or unwilling (especially when they themselves are the cause of the displacement in the first instance) to provide any protection.[6]

In 1992, the United Nations Commission on Human Rights[7] called upon the Secretary-General to appoint a representative on the issue of internally displaced persons ('the Representative') and asked that his first task be an 'examination of existing international human rights, humanitarian and refugee law and standards and their applicability to the protection of and relief assistance to internally displaced persons.'[8] Secretary-General Boutros Boutros-Ghali appointed Francis M. Deng, a former Sudanese diplomat, to the post that same year.

The Representative convened a team of legal experts and consulted widely among states, international organizations, non-governmental organizations (NGOs) and other interested parties on the questions presented.[9] In 1993, he presented a preliminary study,[10] followed in 1996 and 1998, by a two-part 'Compilation and Analysis of Legal Norms' related to internal displacement.[11] The compilation found that 'existing law cover[ed] many aspects of particular relevance to internally displaced persons' but that 'there remain[ed] areas in which the law fail[ed] to provide sufficient protection for them.'[12]

Specifically, it identified two 'categories of insufficient protection': (a) instances where a norm existed in human rights law but not humanitarian law, or vice versa, meaning that the particular norm was not applicable in all situations, and (b) instances where general norms existed (for example the right of freedom of movement) but the specific corollary right relevant to the experience of internally displaced persons had not been explicitly articulated (for example, the right not to be confined in camps).[13] Also very much in the Representative's mind was the confusion among relevant actors about applicable law in light of the wide dispersal of relevant provisions among many different instruments.[14] The Representative therefore recommended that a new instrument be developed to focus specifically on internally displaced persons.[15]

The Commission responded with a resolution calling upon the Representative, 'on the basis of his compilation and analysis of legal norms, to develop an appropriate framework in this regard for the protection of internally displaced persons[...]'.[16] Accordingly, the Representative and his legal team turned to the question of what form the 'appropriate framework' should take and what it should contain.

The Format and Legal Foundations of the Guiding Principles

On the question of format, one obvious path would have been to press for a new international convention on internal displacement. However, the Representative and his legal team worried that promulgating a new treaty could entail a number of risks.[17] First, they noted that treaty-making in the field of human rights is becoming an increasingly difficult process, with no guarantee that states will reach agreement, and even where they can, requiring many years for them to do so. Even if initial agreement is reached, many more years may pass before a sufficient number of ratifications can be gathered for a treaty to enter into force. This has been the story, for example, of the Convention on the Protection of the Rights of All Migrant Workers and Members of Their Families ('Migrants

Convention'), which required over a dozen years after it was first adopted by the General Assembly to enter into force.[18] Moreover, even if a treaty obtains enough state parties to enter into force, the states most affected by the problem it means to address may not be among them. This has been another failing of the Migrants Convention which, to date, boasts no significant migrant-receiving states (its primary targets) among its members.[19]

Another important concern was that, in the process of negotiating a new text, already-existing standards might be 'renegotiated' by states with the end result of reduced, rather than enhanced, rights for internally displaced persons.[20] The International Committee of the Red Cross, as primary international promoter of what today seems to be an increasingly fragile international consensus on humanitarian standards (notwithstanding the firm law on the subject), was particularly worried about this possibility.[21]

Instead, the Representative and his team decided to formulate a non-binding instrument that would compile, restate and interpret existing law. The primary sources they relied upon were instruments of humanitarian law (also known as 'the law of war'), human rights law and refugee law.

In the first category, the most important instruments are the Geneva Conventions of 1949, and in particular the fourth convention, known as the Convention Relative to the Protection of Civilian Persons in Time of War, as well as their two additional protocols, the first of which extends the number of rights guaranteed to non-combatants and the second of which extends a greater number of rights to non-combatants in non-international (that is internal) conflicts. The Geneva Conventions have enjoyed nearly universal accession, including by all of the states addressed by the other authors of this volume.[22] Although the two additional protocols have also been widely embraced, they have not been as entirely successful as the original Geneva Conventions and only one of the states addressed in this book—Bangladesh—has adhered to them.[23] However, it is considered by many international legal scholars that a good number of the provisions of both protocols are also guaranteed by customary international law[24] and are therefore independently binding on all states.[25]

In the area of human rights, the Guiding Principles rely on a range of instruments including (but not exclusive to) the Universal Declaration of Human Rights (UDHR),[26] the International Covenant on Civil and Political Rights (ICCPR) and the International Covenant on Economic, Cultural and Social Rights (ICECSR), the Convention on the Elimination of All Forms of Racial Discrimination (CERD), the Convention on the

Elimination of All Forms of Discrimination against Women (CEDAW), the Convention Against Torture and Other Cruel, Inhuman or Degrading Treatment (CAT), and the Convention on the Rights of the Child (CRC). These instruments have been ratified or acceded to by most of the states discussed in this book.[27]

The authors of the Guiding Principles also looked to concepts in refugee law that might be applied by analogy, such as the right not to be returned to persecution in one's area of origin (in refugee law, the right to *non-refoulement*) which is echoed in Principle 15(d) (asserting that displaced persons have the 'right to be protected against forcible return to or resettlement in any place where their life, safety and/or health would be at risk'). However, each of the rights so articulated can also find a basis in more generally-stated norms of humanitarian and human rights law.[28]

THE CONTENT OF THE GUIDING PRINCIPLES

The Guiding Principles consist of an introduction followed by 30 individual principles, organized by the three 'phases' of displacement (before, during and after) as well as a particular section concerning the rights and obligations of humanitarian aid providers. I will discuss them here under a framework of basic questions that the Guiding Principles seek to answer.

Who do the Guiding Principles Address?

The Guiding Principles are principally addressed to governments, taking as their point of departure, a 'positive' notion of sovereignty not as a barrier to the realization of rights but as an affirmative duty.[29] As stated by Principle 3: 'National authorities have the primary duty and responsibility to provide protection and humanitarian assistance to internally displaced persons within their jurisdiction.'

At the same time, the Guiding Principles call for observance of the rights they articulate not solely by governments but by 'all authorities, groups and persons irrespective of their legal status' (Principle 2). Thus, by their terms, the Guiding Principles address rebel groups (sometimes euphemistically called 'non-state actors'), humanitarian organizations, civil society, and any other persons or entities that might impact upon the internally displaced. While international norms have traditionally been considered to be binding only upon governments, this approach is consistent with humanitarian law, which binds rebel armies in addition to state forces in situations of armed conflict,[30] as well as with a modern trend in other areas of international law to extend their reach beyond states to other entities and even to individuals (as evidenced, for example, by the growth of the application of international criminal law, in particular crimes against humanity).[31]

Who are 'Internally Displaced Persons'?

One of the most important contributions of the Guiding Principles is their definition of the term 'internally displaced persons':

> persons or groups of persons who have been forced or obliged to flee or to leave their homes or places of habitual residence, in particular as a result of or in order to avoid the effects of armed conflict, situations of generalized violence, violations of human rights or natural or human-made disasters, and who have not crossed an internationally recognized state border.[32]

As is evident from the text, this definition is purposefully broad. Previous definitions used at the international and regional levels had limited the term to persons who would be considered refugees if they crossed a border, or were in 'refugee-like' situations.[33] The drafters of the Guiding Principles wished instead to include a wider range of persons, including those fleeing natural disaster, as experience had shown that they frequently faced challenges similar to those fleeing armed conflict.[34] Likewise, although it is not explicitly mentioned, so-called 'development-induced displacement' is considered to be included within the definition, as made clear by later provisions on arbitrary displacement, addressed below.[35]

Inasmuch as it was not their intention to create a specific status for internally displaced persons, there was no need for the drafters to ensure the degree of specificity required, for example, for the definition of 'refugee', given the latter term's legal ramifications. At the same time, the drafters wished to keep their definition of internally displaced persons operationally useful and therefore economic migrants, current and former soldiers, and other travellers were not intended to fall within the internally displaced category.[36]

The primary elements, therefore, of the Guiding Principles' definition are: (a) coercion and (b) movement within borders. Included among the many persons discussed in this book would be not only those deliberately forced from their homes by government armed forces (for example, the Karenni in Myanmar), but also those fleeing the general effects of armed conflict (for example, persons fleeing during the war in Afghanistan in 2003), those fleeing or forced to leave by rebel groups (for example those fleeing Maoist attacks in Nepal) or inter-ethnic fighting (for example Bengalis in Meghalaya), those fleeing natural disasters, whether sudden or gradual (for example erosion on the Jamuna river in Bangladesh), as well as those required to leave their lands in favour of development projects (such as the many dam projects in Pakistan and India).

What Types of Displacement are Prohibited?

Principle 6 affirms that '[e]very human being shall have the right to be protected against being arbitrarily displaced from his or her home or place of habitual residence.' Support for this proposition can be found in humanitarian law[37] and also in the right to movement, guaranteed by a number of human rights instruments, which can be reasonably expected to have as its corollary the 'right not to move'.[38] Moreover, the drafters also looked to important developments in the operational guidance of the World Bank and at the Organization for Economic Cooperation and Development.[39]

It is important to note that the Guiding Principles do not claim that displacement is *always* prohibited. In both humanitarian and human rights law, exceptions to the general rule are available. Rather it is '*arbitrary displacement*' that must be avoided and Principle 7 provides a sort of road-map for avoiding arbitrariness.

First, all feasible alternatives to displacement must be explored. In situations of armed conflict, this means that a determination must be made either that the security of the population or 'imperative military reasons' require displacement before it can be carried out.[40]

Where displacement is to occur outside the context of armed conflict, Principle 7 provides a list of procedural protections that must be guaranteed, including decision-making and enforcement by appropriate authorities, involvement of and consultation with those to be affected and the provision of an effective remedy for those wishing to challenge their displacement. These provisions are, of course, of particular interest to those facing displacement for development projects.

Moreover, in either context, 'all measures' must be taken to minimize the effects and duration of the displacement and the responsible authorities are required to ensure 'to the greatest practicable extent' that the basic needs of those displaced (for example, shelter, safety, nutrition, health, and hygiene) are met.

It should also be noted that Principle 9 articulates a 'special obligation' to protection against displacement of a number of groups whose special attachment to territory has been recognized in international law, including indigenous persons, minorities, peasants, and pastoralists.[41]

How do these rules apply in practice? To take one example highlighted in this volume, it is reported that the armed forces of Myanmar (Tatmadaw) have systematically destroyed villages along the Thai border, forcing all residents to move to new resettlement areas where they are confined with inadequate food, sanitation, educational facilities and livelihood opportunities.[42] The village relocation scheme is part of an explicit army strategy (the Four Cuts) to deprive ethnic armies of any civilian support base. Is this 'arbitrary' displacement as understood by the Guiding Principles and its underlying law?

Yes. Inasmuch as at least many of the relocations arguably occur in an area of armed conflict, the Tatmadaw might argue that the procedural protections articulated in Principle 7 do not apply. However, even in situations of armed conflict, forced displacement of the civilian population is not allowed, except for temporary evacuations required for the security of the civilians involved or 'imperative military reasons.' In this case, the relocations are clearly intended to be permanent, as soldiers allegedly burned villages. The exception for civilian security does not apply, as there is no pretence that the displacements are effectuated to protect the villagers themselves.

Likewise, the exception for 'imperative military reasons' does not apply. Although it is plain that ridding a contested area of civilian habitation can bring military advantage, the International Committee of the Red Cross has noted that 'the adjective "imperative"' in 'imperative military reasons' as used by the humanitarian law underlying Principle 7 (the fourth Geneva Convention and its second Additional Protocol) 'reduces to a minimum cases in which displacement may be ordered. Clearly, imperative military reasons cannot be justified by political motives.'[43] As another commentator has further explained,

> ...[t]he purpose of this exception is to strike the balance between the two countervailing and guiding principles which lay at the heart of humanitarian law: humanity versus military necessity.... As a rule of construction, the notion of 'military necessity' has to be narrowly interpreted because considerations of military necessity are already taken into account in framing the rules of humanitarian law. A state cannot, therefore, be allowed to invoke military necessity as justification for upsetting that balance by departing from those rules.[44]

In light of these considerations, the military advantage that would come from systematically eradicating a civilian population in a large swathe of territory could not be considered to be included in the exception for 'imperative military reasons', or the exception would entirely swallow the rule.

Finally, in addition to violating international norms with regard to the displacement in the first instance, the reported acts of Tatmadaw further violate humanitarian law by failing to provide adequate shelter, food and other needs for those displaced by its deliberate policy.

What Rights do Persons Have Once Displaced?

Displaced persons enjoy the full range of rights enjoyed by civilians in humanitarian law and by every human being in human rights law. These include the rights to life, integrity and dignity of the person (for example freedom from rape and torture), non-discrimination, recognition as a person before the law, freedom from arbitrary detention, liberty of movement, respect for family life, an adequate standard of living (including access to basic humanitarian needs), medical care, access to legal remedies, possession of property, freedom of expression, freedom of religion, participation in public life and education, as set out in Principles 10-23.[45]

In several instances, the Guiding Principles specify how generally expressed rights apply in situations of displacement. These should be of particular interest to those designing and assessing domestic policies on internal displacement. For example, Principle 12 provides that, to give effect to the right of liberty from arbitrary detention, internally displaced persons 'shall not be interned in or confined in a camp' other than in 'exceptional circumstances' and that they shall not be subject to discriminatory arrest 'as a result of their displacement'. Likewise Principle 20 provides that the right to 'recognition everywhere as a person before the law' should be given effect for displaced persons by authorities facilitating the issuance of 'all documents necessary for the enjoyment and exercise of their legal rights, such as passports, personal identification documents, birth certificates and marriage certificates'.

As pointed out in a dedicated chapter of this book,[46] the Guiding Principles provide for special consideration of the needs of women and children (including 'positive discrimination' or affirmative activities on behalf of governments to model assistance and protection to their particular needs, consultation and involvement in decisions regarding their displacement and return or resettlement, protection against recruitment of minors and free and compulsory education), as well as for other especially vulnerable groups, such as the elderly and disabled.

What Rights and Obligations do Humanitarian Organizations Have?

The Guiding Principles also lay out a number of rights and obligations of humanitarian organizations in Principles 24–27. This section again stresses the point that '[t]he primary duty and responsibility for providing humanitarian assistance to internally displaced persons lies with national authorities' (Principle 25[1]). In carrying out this duty, national authorities must not 'arbitrarily withhold' consent to international humanitarian organizations' offer of services to the internally displaced, and must 'grant and facilitate' their free passage to areas where assistance is needed. Humanitarian personnel, material, and supplies are not to be attacked or diverted for other purposes. For their part, humanitarian organizations must carry out their operations 'in accordance with the principles of humanity and impartiality and without discrimination' and should 'give due regard to the protection needs and human rights of internally displaced persons' and not just their needs for assistance.

Humanitarian access is a critical issue in many crisis areas around the globe. In South Asia, Afghanistan serves as a particularly poignant example of this problem, as pointed out by the chapter in this volume on that country. As of 2004, the killing of humanitarian personnel had led to a substantial reduction of international humanitarian presence in many areas of Afghanistan, and the government lacked the capacity to exercise control. In this respect, it is important to reiterate that the Guiding Principles and (in this instance at least) their underlying law apply equally to non-state actors and government forces.[47]

What Help Should Displaced Persons Expect with Return, Reintegration and Resettlement?

In their final section, the Guiding Principles provide that competent authorities have 'the primary duty and responsibility' to assist displaced persons by providing the means as well as by establishing conditions for return to their places of origin, or for resettlement in another part of the country (Principle 28). Any return or resettlement must be voluntary and carried out in conditions of safety and dignity for those involved.

As a corollary to the right to free movement, therefore, displaced persons have the right to return to their homes.[48] Although the right to return or resettle is not expressly stated in any particular human rights instrument, this interpretation of the right of free movement is strongly supported by resolutions of the Security Council,[49] decisions of treaty monitoring bodies,[50] and other sources of authority.[51]

Moreover, although the displaced have the right to return, Principle 28 carefully specifies that they must not be forced to do so, particularly (but not only) when their safety would be imperilled. The issue of the voluntariness of return or resettlement is recurrent in protracted displacement situations around the world. In many places, governments and insurgent groups have ceded to the temptation to use the return or resettlement of displaced persons as a political tool. In this volume, for instance, Samir Kumar Das describes instances in which Indian officials pressured Muslims displaced after riots in Ahmedabad to return home notwithstanding an ongoing atmosphere of intimidation in the city to foster electoral advantage. On the opposite end of the spectrum, as Joe William's chapter reports, the government of Sri Lanka has set up large 'High Security Zones' in Jaffna to which original residents will not be allowed to return. Both cases violate Principle 28.

Principle 29 provides that authorities also have 'the duty and responsibility' to assist displaced persons to recover 'to the extent possible' their property and possessions, and where restitution is not possible to provide or assist the displaced persons to obtain appropriate compensation. Like the preceding principle, this one relies on general precepts of the right to property, the right to remedy for violations of international law, as well as a growing adherence to Security Council resolutions, treaties, national law and other sources of authority.[52]

This right to restitution or compensation comes quickly to the fore in many return situations where displaced persons find their homes destroyed or occupied (sometimes for long periods) by others. Domestic property law is frequently ill prepared to deal with sorting out the resulting claims to ownership and possession, although international law in this area continues to develop.[53]

STANDING OF THE GUIDING PRINCIPLES

As noted above, the Guiding Principles were not negotiated or ratified by states. It is therefore reasonable to ask: What is their status? Are they law? What authority do they have?

In answer to the first question, the Guiding Principles are part of a growing number of 'soft law' instruments that have come to characterize norm-making in the human rights field as well as other areas of international law, in particular environmental, labour and finance.[54] While there is no one universally-accepted definition of soft law instruments,[55] they are generally understood to have some normative character inviting observance but one that is less than strictly binding; thus occupying a 'grey zone between law and politics.'[56] Such instruments range from treaties, but which include only soft obligations . . . , to non-binding or voluntary resolutions and codes of conduct formulated and accepted by international and regional organizations . . . , to statements prepared by individuals in a non-governmental capacity, but which purport to lay down international principles.[57]

Over time, the provisions of soft law instruments can evolve into binding customary law. Many scholars believe that this has happened with respect to the provisions of the Universal Declaration of Human Rights.[58] Even without this 'legal' recognition, however, a number of soft law instruments, including those drafted by 'experts', such as the Principles Relating to the Status and Functioning of National Institutions for Promotion of Human Rights ('Paris Principles'),[59] have inspired an impressive degree of voluntary observance by governments.

With regard to the second question, it should be re-emphasized that the many provisions of the Guiding Principles that simply restate existing law are indisputably binding on any state parties to the underlying 'hard law' instruments. In this sense, the precepts they contain are certainly 'law'. Whether other provisions that move into greyer areas can be said to be 'law' will depend upon their reception by states and other relevant actors.

In their few years of existence, the Guiding Principles have in fact obtained a high level of recognition. When they were first presented in 1998, the Commission on Human Rights merely 'noted' them and the intention of the Representative to use them in his dialogue with states.[60] Over time, however, the language of regular resolutions in the Commission, the Economic and Social Council (ECOSOC) and the General Assembly has grown increasingly warmer. In 2003, for instance, both the Commission and the General Assembly

welcome[d] the fact that an increasing number of States, United Nations agencies and regional and non-governmental organizations are applying them as a standard, and encourages all relevant actors to make use of the Guiding Principles when dealing with situations of internal displacement[.][61]

They have also been acknowledged at the level of the Security Council,[62] at international conferences,[63] and adopted by the U.N. and wider humanitarian community as their standard.[64]

The Guiding Principles have been well received by multilateral organizations at the regional level. They have been welcomed in resolutions, declarations and statements by organs of the Organization of African Unity (OAU) (now known as the African Union), Economic Community of West African States (ECOWAS), Inter-Governmental Authority on Development (IGAD), Organization of American States (OAS), Organization for Security and Cooperation in Europe (OSCE), the Parliamentary Assembly of the Council of Europe (CoE) and the Commonwealth.[65]

Most importantly, the Guiding Principles have started to make an impact at the national level, where they are most needed. A number of governments, including Angola,[66] Burundi,[67] Colombia,[68] and Liberia,[69] have expressly referred to them in domestic laws and policies on internally displaced persons. The Colombia Constitutional Court has gone so far as to hold, in three separate decisions, that national authorities are bound to follow the Guiding Principles as an authoritative compendium of international norms.[70]

Among states discussed in this volume, Sri Lanka has similarly relied upon the Guiding Principles in the formulation of its National Framework for Relief, Rehabilitation and Reconciliation.[71] Likewise, civil society institutions have made increasing use of the Guiding Principles to assess domestic policy and practice concerning displaced persons. In Sri Lanka, the Consortium of Humanitarian Agencies (CHA) produced a 'Toolkit' to make the Guiding Principles more accessible and uses them in its training of government and other actors.[72] The CHA is also currently preparing an additional 'Practitioners' Kit' on return issues relying on the Guiding Principles. In India, moreover, the Calcutta Research Group (CRG) has been very active in educating and training civil society on displacement issues at the national and regional level using the Guiding Principles as an important reference. This book is one of the fruits of CRG's many dedicated efforts.

Thus, in answer to the final question posed above (that is, what rights and obligations do humanitarian organizations have?), regardless of whether the Guiding Principles, as an instrument, are technically binding law, it can be argued with some force that they represent a large and growing international consensus about how internally displaced persons should be treated. Governments formulating policy, members of civil society analysing existing policy, advocates seeking to advance the rights of the internally displaced and the internally displaced themselves would do well therefore to take the Guiding Principles into account and make use of them as others are doing in similar circumstances around the world.

CONCLUSION

The Guiding Principles were never meant to be a revolutionary document. Their underlying premise—that states owe a duty of protection and assistance to civilians within their borders—are familiar in international law, finding precedents in the UN Charter, the Universal Declaration of Human Rights and many other fundamental instruments of the human rights firmament. Long before, the obligations of belligerents to spare civilians to the extent possible from the ravages of war were settled and universally agreed. What *is* very new in the Guiding Principles is the focus on the rights of the internally displaced as a specific group with particular needs.

In clearly setting out the rights of internally displaced persons relevant to the needs they encounter in different stages of displacement, the Guiding Principles provide a handy schematic of how to design a national policy or law on internal displacement that is focused on the individuals concerned and responsive to the requirements of international law. It is to be hoped that other states in the region will follow the lead of Sri Lanka in creating such laws and policies. Similarly, the Guiding Principles can be used by governments (and particularly national human rights institutions where they exist), advocates, and displaced persons as a means to measure the compliance of existing laws and policies with international standards. Finally, their simplicity allows the Guiding Principles to effectively inform the internally displaced themselves of their rights.

While the Guiding Principles have already gained an impressive degree of recognition at the international, regional and national levels, more remains to be done to foster their use, particularly in South Asia, where many states with large displacement problems lack comprehensive policies or effective remedies for those. It is to be hoped that this book will itself encourage that process.

NOTES

1. U.N. Doc. No. E/CN.4/1998/53 Add.2 (1998). The Guiding Principles have been translated into 28 languages (including Burmese, Pashto & Dari, Sqaw Karen, Tamil and Sinhala), many of them available online at the websites for the Brookings Institution-

SAIS Project on Internal Displacement (http://www.brookings.edu/fp/projects/idp/gp_page.htm) and the Office of the High Commissioner for Human Rights (http://www.unhchr.ch/html/menu2/7/b/principles_lang.htm).

2. At the international level, the primary refugee instruments are the 1951 Convention Relating to the Status of Refugees, 189 U.N.T.S. 105 ('1951 Refugee Convention') and its 1967 Protocol, 66 U.N.T.S. 267. Two regional instruments, the Convention Governing the Specific Aspects of Refugee Problems in Africa, 1001 U.N.T.S. 45 ('African Refugee Convention') and the Cartagena Declaration on Refugees, OAS Doc. OEA/Ser.L/V/II.66/doc.10, rev. 1, at 190-93 (1984-85) ('Cartagena Declaration') have expanded upon the provisions of the 1951 Convention, exerting an influence well beyond their state signatories.

3. United Nations High Commissioner for Refugees, Note on International Protection, U.N. Doc. A/AC.96/830 (1994).

4. In all of the relevant instruments, crossing a border (or already being outside one's country in the case of the so-called 'refugees sur place') is one of the prerequisites for refugee status. See, e.g., 1951 Refugee Convention art. 1(A)(2); African Refugee Convention art I(1); Cartagena Declaration para. 3. This is not to suggest that the right to flee across borders is neglected by international law. The right to leave one's country is guaranteed both in humanitarian law (see, e.g., Geneva Convention Relative to the Protection of Civilian Persons in Time of War, 75 U.N.T.S. 287 (1950) ('GC IV'), art. 35) and human rights law (see, e.g., Universal Declaration of Human Rights, G.A. res. 217A (III), U.N. Doc A/810 at 71 (1948), art. 13, International Covenant on Civil and Political Rights, G.A. res. 2200A (XXI), 21 U.N. GAOR Supp. (No. 16) at 52, U.N. Doc. A/6316 (1966), 999 U.N.T.S. 17, art. 12). However, it is not directly addressed by the refugee instruments cited above as they are aimed at refugee-receiving rather than sending states.

5. See Report of the Representative of the Secretary-General for internally displaced persons, U.N. Doc. E/CN.4/2003/86 (2003), para. 5.

6. See Roberta Cohen and Francis Deng, *Masses in Flight: The Global Crisis of Internal Displacement* (Brookings Institution Press, 1998), 2.

7. The Commission on Human Rights is an organ of the United Nations. Its membership consists of 53 UN member states that are elected for a period of two years each. The Commission passes resolutions on issues related to human rights, receives reports from the Secretary-General and other sources, and also creates (or calls upon the Secretary-General to create) 'human rights mechanisms', such as working groups, rapporteurs, and experts, to report upon particular issues.

8. U.N. Doc. No. E/CN.4/1992/73 (1992), para. 2.

9. See Simon Bagshaw, *Developing the Guiding Principles on Internal Displacement: The Rise of a Global Public Policy Network* (Global Public Policy Network 2000), available at www.gppi.net.

10. U.N Doc. E/CN.4/1993/35 (1993).

11. The first volume of the Compilation (U.N. Doc. No. E/CN.4/1996/52/Add.2 [1996]) ('Compilation, Vol. I'), released in 1996, gave a comprehensive description of the rights of internally displaced persons. The second volume (U.N. Doc. No. E/CN.4/1998/53/Add.1 (1998)) ('Compilation, Vol. II'), released in 1998, focused on the right to avoid arbitrary displacement in the first instance.

12. Compilation, Vol. I, supra note 11, para. 410.

13. Ibid., para. 411.

14. See Cohen and Deng, 1998, 257.
15. Compilation Vol. I, 1996, para. 413.
16. U.N. Doc. E/CN.4/1996/52 (1996), para. 9.
17. See Walter Kälin, *How Hard is Soft Law? The Guiding Principles on Internal Displacement and the Need for a Normative Framework* (Lecture sponsored by the Brookings-CUNY Project on Internal Displacement at the City University of New York Graduate Center, 19 December 2001), reprinted in Brookings-CUNY Project on Internal Displacement, *Recent Commentaries about the Nature and Application of the Guiding Principles on Internal Displacement* (April 2002).
18. Human Rights Watch, Migrant Workers Need Protection: UN Treaty Comes into Force (Press Release 1 July 2003).
19. Ibid.
20. Ibid.
21. See Jean-Philippe Lavoyer, *Refugees and Internally Displaced Persons: International Humanitarian Law and the Role of the ICRC*, International Review of the Red Cross, No. 305 (1995), 162–80.
22. See International Committee of the Red Cross, *States Party to the Geneva Conventions and their Additional Protocols* (20 May 2003).
23. Ibid.
24. There are a number of sources of international law, of which treaties are the best known to the general public. Even in the absence of a treaty, however, international law can be formed by the repeated behaviour of states. In order for such 'custom' to be recognized as law, there must be 'a general practice' by states and an acknowledgement that the practice is required, known as 'opinio juris'. See Peter Malanczuk, *Akehurst's Modern Introduction to International Law*, 7th edn (Routledge, 1997), 39.
25. See, e.g., Theodor Meron, *Human Rights and Humanitarian Norms and Customary Law* (Oxford: Clarendon Press, 1989), 62–78.
26. Afghanistan, Burma (now Myanmar), India and Pakistan were among the 48 General Assembly member states who voted in favour of the UDHR in 1948. Since its adoption, the stature of the UDHR has grown so high that many scholars consider many, if not all, of its provisions as binding on all states either as customary law or as an interpretation of the UN Charter. See Henry Steiner and Philip Alston, *International Human Rights in Context*, 2nd edn (Oxford University Press, 2000), 143.
27. All of the states discussed in this volume with the exception of Pakistan and Myanmar have ratified or acceded to both the ICCPR and ICECSR. All with the exception of Myanmar have ratified or acceded to CERD. All have ratified or acceded to CEDAW and the CRC. Afghanistan, Bangladesh and Nepal have ratified or acceded to CAT. See Office of the High Commissioner for Human Rights, 'Status of Ratifications of the Principal International Human Rights Treaties,' available at www.ohchr.org.
28. See generally, Walter Kälin, *Guiding Principles on Internal Displacement—Annotations*, American Society of International Law, Studies in Transnational Legal Policy, No. 32 (1998) (hereinafter '*Annotations*') (and, in particular, with regard to Principle 15's right analogous to '*non-refoulement*,' pages 37–39, which cited provisions of the European Convention on Human Rights and the ICCPR).
29. This notion has been central to the Representative's thinking on internal displacement throughout his mandate. See, e.g., Report of the Representative of the Secretary-General in internally displaced persons, U.N. Doc. E/CN.4/2004/77 (2004) paras. 61-66. It has also enjoyed increasing acceptance among states, as evidenced, for example, by the

recent report of the International Commission on Intervention and State Sovereignty: 'The Responsibility to Protect' (December 2001), paras 2.14-2.15.

30. See *Annotations*, 1998, 9. This entire book is available online at http://www.asil.org/study_32.pdf.
31. See Malanczuk, 1997, 91.
32. Guiding Principles, para. 2.
33. See Cohen and Deng, 1998, 17-18.
34. Ibid.
35. See subsection 3 below as well as W. Courtland Robinson, *Risks and Rights: The Causes, Consequences and Challenges of Development-induced Displacement* (Brookings-SAIS Project on Internal Displacement, May 2003), 6-8.
36. Ibid.
37. With certain exceptions, article 49 of the fourth Geneva Convention provides that '[i]ndividual or mass forcible transfers, as well as deportations of protected persons from occupied territory to the territory of the Occupying Power or to that of any other country, occupied or not, are prohibited, regardless of their motive.' Likewise, article 17 of the second Additional Protocol provides: 'The displacement of the civilian population shall not be ordered for reasons related to the conflict unless the security of the civilians involved or imperative military reasons so demand.'
38. See Maria Stavropoulu, *The Right Not to be Displaced*, American Univ. Journal of International Law & Policy, vol. 9 (1994), 737-38.
39. *Annotations*, op. cit., at 14-16.
40. GC IV art. 49.
41. See *Annotations*, 1998, 22-23.
42. See Sabyasachi Basu Ray Cahudhury, *Escape to Ordeal: IDPs in Contemporary Burma* in this volume; see also generally Norwegian Refugee Council Global IDP Project, 'Myanmar' (November 2003) www.idpproject.org.
43. Jean Pictet, Commentary on the Protocol Additional to the Geneva Conventions of 12 August 1949, and relating to the Protection of Victims of Non-International Armed Conflicts (Protocol II), 8 June 1977 (ICRC, 1960), paras. 4853-54 (commenting on article 17 of the second Additional Protocol and article 49 of the fourth Geneva Convention).
44. See Bonaventure Rutinwa, *Refugee Claims Based on Violation of International Humanitarian Law: The 'Victim's' Perspective*, Georgetown Immigration Law Journal, vol. 15 (2001), 500-01 (internal citations omitted).
45. Technically, as noted by the Representative's Compilation and Analysis of Legal Norms discussed above, some of the laws underlying the humanitarian and human rights norms articulated by the Guiding Principles do not apply in every situation. Humanitarian law, for instance, only applies in situations of armed conflict (and not, therefore, in situations of generalized violence or riot not amounting to 'armed conflict'). Different rules apply in international and internal conflicts. A number of human rights norms may be 'limited' or 'derogated' in particular circumstances. These various exceptions and limitations are not reproduced in the Guiding Principles, inasmuch as they were designed to be 'principles' rather than a binding text. It should be noted, however, that there is a growing trend of overlap between humanitarian and human rights of law, such that situations in which neither type of law might apply because of such exceptions are becoming very few. See Kälin, *How Hard is Soft Law?*, 2002, 6. The Guiding Principles reflect and contribute to this progressive trend.

46. See Paula Banerjee, *Internally Displaced Women in South Asia*, in this volume.
47. Likewise, in a parallel development of humanitarian law on this subject, the International Criminal Court (ICC) has jurisdiction over war crimes committed by *individuals* related to blocking humanitarian aid and attacks on humanitarian personnel. See Rome Statute of the International Criminal Court, U.N. Doc. A/CONF.183/9 (1998), art. 8(2)(b)(ii), (iii), (xxiv), & (xxv), and 8(2)(e)(ii) & (iii). Afghanistan (alone among states discussed in this book) has acceded to the Rome Statute. See www.iccnow.org for an updated list of state parties.
48. See *Annotations*, 1998, 69–70.
49. See, e.g., U.N. Doc. S/RES/1124 (1997) (on Georgia), para. 11 ('[r]eaffirm[ing] the right of all refugees and displaced persons affected by the conflict to return to their homes in secure conditions in accordance with international law'); U.N. Doc. S/RES/1239 (1999) (on Kosovo), para. 4 ('[r]eaffirm[ing] the right of all refugees and displaced persons to return to their homes in safety and in dignity'); S/RES/1483 (2003) (on Iraq) (calling on the Secretary-General to appoint a special representative with responsibility, inter alia, for 'promoting the safe, orderly, and voluntary return of refugees and displaced persons').
50. See, e.g., Committee on the Elimination of Racial Discrimination, General Recommendation XXII: Article 5 and Refugees and Displaced Persons, U.N. Doc. A/51/18 (1996), 126 ('All . . . refugees and displaced persons have the right freely to return to their homes of origin under conditions of safety. . . . States parties are obliged to ensure that the return of such refugees and displaced persons is voluntary . . . ').
51. See, e.g., World Conference Against Racism, Racial Discrimination, Xenophobia and Related Intolerance, Declaration, Agenda item 9, adopted on 8 September 2001 in Durban, South Africa, para. 54. ('We underline the urgency of addressing the root causes of displacement and of finding durable solutions for refugees and displaced persons, in particular voluntary return in safety and dignity to the countries of origin, as well as resettlement in third countries and local integration, when and where appropriate and feasible[.]')
52. See *Annotations*, 1998, at 71–74.
53. See Scott Leckie, ed., *Returning Home: Housing and Property Restitution Rights for Refugees and Displaced Persons* (Transnational Publishers, 2003), ch. 1.
54. Edith Brown Weiss (ed.), *Introduction, in International Compliance with Nonbinding Accords* 3 (1997).
55. See Dinah Shelton, *Compliance with International Human Rights Soft Law, in International Compliance with Nonbinding Accords*, 1997, 120.
56. See Malanczuk, 1997, at 54.
57. C.M. Chinkin, *The Challenge of Soft Law, Development and Change in International Law*, 38 International and Comparative Law Quarterly, vol. 38, 851 (1989).
58. See Steiner and Alston, 2000, at 143.
59. U.N. Doc. E/CN.4/1992/54, Annex (1992).
60. U.N. Doc. E/CN.4/RES/1998/59 (1998), operative paras. 1 & 6.
61. U.N. Doc. A/RES/58/177 (2003), operative para. 7; U.N. Doc. E/CN.4/RES/2003/51 (2003), operative para. 7.
62. See, e.g., U.N. Doc. S/RES/1286 (2000), preamb. para. 6 (on Burundi) ('[n]*oting* that the United Nations agencies, regional and non-governmental organizations, in cooperation with host Governments, are making use of the Guiding Principles on Internal Displacement [E/CN.4/1998/53 and Add.1-2], *inter alia*, in Africa'); U.N. Doc. S/PRST/

2000/1 (2000), at 2 ('The Council further notes that the United Nations agencies, regional and non-governmental organizations, in cooperation with host Governments, are making use of the Guiding Principles on Internal Displacement, *inter alia*, in Africa').

63. See, e.g., Report of the World Conference against Racism, Racial Discrimination, Xenophobia and Related Intolerance, Durban, 31 August–8 September 2001, U.N. Doc. A/CONF.189/12 (2001), para. 65 ('[e]ncourag[ing] the bodies, agencies and relevant programmes of the United Nations system and States to promote and make use of the Guiding Principles on Internal Displacement [E/CN.4/1998/53/Add.2], particularly those provisions relating to non-discrimination').

64. Inter-Agency Standing Committee Summary Record (26 March 1998), agenda item 5.1 (welcoming the Guiding Principles and encouraging member agencies to share them with their executive boards and staff and 'to apply the Guiding Principles in their activities on behalf of internally displaced persons'). See also Inter-Agency Standing Committee, Protection of Internally Displaced Persons, Inter-Agency Standing Committee Policy Paper (1999) at 5 ('Having gained broad consensus, the Principles provide solid guidance on how protection activities should be oriented in order to be effective').

65. See Report of the Representative of the Secretary-General on internally displaced persons, U.N. Doc. E/CN.4/2003/86 (2003) (hereinafter '2003 CHR Report'), paras. 30-35; Report of the Representative of the Secretary-General on internally displaced persons, U.N. Doc. E/CN.4/2004/77 (2004), para. 16.

66. Norms on the Resettlement of Internally Displaced Populations, Council of Ministers Decree No. 1/01 (5 January 2001).

67. Framework for Consultation on Protection of Internally Displaced Persons (February 2001).

68. Presidential Decree No. 6: Instructions for Strengthening Comprehensive Attention to the Population Displaced by Violence (28 November 2001).

69. Declaration of the Rights and Protection of Liberian Internally Displaced Persons (IDPs) (26 September 2002).

70. See Constitutional Court Decisions T-025 (22 January 2004); SU-1150 (August 2000); T-327 (March 2001).

71. 'The universally accepted rights of the internally displaced—to protection, to liberty and security of person, to humanitarian assistance and to their return, resettlement and integration in society—are enshrined in the *Guiding Principles on Internal Displacement*, a document drawn up at the request of the United Nations Commission on Human Rights and General Assembly. Having been developed over the past eight years in consultation with a number of concerned governments, the *Guiding Principles* unquestionably also apply to the situation in Sri Lanka.' The National Framework for Relief, Rehabilitation and Reconciliation (June 2002), at 11.

72. Consortium of Humanitarian Agencies, *Guiding Principles on Internal Displacement: A Toolkit for Dissemination, Advocacy and Analysis* (2001).

APPENDIX

THE UN GUIDING PRINCIPLES ON THE INTERNALLY DISPLACED PERSONS*

INTRODUCTION—SCOPE AND PURPOSE

1. These Guiding Principles address the specific needs of internally displaced persons worldwide. They identify rights and guarantees relevant to the protection of persons from forced displacement and to their protection and assistance during displacement as well as during return or resettlement and reintegration.

2. For the purposes of these Principles, internally displaced persons are persons or groups of persons who have been forced or obliged to flee or to leave their homes or places of habitual residence, in particular as a result of or in order to avoid the effects of armed conflict, situations of generalized violence, violations of human rights or natural or human-made disasters, and who have not crossed an internationally recognized State border.

3. These Principles reflect and are consistent with international human rights law and international humanitarian law. They provide guidance to:

   (a) The Representative of the Secretary-General on internally displaced persons in carrying out his mandate;

   (b) States when faced with the phenomenon of internal displacement;

   (c) All other authorities, groups and persons in their relations with internally displaced persons; and

   (d) Intergovernmental and non-governmental organizations when addressing internal displacement.

4. These Guiding Principles should be disseminated and applied as widely as possible.

---

*Extract from the document E/CN.4/1998/53/Add.2, dated 11 February 1998.

SECTION I—GENERAL PRINCIPLES

Principle 1

1. Internally displaced persons shall enjoy, in full equality, the same rights and freedoms under international and domestic law as do other persons in their country. They shall not be discriminated against in the enjoyment of any rights and freedoms on the ground that they are internally displaced.
2. These Principles are without prejudice to individual criminal responsibility under international law, in particular relating to genocide, crimes against humanity and war crimes.

Principle 2

1. These Principles shall be observed by all authorities, groups and persons irrespective of their legal status and applied without any adverse distinction. The observance of these Principles shall not affect the legal status of any authorities, groups or persons involved.
2. These Principles shall not be interpreted as restricting, modifying or impairing the provisions of any international human rights or international humanitarian law instrument or rights granted to persons under domestic law. In particular, these Principles are without prejudice to the right to seek and enjoy asylum in other countries.

Principle 3

1. National authorities have the primary duty and responsibility to provide protection and humanitarian assistance to internally displaced persons within their jurisdiction.
2. Internally displaced persons have the right to request and to receive protection and humanitarian assistance from these authorities. They shall not be persecuted or punished for making such a request.

Principle 4

1. These Principles shall be applied without discrimination of any kind, such as race, colour, sex, language, religion or belief, political or other opinion, national, ethnic or social origin, legal or social status, age, disability, property, birth, or on any other similar criteria.

2. Certain internally displaced persons, such as children, especially unaccompanied minors, expectant mothers, mothers with young children, female heads of household, persons with disabilities and elderly persons, shall be entitled to protection and assistance required by their condition and to treatment which takes into account their special needs.

Section II—Principles Relating to Protection from Displacement

Principle 5

All authorities and international actors shall respect and ensure respect for their obligations under international law, including human rights and humanitarian law, in all circumstances, so as to prevent and avoid conditions that might lead to displacement of persons.

Principle 6

1. Every human being shall have the right to be protected against being arbitrarily displaced from his or her home or place of habitual residence.
2. The prohibition of arbitrary displacement includes displacement:
   (a) When it is based on policies of apartheid, 'ethnic cleansing' or similar practices aimed at/or resulting in altering the ethnic, religious or racial composition of the affected population;
   (b) In situations of armed conflict, unless the security of the civilians involved or imperative military reasons so demand;
   (c) In cases of large-scale development projects, which are not justified by compelling and overriding public interests;
   (d) In cases of disasters, unless the safety and health of those affected requires their evacuation; and
   (e) When it is used as a collective punishment.
3. Displacement shall last no longer than required by the circumstances.

Principle 7

1. Prior to any decision requiring the displacement of persons, the authorities concerned shall ensure that all feasible alternatives

are explored in order to avoid displacement altogether. Where no alternatives exist, all measures shall be taken to minimize displacement and its adverse effects.

2. The authorities undertaking such displacement shall ensure, to the greatest practicable extent, that proper accommodation is provided to the displaced persons, that such displacements are effected in satisfactory conditions of safety, nutrition, health and hygiene, and that members of the same family are not separated.

3. If displacement occurs in situations other than during the emergency stages of armed conflicts and disasters, the following guarantees shall be complied with:

   (a) A specific decision shall be taken by a State authority empowered by law to order such measures;

   (b) Adequate measures shall be taken to guarantee to those to be displaced full information on the reasons and procedures for their displacement and, where applicable, on compensation and relocation;

   (c) The free and informed consent of those to be displaced shall be sought;

   (d) The authorities concerned shall endeavour to involve those affected, particularly women, in the planning and management of their relocation;

   (e) Law enforcement measures, where required, shall be carried out by competent legal authorities; and

   (f) The right to an effective remedy, including the review of such decisions by appropriate judicial authorities, shall be respected.

Principle 8

Displacement shall not be carried out in a manner that violates the rights to life, dignity, liberty and security of those affected.

Principle 9

States are under a particular obligation to protect against the displacement of indigenous peoples, minorities, peasants, pastoralists and other groups with a special dependency on and attachment to their lands.

Section III—Principles Relating to Protection during Displacement

Principle 10

1. Every human being has the inherent right to life, which shall be protected by law. No one shall be arbitrarily deprived of his or her life. Internally displaced persons shall be protected in particular against:
   (a) Genocide;
   (b) Murder;
   (c) Summary or arbitrary executions; and
   (d) Enforced disappearances, including abduction or unacknowledged detention, threatening or resulting in death.
   Threats and incitement to commit any of the foregoing acts shall be prohibited.
2. Attacks or other acts of violence against internally displaced persons who do not or no longer participate in hostilities are prohibited in all circumstances. Internally displaced persons shall be protected, in particular, against:
   (a) Direct or indiscriminate attacks or other acts of violence, including the creation of areas wherein attacks on civilians are permitted;
   (b) Starvation as a method of combat;
   (c) Their use to shield military objectives from attack or to shield, favour or impede military operations;
   (d) Attacks against their camps or settlements; and
   (e) The use of anti-personnel landmines.

Principle 11

1. Every human being has the right to dignity and physical, mental and moral integrity.
2. Internally displaced persons, whether or not their liberty has been restricted, shall be protected in particular against:
   (a) Rape, mutilation, torture, cruel, inhuman or degrading treatment or punishment, and other outrages upon personal dignity, such as acts of gender-specific violence, forced prostitution and any form of indecent assault;
   (b) Slavery or any contemporary form of slavery, such as sale into marriage, sexual exploitation, or forced labour of children; and

(c) Acts of violence intended to spread terror among internally displaced persons.

Threats and incitement to commit any of the foregoing acts shall be prohibited.

Principle 12

1. Every human being has the right to liberty and security of person. No one shall be subjected to arbitrary arrest or detention.
2. To give effect to this right for internally displaced persons, they shall not be interned in or confined to a camp. If in exceptional circumstances such internment or confinement is absolutely necessary, it shall not last longer than required by the circumstances.
3. Internally displaced persons shall be protected from discriminatory arrest and detention as a result of their displacement.
4. In no case shall internally displaced persons be taken hostage.

Principle 13

1. In no circumstances shall displaced children be recruited nor be required or permitted to take part in hostilities.
2. Internally displaced persons shall be protected against discriminatory practices of recruitment into any armed forces or groups as a result of their displacement. In particular, any cruel, inhuman or degrading practices that compel compliance or punish non-compliance with recruitment are prohibited in all circumstances.

Principle 14

1. Every internally displaced person has the right to liberty of movement and freedom to choose his or her residence.
2. In particular, internally displaced persons have the right to move freely in and out of camps or other settlements.

Principle 15

Internally displaced persons have:
   (a) The right to seek safety in another part of the country;
   (b) The right to leave their country;
   (c) The right to seek asylum in another country; and
   (d) The right to be protected against forcible return to or resettlement in any place where their life, safety, liberty and/or health would be at risk.

Principle 16

1. All internally displaced persons have the right to know the fate and whereabouts of missing relatives.
2. The authorities concerned shall endeavour to establish the fate and whereabouts of internally displaced persons reported missing, and co-operate with relevant international organizations engaged in this task. They shall inform the next of kin on the progress of the investigation and notify them of any result.
3. The authorities concerned shall endeavour to collect and identify the mortal remains of those deceased, prevent their despoliation or mutilation, and facilitate the return of those remains to the next of kin or dispose of them respectfully.
4. Grave sites of internally displaced persons should be protected and respected in all circumstances. Internally displaced persons should have the right of access to the grave sites of their deceased relatives.

Principle 17

1. Every human being has the right to respect of his or her family life.
2. To give effect to this right for internally displaced persons, family members who wish to remain together shall be allowed to do so.
3. Families which are separated by displacement should be reunited as quickly as possible. All appropriate steps shall be taken to expedite the reunion of such families, particularly when children are involved. The responsible authorities shall facilitate inquiries made by family members and encourage and cooperate with the work of humanitarian organizations engaged in the task of family reunification.
4. Members of internally displaced families whose personal liberty has been restricted by internment or confinement in camps shall have the right to remain together.

Principle 18

1. All internally displaced persons have the right to an adequate standard of living.
2. At the minimum, regardless of the circumstances, and without discrimination, competent authorities shall provide internally displaced persons with and ensure safe access to:
   (a) Essential food and potable water;
   (b) Basic shelter and housing;
   (c) Appropriate clothing; and
   (d) Essential medical services and sanitation.

3. Special efforts should be made to ensure the full participation of women in the planning and distribution of these basic supplies.

Principle 19

1. All wounded and sick internally displaced persons as well as those with disabilities shall receive to the fullest extent practicable and with the least possible delay, the medical care and attention they require, without distinction on any grounds other than medical ones. When necessary, internally displaced persons shall have access to psychological and social services.
2. Special attention should be paid to the health needs of women, including access to female healthcare providers and services, such as reproductive healthcare, as well as appropriate counselling for victims of sexual and other abuses.
3. Special attention should also be given to the prevention of contagious and infectious diseases, including AIDS, among internally displaced persons.

Principle 20

1. Every human being has the right to recognition everywhere as a person before the law.
2. To give effect to this right for internally displaced persons, the authorities concerned shall issue to them all documents necessary for the enjoyment and exercise of their legal rights, such as passports, personal identification documents, birth certificates and marriage certificates. In particular, the authorities shall facilitate the issuance of new documents or the replacement of documents lost in the course of displacement, without imposing unreasonable conditions, such as requiring the return to one's area of habitual residence in order to obtain these or other required documents.
3. Women and men shall have equal rights to obtain such necessary documents and shall have the right to have such documentation issued in their own names.

Principle 21

1. No one shall be arbitrarily deprived of property and possessions.
2. The property and possessions of internally displaced persons shall in

all circumstances be protected, in particular, against the following acts:

(a) Pillage;

(b) Direct or indiscriminate attacks or other acts of violence;

(c) Being used to shield military operations or objectives;

(d) Being made the object of reprisal; and

(e) Being destroyed or appropriated as a form of collective punishment.

4. Property and possessions left behind by internally displaced persons should be protected against destruction and arbitrary and illegal appropriation, occupation or use.

Principle 22

1. Internally displaced persons, whether or not they are living in camps, shall not be discriminated against as a result of their displacement in the enjoyment of the following rights:

(a) The rights to freedom of thought, conscience, religion or belief, opinion and expression;

(b) The right to seek freely opportunities for employment and to participate in economic activities;

(c) The right to associate freely and participate equally in community affairs;

(d) The right to vote and to participate in governmental and public affairs, including the right to have access to the means necessary to exercise this right; and

(e) The right to communicate in a language they understand.

Principle 23

1. Every human being has the right to education.

2. To give effect to this right for internally displaced persons, the authorities concerned shall ensure that such persons, in particular displaced children, receive education which shall be free and compulsory at the primary level. Education should respect their cultural identity, language and religion.

3. Special efforts should be made to ensure the full and equal participation of women and girls in educational programmes.

4. Education and training facilities shall be made available to internally displaced persons, in particular adolescents and women, whether or not living in camps, as soon as conditions permit.

Section IV—Principles Relating to Humanitarian Assistance

Principle 24

1. All humanitarian assistance shall be carried out in accordance with the principles of humanity and impartiality and without discrimination.
2. Humanitarian assistance to internally displaced persons shall not be diverted, in particular for political or military reasons.

Principle 25

1. The primary duty and responsibility for providing humanitarian assistance to internally displaced persons lies with national authorities.
2. International humanitarian organizations and other appropriate actors have the right to offer their services in support of the internally displaced. Such an offer shall not be regarded as an unfriendly act or an interference in a State's internal affairs and shall be considered in good faith. Consent thereto shall not be arbitrarily withheld, particularly when authorities concerned are unable or unwilling to provide the required humanitarian assistance.
3. All authorities concerned shall grant and facilitate the free passage of humanitarian assistance and grant persons engaged in the provision of such assistance rapid and unimpeded access to the internally displaced.

Principle 26

Persons engaged in humanitarian assistance, their transport and supplies should be respected and protected. They shall not be the object of attack or other acts of violence.

Principle 27

1. International humanitarian organizations and other appropriate actors when providing assistance should give due regard to the protection needs and human rights of internally displaced persons and take appropriate

measures in this regard. In so doing, these organizations and actors should respect relevant international standards and codes of conduct.

2. The preceding paragraph is without prejudice to the protection responsibilities of international organizations mandated for this purpose, whose services may be offered or requested by States.

Section V—Principles Relating to Return, Resettlement and Reintegration

Principle 28

1. Competent authorities have the primary duty and responsibility to establish conditions, as well as provide the means, which allow internally displaced persons to return voluntarily, in safety and with dignity, to their homes or places of habitual residence, or to resettle voluntarily in another part of the country. Such authorities shall endeavour to facilitate the reintegration of returned or resettled internally displaced persons.

2. Special efforts should be made to ensure the full participation of internally displaced persons in the planning and management of their return or resettlement and reintegration.

Principle 29

1. Internally displaced persons who have returned to their homes or places of habitual residence or who have resettled in another part of the country shall not be discriminated against as a result of their having been displaced. They shall have the right to participate fully and equally in public affairs at all levels and have equal access to public services.

2. Competent authorities have the duty and responsibility to assist returned and/or resettled internally displaced persons to recover, to the extent possible, their property and possessions, which they left behind or were dispossessed of upon their displacement. When recovery of such property and possessions is not possible, competent authorities shall provide or assist these persons in obtaining appropriate compensation or another form of just reparation.

Principle 30

All authorities concerned shall grant and facilitate for international humanitarian organizations and other appropriate actors, in the exercise of their respective mandates, rapid and unimpeded access to internally displaced persons to assist in their return or resettlement and reintegration.

NOTES ON EDITORS AND CONTRIBUTORS

The Editors

Paula Banerjee is a member of the Calcutta Research Group and teaches at the Department of South and South East Asian Studies, University of Calcutta, Kolkata. She specializes in issues of peace and conflict in South Asia as also in diplomatic history besides being a women's rights activist. She has authored two books and numerous journal articles and received the WISCOMP Fellow of Peace Award in 2001–02.

Sabyasachi Basu Ray Chaudhury is a Reader in the Department of Political Science, Rabindra Bharati University, Kolkata, and a member of the Calcutta Research Group. His areas of interest include global politics, democracy, refugee studies and human rights. He has co-authored two books and is also a regular contributor to national and international journals as also to dailies and periodicals.

Samir Kumar Das, a member of the Calcutta Research Group, teaches at the Department of Political Science, University of Calcutta. He specializes in issues of ethnicity, security and migration and has written numerous books and journal articles in these areas.

The Contributors

Bishnu Adhikari, a human rights activist, was earlier a researcher at CENAS (Centre for Nepal and Asian Studies, Tribhuvan University, Kathmandu), and now works for USAID, Nepal.

Suraiya Begum is currently Programme Officer at Research Initiatives Bangladesh. She has written extensively on women's political participation in both East and West Bengal and on women and governance issue. She is also co-editor of *Samaj Nirikshan* and the *Journal of Social Studies*.

Subir Bhaumik is the Eastern India Bureau Chief of the BBC. He is the author of numerous articles and two books on insurgency in the northeast.

David Fisher, a jurist, is a legal adviser to the Brookings Institution, and is based in Geneva. He works closely with the UN Human Rights Commission.

Meghna Guhathakurta is Professor, Department of International Relations, University of Dhaka. She is currently Executive Director of Research initiatives Bangladesh a research support organization for action research for poverty alleviation. Dr Guhathakurta has been involved with the women's movement for a long time and is also a member of a number of national and international civil liberties organizations.

Mossarat Qadeem teaches political science at the University of Peshawar, Peshawar. She works on various human rights and humanitarian issues of Pakistan and Afghanistan.

Atta ur Rehman Sheikh works for the Aurat Foundation, Lahore and is one of the well-known young human rights activists of Pakistan.

Manesh Sreshtha is an educationist of Nepal and is the organizer in the Himal Foundation, which holds the annual South Asia Film Festival, Kathmandu.

Joe William, earlier the executive director of the National Peace Council, Sri Lanka, is now the senior development officer, Canadian International Development Agency (CIDA), Colombo. He is well known for his many contributions to, and experience in, humanitarian work and peace campaigns in conflict-affected areas in Sri Lanka.

INDEX

return, reintegration and resettlement,
172, 325–26; in Bangladesh, 209–10,
234; United Nations Guiding
Principles relating to, 13, 21–32,
345–46
rights against displacement and non-
derogable rights, 23, 24, 114, 320,
336
rights-based argument, 23–24
Rihand dam, Uttar Pradesh, 120
rivalry, 25
river erosion and displacement in
Bangladesh, 19, 177–79, 199,
207
Rohingya Muslims of Burma, 223, 224,
225–26, 227, 287
Rohri, Pakistan: disaster and displacement, 101
Rolpa, Nepal: Kholagaun Village
Development Committee (VDC),
244; women and children,
displacement, 304
Romeo operation, 241
Rotary International, 28n 10
Roy, B.C., 150
Rubi Ramdas, 91
Rukum, Nepal, 251

Sabarkantha, Gujarat: communal clashes
and displacement, 128
Sabarmati Ashram, Gujarat, 130
Sabarmati Express, see Godhra incident
Sachar, Justice Rajinder, 136
Sadar, displacement of Bengalis, 159
Sahmat, 131
Saikia, Hiteshwar, 151
Saleemi, Ibrahim, 51
Sambalpur, Orissa: anti-dam agitation, 121
Sanmilito Janoghostiya Sangram Samity
(SJSS), United Nationalities Struggle
Committee, 156
Santhals, 26, 148, 306
Saraighat, 144
Sardar Sarovar Project (SSP), 15, 116,
126–27, 297–300
Sarder, Karunamayee, 198–99
Satkhira, Bangladesh, 194; discrimina-
tion against Hindus, 188

Sawabi, NWFP, Pakistan, disasters and
displacement, 100
seasonal migrants from Nepal to India,
253
SEBCON Private Limited, Pakistan, 82
seclusion, 46
sectarianism, 31, 63
secularism, 176, 210
security conditions, 36, 209
self-consciousness, 22
self-help, 25
Semas, 152
Semiyas, 152
Senapati, Manipur: ethnic violence, 162
Sengupta, Justice Moloy, 136
separatist groups in North-east, 144–45
Setalvad, Teesta, 130
sex workers, forced eviction in
Bangladesh, 203–6
sexual violence against women, 50, 53,
206, 302; in Gujarat, 295–96; in Sri
Lanka, 267–68, 281, 284
Shafqat Mehmood, 98
Shakargarh, Pakistan, effect of India–
Pakistan border conflict, 93
Shans, Shan state, Burma, 215, 224, 287;
armed conflicts, ethnic clashes, 216,
225, 227; forced relocation, 288;
IDPs, 224; international response to
displacement, 232; right of secession,
226
Shangla, NWFP, Pakistan, disasters and
displacement, 100
Shanti Bahini, 148, 181, 184, 302
Shantipur, West Bengal: affected by
Ganges erosion, 137
Shanty Abhiyan, 294
Sharia, Islamic law in Afghanistan, 33
Sharif, Mohammad Nawaz, 75, 88
Shi'as, 30
Shillong, Meghalaya: violence against
Bengalis, 157
Shiv Sena, 117, 126
Shonghoti, Bangladesh, 204
shrimp cultivation in Bangladesh, 18,
194–99, 282
Shyambazar, Kolkata, West Bengal:
eviction of hawkers, 135